Italy and the Environmental Humanities

Under the Sign of Nature: Explorations in Ecocriticism

EDITORS
Michael P. Branch, Kate Rigby, John Tallmadge

Italy and the Environmental Humanities

LANDSCAPES, NATURES, ECOLOGIES

Edited by Serenella Iovino, Enrico Cesaretti,
and Elena Past

UNIVERSITY OF VIRGINIA PRESS   CHARLOTTESVILLE AND LONDON

University of Virginia Press
© 2018 by the Rector and Visitors of the University of Virginia
All rights reserved
Printed in the United States of America on acid-free paper

First published 2018
ISBN 978-0-8139-4106-6 (cloth)
ISBN 978-0-8139-4107-3 (paper)
ISBN 978-0-8139-4108-0 (ebook)

9 8 7 6 5 4 3 2 1

Library of Congress Cataloging-in-Publication Data is available from the Library of Congress.

Contents

Acknowledgments   ix

Introduction   1

1 NATURES AND VOICES

Gianni Celati's Voicing of Unpredictable Places   17
  PATRICK BARRON

An Ecology of Voices: The Soundscapes of Tuscany's Lunigiana   28
  ALMO FARINA

"Birds Who Speak My Dialect": Poetry, Birds, and Landscape in Andrea Zanzotto   37
  DAMIANO BENVEGNÙ

Witnessing the Slaughter: Human and Nonhuman Animals in Ivano Ferrari's Poetry   47
  MATTEO GILEBBI

Dialogo ergo sum: My Pathway into Posthumanities   57
  ROBERTO MARCHESINI

2 PLACES AND LANDSCAPES

Italo Calvino and the Landscapes of the Anthropocene: A Narrative Stratigraphy   67
  SERENELLA IOVINO

Resisting Erasure: Landscape, Folklife, and Ethics in the Calabrian and Arbëreshë Novels of Carmine Abate   78
  VIKTOR BERBERI

Terra in Dino Buzzati's Fantastic Landscapes   88
SERENA FERRANDO

Aeropittura: Modern Aviation and the Fascist Idealization of the Italian Landscape   98
SOPHIA MAXINE FARMER

On Places and Looking: Italy's Silent Epiphanies   110
FRANCO ARMINIO

3   ECOLOGIES AND ENVIRONMENTS

Thinking Like a Parasite: Malaria, Plasmodium, and Sardinia's Extraordinary Longevity   117
MARCUS HALL

Ascending Underground: An Ecocritical Way through the Susa Valley   129
LUCA BUGNONE

Thinking on Foot in the Hydrocarbon Sublime: Paolo Sorrentino's Petrocultures   139
ELENA PAST

Slow Food and Terra Madre: A Conversation with Carlo Petrini on Ecology, Rural Traditions, and New Food Cultures   150
ILARIA TABUSSO MARCYAN

4   BODIES AND POLLUTIONS

An Environmental Historian among Activists: The Political, the Personal, and a Project of Guerrilla Narrative   163
MARCO ARMIERO

We Will Not Tremble: Healing the Body Politic in Post-Earthquake Emilia-Romagna   173
ANDREA HAJEK

Thinking through Taranto: Toxic Embodiment, Eco-catastrophe, and the Power of Narrative   184
MONICA SEGER

Room with a View (of a Landfill): The Making of Verdenero   194
MARCO MORO

5 IMAGINATIONS AND (RE)VISIONS

This Nostrum That Is Neither Sea nor Remedy: Mediterranean Re-visions   203
PASQUALE VERDICCHIO

Eco-Futurism? Nature, Matter, and Body in Filippo Tommaso Marinetti   215
ENRICO CESARETTI

Nature's Creative Balance: On Italian Eco-art   225
ANDREA LERDA

Walking Roots: Knitting Past and Future through Italy's Woods   235
TIZIANO FRATUS

Afterword: The Proper Study of the Humanities Is No Longer "Man"   242
ROSI BRAIDOTTI

Notes on Contributors   247

Index   255

Acknowledgments

A book is a wonderful prism. Through it, authors can see the size of their debts, the extension of their entanglements, and the length of their roots. When the book is, like this one, the outcome of so many exchanges and intersections, the prism ends up reflecting a sort of friendly reunion, and gratitude turns into a declaration of interdependence.

The first person we wish to thank is Boyd Zenner, our acquisitions editor at University of Virginia Press. Boyd's professional energy, personal encouragement, and unique *joie de vivre* were a constant source of motivation: the image of her sitting at her desk on Sprigg Lane, amidst her landscape of books and curious objects, has been a reassuring companion during occasional moments of difficulty. At UVA, we also wish to thank to our project editor Mark Mones and Siobhan Drummond, who assisted us during the copyediting process. Our deepest appreciation also goes to the two anonymous reviewers of this volume, who provided us with encouragement, stimulating criticism, and luminous suggestions.

Unconditioned gratitude also binds us to the scholarly collectives that enabled all the human and intellectual entanglements at work in this volume: the American Association for Italian Studies (AAIS), the Association for the Study of Literature and Environment (ASLE), and the European Association for the Study of Literature, Culture, and Environment (EASLCE). Thank you for bringing together lively communities of people who believe in the existence of reality more than in disciplinary boundaries, and for whom the whole is always something more than the sum of its parts.

Thanks go to the numerous colleagues and friends who provided useful feedback along the way, giving us the chance to test our ideas in conversations, conference presentations, e-mails, Skype meetings, lunches, dinners, and an entirely reasonable number of *aperitivi*: Joni Adamson, Eleonora Adorni, Deborah Amberson, Aurelio Angelini, Stefania Barca, Christina Ball, Elisa Bolchi,

Antonello Borra, Paolo Chirumbolo, Jeffrey J. Cohen, Roberto Dainotto, Cristina Della Coletta, Rossella Di Rosa, Lowell Duckert, Rebecca Falkoff, Thomas Harrison, Federico Luisetti, Massimo Lollini, Serpil Oppermann, Karen Pinkus, Kate Rigby, Silvia Ross, Domenico Scarpa, Mario Salomone, Ed Slesak, Heather Sullivan, Antonella Tarpino, Maurizio Valsania, Louise Westling, Bertrand Westphal, Hubert Zapf. We also recognize those who should appear here, but who our fallible memories have forgotten: as Borges or Calvino would remind us, a complete list would be impossible in any case.

For their creativity and spirit of initiative, we also wish to thank the graduate students who organized conferences and seminars on topics related to the ones in this book: Federica Di Blasio, Marianna Nespoli, and Rebecca Rose (UC Los Angeles), Maria Pia Arpioni (Università di Venezia Ca' Foscari), Emiliano Guaraldo (University of North Carolina Chapel Hill).

Within and across the scholarly community, Salvatore Settis and Luca Mercalli deserve particular gratitude for being unique inspirational examples of cultural activism on behalf of landscape, citizenship, and environmental protection. Through their insightful work, they confirmed our conviction that Italy matters in conversations about the future of our shared planet. And *grazie* to Rosi Braidotti, a great philosopher who crosses countries and disciplines, for inspiring this book with her insightful address to the AAIS in Zurich, and then for completing it with her brilliant afterword.

Finally, we wish to thank all our authors for their generosity, patience, and professionalism. Contributing to a book as unusual as this one is no easy task. They all took up the challenge with cheerfulness and scholarly zeal, and we hope you will enjoy the result.

This book is dedicated to our partners and families—across lands, species, and spatio-temporal borders, in the dream of ever-new entanglements and prismatic visions of interdependence.

Gerardo Dottori's *La Virata* (1931) is reproduced by permission of the Casa Museo Boschi di Stefano, Milan, Italy. All rights reserved. Many thanks to Chiara Fabi and Martina Viganò for their invaluable help.

Gerardo Dottori's *Mussolini: Anno XI* (a.k.a.) *Ritratto del Duce* is reproduced by permission of the Museo del Novecento, Milan, Italy. All rights reserved. Thank you to Maria Grazia Conti and Danka Giacon for their kindness and responsiveness to our last-minute inquiries.

Despite our best efforts, we were unable to determine the copyright owner of Alessandro Bruschetti's *Aeroveduta con laghi vulcanici* (1933). It has been reproduced in this book following a good faith effort.

A more extended version of Serenella Iovino's "Italo Calvino and the Landscapes of the Anthropocene: A Narrative Stratigraphy," titled "Sedimenting Stories: Italo Calvino and the Extraordinary Strata of the Anthropocene," originally appeared in *Neohelicon* 44.2 (2017), DOI 10.1007/s11059-017-0396-7. Portions of that text are reproduced in reviewed form with permission of the publisher. Copyright by Akadémiai Kiadó Zrt., Budapest (2017). Gratitude is due to Peter Hajdu and Nikoletta Schalbert at the Akademiai Kiadó for their valuable help.

A longer version of Enrico Cesaretti's "Eco-Futurism? Nature, Matter, and Body in Filippo Tommaso Marinetti" originally appeared in Nicolás Fernández-Medina and Maria Truglio, eds., *Modernism and the Avant-garde Body in Spain and Italy* (New York: Routledge, 2016), 232–48. The text is reproduced in reviewed form with permission of the publisher.

Turin
Charlottesville
Detroit
May 1, 2017

Italy and the Environmental Humanities

Introduction

"How does this hotel called Italy feel?" asks the poet and writer Guido Ceronetti in his book *Albergo Italia* (1985). He answers: "I've got a nice room . . . with curtains through which one can see and not see; little by little, the view from my window has lost grace indeed; it moves—time and again being touched by the inexplicable: a hill disappears, and smoke and steel take its place . . . the good fragrances of food and garden I used to smell are taken over by fumes that burn your throat" (ix).[1]

How does this place called Italy feel? Not so good, lately. As we write, one of the country's biggest oil refineries, near Pavia, is burning. Meanwhile, in Sicily, hundreds of migrants from Syria, Libya, and other Mediterranean lands are mooring in the docks, waiting to be transferred to temporary reception centers or scattered across the country. It is a sunny December morning; but still, it is a cold day for the thousands of people who lost their homes in the earthquakes that continue to shake central Italy, destroying inestimable pieces of the country's artistic and historical heritage. Somewhere, in illegal dumps, hidden from indiscreet eyes, criminal organizations are burying toxic waste that will one day return in new cellular formations and epidemiological reports.

This perhaps graceless image is what one sees, looking through the curtains of our room with a view. But if for a moment you direct your gaze away from this worrisome panorama, you also see something else. You see that Italy resists. This resistance is visible in the movements of citizens who defend the commons and ecological health, in the work of public intellectuals against the ruin of environment and landscape, in the reevaluation of food culture as eco-anthropological presidium, and even in the creation of new words, such as "ecomafia," which inspired long-awaited legislation against environmental crimes. It is a *cultural* resistance that, although inconclusive and certainly still incomplete, is a sign that something is changing vis-à-vis the dominance of what Ceronetti calls "the inexplicable," namely, the strange mechanism that transforms cultural richness into misery, and public good into a private supply for short-term speculations. Strongly rejecting the separation of "the natural" from "the cultural," this resistance—slowly but irresistibly—is changing the scene of Italian studies, too.

Italy and the Environmental Humanities: Landscapes, Natures, Ecologies is part of this culture of resistance. The idea for the book came to us in the spring of 2014 in Zurich, at the conference of the American Association for Italian Studies. An interesting phenomenon unfolded at that Swiss-Italian-American meeting of Italianists: for the first time, a number of panels and presentations explicitly dedicated to ecocriticism and environmental humanities were being held and copiously attended, indicating a meaningful turn of the dial in the critical canon of Italian studies. What most inspired us, however, was Rosi Braidotti's keynote lecture, "Posthumanist Paradoxes." On that memorable afternoon, we heard ideas that, filtered through our notes, read like this: *We need new figurations for the humanities. We need to explore intellectual pathways in which critique goes together with creativity. We need critical practices that, defamiliarizing consolidated patterns of thinking, escort us out of the safety zones in which anthropocentrism, Eurocentrism, sexism, speciesism, ableism, constitute the normal discourse of our cultural paradigms.*

For convinced eco-scholars like us, this subversive call marked the joyful advent of a long-awaited revolution. Intervening in a debate in which traditional humanistic approaches have always played a major role, and in a context that has historically privileged single specializations and critical methodologies, Braidotti courageously urged the audience to think beyond the usual disciplinary categories and to embrace the more hybrid, inclusive, and participatory mode of the environmental humanities.

Braidotti's call could hardly have been more timely or more sensible. We undeniably face critical times: critical for our planet and its collapsing life-support systems; critical for our societies, ravaged by biopolitical tragedies and global uncertainties; and critical for cultural imagination, now more than ever challenged by one-sided discourses that fail to address the intertwined matters of our lives. The truth is that the "safety zones" of self-referential paradigms dissolve every day in the faces of displaced people, in the decay of biomes and landscapes, in the visible and invisible contamination of cells and places, and in all the multilayered turbulence of the Anthropocene. As these emergences prove, the environment is not just "out there." It is everywhere, outside and inside our bodies *and* discourses; it is at once a background, an issue, and an actor in our social and biological life. If subjects, agents, and dynamics are collective and elementally intermingled, the traditionally conceived humanities can no longer critically deal with the world alone but must engage in conversation with scientific fields of study. From this need—the need to see how human stories emerge from and converge with the stories of the more-than-human beings around and within us—come the environmental humanities.

A burgeoning area of transdisciplinary inquiry, the environmental humanities is an umbrella term that "brings the social sciences, the humanities, and the natural sciences together in diverse ways to address the current ecological crises from closely knit ethical, cultural, philosophical, political, social, and biological perspectives" (Oppermann and Iovino 2017, 2). The distinctive trait of the environmental humanities is that they are practiced in the form of research collectives, where highly specialized results achieved in single disciplines are complemented by other concurring areas, explicitly integrating scientific and humanistic methodologies. Rejecting the reductionism of eco-technocracy and of a "managerial approach to human-environment interaction" (Castree 2014, 249), this cooperative discourse infers that environmental research can have a meaningful impact on society only if climatologists and economists team up with historians and political scientists, biologists join forces with philosophers and geographers, and hard-science researchers work together with humanities scholars and educators, supplementing efforts in public policy with more sustainable cultural models. The point here is that no single discipline can provide satisfactory answers when the problems to be tackled are embedded in complex systems. To really know what "environment" means and what "ecological crisis" implies, we must, in other words, move beyond unilateral approaches and engage in cooperative conversations that boost our imagination of reality. Rejecting the divide between the "two cultures" (Snow 1961), as well as autarchic ontologies of the human, the environmental humanities invite us to rethink the humanities themselves as critical posthumanities, in an attempt to move beyond human-centered individualism and universality. This intellectual shift does not intend to reject the methods and insights of the humanistic tradition but rather "spells the end of the idea of a de-naturalized social order disconnected from its environmental and organic foundations, and calls for more complex schemes of understanding the multilayered form of inter-dependence we all live in" (Braidotti 2013, 159–60). The educational impact of this vision is momentous, for it has the power to reaffirm the crucial role of the humanities "at a time when a neoliberal agenda of economic utilitarianism, along with empirical-quantitative models of science, threatens to dominate universities" (Zapf 2016, 1).

Faced with the potentialities of this approach, we therefore understand Braidotti's call as something more than an invitation to explore new disciplinary territories. We read it as the urge to move toward a radical sea change in our worldviews, overcoming the anthropocentrism and dualisms that characterize the humanities. This does not mean that, as we focus our attention beyond the sphere of the human, we wish to radically remove the human subject from the picture and devaluate or reject human life and concerns. As Christopher Breu (2014) argues, "there are too many forces in contemporary life that degrade human life, such as neoliberalism, neoimperialism, global warfare, and various discourses of social exclusion and exploitation, for it to be acceptable that theory even unconsciously participates in the denigration of the human" (194). However, when humans are vulnerable, but also largely responsible for our "messy era of ruinous hyper-industrial civilization" (Cohen 2016, 24), we believe that the focus of academic inquiry should shift from being exclusively (and hubristically) centered on human life and subjectivity. To better understand (and possibly disentangle) the troubling predicaments of our era, the humanities are called to encompass and make sense of the role and agency of more-than-human reality as a whole, in the hope that this "discursive change . . . will create and implement more sustainable economic practices, social behaviors, and moral paradigms" (Oppermann and Iovino 2017, 5). We respond to Braidotti's call by imagining that the human must acknowledge, collaborate with, and curate the stories of the nonhuman others that traverse, compose, and surround us. The environmental humanities, in this way, embody a discourse of liberation, a renewed humanism that is at once critical and nonanthropocentric.

In a nutshell, this discourse means that we need to be able to read the texts of the world from many angles, whether informed by arts or sciences, and whether these angles are human or not. And we need to be able to articulate what we read in critical narratives that can provide the ground for wider pedagogies in which the human world is an element rather than an end in itself. We need more creativity in our critical ventures, and we need to work together, across the abstract margins of our fields. In other words, *we need new figurations for the humanities.*

Innovatively blending critique with creative prose, the twenty-two essays of *Italy and the Environmental Humanities: Landscapes, Natures, Ecologies* seek to distinctively situate Italian studies on this horizon. To couple Italy and the environmental humanities is not a demanding task: Italy's history, its significant literary and artistic heritage, its importance in shaping the Western construction, appreciation, and aesthetics of nature and landscape offer excellent starting points. Our collection, however, is motivated less by a parochial eco-renaissance than by the aspiration to show how this particular country, with its problems, ambivalences, and resources, is at once unique and exemplary in the panorama of the environmental humanities.

Italy is indeed a nation systematically affected by political corruption and infrastructural deficiencies—and yet the Italian government periodically earmarks substantial amounts of public money to build a "mythical" bridge over the highly seismic area of the Strait of Messina, which is supposed to link the mainland to Sicily.[2] Unregulated building development results in severe hydrogeological risk, flirting dangerously with intricate webs of fault lines, rugged terrain, and tens of thousands of kilometers of increasingly eroding coast. Almost daily, the country faces ethical, geographic, and sociopolitical challenges with thousands of refugees crossing the Mediterranean to reach its shores. The magnificent capital city, itself always on the verge of collapse, is surrounded by "a belt of *favelas*, made of decrepit huge building blocks, aborted streets, and fake squares invaded by rubbish" (Settis 2012, 8). Environmental business—for example, waste disposal, building development, and even farming—is often in the hands of the ecomafia, with tragic consequences for living beings and territories. Meanwhile, tiny alien parasites are destroying countless acres of iconic olive trees, thus bringing the agricultural economies of entire regions to their knees.

The interlaced landscapes of matter and stories that we see from our hypothetical window require us to transform Braidotti's incitement into a number of questions. For instance, how urgent is it to reconsider the limits of both the humanities and the environment? What does this reconsideration mean for a country steeped in the tradition of humanism and the Renaissance, with their emphasis on human potential and accomplishments, and later shaped by the neo-idealistic philosophy of figures such as Benedetto Croce and Giovanni Gentile and their privileging of a dematerialized mind over the tangible claims of the physical world? And how might the novel, post-dualistic humanities merge with a culture that has contributed to a radical critique and rethinking of the contemporary social and political world? Italy, in fact, is also to be found in the work of intellectuals such as Antonio Negri, Giorgio Agamben, Roberto Esposito, Maurizio Ferraris, and the so-called New Italian Theory; it is present in a strong tradition of feminist scholarship, which includes seminal figures like Adriana Cavarero, Luisa Muraro, and the nomadic Braidotti herself; it is the reassessment of modernity from the southern, Mediterranean perspectives of Franco Cassano and Franco La Cecla; more recently, it is the reconsideration of the nonhuman—this "ontological South"—in the posthumanist philosophies of Roberto Marchesini and Francesca Ferrando. It is advocacy for including places and their artistic heritage on our horizon of political values, initiated by Antonio Cederna and Eugenio Turri, and powerfully epitomized today by Salvatore Settis and Tomaso Montanari's struggles for a joint safeguard of Italy's cultural landscape and constitutional principles. And so, how can this rich tradition of Italian culture and Italy itself, in its multiple, historical, imagined, and material-discursive forms, contribute to these challenges? Where does this country, with both its texts and contexts, locate itself within the expanding critical debate of the environmental humanities?

In order to answer these questions, we believe it is necessary to defamiliarize the imagination of Italy—too often frozen in essentialist anthropological categories, romanticized in the aesthetic cliché of the "beautiful land," and fixed in the human-centered discourse of classical humanist thinking—and to engage with the voices emerging from the Italian cultural horizon. In the past several years, indeed, Italian scholars and Italianists have been increasingly rethinking how they tell their stories, and what they want to tell stories about. These voices and narratives are so numerous that a complete list is impossible, and yet some of the major steps toward the making of the Italian environmental humanities must be noted in this introduction. They are here to prove that, as we considered how our volume might enrich this debate, we mused in good company.

A map of the Italian environmental humanities *avant la lettre* might begin with the trailblazing contributions of Eugenio Turri, a prolific geoanthropologist who has literally changed the way we look at landscapes, especially those of the Po Valley and of the Italian Nord-Est, and whose legacy lives in the important works of scholars such as Francesco Vallerani, Marcello Zunica, and Nadia Breda. Italy's landscapes have also spoken to and through a number of eminent environmental historians. A few major examples: Piero Bevilacqua's pioneering and wide-ranging works delve into the history of land reclamation, agriculture, and landscape photography; Marco Armiero and Marcus Hall's *Nature and History in Modern Italy* (2010) brings a broad view of Italian environmental history to English language readers; Armiero's monographic *A Rugged Nation: Mountains and the Making of Modern Italy* (2011, translated into Italian as *Le montagne della patria*, 2013) compellingly shows how the Italian mountains contributed to the making of the nation and how the nation shaped and modified the rocky landscape; Stefania Barca's *Enclosing Water: Nature and Political Economy in a Mediterranean Valley, 1796–1916* (2010) sheds light on the power of water to shape proto-industrial landscapes and stir up early forms of ecological awareness, citing the Liri valley as an exemplary case; and Giacomo Parrinello's *Fault Lines: Earthquakes and Urbanism in Modern Italy* (2015) uncovers the powerful geological force and historical agency of two of the major seismic disasters in the history of modern Italy (Messina and the Belice valley). Populated by vital nonhuman protagonists—earthquakes, landslides, and mobile waterways—this original scholarship has shifted the terrain of Italian studies, showing that, long before a political entity called "Italy" had been officially imagined, a compelling geo-cultural mesh of stories was emerging from the peninsula and its inhabitants. Antonella Tarpino's recent *Il paesaggio fragile* (The fragile landscape, 2016), as well as her previous works *Geografie della memoria* (Geographies of memory, 2008) and *Spaesati* (Dis-placed, 2012), can also be situated in this lineage; with considerable interdisciplinary skillfulness, she retraces the stories and imagination of Italy's often ignored marginal areas (abandoned mountains, ancient roads, critical borders), explicitly calling into question the country's official "political cartography." The work of environmental sociologists such as Aurelio Angelini and Mario Salomone are also crucial references, not the least because they complement their studies with important projects of eco-pedagogy and landscape valorization. Donatella Della Porta, Mario Diani, and Pietro Saitta research environmental movements, activism, and models of political ecology in Italy and give voice to both environmental struggles and vibrant strategies of resistance.

From our own vantage point as ecocritical scholars, we cannot fail to emphasize the role played by literature on this horizon. Italian literature—from Dante to Machiavelli to Manzoni—helped create the Italian polis and its language in ways that have been well documented. The manifold ways in which Italian literature and cinema participate reciprocally in a more-than-human world, however, have just begun to emerge in academic work. With *Italian Environmental Literature: An Anthology* (2003), Patrick Barron and Anna Re curated a valuable reading list from which to begin this process. Serenella Iovino's long engagement as a theorist and literary scholar subsequently provided fertile ground for environmental cultural studies, paving the way for a new generation of Italian scholars to reenvision their position in material and scholarly worlds. Her seminal *Ecologia letteraria* (Literary ecology, 2006) traces the relationship between environmental ethics and literary theories and methodologies, while her transdisciplinary *Ecocriticism and Italy: Ecology, Resistance, and Liberation* (2016) brings material ecocriticism to bear on the Italian context and landscape, offering a roadmap to a transverse narrative practice of liberation—a practice with deep ethical implications beyond Italy.

Monica Seger's monograph *Landscapes In Between: Environmental Change in Italian Literature and Film* (2015) and Pasquale Verdicchio's edited collection *Ecocritical Approaches to Italian Culture and Literature: The Denatured Wild* (2016) continue the work of rereading Italy and its many eco-cultural texts in ethically engaged, ontologically open ways, drawing more cities, geological forces, and environmental pollution into the unfolding conversation. Deborah Amberson and Elena Past's edited volume *Thinking Italian Animals: Human and Posthuman in Modern Italian Literature and Film* (2014) calls on the nonhuman animals, biopolitical and posthumanist questions that animate and trouble Italian cultural productions. From a more geographically defined standpoint, Silvia Ross's *Tuscan Spaces: Literary Constructions of Place* also provides an insightful contribution to the debate. Most recently, Enrico Cesaretti organized a Mellon symposium on environmental posthumanities at the University of Virginia. The day of collaborative, engaged meetings convened Italianists, comparativists, and some of the most vibrant voices in the environmental humanities, performing the kind of work this volume wishes to continue.

In the essays that follow, we aim to shape a critical approach to Italy that, in creative and rigorous ways, heeds territories, bodies, animals, and more-than-human beings. *Territories* are here taken as the basis of a new anthropology of nature, namely, as a way to reinforce the mutual formative bond of humans and places, something which should constitute the premise for a healthy life, both in physical and political terms. Implicitly resonating with the social implications of Gregory Bateson's ecology of mind, Salvatore Settis refers to a healthy territorial life as a "*sanità* dello spazio"—a healthiness of space, to be intended both literally and culturally (Settis 2012, 52). It is evident, in fact, that the decline of a landscape, and of a shared environment in general, is a decline of citizenship, and of citizens' basic rights. Far from being active players in democratic decision making, individuals are often forcibly separated from both their social and territorial identities. This, of course, is a political problem, but it is also an ethical matter. The lack of a bond between cultural identity, social awareness, and environmental protection is indeed at the core of the ecological crisis. Within these territories and landscapes, *bodies*—human or not—are nodes of ecological dynamics, political actions, and worldviews. Considering them often, but not exclusively, within the theoretical framework of material ecocriticism, the bodies examined in this volume are read both as litmus tests to evince environmental criticalities and as fronts of resistance against the infiltrating violence hidden in the corners of development. Finally, *animals* and *nonhuman beings* are here taken as full-fledged material-semiotic subjects, and not as merely symbolic or metaphoric matter. They are holders and agents of interlaced stories and not simply backgrounds for human enterprises.

The Italian landscapes discussed in this volume thus mark a shift from the idealized Grand Tour representations to the living nightmares of ecomafia and the post-seismic rubble, also traversing the linguistic territories, both cradles and enclaves, in which this country expresses its mind. Italy's natures embrace nonhuman creatures from eloquent birds to storied trees, resident parasites, and stratifying geo-social layers; its ecologies entail the beauty of Alpine regions as well as the cellular intricacies of pollution and maldevelopment that contaminate Italian bodies and elements. In short, the stories we record are stories of life forms and signs, justice and violence, food and places, uncertain borders and oil, dissident communities and interspecies dialogues, poetry and slaughterhouses, industry and art, sea and roots.

The first section, "Natures and Voices," features essays that, from various perspectives, underline the complex interrelations and entanglements between living beings and their natural and artificial surroundings. If the voices we hear in Patrick Barron's study of Gianni Celati are those of the ordinary, often overlooked ecologies in which we all live and move, those in Almo Farina's and Damiano Benvegnù's essays are those of birds who sing, respectively, in the woods of Lunigiana and in the poetry of Andrea Zanzotto. In Matteo Gilebbi's essay the sounds, real and metaphoric, muffled and violent, are instead the dreadful ones coming from the abattoirs powerfully evoked in Ivano Ferrari's poetry. This initial section ends with a short piece by writer, philosopher, and zoo-anthropologist Roberto Marchesini, who engages in a dialogue between his personal path and the Italian intellectual scenery. In this autobiographical account *en philosophe*, Marchesini shows how posthumanist ontology has become a philosophy of codependence, where animals, as forms of embodied "epiphany," show us the impossibility of understanding the human divided from its relation with the other.

The critical essays that compose part 2, "Places and Landscapes," share an interest in charting and deciphering the meanings inscribed in a number of physical, artistic, and literary Italian landscapes. Starting from the industrial North, but with a look at larger dynamics, Serenella Iovino uses Italo Calvino's early urban works as tools for a "narrative stratigraphy." Calvino's imaginative dealings with the material world, she argues, emerge and evolve along with the landscapes of the Anthropocene that stratify over and within Italy's bodies. And stratifications—this time linguistic as well as ethno-anthropological—come from the region of Calabria, which provides the background of Viktor Berberi's essay on the literary works of Carmine Abate. The interpenetration of landscape and folklife—an Italo-Albanian hybrid compound—in some of Abate's novels engenders, Berberi maintains, a sense of social engagement and a possibility for resistance. Serena Ferrando's contribution shifts our attention to northern Italy again and the Alpine landscape of the Dolomites, a familiar playground of writer and journalist Dino Buzzati. His works, Ferrando contends, outline a liminal, fantastic territory made of rock, sand, mud, and Dolomitic peaks that is both human and elusively more-than-human. In the fourth essay we encounter the Italian landscape as an artwork to be looked at from above. Here, Sophia Maxine Farmer, an art historian, argues that the Futurist sub-movement of aeropainting portrayed the fantasy of a conquered Italian land and of a national identity associated with the transformation of wilderness into a productive agricultural landscape. Implicitly rejecting nationalistic epopees for the ancient silences of peripheral lands, the writer, poet, and theorist of *paesologia* (placeology) Franco Arminio provides a creative conclusion to this section with an alternative Grand Tour across Italy's peripheral and abandoned sites and villages. Lost and dispersed in a voracious history, Italy's minor places are here populated by stones and empty squares, by weeds and rusty tools—all things that glint with unexpected narrative power. More than merely mapping this marginal geography, Arminio uses *paesologia*—a poetic eco-phenomenology of places—as a way to preserve the material horizon of domestic intimacy, a "form of intimate resistance," and a therapeutic art of inhabiting place.

The notion of resistance also informs much of the third section, "Ecologies and Environments." The four essays in this part, shifting focus between the regions of Piedmont and Sardinia, also emphasize unavoidable ecological continuities between landscapes, bodies, and ideas. In Marcus Hall's opening essay on malaria in Sardinia, resistance, in the sense of immunity, may paradoxically emerge from contamination, as he shows us how the microinhabitants living inside us alter our physiology as well as cognition, and promote sickness as well as good health. In the second essay, Luca Bugnone compares the enthusiastic response to the opening of the Fréjus rail tunnel in 1871 with the contemporary dissent against the environmentally devastating construction of a transalpine high-speed railway linking Turin and Lyon. Examining the transnational landscapes of Paolo Sorrentino's films, Elena Past identifies the director's relentless attention to the hydrocarbon cultures that drive people apart but that also fuel the filmmaking industry. Sorrentino's cinema, she argues, enacts a Mediterranean form of resistance by "thinking on foot" about how to live in the Anthropocene. How to resist food's far-from-ecological transformation into a global commodity in a reality of land-grabbing and environmental crisis is the crucial question Ilaria Tabusso Marcyan asks both herself and, in an exclusive interview, Carlo Petrini, the globally renowned founder of the Slow Food movement.

The fourth section, "Bodies and Pollutions," includes essays in which pressing issues of environmental justice and politics dialogue with creative literary and cinematic texts that have helped to aesthetically translate the Anthropocene. Within this framework, Marco Armiero's personal, scientific, and political reflections on his research experience and "guerrilla narrative project" on the waste crisis in Campania are followed by Andrea Hajek's discussion of how two recent earthquakes in the region of Emilia-Romagna changed not only the natural environment but also people's living and working practices, forcing them to rebuild their body politic by rejoining the material territory, the social environment, and the community at large. In the third contribution, the highly polluted city of Taranto, in the southeastern region of Puglia, is at the center of Monica Seger's investigation on local forms of creative resistance. This section ends with the story of the environmental eco-noir book series Verdenero. Marco Moro, the editor-in-chief of Edizioni Ambiente, Italy's only publishing house exclusively devoted to environmental issues, shares his view of an initiative of cultural activism that coincided with the emergence of a new Italian "social novel" and introduced issues long hidden by the collusion between politics and organized crime.

In the final, fifth section, "Imagination and (Re)visions," onto-epistemological and ethical questions continue to resonate, as our attention is drawn to new material and intellectual landscapes. It opens with Pasquale Verdicchio's provocative reconsiderations of our common perceptions of the Mediterranean. Against a backdrop of cultural beliefs that emphasize a natural blending of human and sea life, he contends that the remains of drowned migrants decaying on the sea bottom retain a sort of agency stemming from transformative processes that incorporate the basic elements of human bodies into the body of the sea. Reconnecting with Farmer's essay, Enrico Cesaretti's contribution provocatively suggests ways in which Italian Futurism may be approached from an ecocritical perspective. Cesaretti draws attention to potential affinities, parallelisms, and, to use Deleuze and Guattari's term, "adjacencies" between the way Futurism imagined the interrelated notions of nature, matter, and corporeality and some of the current positions of postmodern, material ecocriticism. The final two essays of this section are by eco-art gallery curator Andrea Lerda, who addresses the often prescient relevance of Italian contemporary art in raising environmental awareness, from Arte Povera in the 1960s until today, and by contemporary writer, poet, and "tree seeker" Tiziano Fratus, who takes us for a deep natural-cultural immersion into some important Italian forests, elaborating an imaginative anthropology of woods in which roots, landscape, sounds, and time converge in his notion of "dendrosophy," a theory of arboreal wisdom and an art of living. An ideal conclusion to the volume, Rosi Braidotti's afterword, "The Proper Study of the Humanities Is No Longer 'Man,'" reconnects the large scope of the environmental humanities with the theoretical principles of feminist philosophy in a common front of cultural and material liberation.

"A general explanation of the world and of history must first of all take into account the way our house was situated," writes Italo Calvino in his autobiographical piece *The Road to San Giovanni* (1993, 3). Far from providing general explanations of history and the world, the modest ambition of this book is to describe, in different ways and from different angles, the terrain where this house of ours is situated and some of the inhabitants that animate it. Perhaps you will not see an ideal "Beautiful Land" from this window view.

But maybe Italy was never *just* a beautiful land—and this might indeed be a source of its enduring creativity. Through its dystopian, dissonant, disturbing, yet ever resistant and resilient stories, we have tried to show that this old country, with its hybrid roots and evolving mind, can still provide new figurations for the humanities.

NOTES

1. Unless otherwise indicated, all translations in this introduction are our own.
2. For a critical history of the bridge, and for its definition as "mythical," see Angelini (2011).

WORKS CITED

Amberson, Deborah, and Elena Past, eds. 2014. *Thinking Italian Animals: Human and Posthuman in Modern Italian Literature and Film*. New York: Palgrave Macmillan.

Angelini, Aurelio, ed. 2011. *Il mitico Ponte sullo stretto di Messina. Da Lucio Cecilio Metello ai giorni nostri: La storia, la cultura e l'ambiente*. Milan: Franco Angeli.

Armiero, Marco. 2011. *A Rugged Nation: Mountains and the Making of Modern Italy*. Cambridge, UK: White Horse Press.

Armiero, Marco, and Marcus Hall, eds. 2010. *Nature and History in Modern Italy*. Athens: Ohio University Press.

Barca, Stefania. 2010. *Enclosing Water: Nature and Political Economy in a Mediterranean Valley 1796–1916*. Cambridge, UK: White Horse Press.

Barron, Patrick, and Anna Re, eds. 2003. *Italian Environmental Literature: An Anthology*. New York: Italica Press.

Braidotti, Rosi. 2013. *The Posthuman*. Cambridge, UK: Polity Press.

Breu, Christopher. 2014. *Insistence on the Material: Literature in the Age of Biopolitics*. Minneapolis: University of Minnesota Press.

Calvino, Italo. 1993. *The Road to San Giovanni*. Translated by Tim Parks. New York: Pantheon Books.

Castree, Noel. 2014. "The Anthropocene and the Environmental Humanities: Extending the Conversation." *Environmental Humanities* 5: 233–60.

Ceronetti, Guido. 1985. *Albergo Italia*. Turin: Einaudi.

Cohen, Tom. 2016. "Trolling 'Anthropos'—Or, Requiem for a Failed *Prosopopeia*." In *Twilight of the Anthropocene Idols*, by Tom Cohen, Claire Colebrook, and J. Hillis Miller, 20–80. London: Open Humanities Press.

Iovino, Serenella. 2016. *Ecocriticism and Italy: Ecology, Resistance, and Liberation*. London: Bloomsbury.

———. 2006. *Ecologia letteraria: Una strategia di sopravvivenza*. Milan: Edizioni Ambiente.

Oppermann, Serpil, and Serenella Iovino. 2017. "The Environmental Humanities and the Challenges of the Anthropocene." In *Environmental Humanities: Voices from the Anthropocene*, edited by Serpil Oppermann and Serenella Iovino, 1–21. London: Rowman and Littlefield International.

Parrinello, Giacomo. 2015. *Fault Lines: Earthquakes and Urbanism in Modern Italy*. New York: Berghan Press.

Ross, Silvia. 2010. *Tuscan Spaces: Literary Constructions of Place*. Toronto: Toronto University Press.
Seger, Monica. 2015. *Landscapes in Between: Environmental Change in Modern Italian Literature and Film*. Toronto: Toronto University Press.
Settis, Salvatore. 2012. *Paesaggio, costituzione, cemento: La battaglia per l'ambiente contro il degrado civile*. Turin: Einaudi.
Snow, C. P. 1961. *The Two Cultures and the Scientific Revolution: The Rede Lecture 1959*. Cambridge: Cambridge University Press.
Tarpino, Antonella. 2008. *Geografie della memoria: Case, rovine, oggetti quotidiani*. Turin: Einaudi.
———. 2016. *Il paesaggio fragile: L'Italia vista dai margini*. Turin: Einaudi.
———. 2012. *Spaesati: Luoghi dell'Italia in abbandono tra memoria e futuro*. Turin: Einaudi.
Verdicchio, Pasquale, ed. 2016. *Ecocritical Approaches to Italian Culture and Literature: The Denatured Wild*. Lanham, MD: Lexington Books.
Zapf, Hubert. 2016. "Introduction." In *Handbook of Ecocriticism and Cultural Ecology*, edited by Hubert Zapf, 1–18. Berlin: DeGruyter.

1

NATURES AND VOICES

PATRICK BARRON

Gianni Celati's Voicing of Unpredictable Places

The first book that I read by Gianni Celati was *Narratori delle pianure* (1985; *Voices from the Plains*, 1990), a collection of stories informally gathered during wandering journeys along the Po River, so ordinary and unfiltered that they often seem hyperrealistic. When I chanced upon it in a bookstore in Ferrara, a town in northern Emilia-Romagna where I used to live, the cover photograph immediately captured my attention. In it, a man stands somewhat crookedly on a snowy dirt road, facing away from us toward a snowy flat landscape marked by an indistinct edge, likely a bank of the Po River or one of its tributaries. The man in the photograph I later came to realize is Celati, and the photographer his friend and collaborator Luigi Ghirri, renowned for his images of landscapes. As I opened the book, I saw a map of the Po Valley that roughly charts the geographic and narrative flow of the stories Celati recounts, from near Milan east across northern Italy, passing just to the north of Ferrara where I stood, then flowing into the Adriatic Sea about fifty miles south of Venice. I had been searching for works of Italian literature engaged with landscape and ecology, and in *Narratori delle pianure* found a text that seemed to hold environmental insights at once immediately local and more distant.

The interrelationships between images, maps, and words hinted at in this initial perusal of *Narratori delle pianure* indeed become increasingly complex as various stories unfold in this and similarly situated work. These narratives — mundane, improbable, random — form a complex spatiotemporal awareness of the Po Valley and recount various oscillating human and nonhuman phenomena in mutable, overlaying localities within an immense enveloping bioregional watershed. This awareness has many phenomenological strands, from the visual to the sonic, calling into question the membranous interface between what and how we perceive and the means by which we express this perception. Celati's work, ranging from stories and essays to translations and films, is indeed multisensorial, drawing on as it questions field-based observations of sights, sounds, textures, and smells. It is also multidisciplinary, delving into various fields of environmental study, from geology and cultural geography, to fluvial hydrology and urban studies. He affectionately describes everyday places, giving voice to spatial realities that are often overlooked. He not only speaks about and for places but attempts to answer the question of how we might better listen to the voices of places themselves.

By performing an itinerant "reinhabitation" of ordinary places within the Po Valley, Celati consistently makes evident the "separation between conscious human identity and locatedness" and, in so doing, helps to answer Peter Berg's (2015) question: "How do we rediscover where we actually live?" (62, 61). As Serenella Iovino (2012) argues, "bioregional narratives" such as Celati's can help "'restore the imagination' of place" (100). This is the case even if, as the nomadic Celati claims somewhat slyly in the film *Mondonuovo*, "I don't believe in local identity . . . and I don't believe in belonging to an area, and I don't believe in so-called roots" (Ferrario and Celati 2003). It is perhaps his intense, peripatetic, and at times paradoxically nearly alien engagement with places to which he was once native, that spurs Celati to develop his complex spatial awareness of the Po Valley—in part by a careful study of what Henri Lefebvre (1991) calls "natural rhythms, and of the modification of those rhythms and their inscription in space by means of human actions," by an almost constant concern with "the relations between language and space," and by resisting the temptation to claim as his own images "at once true and false" that the landscape offers (117, 130, 189).

Out of the overarching range of Celati's interests, I am here most interested in how he voices interconnected marginal places in order to draw attention to the ordinary, often overlooked ecologies in which we all live and move. Or, put another way, how he draws various sensations—in particular sounds, words, and images—directly from the landscape to render as immediately as possible the tangled and transitory interrelations between living beings and their organic and inorganic surroundings, whether agricultural, wild, industrial, urban, or suburban. Celati is especially attentive to interstitial *terrains vague*, "seemingly abandoned or overgrown sites where the landscape has gone to seed and been left to its own devices," such as vacant lots, derelict industrial sites, or leftover border areas (Barron 2013, 1). One of the many reasons he is drawn to such caesuras in the landscape is that human-caused disruptions and noises are often muted therein, and other traces and sounds more present. A keen listener, Celati is attuned not only to sonic geographies (distinctive local speech patterns and dialects; Boland 2010), but to greater soundscape ecologies composed of matrices of biological (biophony), geophysical (geophony), and human-produced (anthrophony) sounds (Pijanowsky et al. 2011). Celati's attention to the larger soundscape enables him, as Iain Foreman (2010) argues in relation to W. G. Sebald's similarly *dérive*-based, psychogeographic writing, to hear "the world in simultaneous, interlocking times and spaces where the Other, both temporally and spatially situated, resounds" (9). In his attempt to give voice to the nearly ineffable, Celati gives us a method for re-perceiving the world, for listening to its stories more closely. If we pause to intensely observe wherever we happen to be, distinctions and certainties begin to waver, from where one place ends and another begins, to where what we perceive overlaps with our perceptions, our bodies and selves. Pushed to this edge, language falters as it is also spurred on. As Celati (2011a) puts it, "encounters with places are always unpredictable, attracting us to something we don't know, to something we don't know what to call" (8).[1]

I focus here on *Verso la foce* (1989; *Towards the River's Mouth*, forthcoming), a contemplative travelogue of "stories of observation" that recount slow journeys across the Po Valley, and on the film *Strada provinciale delle anime* (Provincial road of the souls, [1991] 2011), a pseudo-documentary of a bus journey by friends and family to decidedly non-touristic places, many of which also appear in *Verso la foce*. All of Celati's films, while resisting easy categorization, might be called anti-documentary documentaries, in that they recount how any comprehensive sense of the reality of the external world is ultimately un-documentable. They perform what Scott MacDonald (2013) calls the key task of ecocinema, "to provide *new kinds of film experience* that demonstrate an alternative to conventional media-spectatorship and help to nurture a more environmentally progressive mindset" (20). Some techniques that Celati employs to "'retrain' our perceptions of natural (and human) processes" include what Adrian Ivakhiv (2013a) terms "the use of silence and natural sounds, and [the] foregrounding of subjects—places, landscapes, rivers, changing seasons, and everyday visual and sensory occurrences—that usually serve only as background in mainstream cinema" (129). One difference between Celati's films and much of the more radically avant-garde cinema that MacDonald tends to focus on is that while experimental and landscape-scaled, they are built on human narratives, albeit largely unscripted ones.

Verso la foce and *Strada provinciale delle anime* both ask us to carefully and affectionately examine our surroundings while attempting to step back from habitual ways of perceiving and moving through space. The book originated in the company of photographers seeking to document the "new Italian landscape" where divisions between the urban and rural were being blurred into what Celati (1989) describes as "a new variety of countryside where one breathes an air of urban solitude" (9). In the nearly thirty years since *Verso la foce* was first published, this phenomenon of what Eugenio Turri (2004, 20) calls "space built on a diffuse urban fabric" has become even more common, symptomatic of the immense megalopolis that sprawls over vast portions of the Po Valley, growing in intensity near larger urban centers, which are often connected by unbroken strips of urban growth along major roads. Stretching over four hundred miles across northern Italy, the Po Valley contains nearly one-third of the country's total human population, many industries, and some of the most intensively cultivated land in Europe. Water and air pollution continue to plague the area, millions of cubic yards of sand and gravel are dredged (often illegally) from the riverbed, long stretches of the river's banks are dominated by geometric plantations of poplars that are harvested for cellulose, and countless former small farms have been abandoned as large-scale industrial agricultural holdings have proliferated. As Iovino (2012) points out, rather than a bioregion, the Po Valley often resembles a "necroregion" wherein "the 'stories' and 'wisdom' of places seem on the verge of extinction" (102). There are a few protected areas that partially offset the relative sterility of the more intensively exploited zones, notably the Po Delta Regional Park where the river fans out and runs into the Adriatic Sea, an area of about two hundred square miles that has in recent years seen the return of various species of wildlife. There are also many fascinating older urban centers and various early canal systems, some from the sixteenth century that over time have partially melded into surrounding landscapes—yet dead zones of speculation or abandonment are never far away.

Verso la foce traverses the valley in four narrative sections beginning with journeys taken in the days following the 1986 Chernobyl disaster, and then—stepping back and forth in time—wanders downstream along levees, in and out of towns, through areas of reclaimed land, and ends in the delta. The book resists formal literary narrative structures, bringing together moments of perception, observation, and reflection with situated writing in order to render a sense of space as "multiplicity always unraveled, always unraveling" (Celati 2006, 120). As much an exploration of perception and memory as it is of place and space, the book is a series of carefully selected, often filmic observations of riverine landscapes at turns depressingly degraded and at others unexpectedly welcoming in their palimpsest entanglements of human and nonhuman presence. Celati's observational gaze treats every scene as something at once immediately encountered yet also countlessly remembered along "numerous approaches or stimuli [that] converge upon it and lead to it," creating place-based "radial systems" of illuminative "words, comparisons, [and] signs" that he builds around each set of images (Berger [1980] 1991, 67). Celati seeks to expose each location that he describes—in the spirit of John Berger's ordinary-extraordinary field—simultaneously as "a space awaiting events," as a space containing various partly perceived events, and as "an event in itself" (Berger [1980] 1991, 204).

In spare, concentrated prose focused on close-up details of the external world, Celati attempts the difficult task, as Monica Seger (2015) notes, of imbuing "his writing with the not-yet-filtered sensation of initial comprehension" (75). He looks for meaning by seeking the uncertain limits of our ability to discern everyday surroundings. "Every observation," as he writes in his introductory note to *Verso la foce*, "needs liberate itself from the familiar codes it carries, to go adrift in the middle of all things not understood, in order to arrive at an outlet, where it must feel lost" (1989, 10). Berger writes in his essay "The River Po" that the films of Michelangelo Antonioni "question the visible until there's not enough light to see any more" (2001, 136). Celati's writings have a similar quality, and a similar hope that "as we peer, something will come to meet us, something that almost escaped him, something so real that it doesn't have a name" (Berger 2001, 136).

Celati, who like Antonioni grew up in Ferrara close to the Po River and was similarly influenced by the enigmatic landscapes of the surrounding plain, writes of a "reopening" of environmental awareness in Antonioni's films—in their many "still moments, lingering aimless gazes and gestures, the steadiness of the frontal views" (2011d, 30). With this sense of sustained outward perception, "all places become observable," beautiful and ugly alike, with the very act of pausing to linger in places becoming a sign of "our inhabiting the earth, in the realm of the indeterminate. When we stop sensing the landscape as the realm of the indeterminate, and thus beyond description, it means that our environmental comprehension has gone to pot" (31). This lingering in places in order to heighten complex areal perception is evident throughout *Strada provinciale delle anime*, which revisits many ideas and places earlier encountered in *Verso la foce*, with the shared aim to give vocal and visual substance to "spaces marginalized or simply ignored by memory-tradition" (Celati 1975, 221). As Rebecca West (1992) notes, the film "seeks to transcend the limits of traditionally linguistic representations by heightening our awareness of the eloquence of silence, of seeing and being seen, and of the body's role in imagining and reasoning alike" (370).

Strada provinciale certainly has many quiet moments and images of people moving slowly through or resting in outdoor spaces, drawing on what Celati (2011a) calls "il disponibile quotidiano" (the accessible everyday)—everything in landscapes, welcoming and unwelcoming alike, that passes on around us (10). The diegetic soundtrack of the film is attuned to the encompassing soundscape of the journey and shifts from anthropophonic sounds such as the voices of the passengers or the rumble of the bus's engine, to biophonic sounds such as the songs of frogs and insects in a canal, to geophonic sounds such as the wind blowing through plants. Non-diegetic sounds, notably Celati's narrative commentary, occasional voiceovers of fellow travelers, and music, tend not to overwhelm sounds originating from within the immediate world of the film. Celati (2011b) often prefers to leave commentary and music out entirely, mentioning that adding even a minimal amount of external sound causes "an image to disappear" or "to suddenly become conventional."

The roughly thirty friends and relatives that accompany Celati in the film create a sense of companionship that Celati considers integral to making a documentary, in contrast to the solitary activity of writing. The presence of the fellow travelers punctuates the traversed landscapes, however seemingly desolate or anonymous, with "points of affection" and counterbalances to a degree the marginalized and alienated human figures Celati often writes about, including himself (2011a, 12). To follow the voices of his fellow travelers and those of randomly encountered other people is, as Celati writes in *Verso la foce*, "like following the banks of a river in which something flows that cannot be understood abstractly" (1989, 57). The stories of others also counterbalance judgmental worry about environmental and moral degradation: "It's better to listen carefully to others: the sound of voices that come to the ear, all these outpourings of breath that rise up towards the sky" (Celati 1989, 18).

In a brief narrative preface before the opening credits, Celati (2011) sketches in a voiceover the background of the film, recounting that "in the winter months we crisscrossed the Po River Delta in what you might call a triangle, from Ferrara to the Valley of Comacchio, and from here to the farthest point of the Veneto. In the early summer we re-traversed the same landscape in a blue bus together with thirty people because we wanted to see it in another way, that is, with other people. This is how it went. The trip lasted a number of days and everything that happened we'll recount to you—as we remember it." Celati here blurs the individual and the collective, as it is unclear who the "we" is that he mentions—presumably the film crew and other close collaborators, some of whom are also among the thirty people on the bus. The film leaves many aspects ambiguous, from the number of days the journey lasted to when one day ends and another begins. It soon becomes apparent that the remembered story—filled with marginal voices and places—is fragmentary, shared, dreamlike, and without a clear end. With its celebration of memory as collective and imperfect, the film becomes an experiment in mobile collaborative narration in which filmmaking and writing are used as complementary tools to recount a journey through everyday places. As Celati (2011c) explains, one of the main objectives of documentary filmmaking is to record "the exposure to something that can be thought of as an area of the subconscious, composed entirely of ordinary things, with all that which is outside of ourselves: something anonymous and collective, that can't be controlled or presumed" (73). And, as he states later, "my idea is to make documentaries as unpredictable as dreams. Unpredictable not only for the spectators, but even more so for those who make them" (78). What Ivakhiv (2013a, 62) refers to as the "reality-referent" of the surrounding ordinary world taken as a basic premise in most documentaries, in Celati's films appears disruptive and random, continually pointing to the "extra-filmic world" hinted at but always just outside the frame.

Celati ends his narrative preface by glossing the film's title, stating that the "Strada provinciale delle anime," an actual (dead end) road encountered early on, served as a "point of reference for the exploration of these landscapes . . . perhaps because of its name, or because at the moment it doesn't go anywhere" ([1991] 2011). This sense of the landscape as local, immediate, and holding deep meaning, while at the same time being ineffable, full of misleading appearances, and always just out of reach, pervades both *Strada provinciale* and *Verso la foce*.

After Celati's preface and the opening credits, an older man speaks in a voiceover of his impressions of the journey as the camera's gaze wanders around the edges of Piazza San Giorgio in Ferrara, at times following the movements of people and traffic, at other times pausing at a wall, a corner of a park, a railing, sign, curb, or statue. His voice begins by reminiscing about how in the past the busy life of the piazza was the equivalent of people's television and that now people feel the need to travel to far-flung places—in order "to see what?" The vision of the piazza in the film gives the impression of little human activity apart from a few isolated elder residents and the steady passage of cars and buses. The voice goes on to say, "I'll tell you the truth—on this trip we didn't see anything spectacular, but I didn't mind it. We saw lots of places, and everywhere there were many houses like here, and everywhere there were people like us." We are thus given a sense of the end of the journey into the ordinary before it has begun—underlining the reflective nature of the film, which increasingly seems less a journey through linear time than one through memories and situated encounters.

By the time the crew, friends, and relatives board the bus, the film has given us views from all around the piazza, which is bordered on one side by a church and semi-deserted side streets, and on the other by a busy intersection and a bridge over the Po di Volano, a tributary of the Po. Close-up shots of people and buildings are mixed with panning and zooming shots, at times including members of the production crew, who we quickly come to realize will not remain hidden in the background but become part of the film. Piazza San Giorgio seems to lack a central point of interest—as do virtually all places explored in the film. Even the church, whose façade faces away from the grassy open area and the main road toward a slightly forlorn-looking neighborhood, seems to have lost its importance to the greater city. There is some irony here, as this is the oldest area of Ferrara but is just outside the walls and has become primarily an area of transit. The center long ago moved on. Celati seems to delight in this richly layered yet overlooked space at the edge of more concentrated city along a main route leading elsewhere. Here, as in virtually all the predominantly marginal spaces encountered in the film, there are no minutiae unworthy of attention.

Later in the film the bus stops beneath a levee to let the troupe off near a boat bridge in Gorino. The film portrays a complex, layered place filled with human and nonhuman voices, overlaid with boundaries that are difficult to determine. We see a group of people walking up a gravel road to the top of a levee accompanied by a mix of biological, geophysical, and human-produced sounds. Behind the people stretches a view over a vast countryside, as we hear muffled talking mixed with the sounds of insects and birds, then water, wind, and rustling plants. As the river draws nearer, telephoto and wide-angle shots predominate, punctuated with a slow-panning group shot on the bridge after a loud voiceover call for "silence please." All sound is cut, diegetic and non-diegetic alike, and the camera slowly examines the group, once again calling meta-cinematic attention to not only the filmmaking process but to the variety of sounds to which we have just been listening—by their sudden removal. This moment of enforced silence, mimicking the directions of the photographer for the subject to remain still, underlines all narrative and documentary components of the film as fictional, in keeping with Celati's notion of "the belief-giving potential of everyday stories, or what he calls 'fictions in which to believe'" (West 2000, 5). *Strada provinciale* continually makes evident the capacity of cinema, as Ivakhiv (2013b) argues, to produce or disclose anthropomorphic, geomorphic, and biomorphic worlds "of subjects, objects, and things in between"—causing "an interactive oscillation between the cinematic world and the extra-cinematic world" (88). Celati delights in raising the curtain on the film's borders (or what seem to be the film's borders), showing us members of the camera and sound crew, letting us listen to their comments and directions, and in this case, making evident the construction of the soundtrack by taking it away. As he mentions in an interview, such inclusions of meta-cinema combat the sensation of falseness that can arise in documentaries when the external world presented appears overly determined, defined, or real (Celati 2011b).

As the film continues and sound is eventually restored, we see Luigi Ghirri photographing, a fisherman pulling in a carp, details of the bridge and water, a few slowly passing cars, a seagull, and river plants. The voices of two crew members, worried about time, futilely call for the group to return, with one imploring comically to the other, "What's there to see in the Veneto?" Taking this as a cue, the camera explores the landscape on the far side of the northern levee, focusing on a row of pieced-together rural houses and a church, hung laundry flapping in the wind, fields with newly planted crops in lines, and blowing dust. The effect of this sequence, as of many others in the film, is to blur the line between spectator and spectacle, between interior and exterior. The crossing—of the water, of regions, of modes of perception—is a brief but meaningful pausing in space, a slowed-down sequence of places that allows for a more intimate interaction with the landscape.

To end I offer Celati's description of the main piazza in a small town called Pomponesco. It appears toward the end of the first section of *Verso la foce* in between descriptions of two nearby areas—"an immense mazelike industrial area" and a sea of strange invasive plants that seem "artificially green," perhaps due to nuclear fallout, and made of a "faintly monstrous plastic material that in some unknown manner has taken on a shape of nature, by now indistinguishable from nature" (Celati 1989, 46, 47). The piazza, to which Celati returns in two later films, *Il mondo di Luigi Ghirri* and *Case sparse*, is a place of repose and hope despite so much evidence to the contrary, where from the intersection of built and open space there arises the possibility of readjusting our perceptual habits to recognize and embrace a collective sense of belonging to the world:

> The town extends out from around the marvelous rectangular piazza, not humiliated by concrete and the new. The perspective down the piazza is delimited by two columns just below the levee, the narrowed end of a quiet street with beautiful old houses, and carries the eye towards open space. There at the end, the open space arises from behind a horizon, causing a sensation of indistinct distance that gives a sense of our spatial relatedness. The piazza almost always empty, where the emptiness reveals itself as welcoming—where welcomed, we were able to notice other welcomed passersby, without the usual sensation of unease. (Celati 1989, 46)

In narrating this multifaceted layering of ordinary places—the piazza, the levee, the unseen water and countryside beyond—Celati reveals an emptiness that is rather a fullness of attention, a decelerated and affectionate moving in and with space, a focus on edges such that they begin to dissolve. It is then up to us to seek out our own intense observations of the external world where place, body, and language at once gain and lose definition, where bemused we begin to make sense of the very stuff of life.

NOTE

1. All translations, unless otherwise noted, are my own.

WORKS CITED

Barron, Patrick. 2013. "Introduction: At the Edge of the Pale." In *Terrain Vague: Interstices at the Edge of the Pale*, edited by Manuela Mariani and Patrick Barron, 1–23. London: Routledge.

Berg, Peter. 2015. *The Biosphere and the Bioregion: Essential Writings of Peter Berg*. Edited by Cheryll Glotfelty and Eve Quesnel. London: Routledge.

Berger, John. (1980) 1991. *About Looking*. New York: Vintage.

———. 2001. *The Shape of a Pocket*. New York: Pantheon.

Boland, Philip. 2010. "Sonic Geography, Place and Race in the Formation of Local Identity." *Geografiska Annaler: Series B, Human Geography* 92(1): 1–22.

Celati, Gianni. 1975. *Finzioni occidentali: Fabulazione, comicità e scrittura*. Turin: Einaudi.

———. 1985. *Narratori delle pianure*. Milan: Feltrinelli.

———. 1989. *Verso la foce*. Milan: Feltrinelli.

———. (1991) 2011. *Strada provinciale delle anime*. In *Cinema all'aperto: Tre documentari e un libro*. Rome: Fandango. DVD.

———. 2006. Interview with Marina Spunta. In *Il romanzo contemporaneo: Voci italiane*, edited by Franca Pellegrini and Elisabetta Tarantino, 117–31. Leicester, UK: Troubador.

———. 2011a. Interview with Fabrizio Grosoli. In *Documentari imprevedibili come i sogni: Il cinema di Gianni Celati*, edited by Nunzia Palmieri, 7–16. Rome: Fandango.

———. 2011b. Interview with Matteo Bellizzi. In *Doppiozero*. http://www.doppiozero.com/materiali/speciali/intervista-di-matteo-bellizzi-gianni-celati.

———. 2011c. Interview with Sarah Hill. In *Documentari imprevedibili come i sogni: Il cinema di Gianni Celati*, edited by Nunzia Palmieri, 71–85. Rome: Fandango.

———. 2011d. "La veduta frontale: Antonioni, *L'avventura* e l'attesa." In *Documentari imprevedibili come i sogni: Il cinema di Gianni Celati*, edited by Nunzia Palmieri, 27–32. Rome: Fandango.

———. Forthcoming. *Towards the River's Mouth*. Translated and edited by Patrick Barron. Lanham, MD: Lexington.

Ferrario, Davide, Dir., with Gianni Celati. 2003. *Mondonuovo*. DVD. Bologna: Movie Movie.

Foreman, Iain. 2010. "Vertiginous Spaces, Phantasmagorical Geographies: Soundscape Composition after Sebald." *Soundscape* 10(1): 7–10.

Iovino, Serenella. 2012. "Restoring the Imagination of Place: Narrative Reinhabitation and the Po Valley." In *The Bioregional Imagination*, edited by Tom Lynch, Cheryll Glotfelty, and Karla Armbruster, 100–117. Athens: University of Georgia Press.

Ivakhiv, Adrian. 2013a. *Ecologies of the Moving Image*. Waterloo, ON: Wilfrid Laurier University Press.

———. 2013b. "An Ecophilosophy of the Moving Image." In *Ecocinema Theory and Practice*, edited by Stephen Rust, Salma Monani, and Sean Cubitt, 87–105. New York: Routledge.

Lefebvre, Henri. 1991. *The Production of Space*. Translated by Donald Nicholson-Smith. London: Blackwell.

MacDonald, Scott. 2013. "The Ecocinema Experience." In *Ecocinema Theory and Practice*, edited by Stephen Rust, Salma Monani, and Sean Cubitt, 17–41. New York: Routledge.

Pijanowsky, Bryan, Luis Villanueva-Rivera, Sarah Dumyahn, Almo Farina, Bernie Krause, Brian Napoletano, Stuart Gage, and Nadia Pieretti. 2011. "Soundscape Ecology: The Science of Sound in the Landscape." *BioScience* 61(3): 203–16.
Seger, Monica. 2015. *Landscapes In Between: Environmental Change in Modern Italian Literature and Film.* Toronto: Toronto University Press.
Turri, Eugenio. 2004. *La megalopoli padana.* Venice: Marsilio.
West, Rebecca. 1992. "Gianni Celati's *La strada provinciale delle anime*: A 'Silent' Film about Nothing." *Romance Languages Annual* 4(1): 367–74.
———. 2000. *Gianni Celati: The Craft of Everyday Storytelling.* Toronto: Toronto University Press.

ALMO FARINA

An Ecology of Voices: The Soundscapes of Tuscany's Lunigiana

The influence of the environment on the life of organisms is a pillar of the theory of ecology, and this assumption can be used as metaphor to explain which factors inspire the scientific research on natural phenomena. In my case, the choice to study sounds from an ecological perspective has been inspired by the environment in which I have for a long time spent my professional life as a field naturalist. This is Lunigiana, a small subregion located between Tuscany and Liguria, in which sea and mountains, lowlands and steep slopes support a finely grained mosaic of rural patches and human settlements scattered according to invisible rules, written by the distribution of potential resources.

This area contains an amazing diversity of physical, biological, and cultural entities (Farina 1980) that create an ecological puzzle hard to solve when approached with the tools of traditional "spatial" ecology. With the help of new digital hardware and supported by innovative metrics, I have used environmental sounds as a model to investigate the ecological complexity of this region. This model has also been successfully exported to other environmental contexts far from this European location.

Principles of Ecoacoustics

Sounds are fundamental biosemiotic tools used by many animals to establish intra- and interspecific communication, to memorize their individual environment or *umwelt* (von Uexküll 1982), and to orient themselves across individually based cognitive landscapes (Farina 2010, 19).

Depending on the sources, sounds are distinguished in geophonies (when the source is constituted by geophysical agents: running water, wind, thunder, etc.), biophonies (when it results from animal voices: songs, calls, vocalizations), and technophonies (when it results from human machinery: engines and dynamic machines of all types). These three sources, when combined, create unique acoustic signatures or soundscapes (Pijanowski et al. 2011) that are composed of acoustic patches or sonotopes (Farina 2014, 16–17). Sonotopes are further divided according to a functional criterion into soundtopes or acoustic communities (Farina and James 2016). These emergent patterns are highly dynamic and respond to environmental variables and to animal and human behavior as well (Farina 2014).

Recently, sounds have been recognized as an ecological indicator to assess the quality of habitats (Pijanowski et al. 2011), and as important proxies of environmental functioning (Towsey et al. 2014). In particular, sounds can help detect early signs of animal stress connected to climate change (Krause and Farina 2016), and to assess the consequences of acoustic pollution caused by human intrusion in the environment (Pivato 2011; Farina 2015). Sounds have also been used as proxies for biodiversity (Sueur et al. 2008), and passive recording of animal acoustics using digital voice recorders is particularly effective in areas that are hard to visit because of their remoteness or difficult climatic conditions, like forests in the tropics (e.g., Ochoa, O'Farrell, and Miller 2000) and circumpolar boreal forests (Mullet 2015).

Ecoacoustics, a recent discipline that offers theoretical and methodological support for exploring acoustic complexity across a broad spectrum of perspectives, focuses on the ecological role of sounds. This discipline has been defined by Sueur and Farina (2015) as "a theoretical and applied discipline that studies sound along a broad range of spatial and temporal scales in order to tackle biodiversity and other ecological questions" (494). By "covering all ecological organization levels, ecoacoustics includes *ipso facto* soundscape ecology, which is a field of research specifically dedicated to the study of the sounds emerging from the landscape" (494).

The advancement of ecoacoustics studies has been possible thanks to the availability of new technologies for passive recording, using digital recorders to sample sounds at a scheduled time and sampling rate. Additionally, new indices that capture acoustic information have been written and tested in different biomes (Gage and Axel 2014; Gage, Napoletano, and Cooper 2001; Fuller et al. 2015; Towsey et al. 2014; Sueur et al. 2008; Sueur et al. 2014).

Opportunities for Ecoacoustic Studies in Lunigiana

Recent advancements in theory, concepts, and application of ecoacoustics carried out by myself and my collaborators during the last ten years have been facilitated by the possibility of conducting ecoacoustics research in the environmental context of Lunigiana. This area is an extraordinary field laboratory. Extending nearly 155 square miles, it offers an unexpected variety of landscapes and soundscapes (Farina 1980). At the border between Tuscany and Liguria, Lunigiana is an intermontane basin located on the western side of the Tuscan-Emilian Apennines mountain range, delimited on its western side by the Tyrrhenian Sea. Lunigiana has a complex morphology dominated by alluvial plains, steep hills, and low mountains (the highest peak is 6,500 feet; Page 1962). The complexity of a finely grained pattern of cultivated forest patches and sparse human settlements represents an example of a "full world anthropogenic model" (Farina et al. 2003, 16), that is to say, a place where, over thousands of years, indigenous people have modified many of the ecological assets of the landscape, preserving necessary resources (Farina 2012) and enforcing resilient strategies that have preserved a substantial biodiversity. A Mediterranean sub-humid maquis along the coast and a mesophyll woodland are the dominant forest cover (Ferrarini 1972, 1979, 1988). Olive orchards, vineyards, and crop fields create a patchy mosaic on the warmest southern and western hill slopes, which were transformed into a terraced rural landscape over a long history of settlement by the Ligurian-Apuan tribes who historically inhabited this region (Ambrosi 1981). Today, the Lunigiana is suffering the effects of land abandonment and lowland urbanization, and these factors are, in turn, added to the evident effects of climate change with regard to the distribution and dynamics of animal communities.

The International Institute of Ecoacoustics was founded in collaboration with the University of Urbino in 2015 in Fivizzano (a village located in the eastern part of Lunigiana, in the province of Massa-Carrara, Tuscany) in order to develop ecoacoustic research in this region.[1] This is a nonprofit research institute devoted to the dissemination of ecoacoustic theories and methodologies. In particular, pioneering studies on the ecoacoustics of birds have been carried out in this area using, for the first time, the Acoustic Complexity Index (ACI), a metric I conceived in 2008 (Farina and Morri 2008) and later implemented with my collaborators (Pieretti, Farina, and Morri 2011), which proved to be particularly efficient as a way to measure the amount of information present in an acoustic file. This metric is based on the information conveyed by the difference in amplitude between successive pulses along the frequency bins of a spectrogram; it has been subsequently used in different geographical contexts, both in terrestrial habitats (Farina, Pieretti, and Morganti 2013; Farina, Pieretti, and Piccioli 2011; Pieretti and Farina 2013; Lozano, Farina, and Márquez 2014; Bobryck et al. 2015; Duarte et al. 2015) and in marine systems (McWilliam and Hawkins 2013; Staaterman et al. 2013; Kaplan et al. 2015).

The ecoacoustic research that I conducted in recent years in Lunigiana under the endorsement of the University of Urbino and, even more recently, of the International Institute of Ecoacoustics, has focused on six main project goals:

- Test the performance of the Acoustic Complexity Index (ACI) metrics
- Test the new, low-cost digital recorder, Soundscape Explorer Terrestrial (SET) and the open access software (Soundscape Meter, release 1.0 and 2.0)
- Investigate the seasonal dynamics of acoustic communities
- Investigate the acoustic patterns of bird choruses at dawn
- Establish a net of acoustic sensors to investigate long-term effects due to change of climate and change of land use
- Test the biosemiotic acoustic event model in order to mine big data and to extract meaningful information to be applied in land management and resource protection

Since 2008, the ACI has been tested in different typologies of field recorders and has proven to be correlated with bird diversity (Pieretti, Farina, and Morri 2011).

The Soundscape Explorer (with its two versions, Terrestrial [SET] and Aquatic [SEA]), in particular, offers new, exclusive performances and can be considered in the category of low-cost digital recorders (Farina et al. 2015).[2]

The terrestrial device (SET), which my colleagues and I have been using in Lunigiana, has two microphones with sampling capacities of 48 kHz and 192 kHz, respectively, and four sensors (measuring humidity, pressure, temperature, and light) that operate during sound recording. SET processes in real time the acoustic data which is stored in .wav format, using the indices $ACIt_f$ and $ACIf_t$ (Farina and Morri 2008; Pieretti, Farina, and Morri 2011; Farina et al. 2016).

During the spring and summer of 2011, and then again in 2012, we conducted surveys at the Deiva Marina maquis and assessed the dynamics of the local acoustic community. We noticed interesting patterns in this acoustic community, and we paid special attention to the distribution of the acoustic information according to the frequency bins. In particular, we noted that frequencies lower than 1,500 Hz and empirically associated to geophonies and technophonies are particularly abundant in the winter. Frequencies larger than 1,500 Hz and associated to biophonies are present especially during the breeding period, with an increased presence in October. This second pattern has been associated with birds' migratory time, which confirms the stopover function of this area and its role as an important bridge during the seasonal migrations between northern Europe and Africa. During the spring and summer of 2014, we investigated the acoustic patterns of bird choruses at dawn. Choruses are an important moment in the dynamic of acoustic communities. Recent investigations conducted in different habitats with different levels of potential resources for birds revealed interesting patterns among them (Farina et al. 2015). In particular, we observed that a dawn chorus is more relevant when compared with daily acoustic activity in habitats with low resources. This is a finding that confirms the importance of food resources for maintaining a high level of song activity all day long.

During 2015, the International Institute of Ecoacoustics established a total of five permanent recording stations that operate to assess the changes occurring in the landscape structure and in climatic conditions. This project, called Lunigiana Ecoacoustic Monitoring (LEM), aims to illustrate the results obtained by the ecoacoustic processing. Moreover, this project intends to monitor the effects of climate change on bird populations and communities and to demonstrate the importance of an ecoacoustic approach as a means for low-cost remote sensing in situ, one that could be used by engaged citizen scientists and by local governments as well. As a matter of fact, the ecoacoustics methodology is not expensive and allows us to investigate phenomena on a small spatial scale. Climate change has an impact on both the sound performance of vocal species and on the geophonic soundscape as well. We maintain that our ecoacoustic approach is affordable and that it is definitely a good instrument to measure the challenges posed by climate change and its effects on species, populations, and communities. Biophonies, in fact, are life traits characterized by a high plasticity; they may change earlier than other environmental characteristics, such as vegetation in its composition and geographical shift. This characteristic of biophonies is thus extremely important for policymakers and stakeholders seeking to discover early symptoms of environmental changes. Ecoacoustics may therefore provide the tools necessary to conceive advance remediation actions to reduce the risk that an ecological debt (Tilman et al. 1994) will later produce irreversible changes in species composition, up to potential extinction.

That said, the use of passive recording in long-term studies addressing environmental complexity still presents difficulties because of the great amount of acoustic data that must be processed. This often forces researchers to adopt a sampling strategy instead of doing continuous surveys (Wimmer et al. 2013; Pieretti et al. 2015). Furthermore, in many cases, the ecoacoustic indices are not informative enough to interpret the complex patterns created by acoustic phenomena, and biosemiotics models are required (Farina 2010, 128). In order to look for solutions to these problems, I have recently proposed a new methodology for acoustic data mining: the ecoacoustics event detection and identification (EEDI) model. This model facilitates the survey of big data, reduces processing time, and identifies acoustic patterns. EEDI is based on the detection and identification of ecoacoustic events that are defined as a phenomenological acoustic category, one that is empirically fixed when the sources of sounds are not considered in isolation but as part of an emergent acoustic pattern that should fulfill specific functions (Farina et al. 2016). For instance, an ecoacoustic event may happen when birds are singing in a heavy rainfall or when a chorus of stopover migratory birds occurs in the early afternoon.

The EEDI model is particularly important in Mediterranean landscapes where the patchy distribution of habitats and a diffuse human presence reduce the efficiency of assessing the dynamics of species, populations, and communities via traditional ecological methods, such as point counts or line transects (Bystrak 1981; Ralph and Scott 1981; Verner 1985; Bibby, Burgess, and Hill 1992). The EEDI strategy is based on the possibility of restricting the range of analysis of the acoustic files; that is, it excludes from the computation all the conditions that are not relevant to the investigation. This reduction of the computational effort is achieved by selecting the thresholds to apply to environmental variables, such as temperature, light, humidity, or time of day, and to ACI metrics ($ACIt_f$ and $ACIf_t$). The EEDI model is based on the assumption that a combination of ACI metrics discriminate among ecoacoustic events. The EEDI model comprises two steps. After having fixed a specific range of values of certain environmental conditions, such as temperature and light, the first step involves plotting $ACIf_t$ with its evenness ($ACIf_{te}$), creating an ecoacoustic event space in which only data that responds to the selected conditions appears. The second step identifies an event using the computation of the level of correlation/similarity between the detected event(s) and the acoustic signatures ($ACIt_f$) selected from a library of identified events

The entire procedure, from the recording moment to the real-time calculation of the ACI metric executed by the onboard software of SET, is carried out automatically using the Soundscape Explorer 2.0 routine. EEDI is thus an important procedure, able to distinguish and identify several ecoacoustic events, such as heavy rain, thunder, wind, the alarm call of a bird, dawn and dusk choruses, the passage of a car or an airplane, and so on. The philosophy behind this procedure is based on the premise that sounds are often not perceived in isolation by a cognitive animal but rather as a whole soundscape which carries meaning. Every soundscape perceived by individual species is the result of both a perceptive capacity and a cognitive elaboration based on the memory of the meaning of signals. One may say that ecoacoustic events are thus empirical cognitive patterns that depend on the individual species considered as the sum of its experience and its physiological and behavioral status. EEDI opens a new way to interpret and classify soundscapes responding to empirical models that can be designed according to the goals of a specific analysis, and it represents a good example of an application of biosemiotic models to quantitative data.

The ecoacoustic approach is a particularly efficient way to study the complexity of ecological phenomena over a broad range of temporal and spatial scales, in both terrestrial and aquatic environments. The great sensitivity of sound performances to environmental variables makes sounds proxies for relevant phenomena such as climate change, noise pollution, and loss of biodiversity, which are creating concern in modern societies. The new theories, models, methods, and technologies that I have illustrated are particularly efficient when the empirical tests are carried out in appropriate environmental conditions like those found in Lunigiana. The complexity of the Mediterranean landscape is well represented in this relatively small area, and the ecoacoustic approach seems apt to capture the variability of the land mosaic and to differentiate human intrusion. At the same time, the Lunigiana ecoacoustic research model might also be successfully exported to many other regions across the Mediterranean and, in particular, LEM and EEDI could be respectively located and applied in regions where ecological investigation is minimal and where economic resources to conduct ecological research are scarce.

NOTES

1. For more on the insitute, visit www.iinsteco.org.
2. These are designed by the International Institute of Ecoacoustics and manufactured by Lunilettronik, in Fivizzano, Italy.

WORKS CITED

Ambrosi, C. A. 1981. *Lunigiana: La preistoria e la romanizzazione.* Vol. I: *La preistoria.* Aulla, Italy: Centro Aullese di Ricerche e di Studi Lunigianesi.

Bibby, C. J., N. D. Burgess, and D. A. Hill. 1992. *Bird Census Techniques.* London: Academic Press.

Bobryk, W. C., C. C. Rega, S. Bardhan, A. Farina, H. S. He, and S. Jose. 2015. "Utility of Soundscape Assessment for Understanding Conservation Benefits of Temperate Agroforestry Systems." *Agroforestry Systems* 90: 997–1008.

Bystrak, D. 1981. "The North American Breeding Bird Survey." *Studies in Avian Biology* 6: 34–41.

Duarte, M. H. L., R. S. Sousa-Lima, R. J. Young, A. Farina, M. Vasconcelos, M. Rodrigues, and N. Pieretti. 2015. "The Impact of Noise from Open-Cast Mining on Atlantic Forest Biophony." *Biological Conservation* 191: 623–31.

Farina, A. 1980. *Itinerari educativi. Lunigiana: L'ambiente e i suoi caratteri.* Centro Aullelse di Ricerche e di Studi Lunigianesi. La Spezia, Italy: Tipografia Ambrosiana.

———. 2010. *Ecology, Cognition and Landscape: Linking Natural and Social Systems.* Dordrecht, Netherlands: Springer.

———. 2012. "A Biosemiotic Perspective of the Resource Criterion: Toward a General Theory of Resources." *Biosemiotics* 5: 17–32.

———. 2014. *Soundscape Ecology: Principles, Patterns, Methods and Applications.* Dordrecht, Netherlands: Springer.

———. 2015. "Animals in a Noisy World." In *Thinking about Animals in the Age of Anthropocene,* edited by Ratasepp Tønnessen and Oma Armstrong, 37–52. Lanham, MD: Lexington Books.

Farina, A., A. R. Johnson, S. J. Turner, and A. Belgrano. 2003. "'Full' World versus 'Empty' World Paradigm at the Time of Globalisation." *Ecological Economics* 45: 1–18.

Farina, A., M. Ceraulo, C. Bobryk, N. Pieretti, E. Quinci, and E. Lattanzi. 2015. "Spatial and Temporal Variation of Bird Dawn Chorus and Successive Acoustic Morning Activity in a Mediterranean Landscape." *Bioacoustics* 24(3): 269–88.

Farina, A., and P. James. 2016. "The Acoustic Communities: Definition, Description and Ecological Role." *Biosystems* 147: 11–20.

Farina, A., and D. Morri. 2008. "Source-sink e eco-field: Ipotesi ed evidenze sperimentali." In *Atti del X congresso nazionale della SIEP-IALE. Ecologia e governance del paesaggio: esperienze e prospettive*, edited by P. Mairota, M. Mininni, R. Lafortezza, and E. Padoa-Schioppa, 365–372. Bari, Italy: SIEP-IALE.

Farina, A., N. Pieretti, and N. Morganti. 2013. "Acoustic Patterns of an Invasive Species: The Red Billed Leiothrix (Leiothrix lutea Scopoli 1786) in a Mediterranean Shrubland." *Bioacoustics* 22(3): 175–94.

Farina, A., N. Pieretti, and L. Piccioli. 2011. "The Soundscape Methodology for Long-Term Bird Monitoring: A Mediterranean Europe Case-Study." *Ecological Informatics* 6: 354–63.

Farina, A., N. Pieretti, P. Salutari, E. Tognari, and A. Lombardi. 2016. "The Application of the Acoustic Complexity Indices (ACI) to Ecoacoustic Event Detection and Identification (EEDI) Modeling." *Biosemiotics* 9(2): 227–46.

Ferrarini, E. 1972. "Carta della vegetazione delle Alpi Apuane e zone limitrofe: Note illustrative." *Webbia* 27: 551–82.

———. 1979. "Studi sulla vegetazione dell'Appennino settentrionale (Dal Passo della Cisa al Passo delle Radici)." *Memorie dell'Accademia Lunigianese di Scienze* 43/44: 1–157.

———. 1988. "Carta della vegetazione dell'Appennino settentrionale dalla Cisa al Gottero e alle Cinque Terre: Note illustrative." *Memorie dell'Accademia Lunigianese di Scienze* 51/53: 173–92.

Fuller, S., A. C. Axel, D. Tucker, and S. H. Gage. 2015. "Connecting Soundscape to Landscape: Which Acoustic Index Best Describes Landscape Configuration?" *Ecological Indicators* 58: 207–15.

Gage, S. H., and A. C. Axel. 2014. "Visualization of Temporal Change in Soundscape Power of a Michigan Lake Habitat over a Four-Year Period." *Ecological Informatics* 21: 100–109.

Gage, S. H., B. M. Napoletano, and M. C. Cooper. 2001. "Assessment of Ecosystem Biodiversity by Acoustic Diversity Indices." *Journal of the Acoustical Society of America* 109(5): 2430.

Kaplan, B. M., T. A. Mooney, J. Partan, and R. A. Solow. 2015. "Coral Reef Species Assemblages Are Associated with Ambient Soundscape." *Marine Ecology Progress Series* 533: 93–107.

Krause, B., and A. Farina. 2016. "Using Ecoacoutic Methods to Survey the Impacts of Climate Change on Biodiversity." *Biological Conservation* 195: 245–54.

Lozano, A., A. Farina, and R. Márquez. 2014. "ACI (Acoustic Complexity Index): A New Tool to Study Anuran Calls." *Quehacer Científico en Chiapas* 9(2): 17–27.

McWilliam, J. N., and A. D. Hawkins. 2013. "A Comparison of Inshore Marine Soundscapes." *Journal of Experimental Marine Biology and Ecology* 446: 166–76.

Mullet, T. 2015. "Temporal and Spatial Variation of a Winter Soundscape in South-Central Alaska." *Landscape Ecology* 31: 1117.

Ochoa, G. J., J. M. O'Farrell, and W. B. Miller. 2000. "Contribution of Acoustic Methods to the Study of Insectivorous Bat Diversity in Protected Areas from North Venezuela." *Acta Chiropterologica* 282: 171–83.

Page, B. 1962. "Geology South and East of Passo della Cisa Northern Apennines." *Bollettino della Società Geologica Italiana* 81(3): 147–94.

Pieretti, N., M. H. L. Duarte, R. S. Sousa-Lima, M. Rodrigues, R. J. Young, and A. Farina. 2015. "Determining Temporal Sampling Schemes for Passive Acoustic Studies in Different Tropical Ecosystems." *Tropical Conservation Science* 8(1): 215–34.

Pieretti, N., and A. Farina. 2013. "Application of a Recently Introduced Index for Acoustic Complexity to an Avian Soundscape with Traffic Noise." *Journal of the Acoustical Society of America* 134(1): 891–900.

Pieretti, N., A. Farina, and D. Morri. 2011. "A New Methodology to Infer the Singing Activity of an Avian Community: The Acoustic Complexity Index (ACI)." *Ecological Indicators* 11: 868–73.

Pijanowski, B. C., L. J. Villanueva-Riiera, S. L. Dumyahn, A. Farina, B. L. Krause, M. Napoletano, S. H. Gage, and N. Pieretti. 2011. "Soundscape Ecology: The Science of Sound in the Landscape." *BioScience* 61: 203–16.

Pivato, S. 2011. *Il secolo del rumore*. Milan: Il Mulino.

Ralph, C. J., and J. M. Scott, eds. 1981. "Estimating Numbers of Terrestrial Birds." In *Studies in Avian Biology*, vol. 6. Los Angeles: Cooper Ornithological Society.

Staaterman, E., A. N. Rice, D. A. Mann, and C. B. Paris. 2013. "Soundscapes from a Tropical Eastern Pacific Reef and a Caribbean Sea Reef." *Coral Reefs* 32(2): 553–57.

Sueur, J., and A. Farina. 2015. "Acoustics: The Ecological Investigation and Interpretation of Environmental Sound." *Biosemiotics* 8: 493–502.

Sueur, J., A. Farina, A. Gasc, N. Pieretti, and S. Pavoine. 2014. "Acoustic Indices for Biodiversity Assessment and Landscape Investigation." *Acta Acustica United with Acustica* 100: 772–81.

Sueur, J., S. Pavoine, O. Hamerlynck, and S. Duvail. 2008. "Rapid Acoustic Survey for Biodiversity Appraisal." *PLoSONE* 3: 1–9.

Tilman, D., R. M. May, C. L. Lehman, and M. A. Nowak. 1994. "Habitat Destruction and the Extinction Debt." *Nature* 371, 65–66.

Towsey, M., J. Wimmer, I. Williamson, and P. Roe. 2014. "The Use of Acoustic Indices to Determine Avian Species Richness in Audio–Recordings of the Environment." *Ecological Informatics* 21: 110–19.

Verner, J. 1985. "Assessment of Counting Techniques." *Current Ornithology* 2: 247–302.

von Uexküll, J. 1982. "The Theory of Meaning." *Semiotica* 42(1): 25–82.

Wimmer, J., M. Towsey, P. Roe, and I. Williamson. 2013. "Sampling Environmental Acoustic Recordings to Determine Bird Species Richness." *Ecological Application* 23(6): 1419–28.

DAMIANO BENVEGNÙ

"Birds Who Speak My Dialect": Poetry, Birds, and Landscape in Andrea Zanzotto

In the introduction to her *Penguin Book of Bird Poetry* Peggy Munsterberg claims that if Julius Caesar were to come back to Britain today, he would recognize nothing of the landscape but the gulls screaming around the boats, because they are the same today as they were when he arrived in 55 BCE (1980, 25). Her statement highlights our hearing the birds rather than our usual seeing them; it thus indicates that sound is a fundamental property of the landscape.[1] Yet, it is likely inaccurate: in modern times, birds have become extinct at an exceptionally high rate, and even many common bird species, such as gulls, are in dramatic decline (BirdLife International 2014). This decline had already proven an ominous sign for the ecosystemic balances of industrialized countries in 1962 when Rachel Carson (2002) significantly titled her seminal book *Silent Spring*, as large areas of the United States were becoming "strangely silent where once they were filled with the beauty of bird songs" (103).

According to Carson, this sudden silencing was the consequence of the mutation of traditional agro-pastoral practices, in particular the indiscriminate use of pesticides. A recent study sponsored by the Italian government proves her claim, affirming that avifauna is an effective biodiversity indicator when it comes to agricultural landscapes and rural habitats, and this is particularly patent in Italy (Rete Rurale Nazionale & LIPU 2011, 6–11). More specifically, the Italian League for Bird Protection (LIPU) in 2009 established that forty-five of the eighty-eight species of birds that regularly nest in this country are vulnerable or endangered due to the increasing disappearance of the traditional agro-pastoral landscape (Brambilla, Celada, and Gustin 2010, 1150–51; see also Cecere et al. 2012, 11–23). The extremely rapid and radical changes in Italy's economic structure have thus not only created "a semantic vacuum in the ways of considering the relationships between the physical environment and society" (Soriani, Vallerani, and Zanetto 1996, 71), but also a decrease in bird populations at least as dramatic as the disappearance of fireflies famously denounced by Pier Paolo Pasolini in 1975 (1981, 128–34; see also Iovino 2006, 101–21). The ongoing silencing of Italian birds in fact ratifies the definitive dissolution of the Italian agro-pastoral landscape, whose typical sounds have traditionally been embedded in Italy's natural, as well as cultural, identity.

Few regions in Italy have experienced a more radical mutation in the last two centuries than the Veneto. From the persistence of agro-pastoralism to new models of "diffused industry," this northeastern region has been the object of several studies about the conflicting aspects of our modern cultural and environmental crisis.[2] For instance, between the 1950s and the 1990s the Veneto witnessed a decrease in agro-pastoral employment from almost 46 percent of the population to a marginal 6 percent (Fumian and Ventura 2004, 217). Surprisingly, this major transformation affected the linguistic diglossia of the local communities less and later than other northern Italian regions, testifying to the resistance of an anthropic soundscape indeed capable of reconciling "the local to the global dimension of our perceptional Umwelt" (Farina 2014, 4).[3] Prompted by this apparent paradox of an idiom surviving the mutation of its socioeconomic origins, poets and writers from this area have been particularly concerned with the connections between the transformation of their places, their literary work, and their vernaculars.[4]

This essay examines the significance of birds and bird songs in the literary work of Andrea Zanzotto (1921–2011). Born in the small town of Pieve di Soligo (province of Treviso, Veneto), where he spent almost his entire life, Zanzotto is one of the most important European poets of the twentieth century and particularly meaningful for at least two reasons. According to the poet and literary critic Gian Mario Villalta, Zanzotto understood and described the reality of the Veneto and of a large part of Europe in the last few decades better than any other writer of his generation (Villalta 2001, 13). Although he frequently featured his own geographical location and community in his writing, Zanzotto's work also implies the transformations of that peculiar relationship between human culture and the natural environment that characterize the Italian landscape as a whole.[5] He also wrote both in Italian and in Pieve di Soligo's patois. In so doing, he not only testified to the diglossia of many Italian speakers but also poetically investigated the ties between language, community, and territory. One may say, paraphrasing Gary Snyder, that Zanzotto's poetry is one of the most emblematic examples of global bioregionalism, because his relation to the natural world indeed occurs in a place but is nonetheless grounded in information and experience we can use to interpret and reimagine certain aspects of our tangled contemporary reality at large (Snyder 1990, 39; see also Heise 2009). As we will see, birds in Zanzotto's poetry have in fact the imaginative function of binding the natural sounds of the landscape with the voices of a specific human community and its language. They thereby help us to better understand the evolutionary dynamics connected to the life of a place threatened by destruction, as well as to reflect upon nature and poetry as key elements of the soundscape ecology (Iovino 2012, 100–107).

Although references to birds are present throughout Zanzotto's work, here I focus on three key occurrences. The first belongs to Zanzotto's inaugural book of poetry, *Dietro il paesaggio* (Behind the landscape, 1951), written during and immediately after World War II, at the very beginning of Italian economic mutation. As Mengaldo (2003, 871) has pointed out, in this book Zanzotto identifies the poetic subject with his native language and the language with the landscape as a whole, perceived as both protective and threatening. The poem titled "Lorna" mirrors such a double overlap with a middle section that includes three questions to elements (the sun, the birds, and the river) of the specific environment around Pieve di Soligo. Addressing the birds as "Uccelli che parlate il mio dialetto" ("birds who speak my dialect") he asks them about the "fresh eyelashes" of a mysterious feminine figure that, as often in Zanzotto, can be an actual woman, a personification of poetry, or even nature itself.[6]

As Almo Farina (2014) has pointed out, for both humans and birds dialect "represents variation of the acoustic theme performed by a local population of a species under specific environmental constraints" (91). In Zanzotto's case, these constraints are both historical and environmental, or direct consequences of that *"immorari in loco"* (existing in place) that he sees as the fundamental characteristic of any local language (Zanzotto 1998, 18). Therefore, in "Lorna" the birds speak the same dialect as the humans because they all belong to a common soundscape that is both familiar and paradisiacal (i.e., both heavenly and etymologically separated), evoked by the poet in order to protect himself and his sense of place.[7] As Zanzotto confirmed in a 2004 interview, in *Dietro il paesaggio* nature embodies an objection to the lacerations of human history, and thus the vernacular of both humans and birds is opposed to any rhetorical—and indeed exclusively human—discourse (Carbognin and Mott 2004, 443–44). However, here the poet neither expresses this soundscape in its original language, nor offers a sample of such a dialect, "Lorna" having been written in the Italian of lyric tradition. In *Dietro il paesaggio*, the birds and the language they shared with the poet are simply addressed but not expressed, probably because they both belong to a landscape that in 1951 was not yet perceived as threatened by new development.

It was not until twenty years later, when the Italian economic boom experienced its first downfall, that Zanzotto returned to the language of birds in

"Subnarcosi" (Subnarcosis), a short poem included in *Pasque* (Easters, 1973). In his *Birds in Literature*, Leonard Lutwack (1994) claims that bird songs have always had a strong appeal to poets because they "recognize in the song of a bird their own struggle to express meaning and feelings" (12). "Subnarcosi" focuses precisely on the experience of listening to birds and seems to testify to the contradiction between the necessity and the impossibility of speaking, a contradiction that, according to Armando Balduino (1974), also characterizes the book as a whole. In terms of setting, the poem recalls an actual experience of the poet, who, in the early 1970s, attempted sleep therapy for his anxiety. In the resulting drug-induced semi-hypnotic condition, he was particularly struck by the chirping of some unidentified birds in an outside tree. Zanzotto (2011) links this experience of hearing the birds in a state of partial unconsciousness to both the origin of language and writing poetry. Furthermore, playing on the double meaning of the word "verso" in Italian (both poetic verse and animal call), he actually claims that poetry connects human and nonhuman voices because it preserves a significant amount of primitive orality even when written (Zanzotto 1999, 1231).

Given this context, it is not surprising that the first verse of "Subnarcosi" consists only of the word "uccelli," birds. Gino Tellini (1974) has noted that this poem stages a continuous state of objection, as testified by the triple "ma" (but) that frames its nineteen lines (315). More generally, "Subnarcosi" reveals a contrast between the soundscape perceived by the poet and his attempts to make sense of his experience. The second verse thus gives us the acoustic dimension of the event and the "uccelli" of the previous line are denoted only as a "crudo infinito cinguettio," a raw infinite chirping. Zanzotto considers that such chirping might not speak the truth (verse 5), but it is nonetheless the "scintillio di un possibile/infantilmente aumano" (spark of a possible/childishly a-human; verses 6–7). This relationship between poetry ("scintillio" being a typical signifier for poetry in Zanzotto), childhood ("infantilmente"), and what is a-human ("aumano') is given here only as potential ("possibile"), but it fits within that nostalgia for an expression prior to grammar and writing that marks Zanzotto's (1999) reflection on vernacular poetry (1230). In a sense, the use of the term "a-human"—rather than simply "nonhuman"—suggests in fact a soundscape devoid of the human but still in fieri, that is, open to the possibility of maturation and language, as the adverb "infantilmente" indicates.[8] As a consequence, such nostalgia for an idiom before or even without human linguistic individualization is not merely regressive and leads neither to a pure game of signifiers, nor to Pascoli's *fanciullino* (eternal child) and his epigones.[9] Instead, the last three verses before the final distich offer a partial retraction of the first definition:

un chiuso si-si-significare
nemmeno infantile ma
adulto occulto nella sua minimità.

(a closed me-me-meaning
not even childish but
adult occult in its minimalness)

Here the "ma" (but) denies that the chirping is merely childish or meaningless. Instead, it is minimal and hidden but very much mature, connected to the idea of responsibility Zanzotto also applies to his own dialect. Zanzotto (1999, 1129) believes that the chirping of birds and children—namely, any primordial manifestation of language—must be read as a tension toward expression and responsibility, being, and development. This chirping is in fact the very root of any creative speech and as such is not only attached to the possibility of both writing and memory, that is to say, of a meaningful narrative (Zanzotto 1999, 1163), but also potentially perceived "as a whole soundscape which carries meaning," as Farina points out in his essay included in this volume (p. 33). Yet, the raw infinite chirping of line 2 becomes here a "chiuso si-si-significare," an expression where meaning is indeed present but locked and therefore unreachable by humans. However, this does not mean that it is merely negative: actually, Zanzotto's *trobar clus* encloses a triple, stuttering, almost birdlike "yes" ("*si-si-significare*," my emphasis) that might not succeed yet, but is nonetheless "incoercible, sparkling, and at the same time amazed to have broken free from the *no* that is suffocating us as well as from those multiple *no*'s that have threatened each origin, each budding of reality" (Zanzotto 1999, 1129).[10] What "Subnarcosi" thus offers is the reflection upon a soundscape in which the chirping of birds expresses the minimal manifestation of a *logos erchomenos* ("coming logos") that, according to Zanzotto (1999, 1230), does not hierarchize and divide (not even among species), but sets minimal, affirmative, and inventive connections.[11]

This close relationship between birds and *logos erchomenos* appears one final time in Zanzotto's first work completely in dialect, *Filò* (1976). Here the coming *logos* is declared to be the very place from which dialect comes: a place without grammar, a "vague site in which langue and parole tend to identify themselves and every territoriality vanishes in those that are contiguous" (Zanzotto 1997, 89). Near the end of *Filò*, reflecting in dialect upon the destruction of that natural and cultural landscape that was so fundamental for *Dietro il paesaggio*, Zanzotto addresses directly the vernacular or, as he calls it, his ancient tongue ("vecio parlar"):

> But you, ancient tongue, endure! And even if people
> will someday forget you without noticing it,
> there'll be birds—
> maybe only two or three birds
> who will have flown away from the shooting and the killing—:
> tomorrow on the last branch way down there
> at the end of thickets and meadows,
> birds who learned you long ago,
> they'll speak you in sunshine, and in shadows.[12]

Here Zanzotto returns not only to the idea that birds speak such "vecio parlar" but also that they will speak it even after humans have forgotten it. There are, however, two differences between how this image of the birds speaking dialect appears in *Filò* and in "Lorna." First, in 1976 the referential language and the actual language of the poem overlap, offering a sample of the kind of language that connects humans and nonhumans under a specific, unified landscape. *Filò* is in fact the first work Zanzotto wrote completely in his vernacular and therefore the first written occurrence of that almost foreign "chiuso si-si-significare" he had described three years earlier in "Subnarcosi." Second, in "Lorna" the main tense was the present, an almost paradisiacal present set against history. Here, instead, history forces the poet to use a future tense that actually seems to allude to an eschatological after-history connecting the original linguistic event ("birds who learned you long ago") to a moment of loss and destruction ("flown away from the shooting and the killing"). Although the incentive to write came after Fellini's request for his *Casanova*, the long poem eponymously entitled "Filò" that closes the book is in fact written in Zanzotto's very dialect because it is also directly linked to the history of his local landscape—itself a vernacular landscape. As testified by the initial reference to the almost contemporary earthquake in nearby Friuli, in "Filò" Zanzotto wants to contrast his vernacular with/to the very fiber of both nature and history. He then uses this contrast to denounce the contemporary destruction of his rural landscape by greedy economic development, as exemplified by the tragedy of the Vajont Dam.[13] According to "Filò," the unleashed waters of Italian neo-capitalism were in fact sweeping away not only villages and their inhabitants but also the intricate connection between language, community, and landscape that had traditionally established an ecologically responsible relationship between culture and nature (metonymically expressed as "zhiése e pra," thickets and meadows). "Filò" is thus both a reflexive "eclogue in dialect on the end of dialect" (Bordin 2001, 9) and the actual transcription of the soundscape of an agro-pastoral world at the edge of extinction.[14] The birds are therefore the repositories of a specific place dear to the poet as well as the nonhuman agents capable of preserving the original force of a linguistic and natural environment threatened by irresponsible human progress.

As Steven Feld (1996) noted in his study on the Kaluli people's incorporation of bird calls into their traditional songs, the sounds of avifauna can play an aesthetically fundamental function in signifying human living, motion, centering, and leaving, that is to say "the sense of place" (119). As we have seen, Zanzotto's poetic birds not only visualize the connection between people, language, and place, but they are also an essential component of the place's soundscape as well as the ecological memory of its original becoming life and language. Their voices come both from a very specific landscape that, according to Zanzotto, in recent years has been radically exploited and from the house (*oikos*) of language, where meaning originates following minimal, hidden affirmations.[15] This is the reason why the destiny of birds, according to Zanzotto, is directly linked not only to any human linguistic community and its more-than-human environment but also to the very possibility of poetry itself. As he writes with bitter irony in response to a public letter, when the last birds will be killed by the "legions of hunters who considered themselves ecological," then even poets will no longer be able "to sing as the birds that live in the branches" (Berardinelli 1999, 99).[16] On the environmental-ethical level, this connection between the destinies of birds and poetry reminds us that they belong to the same soundscape, and furthermore that the latter can play an important role in restoring the "material imagination" of a place (Iovino and Oppermann 2012, 81). Zanzotto's poetic birds accomplish what Serenella Iovino (2012, 112) has addressed as the essential components of such an enterprise: they enhance empathy and awareness about the interconnections that constitute the life of a place, as well as implement our sense of responsibility toward a landscape that otherwise risks falling silent.

NOTES

1. On the importance of hearing the birds, see Gannon, *Skylark Meets Meadowlark* (2009, 302). For a critique of "the visualism deeply rooted in the European concept of landscape," see Feld, "Waterfalls of Song" (1996, 91–98). On sound as a dynamic property of the landscape, i.e., on the concept of soundscape, see at least Farina, *Soundscape Ecology* (2014), as well as his essay in this volume.

2. For an introduction, see Turri, *Miracolo economico* (1995), as well as both Baldan Zenoni-Politeo, *Paesaggio e paesaggi veneti* (1999), and Vallerani and Varotto, *Il grigio oltre le siepi* (2005).

3. According to the Oxford Dictionary online, the term "diglossia" refers to a situation in which two languages (or two varieties of the same language) are used under different conditions within a community, often by the same speakers. In Zanzotto's case,

the local dialect would be the colloquial, "low" language, while Italian would be the official, "high" language. On this topic, see De Mauro (2015, 126–41) and Bernardi (1986, 176–77).

4. For the relationships between poetry and language in Triveneto, see Benvegnù (2011). For an anthology of writers from this area on the mutation of the landscape, see Vallerani and Varotto (2005).

5. On landscape "as a balance of nature and culture stratified through centuries of mutual adaptation," see Iovino (2010, 31).

6. Zanzotto was aware of the ambivalences of the term "nature." Actually, his whole poetic work can be interpreted as a series of precarious attempts "to call you nature," as the title of one poem in *Sovrimpressioni* (2001) reads. However, Zanzotto often overlaps nature with both poetry and landscape, the three of them being for him manifestations of an original, authentic, and inquisitive eros capable of gathering human and nonhuman life as well as testifying to the potential relationships between human culture and nonhuman environment. On this topic, see at least Zanzotto, *Luoghi e paesaggi* (2013, 29–38).

7. The term "paradise" comes from an Iranian source similar to Avestan *pairidaeza* ("enclosure, park"), and it is a compound of *pairi-*, "around," and *diz*, "to make, form (a wall)." Etymologically, the paradise is what is thus separated from the rest of the environment by a wall.

8. The term "infant" comes from Latin *infantem* (nominative *infans*) "young child, babe in arms," noun use of adjective meaning "not able to speak," from *in-*, "not, opposite of," and *fans*, present participle of *fari*, "to speak," from the Proto-Indo-European root *bha-*, "to speak, tell, say." Yet Zanzotto claims to perceive in the prefix "in" also the meaning of "toward." "Infantilmente" would thus express the inability to speak as much as a complementary, and more or less conscious, desire for expression. On the relationships between childhood, language, and poetry, see at least Zanzotto's beautiful essay entitled "Infanzie, poesie, scuoletta (appunti)" (1999, 1161–90), where he originally elaborates on his experience as a poet as well as a teacher and engages with a long tradition of linguistic thought that goes from De Saussure to Kristeva.

9. Stefano Agosti was the first literary critic to address the work of the signifier in Zanzotto's poetry (Agosti 1972). On Pascoli's *fanciullino* and his relationship to dialects and orality, see Agamben (2010, 61–72).

10. "Incoercibile, lucente, e insieme stupito del suo scattare dal no che ci sta soffocando come dai no che da sempre hanno minacciato ogni origine, ogni gemmazione della realtà" [all the translations of Zanzotto's work are mine, unless otherwise stated].

11. On this topic, see also Agamben (2010, 96–102), Bignamini (2011, 51–65), and Venturi (2013, 197–212).

12. "Ma ti, vecio parlar, resisti. E si anca i òmi/te desmentegarà senzha inacòrderse,/ ghén sarà osèi—/ do tre osèi/sòi magari/dai sbari e dal mazhelo zoladi via—:/doman su l'ultima rama là in cao/in cao de zhiése e pra,/osèi/che te à inparà da tant/te parlarà inte 'l sol, inte l'onbrìa" (Zanzotto 1997, 82).

13. The Vajont Dam is a disused dam, completed in 1959 in the valley of the Vajont River under Monte Toc, 60 km north of Pieve di Soligo. On October 9, 1963, during initial filling, a massive landslide caused a man-made wave in the lake in which 50 million cubic

meters of water overtopped the dam in a wave 250 meters high, leading to the complete destruction of several villages and towns and 1,917 deaths. For more information, see http://www.vajont.net/.

14. On the project of this actually never completed "eclogue," see Bordin (2001).

15. Toward the end of his life Zanzotto became increasingly vocal about the critical condition of his native environment; see, for example, Zanzotto (2013, 131–34).

16. Zanzotto actually quotes in German from Goethe's *Der Sänger:* "Ich singe, wie der Vogel singt,/Der in den Zweigen wohnet."

WORKS CITED

Agamben, Giorgio. 2010. *Categorie italiane*. Rome-Bari, Italy: Laterza.

Agosti, Stefano. 1972. *Il testo poetico: Teoria e pratiche d'analisi*. Milan: Rizzoli.

Baldan Zenoni-Politeo, Giuliana, ed. 1999. *Paesaggio e paesaggi veneti*. Milan: Guerini e Ass.

Balduino, Armando. 1974. "Zanzotto e l'ottica della contraddizione (impressioni e divagazioni su 'Pasque')." *Studi novecenteschi* 4: 281–313.

Benvegnù, Damiano. 2011. "Uno sguardo dalla periferia: appunti per una storia novecentesca della poesia in dialetto nel Triveneto." *MLN* 126(1): 74–97.

Berardinelli, Alfonso. 1999. *Nel caldo cuore del mondo: Lettere sull'Italia: dialoghi con Geno Pampaloni, Sandro Veronesi, Andrea Zanzotto*. Florence: Liberal.

Bernardi, Ulderico. 1986. *Paese Veneto: Dalla cultura contadina al capitalismo popolare*. Florence: Edizioni del riccio.

Bignamini, Mauro. 2011. "Sull'elaborazione della 'Nota ai testi' di 'Filò': Il dialetto tra 'lettera' e 'voce.'" *Autografo* 46: 51–65.

BirdLife International. 2014. "We have lost over 150 bird species since 1500." *BirdLife State of the World's Birds*. http://www.birdlife.org/datazone/sowb/state/STATE1.

Bordin, Michele. 2001. "Morte e rinascita del 'vecio parlar': Gli inediti. 'Appunti e abbozzi per un'ecloga in dialetto sulla fine del dialetto' di Andrea Zanzotto." *Autografo* 43: 19–48.

Brambilla, Mattia, Claudio Celada, and Marco Gustin, eds. 2010. *Valutazione dello stato di conservazione dell'avifauna italiana*. Rome: Ministero dell'Ambiente e della Tutela del Territorio e del Mare/LIPU.

Carbognin, Francesco, and Glenn Mott. 2004. "Intervista a Andrea Zanzotto." *Poetiche* 3: 443–57.

Carson, Rachel. (1962) 2002. *Silent Spring*. 40th ed. Boston: Mariner.

Cecere, Jacopo, Marco Gustin, Valentina Peronace, and Carlo Rondinini. 2012. "Lista Rossa 2011 degli Uccelli Nidificanti in Italia." *Avocetta Journal of Ornithology* 36(1): 11–58.

De Mauro, Tullio. 2015. *Storia linguistica dell'Italia unita*. Rome-Bari: Laterza.

Farina, Almo. 2014. *Soundscape Ecology: Principles, Patterns, Methods and Applications*. Dordrecht, Netherlands: Springer.

Feld, Steven. 1996. "Waterfalls of Song: An Acoustemology of Place Resounding in Bosavi, Papua New Guinea." In *Senses of Place*, edited by Steven Feld and Keith Basso, 91–135. Santa Fe, NM: School of American Research Press.

Fumian, Carlo, and Angelo Ventura, eds. 2004. *Storia del Veneto*. Vol. 2, *Dal Seicento a oggi*. Rome-Bari: Laterza.

Gannon, Thomas. 2009. *Skylark Meets Meadowlark: Reimagining the Bird in British Romantic and Contemporary Native American Literature*. Lincoln: University of Nebraska Press.
Heise, Ursula K. 2008. *Sense of Place and Sense of Planet: The Environmental Imagination of the Global*. Oxford: Oxford University Press.
Iovino, Serenella. 2006. *Ecologia Letteraria: Una strategia di sopravvivenza*. Milan: Edizioni Ambiente.
———. 2010. "Ecocriticism and Non-Anthropocentric Humanism: Reflections on Local Natures and Global Responsibilities." In *Local Natures, Global Responsibilities. Ecocritical Perspectives on the New English Literatures*, edited by Laurenz Volkmann, Nancy Grimm, Ines Detmers, and Katrin Thomson, 29–53. Amsterdam: Rodopi.
———. 2012. "Restoring the Imagination of Place: Narrative Reinhabitation and the Po Valley." In *The Bioregional Imagination*, edited by Tom Lynch, Cheryll Glotfelty, and Karla Armbruster, 100–117. Athens: University of Georgia Press.
Iovino, Serenella, and Oppermann, Serpil. 2012. "Material Ecocriticism: Materiality, Agency, and Models of Narrativity." *Ecozon@* 3(1): 75–91.
Lutwack, Leonard. 1994. *Birds in Literature*. Gainesville: University Press of Florida.
Mengaldo, Vincenzo. 2003. *Poeti Italiani del Novecento*. Milan: Mondadori.
Munsterberg, Peggy. 1980. *The Penguin Book of Bird Poetry*. New York: Viking.
Pasolini, Pier Paolo. (1975) 1981. *Scritti corsari*. Milan: Garzanti.
Rete Rurale Nazionale & LIPU. 2011. *Gli andamenti di popolazione degli uccelli comuni in Italia 2000–2010*. Milan: MiPAAF.
Snyder, Gary. 1990. *The Practice of the Wild*. New York: North Point Press.
Soriani, Stefano, Francesco Vallerani, and Gabriele Zanetto. 1996. *Nature, Environment, Landscape: European Attitudes and Discourses in the Modern Period. The Italian Case, 1920–1970*. Padova, Italy: University of Padova.
Tellini, Gino. 1974. "La 'subnarcosi' di Zanzotto." *Studi novecenteschi* 4: 315–32.
Turri, Eugenio. 1995. *Miracolo economico: Dalla villa veneta al capannone industriale*. Verona: Cierre.
Vallerani, Francesco, and Mauro Varotto, eds. 2005. *Il grigio oltre le siepi: Geografie smarrite e racconti del disagio in Veneto*. Venice: Nuova Dimensione.
Venturi, Francesco. 2013. "Alle origini della 'trilogia' di Andrea Zanzotto. Il progetto 'lógos erchómenos' e 'Fosfeni.'" *Strumenti critici* 338(132): 197–212.
Villalta, Gian Mario. 2001. "Confessioni dell'altro curatore." *L'immaginazione* 18, 175.
Zanzotto, Andrea. 1951. *Dietro il paesaggio*. Milan: Mondadori.
———. 1973. *Pasque*. Milan: Mondadori.
———. 1976. *Filò*. Venice: Edizioni del Ruzante.
———. 1997. *Peasants Wake for Fellini's "Casanova" and Other Poems*. Edited and translated by John P. Welle and Ruth Feldman. Champaign, IL: University of Illinois Press.
———. 1999. *Poesie e prose scelte*. Milan: Mondadori.
———. 1998. "Una esperienza in comune nel dialetto." *In forma di parole* 3: 17–23.
———. 2001. *Sovrimpressioni*. Milan: Mondadori.
———. 2011. *Il mio Campana*. Bologna: CLUEB.
———. 2013. *Luoghi e paesaggi*. Milan: Bompiani.

MATTEO GILEBBI

Witnessing the Slaughter: Human and Nonhuman Animals in Ivano Ferrari's Poetry

Slaughtering became part of the life of poet Ivano Ferrari in the midseventies when, for several years, he worked at the municipal abattoir of Mantua. The city is situated in an area of northern Italy where animal farms are common and the meat industry is thriving. In this place, where the culture of slaughter is celebrated, Ferrari felt the urgency to witness what he saw and heard: not only the suffering, degradation, and death but also the vitality, sacredness, and redemption of both human and nonhuman animals. His testimony takes the form of short poems with a uniform style and structure, so that they actually connect to each other in forming a single, organic, longer poem. The first part of this longer poem is contained in the book *Macello* (Slaughterhouse), which includes poems written during his period of work at the abattoir but published almost thirty years later, in 2004. The second part can be found in *La morte moglie* (The death wife, published in 2013), which includes both rediscovered poems from his time at the slaughterhouse and more recent poems written after the death of his wife. In this second book, Ferrari concludes his testimony by placing human pain side by side with animal pain, exploring the ways in which these sufferings and deaths are equivalent and intimately connected. As Ferrari writes: "it dies it is dying matter/enormous shadow of the alphabet" (Ferrari 2013, 87).[1] While matter itself disappears, the testimony left by the equivalent existence and suffering of both human and nonhuman animals cannot be erased. Through his poetry, Ferrari tries to keep precisely this aspect alive: the "shadow of the alphabet," the linguistic trace that survives the shared death of humans and animals.

The slaughterhouse described by Ferrari is a real space, but sometimes it is also intended as a metaphorical space. In fact, there is a metaphorical intent in the decision to entitle one of the two collections *Macello*. This is because while in Italian the word *mattatoio* means only "slaughterhouse," *macello* also means "mess," "disaster," "massacre," and "chaos." Therefore, it is likely that Ferrari chose *macello* because this word incorporates a reference to the real and metaphorical mess inside and outside the slaughterhouse. This term conveys the ethical and political message in Ferrari's work and exposes the connection to any physical and metaphorical places where both human and nonhuman animals experience a trauma. In fact, considering the slaughterhouse as a space that metaphorically refers to other traumatic experiences and to other places of suffering, Ferrari in his poems evokes images of war ("A pig with a slit throat commands me:/password!" [Ferrari 2004, 39]), the Holocaust ("the death gas cannot be smelled" [Ferrari 2004, 57]), and class conflict ("tanners, butchers and gravediggers,/the working class." [Ferrari 2013, 31]). Ferrari therefore implies that human violence toward the animal (interspecific violence) is directly related to the violence against other humans (intraspecific violence).

Carno-sado-pornocentric

In *The Sexual Politics of Meat* (1990), Carol Adams exposes the connections between sexism and speciesism, in particular, between male intraspecific dominance and the interspecific dominance linked to human carnivorism. By analyzing and comparing various media representations of female and animal bodies, Adams shows how pornographic images often display a female body dominated through symbols and metaphors derived from animal farming and meat production. The human female body is chained, locked up with collars, and tied by ropes, nooses, and other instruments of control, torture, and domination. These kinds of images create a visual rhetoric that clearly connects male sadistic pleasure to human domination over the animal (Adams 1990, 43).

In addition, the dominated woman no longer has a face or an identity, since she has been dehumanized by the process of animalization and by the replacement of her body by single anatomical parts—parts that were selected as though they were delicious cuts of meat—that the macho pornographic imagination identifies as sources of pleasure: the breasts, the vagina, etc. (Adams 1990, 58). Adams defines this dehumanization and loss of subjectivity as the "absent referent": in these kinds of erotic and pornographic images the female identity is removed from the female body in order to justify its subjugation and to fully enjoy the sadistic pleasure of controlling it. Thus, the human element is the absent referent of the female body reduced to meat. The link between sexism and speciesism, according to Adams, is there: just as the human/woman is the absent referent in pornography and the abused female body, so is the animal the absent referent in the meat production process (1990, 40–43). Therefore, following a strategy typical of sexism, animals (like women) must lose their identity and become a commodity before being consumed. This practice is one of the cornerstones of animal slaughtering, and the *conditio sine qua non* of the slaughterhouse. In his poems, Ferrari works against this objectification process by returning identity to the animal. Objectification emerges especially when Ferrari observes his colleagues—"strange creatures" who, by working "as miners," transform the animals into "frugal nutrients" (Ferrari 2004, 21). In the butcher's mind, the animal exists only qua nourishment, with its identity being replaced by its function as food. The job of the butcher is thus similar to that of a miner: they both work with inanimate elements.

In Ferrari's poems the animal referent, once absent, is now struggling to become present again, both to poet and reader. An opportunity comes with the description of the escape of a bull that "wanders on the overpass" in search of freedom and instead of being killed in the slaughterhouse is executed by a firing squad of "Carabinieri with machine guns" (Ferrari 2004, 25). By escaping the space of the slaughterhouse, the bull also escapes the mechanism of objectification, regaining, in his flight, an identity as a living being. This identity materializes both in the escape, representing the bull's desire to survive the slaughter, and in the moment of death when the animal "whispers something to the flies" (Ferrari 2004, 25). This whispering offers a boost of vitality, a desperate desire to communicate, a survival impulse, and, most particularly, a final testimony of suffering. All these acts lead us to recognize the bull as a single living being able to feel, desire, and suffer, not simply a lifeless piece of meat.

For Adams, the relationship between sexism and speciesism is not only in this parallel condition of absent referent between woman and animal. The loss of identity through absence is just the beginning of these inter- and intraspecific practices of oppression. The most provocative point emerging in *The Sexual Politics of Meat* concerns the erotic tension present in the slaughtering process, a point that leads to a very interesting conclusion: when, in the space of the slaughterhouse, sexual metaphors are communicated, fetishisms emerge, and slaughtering and eroticism overlap, the absent referent of meat becomes not the animal but the woman (Adams 1990, 43, 59). This means that the oppression of the animal, in addition to being related to speciesism and to the capitalistic mechanism of production and consumption, also concerns a form of sadistic pleasure and sexual perversion. According to Adams, the oppression and exploitation of animals contain the same sexual urges present in the sadistic interaction with women. The slaughter excites the erogenous zones of the human male's logic of dominance. Ferrari's poems bring us even more precise examples of this dynamic, showing us the complexity and depth in the relationship between violence against animals and sexual pleasure, between the slaughterhouse and the brothel. In fact, slaughter connects to eroticism in the poem that opens *Macello,* which emphasizes the carno-sado-pornocentric model as the fundamental ingredient of both Ferrari's poetry and the space of the slaughterhouse: "The cubicle at the bottom of the locker room/is called choking your chicken/posted on three walls are photos of women/with hairless vaginas/on the other wall the poster of a cow/unveiling with different colors/its delicious cuts" (Ferrari 2004, 3). In the architecture and organization of the slaughterhouse, there are spaces specifically dedicated to the autoerotic consumption of images of women and animals. The sexual tension that mounts during the slaughtering process must be released in the cubicle, a secluded place isolated inside the slaughterhouse, indicating that the enjoyment that comes from the submission of the animal/woman is fully achieved in the dark core of the abattoir's architecture. Significantly, Ferrari feels the need to shed light on this place in his first poem, at the very beginning of his poetic testimony. In this poem, where the animal is the absent referent of the female erotic body, there emerges a symmetry between the verses "with hairless vaginas" and "its delicious cuts": the choice of a female anatomical part as erotic stimulus occurs according to the same practice of selecting of meat parts. The female body is enjoyed because it has become a selected and dominated piece of meat, and animal flesh is enjoyed because it has become the referent of the domination over the female body. The combination of violence toward the animal and sexual pleasure materializes in the word *sega,* which I have freely translated as "choking your chicken" because in Italian *sega* translates as both "saw" and "masturbation." Therefore, the original Italian term *sega* evokes the tool ("saw") used to dissect the slaughtered animal and directly connects it to the pleasure ("masturbation") experienced by reducing animals to those discrete parts similar to the female erotic sections. The saw/masturbation is the end, but also the means, of the domination over the animal in the erotic space of the slaughterhouse.

In many other poems Ferrari calls on the sexual tension present in different stages of slaughtering. For example, the animals are often described with precise sensual elements, such as the calves hanging on hooks that "show off" (Ferrari 2004, 31), the "limber heifers" smiling (Ferrari 2004, 82), the "elegant young cow" (Ferrari 2013, 8), and the "nymphomaniac bovines" (Ferrari 2004, 72). This sexual tension also emerges from the movements of the workers of the slaughterhouse, whose hands, while "skinning" a bleeding animal, "arrange the raw flesh/of an intern" (Ferrari 2004, 46). Ferrari again aligns slaughtering and the sexual act and emphasizes how the woman is reduced to a scrap of flesh in a butcher shop. Ferrari also bears witness to the sadistic relationship that exists between the human/ruler and animal/victim, such as when he describes a horse as a "faggot dancer" that is sodomized by a butcher with a club and whose death occurs while "offering squirts of organic matter/ to his unseducible rapist" (Ferrari 2004, 71). At this point, inside the slaughterhouse, the human has taken the identity of a pervert and a molester, and his acts of violence carry a sexual pleasure that, sadistically put into practice in the space of the slaughterhouse, has become an essential element of the animal meat we consume. In addition, it is important to notice that in these poems, the man who rules and rapes the animal remains "unseducible" because the sexual pleasure is sadistic and the depiction of the slaughter is pornographic, leaving no chance for intimacy, however perverse. The distance between human and animal is dilated, and speciesism is strengthened by this perverse enjoyment of the suffering and death of the animal, a pleasure that dramatically connects speciesism to sexism.

Ferrari tries to approach the animal in a different, possibly nonviolent way, but even his attempt results in an awkward and embarrassing act of cruelty: "In order to measure the fever of the victim/it is introduced a thermometer into the rectum/or (if female) in the vagina/this operation is done without gloves/and it is not hard to insert/together with the instrument a note/of poems scribbled earlier" (Ferrari 2004, 73). These same poems, written during his time at the abattoir, are composed to become the means for a different relationship with animal otherness, a different approach to the painful condition of the nonhuman animals at the slaughterhouse. But the "poems scribbled" come in contact with the animal through an improper veterinary practice "done without gloves" that recalls more the image of rape and violence than that of intimacy and encounter. Ferrari shows that even the good intention of witnessing the slaughter inevitably falls into the category of a brutal act. It seems that interspecies violence, even when reported, is so ingrained in mankind that it is inevitably always put into practice. This is also an interspecific violence that, inside the slaughterhouse, relentlessly produces practices firmly tied to intraspecific violence: his logocentric act of donating poetry to the animal is performed by penetrating its flesh, through a form of rape that makes any communication with the nonhuman impossible. This is the same form of violence that subjugates and violates the female body. Speciesism and sexism are woven together by a poem that, in witnessing the slaughterhouse, is inevitably contaminated by the same violence that this place perpetuates.

Becoming Animal

The human is animalized, implicitly or explicitly, via a rhetorical mechanism of power that, assuming that the animal condition is inferior, justifies control over those individuals *reduced* to animals. Giorgio Agamben has analyzed this mechanism and presented it as the most typical instrument of modern biopolitical power, and he has renamed this animalization of humans the "anthropological machine," indicating that it is an integral element of the anthropological condition itself (Agamben 2004, 2005). In other words, it comes naturally for the *Homo sapiens* species to control, subjugate, torment, and exterminate other humans by labeling them as inferior species.

However, another kind of animalization exists that could be considered positive. This animalization generally occurs in three forms. In its first iteration, it uplifts the human condition to that of the animal, considering the animal superior to man and therefore a model to imitate. The second form instead advocates for unveiling an animal element that has been always present, but hidden, inside the human and aims to return this hidden animality to an anthropological condition considered incomplete when deprived of this untamed and primitive element. Finally, the third form considers the animalization of humans the necessary condition for reaching a connection and for building a dialogue with animal otherness; it attempts an interspecific contact in which the human seeks to evolve toward an open-minded embrace of the heterospecific condition.[2] Ferrari embraces this third form of animalization, a process that reduces the distance between humans and nonhumans and might offset the inhumanity of the slaughterhouse space. In several of his poems Ferrari describes how the slaughterhouse has become a privileged place for the evolution of inhuman behavior, that is, a lack of understanding for the human and animal condition and an absence of compassion for the suffering that animals experience in the slaughterhouse. This inhumanity often takes the forms of cynical violence: "To strike the beast/with more blows/than it can withstand,/sneering/when it realizes/that it is going to die" (Ferrari 2013, 15). At other times, this inhumanity manifests itself as an abyssal detachment from animal pain directly caused—and witnessed—by humans: "The dying beast/agonizes alone/because no thing/happens held in the arms" (Ferrari 2013, 17). In several other poems the death of the animal is an isolated, painful, secret circumstance, pertaining to the animal alone, with the butcher incapable of demonstrating any empathy. The animal's death remains unknown or ignored, accompanied only by the cold inertia of the inhuman: "Loaded the weapon/the executioner with greenish eye sockets/smiles to it (I lie down between little pieces of fat)/he shoots./The secrets are recomposed/in the extraneousness of death" (Ferrari 2004, 23).

This implies that becoming animal inside the slaughterhouse means resisting inhumanity and seeking empathy and dialogue with the animal condition. This is a process that goes beyond simple piety, beyond that "sadness"—Ferrari writes—that "does not prevent us/from starting the slaughter at seven thirty sharp" (Ferrari 2004, 32). Becoming animal means instead encountering the animal in the space of its (and our) suffering, in order to be able to stop the mechanism of inhumanity, of speciesism, of slaughter.

In an interview with Nicholas Gane, Donna Haraway raises the possibility of animalization as a new category of relations based on mutual curiosity that takes place during the meeting between "mortal, situated, relentlessly relational worlding" (Gane 2006, 143). Therefore, the process of becoming animal starts from curiosity among living beings emanating from their own contingent and relational existence, a post-Heideggerian being there and being toward death that resets the species distance and makes the contact between species innate and spontaneous. As a human species, we must therefore recognize that animalization is a form of interspecific relationships historically and biologically always in place (Gane 2006, 146). What we are as humans, and what we might become, is not acquired in isolation but in the encounter with the nonhuman, the different, the other, the heterospecific, an encounter that often takes the form of a collaboration between "companion species" (Haraway 2008, 17, 155). In my view, the humans start becoming animals when they recognize this collaboration and work toward making these encounters possible. And becoming animal also means, as Roberto Marchesini clearly explains, "to anthropodiscenter" (*antropodecentrarsi*) and "to travel through planes of reality" (Caffo and Marchesini 2014, 21–22). Therefore, this process of animalization brings the human into contact with those different existential possibilities with which we have always found ourselves in dialogue, through which we also have learned how to relate to the world. By anthropodiscentering, our species can explore other forms of existence and recognize them as being as dynamic and valid as the human one. In experiencing this animalization, we also find that these forms of existence are not monads but throbbing seeds that are always open to cross-species contamination. Becoming animal means resisting the uncontaminated and lonely inhuman, to get dirty with reality, to get stuck in new worlds, and to compromise our existence by admitting countless others. This is how, according to Haraway, species come together and *together* transform themselves and evolve, not as heavenly creatures but as terrestrial critters belonging to the mud (Haraway 2008, 3, 19, 27, 72). And to the blood. Because in actuality, the slaughterhouse is one of the ideal spaces for this encounter between species that allows us to become animal, as it is inside the slaughterhouse that the battle between animalization and inhumanity that abhors cross-species contamination is fought.

In the slaughterhouse a dramatically physical contact between species occurs, a literal skin-to-skin interspecific brush in which the human touches the physicality of animal existence and the reality of animal suffering and death. Ferrari witnesses this dramatic interspecific encounter, and his poems give us the tools to understand what happens when species meet and become companions in the space of pain and death. First of all, Ferrari shows us that humans and animals share suffering in the real and metaphorical spilling of the same blood: "Two fingers severed/almost a metaphor/one blood like the other's" (Ferrari 2004, 34). An incident in which the human animal is a victim becomes the epiphanic episode that transforms the pain into a shared event. The accident reveals the existence of a moment of suffering when we can meet with another species. The awareness of having the same animal blood and the same nervous system capable of feeling the same pain is made banal, a common fact of which the human had been unaware. It is "a moment of stillness, like an afterthought" (Ferrari 2004, 34), that for a moment anthropodiscenters us while making us perceive the truth of animal suffering, albeit in relation to ours. Along with suffering comes the "absolute" experience of death (Ferrari 2004, 16) that pushes the human toward a particular animalization: the poet takes on the qualities and attitudes of cattle in order to get near a calf and follow him closely during the slaughtering process. This animalization is necessary because the experience of death in the slaughterhouse belongs completely to an animal; therefore, only the animal victim can truly witness this kind of death. Becoming animal is therefore essential to testifying to death in the slaughterhouse: "Lukewarm, I smell the ass/of the large calf that goes before me/in the race to the absolute" (Ferrari 2004, 16). The poet becomes animal by performing animal motions and sharing the same slaughtering space in which we are metaphorically in line with the animal, who goes before us toward the same fate of annihilation. The animal experiences death in front of the human so he can prepare for it. This is why, in his becoming animal, the poet sniffs the calf: he establishes a sensorial communication with the animal who allows him to gaze at death before it is his turn. Our turn.

Or the turn of those we love the most, those with whom we have shared our existence. Ferrari suggests a form of animalization that carries a deep emotional and moral impact, especially in the poems written about the illness and death of his wife in *La morte moglie*. Through portraying the figure of his sick wife becoming animal, Ferrari presents a relationship between human and animal suffering that is even more intimate than in his previous work. So intimate that any interspecific separation fades to give way to the images of humans and animals existing, feeling, suffering, and dying in the same manner. Ferrari's agonizing wife becomes animal because her body belongs to the slaughterhouse as much as an animal body: like these animals, she lies "on a large table to be eaten" (Ferrari 2013, 43), and finally nothing remains of her body "but a meal" (Ferrari 2013, 50). In death, her face becomes a "surging snout" (Ferrari 2013, 50), and among her human gestures appears the animal trait of "licking the palm of the hand" (Ferrari 2013, 53). This is not simple zoomorphism, because there is neither the use of simile nor a metaphorical intent. Instead, the human *is* biologically animal because it is *recognized* as an animal as it suffers and dies. What Ferrari saw inside the slaughterhouse he now sees in the hospital: a carcass hanging from a hook is identical to a body lying on a stretcher. These poems confirm the intuition Ferrari had in the slaughterhouse: humans and animals suffer the same pain and experience the same death because they are, as Haraway says, "companion species." In the hospital and the slaughterhouse the distance between human and nonhuman animals is eliminated, and Ferrari witnesses the presence of a single species made of undifferentiated, sentient beings. We are all this single animal: "As hard as clotted blood/and as soft as calf's marrow/so I am, if not equal" (Ferrari 2013, 33). These lines, a perfect synthesis of Ferrari's anti-speciesism, trace the path that crosses similarity and arrives at equality. It is a route that moves through bodily elements shared by humans and animals (the blood and bone marrow), filtered through suffering (the clotted blood). Man or animal, everything is equally body, flesh, sentient matter. And Ferrari constantly tries to communicate this truth via a particularly difficult testimony because it still comes from a butcher, and from a species that has been considering itself the dominant one and that now, self-aware and animalized, breaks out crying, "I am a lamb too" (Ferrari 2013, 19).

This animalized poet-butcher now faces the moral necessity of dismantling the slaughterhouse and showing the possibilities of becoming animal to the rest of the slaughterers and meat eaters. Ferrari sketches this new phase by forming hypotheses and questions: "If I broke down the wall of flesh/and hanging from the hook I smiled/what would those say who are paid to dismember/the stamper of tongues/what label would they put on me/how many organs would they discard/and would the vet think *panta rei?*" (Ferrari 2013, 9). The final passage of becoming animal is this hypothetical self-replacing of the animal victim, a sacrifice full of Christological tensions that, by transforming the slaughterhouse into the space of human slaughter, may cause it to short-circuit.

It might. Ferrari does not anticipate the consequences of this hypothetical self-sacrifice of becoming animal; he only questions. The mechanisms of the slaughterhouse, of speciesism, of the control over the animal, and of its eroto-capitalistic transformation into an object seem so ingrained in the practices of our species that they may never be called into question, not even in the face of the human becoming animal. The anthropological machine always uses human animalization as a mechanism of domination: it would become even easier to slaughter fellow humans when they voluntarily replace animals. What remains, then, of Ferrari's poetry is the affirmation that a different animalization, while unlikely, is possible—an animalization realized, according to the moral and philosophical position of painism (Singer 1975, 75; Ryder 2011), through a convergence between humans and animals who understand and share the same, universal suffering.

With *Macello* and *La morte moglie*, Ferrari begins the search for an alternative way of becoming animal, that is, the chance to approach an understanding of the heterospecific in a space built on the solidarity of pain. His poetry testifies that in this space, a space that emerges inside the slaughterhouse, humans can recognize their sadistic practices of control, transcend their inhumanity, and find empathy with fellow human and nonhuman animals.

NOTES

1. All translations of Ferrari's poems are mine.
2. This form of animalization, which can be defined as "posthumanist," is presented and discussed in Marchesini (2002), Haraway (2008), and Braidotti (2013).

WORKS CITED

Adams, Carol. 1990. *The Sexual Politics of Meat: A Feminist-Vegetarian Critical Theory*. New York: Continuum.
Agamben, Giorgio. 2004. *The Open: Man and Animal*. Stanford, CA: Stanford University Press.
———. 2005. *State of Exception*. Chicago: University of Chicago Press.
Braidotti, Rosi. 2013. *The Posthuman*. Cambridge, UK: Polity Press.
Caffo, Leonardo, and Roberto Marchesini. 2014. *Così parlò il postumano*. Aprilia, Italy: Novalogos.
Ferrari, Ivano. 2004. *Macello*. Turin: Einaudi.
———. 2013. *La morte moglie*. Turin: Einaudi.
Gane, Nicholas. 2006. "When We Have Never Been Human, What Is to Be Done? Interview with Donna Haraway." *Theory, Culture & Society* 23(7–8): 135–158.
Haraway, Donna. 2008. *When Species Meet*. Minneapolis: University of Minnesota Press.
Marchesini, Roberto. 2002. *Post-human: Verso nuovi modelli di esistenza*. Turin: Bollati Boringhieri.
Ryder, Richard. 2011. *Speciesism, Painism and Happiness*. Exeter, UK: Imprint Academic.
Singer, Peter. 1975. *Animal Liberation: A New Ethics for Our Treatment of Animals*. New York: Random House.

ROBERTO MARCHESINI

Dialogo ergo sum: My Pathway into Posthumanities

On any literary, philosophical, or scientific path there is always a question or—if you will—a detail that does not add up, a slightly false note, together with the lurking feeling that one has to resolve it. I have felt this since high school, when something disturbed the reception, so to speak, of the knowledge being imparted to me. The contemplative and introspective tenor of much twentieth-century research was dissonant to me, as if a solipsistic disorder emerged from the texts I was reading. During my teenage years, I was fascinated by nature. My feelings, however, seemed to be unreciprocated by other humans. To me, nature was not a cyclical snapshot, a backdrop for inspiration. Rather, it was a life companion, a friend to whom I could turn for advice in the here and now. I used to spend time with my camera, watching the play of light on the landscape, hoping to transform it into intricate black and white embroidery. I wanted the world to show me my own image, to unveil possibility. Everything seemed to flow like a river.

I remember those moments as suspended breaks in the flow of time. It was like looking outside, letting myself be owned and, at the same time, projecting myself into otherness. I believe my true formation as a young man took place in those silent hours of total immersion in nature, of inner welcoming and amazement, of openness toward the lives of others. I found inspiration in my relationship with nature, and my dreams reflected the photographic representations of very distant worlds. For instance, I spent many hours observing the microworld of insects, a perspective that changed my spatial and temporal bearings and turned me into an insect, too: there were slivers of remote sky, minutes dilated into hours, forests of slender flowers and shrubs, sets of improbable and elliptical morphologies. I caught imperceptible fragments that, magnified, gave me the impression that I was shrinking so as to fully participate in that different-sized dimension. A micro-impressionist style inspired my writing, as if I had the smallest of brushes in my hand instead of a pen. Nature, with its continuous stream of forms, did not flow on my skin but rather through it. My being did not remain imprisoned within the impermeable fabric of the body but rather dispersed itself. It was my infinite, my Leopardian sweet shipwreck.

Any life path is always conditioned by a gap to fill, an itch to scratch, a discrepancy to solve knocking on the doors of one's thoughts. I needed a different poetics, a shift that would create the conditions for an equal relationship with otherness. I had the impression that the entire animal world was trying to get in contact with me, and I had to find the right harmony to enter the dialogue, to discover the possible answers to my questions. I felt like nature was alienated in the texts available at the time. It was holographically remote, distant in space and even more so in time, as if it were the light of a star. Nature was a phenomenon to admire or study, to desire or reject, but always outside of any dialogical space. Nature was not present. It could transmit the stillness of beauty or the vertigo of the sublime, it could become a vortex and gravitate toward regression or act as a metaphor and represent the impulses of the soul, but it would always present itself to the author like a fossil. Those seeds were to become the core of my research and poetics over time.

Every life path is unclear because you never know your route, and you get carried away on biographical waves, by fleeting suggestions, by the loves and ghosts cast like a shadow on the background of desire and inexperience. Later you realize that some coordinates were there from the very beginning. They emerge over time. You see it when, reading your early writings, you find the unripe fruits of your thought, already present like the colors on a painter's palette. My first book *Il dio Pan* (The god Pan), published in 1988, was the result of a feverish work begun ten years before, when I tried to turn words into brushstrokes of nature, as if I were painting rather than writing.

My entomological past, which is more poetic than scientific, had dotted my unconscious with small creatures like unstable metamorphic appearances, incredibly fluid on paper. It was a style—a poetics—but also a shift toward my questions about the Dionysian flow of life, or the panic sense. This framework reached maturity during my university years, which were undefined but intense enough to leave behind much nostalgia. A life path is also made up of important encounters, people who help you better see what you are looking for. My encounter with Giorgio Celli is the first one I want to recall. He was an entomologist and ethologist with a strong artistic and poetic energy who was also a member of the Gruppo '63. Celli was a friend more than a teacher, a confidant who encouraged me and saw something worth supporting in my immature propositions. I had a lot in common with him: the poetic interest in nature, the tendency to consider disciplinary boundaries as thresholds to continuously overcome, the inclination to criticize the status quo and the curiosity about minority theories, the awareness that every living being exists as a relation, the tendency to consider the relationship with animals as too often trivialized or misrepresented. Obviously, there were also many differences between Celli and me. These concern poetics and, more particularly, my greater interest in the philosophical problematization of animal life and ontology.

We were both driven by our intent to enhance the relationship with nature as a moment of growth and not just as an ecological, scientific, or economic resource. We thought that Western society had reached a dead end. The total trivialization and devaluation of nature was leading to a gradual erosion of creativity and presence. The human being practiced a blind isolationism, contemplating his own reflection as if it were the only real source of inspiration. But where to begin? Our common interest in animals gave us a hint. The relationship with animals was sick in Western culture. Zoophilia, often flaunted as an emphatic predicate of opulence, actually took place through anthropomorphizations that denaturalized its scope. Therefore, we planned a series of educational projects for primary schools and presented them around Italy with surprising results. In fact, the evidence revealed that we achieved disciplinary objectives as well as other, more generally educational ones.

At that time, I was attending the pedagogy course in the Department of Arts and Philosophy at the University of Bologna, seeking to explore the importance of the relationship with nature in childhood development. This is how the book *Natura e pedagogia* (Nature and pedagogy, 1996) came to life, with a preface by Giorgio Celli. It can be considered my first work of zooanthropology. *Natura e pedagogia* marked an important moment in my path: the achievement of deeper awareness and, simultaneously, the acknowledgment of needs that classical ethology and current anthropology could not answer. The question was always the same: Was the human being an autarchic construction or, on the contrary, was it a hybrid fruit—that is, realized by making identity pervious to external contaminations? My path was diverging from Celli's, but I was still deeply grateful to the scholar who helped me find my way.

The philosophical investigation of the human being was becoming increasingly fascinating to me. In my mind the human being was a fluid and metamorphic condition whose quality paradoxically arose from the hybridization with the nonhuman pluriverse. At the same time, I felt that there was an unavoidable link between this kind of philosophical work and the full and free development of a poetics that would give life in writing to the chaotic flow of hybridizations I saw around me. I wanted to talk about the mystery of this conjugative flow but I had to change my poetic style in order to do so. My writing had to move away from the traditional canon, from its being essentially reflective and introflexive. I had to find a new way. The 1980s were important because of my lonely immersions into nonhuman worlds. I developed a different idea of nature: it was not a remote and external background but rather something affecting my very fabric and innermost feeling. Those plural universes were not the apparatus of an ahistorical mechanism but rather presented me with real situations, stories, singularities. I began to observe nature like a reporter who merely takes note of events and does not presume to extract eternal laws. I was a journalist who speaks about himself through the story he's narrating.

I wrote *Il dio Pan* also thanks to a meeting with poet Roberto Roversi, who was interested in my mix of poetry and fiction, creating a lyrical matrix detached from the classical setting of poetry. My encounter with Roversi helped me search for new poetic solutions that crosscut traditional boundaries. In fact, I was experiencing hybridization myself: the lyrical narrative with a naturalist base allowed me to ask questions through my careful chronicle of events. Therefore, *Il dio Pan* was also the first expression of a research practice that would later find maturity in two essays in the 1990s: *Oltre il muro* (Beyond the wall, 1996) and *Il concetto di soglia: Critica all'antropocentrismo* (The concept of threshold: A critique to anthropocentrism, 1996). My friend Mauro Ceruti, who introduced me to the concept of complexity, strongly influenced these essays, and the second in particular. Over the second half of the 1990s, Mauro gathered a fine group of scholars around the journal *Pluriverso*. I published my first essay on cognitive plurality in the animal world there, exploring theories of chaos and complex phenomena. I used the concept of threshold as a tool to demolish, on the one hand, the presumption of a reflexive ontology based on the cogito rather than dialogue and, on the other hand, a solipsistic epistemology based on the relationship between subject and object.

My primary question could be translated as follows: Is it possible to better understand what we are and how we bring ourselves into the world through a dialogue with nature? That is, what happens when we make nature the protagonist of a revealing encounter, rather than plumbing the depths of our own being and transforming nature into a stage onto which to project our inner self? I thought it was possible indeed, and in those early works I developed what I called a practice of extroversion. This practice transforms what one has experienced/felt into a threshold that can welcome otherness and/or be hosted by it. I thought of the human self not as a finite and impervious being but rather as a threshold being constantly negotiated in the relationship with otherness; I thought about a decentrative evolution, compared to phylogenetic heritage. This let me consider epistemology as a dialogical process with a counterintuitive direction.

This idea, the preparatory core of all my following posthumanistic works, took shape in the book *Il concetto di soglia*, which contains the first germ of relational ontology. Astrophysicist Margherita Hack, with whom I established a fruitful dialogue on the counterintuitive meaning of scientific thought, wrote the preface. Here I must also recall my friendship with Eleonora Fiorani and Sabrina Tonutti, who led me to study the work of Francesco Remotti and Ugo Fabietti, two important Italian anthropologists who addressed the issues of identity through a relational conception that, taken to the extreme, questioned the very concept of identity. If cultures were born and developed through continuous dialogue, could the human condition itself be the result of an ongoing dialogue with the nonhuman universe? What I particularly liked about these two authors was the idea of the human dimension as a work in progress—which is therefore indefinable, since its borders and forms are constantly negotiated and negotiable. I thus began to reflect on the theme of identity from a different perspective—a relational one—and acquired a better understanding of it thanks to zooanthropology. Was it possible to explain human culture as the result of the hybridization with animal otherness? I now had a clearer and more detailed question to work on.

Initially, zooanthropology was not very different from other perspectives in animal studies (like anthrozoology, developed in the English-speaking world, for example), except for its special interest in the cultural aspects of the relationship with animals. The zooanthropology that Giovanni Ballarini and I developed in the second half of the 1980s did not particularly distance itself from Hubert Montagner's and Boris Cyrulnik's Francophone tradition, which stressed the essentially illustrative role of the encounter with animal otherness. This reading convinced me only partially, though, and I did not agree with the thematic structure. More specifically, I did not want to consider the terms of the relationship in an essentialist way, presupposing the imperviousness and the constitutive purity of the two related beings. From my point of view, every relationship led to an asymmetrical contamination between entities because the human being always underwent the deeper ontological change. First of all, it was necessary to investigate why the human being was so interested in other species. Such an interest can indeed be documented in every anthropological field.

The human relationship with other species, I believed, was supported by a set of motivational matrices that, together, constituted a driving force. In this sense, the more human beings absorbed heterospecific predicates in their cultural heritage, the more they were indispensably and directly dependent on the relationship with other species. Thus was born my theory of zootrophy, which dates to the late 1990s. The heterospecific was not only an external entity, objectively phenomenal, but also an entity introjected through the relationship itself. During that decade, my definition of otherness underwent a profound change: it shifted from "other from oneself" to "other with/in oneself." In this regard, Remotti's and Fabietti's considerations were very helpful (even though I needed to cross the Rubicon and extend the idea of hybridization not only to the relationship between cultures but also to that between human and nonhuman). The research on mirror neurons—which, beyond its strictly scientific meaning, urged one to look at the human being's strong tendency to identify—was crucial.

What did human beings see in the heterospecific? Maybe they saw something external that amazed or scared them but that was still "other from oneself." Or maybe they rediscovered themselves in it, perhaps in an approximated or deformed but essentially always-projective shape. Neither of these assumptions convinced me. From my point of view, the human being could see in the heterospecific a possible existential dimension for oneself, an opportunity, a continent to inhabit. In other words, the encounter with animal otherness was an *epiphany* for the human being, a kind of revelation and annunciation of a new potentially reachable existential dimension. Essentially, to identify oneself with the flight of a bird did not only mean to admire its flight or to learn its flying techniques. Before every mimesis there is always an epiphany. For me it meant to *feel* that it is possible to fly, to imagine flight, to experience the thrill of flight by projecting oneself into the bird's body. The concept of animal epiphany, along with the concept of zootrophy, represents the real innovation of my zooanthropological research: a key to reinterpreting dance, music, cosmetics, technology, and, in short, the entire anthropological corpus.

The 1990s were a very fertile decade for Italian research in posthumanistic poetics and ontologies. I remember, for example, the magazine *Virus* edited by Francesca Alfano Miglietti, to which I contributed. The debate at the time focused on the hybrid relationship between human beings and nonhuman otherness (animal and machinic). Moreover, I want to stress that, thanks in part to Karin Andersen's work, theriomorphic poetics were taking root in Italy then, deeply influenced by my research on posthumanity understood as the implicit human condition rather than as a horizon (as in transhumanist thought). In Italy, the debate on human predicates as hybrid fruits paved the way to a new wave of criticism of humanism that took up and integrated French poststructural and deconstructive criticism. The posthumanism that was taking shape in our research could not be seen as antihumanism but rather as a new form of nonanthropocentric humanism. The posthumanistic climate thus developed in Italy between the late twentieth century and the early twenty-first century and differed from the posthumanism of other countries for its criticism of traditional ontological anthropocentrism. There is a common thread between this approach and the works of Donna Haraway and Rosi Braidotti. These facts are the background against which I wrote *Post-human* in 2002.

I consider *Post-human* my most ambitious (though not the most complete) attempt to give explanatory coordinates to human predicates. I took my cue from this preliminary consideration: the human being, as the outcome of a precise phylogenetic trajectory, is not a biologically deficient entity (as reiterated in the humanistic tradition from Pico della Mirandola to Arnold Gehlen) but rather a complex being with a rich heritage. This richness, however, which must be thought of as redundancy rather than lack, results in a huge virtuality of possible identities. Basically, redundancy—rather than emptiness—has allowed for the human's acquisitive capacities by making the relationship between innate and learned—or nature and culture—directly proportional rather than inversely proportional. Furthermore, the motivational matrices—as well as anthropomorphism's empathic and identifying inclinations, which favored the decentralization of the animal epiphany—had to be researched precisely within the phylogenetic heritage.

The human being was thus naturally led to hybridize with otherness and to overcome the very legacy of the species. Human nature was designed to hybridize. This process, however, led to unpredictable outcomes that could not be derived from the contents of the species, as they were attributable to elements that come from nonhuman otherness. Thus, I distanced myself both from the disjunctive vision of nature and culture typical of humanism and from the reductionism deriving culture from nature typical of sociobiology. In *Post-human*, I developed an interpretation of nature and culture that neither opposed nor complemented the two terms. This interpretation of both anthropopoiesis and the human-animal relationship distanced me from Giorgio Agamben's analysis. In fact, Agamben remained within a deeply humanistic framework and denied the nonhuman any effective role in giving rise to the human dimension. Agamben's anthropological machine keeps the distance between human and nonhuman under both an ontological and a relational profile. According to him, the animal is not a referential presence but rather a representation of the human being who operates recursively so as to lay down the coordinates of marginalization. From my point of view, animal otherness directly operates on the human being through animal epiphany. For me, the human being is a never-ending construction realized by continuously hybridizing with otherness, so it is not possible to derive cultural expressions from nature, either in terms of emptiness or in terms of significance. In the decade following the publication of *Post-human*, I explored these issues in dedicated studies such as *Fondamenti di zooantropologia* (Fundamentals of zooanthropology, 2005), *Il tramonto dell'uomo* (The decline of humankind, 2009), and *Epifania animale* (Animal epiphany, 2014).

At this point, my research turned to investigate this referential protagonism of nonhuman otherness, in several recent works: *Intelligenze plurime* (Multiple intelligences, 2008), *Modelli cognitivi e comportamento animale* (Cognitive models and animal behavior, 2011), and, in particular, *Etologia filosofica: Alla ricerca della soggettività animale* (Philosophical ethology: The search for animal subjectivity, 2016). The last text aims to analyze the animal condition—that is, what it means to "be animal" and to own a subjectivity. Subjectivity, I argue, indicates an individual's dialogical openness toward the outside world that aims to build a continuous state of singularity—a real animal *Dasein*. The guiding principle in the philosophical ethology, zooanthropology, and the posthumanistic vision that have consistently marked my work is simple. I have often enunciated it: *dialogo ergo sum*.

PLACES AND LANDSCAPES

SERENELLA IOVINO

Italo Calvino and the Landscapes of the Anthropocene: A Narrative Stratigraphy

Imagine Italy at the end of the 1940s. Imagine a northern city—one that has just emerged from war. Streets with uneven pavements are what you see in this still uncertain black-and-white landscape, courtyards with kids playing games, *case di ringhiera;* rubble, barracks—a setting that resembles a less-charmed reproduction of Vittorio De Sica's *Miracle in Milan.* In the city's downtown—a downtown light-years away from the very idea of one day being gentrified—you see local markets, horses drawing carriages, and people: women carrying bags, men in work clothes, children. There are few cars in the streets, downtown. But there are tramways, and Vespas and Lambrettas, too. What you mostly see, however, are bicycles: bicycles everywhere— outside factories and churches, leaning on brick walls—heavy iron bicycles rolling on the bumpy roads, against the grey sky. Not particularly clean is this city. And the air is thick and dirty because the factories, after the war's forcible break, are slowly getting back to production.

There is nothing more remote from the idea that a new geological epoch might have begun than these fragments of a resilient Italy. Still, according to many scholars, it is in these very postwar years that the "Great Acceleration" was setting off, mutating the maps of power and the landscapes of the world, including this one. This mutation, now recognizable as the Anthropocene, was not occurring merely on the surface but was affecting many interconnected layers: lithosphere, atmosphere, biosphere, and even sociosphere. The stratigraphy of the Anthropocene, the "epoch of the human," includes in fact the ground, the air, life forms and genes, and people—themselves defined by their degree of exposure to environmental risks and pollution. It is easy to see these things in their complexity today: geo-ecological records indeed shape a story that is always readable *post factum.* But what if literature were able to follow the episodes of this story *while*—and not just *after*—it is in the making? The more I read Italo Calvino's early works, the more I have the feeling that, long before Paul J. Crutzen and Eugene F. Stoermer, he understood that something in the world's embodied stories was changing. *Smog, A Plunge into Real Estate, The Argentine Ant,* and *Marcovaldo* might, in other words, provide a narrative stratigraphy of the Anthropocene at the time of the Great Acceleration, following its socio-ecological parable from a very specific observatory: Italy. If *apocalypse* means "revelation," Calvino's imaginative dealing with the material world is therefore apocalyptic in the real sense, emerging and evolving along with the landscapes of the Anthropocene that stratify over and within the peninsula's bodies.

The Anthropocene's Extraordinary Strata

The Anthropocene reveals itself in layers, and these, as the head of the Anthropocene Working Group of the International Commission on Stratigraphy Jan Zalasiewicz (2016) described them, are "extraordinary strata." For the first time in the planet's history, in fact, geological boundaries raise both a chronological and an ontological question. For example, the so-called golden spike—the point within a stratal section where two geological phases are visibly distinct—is debated. Following Crutzen and Stoermer (2000), many scholars situate this boundary around 1800 CE, coinciding with the Industrial Revolution; others (Ruddiman 2003) go back 12,000 years to the Neolithic, when the rise of agriculture took place—which would mean, to paraphrase Bruno Latour (1991), that we have never been Holocenic. An accredited stance, however—and this is Zalasiewicz's opinion—is that we should start counting from 1945–50, a period marking the "spread of radionuclides from atmospheric nuclear weapon tests" and the skyrocketing increase in "the use of natural resources and the emission of pollutants" known as the Great Acceleration (Zalasiewicz, Williams, and Waters 2016, 15).

Whatever its birth date, the Anthropocene's boundaries are blurred by definition—and here comes ontology. The interesting feature of the Anthropocene, indeed, is not so much that one living species has become a geological force—life and geology have always been deeply entangled—but that for the first time techno-industrial processes, military competitions, economic fluxes, and use and consumption habits have become part of the geological record, inscribing themselves into all planetary spheres and impacting the carrying capacity of ecological systems. The Anthropocene, in other words, is both a landscape and a discourse, a dynamic composition of corporeal elements and of sociopolitical narratives: it is the quintessential example of "storied matter" (Oppermann, forthcoming). The extraordinary strata of the Anthropocene are thus together physical and cultural. Unlike ever before, culture and technology are readable in ice cores and scientists are faced with the appearance of post-geological rocks, such as the "enormous city-structures that make up the urban strata, and . . . novel material such as plastics and aluminum and the extraordinarily diverse . . . technofossils . . . into which they are shaped" (Zalasiewicz 2016, 123). Enormous cities, novel materials, future technofossils—and around them pollution, waste, hierarchal accumulation of wealth, social discrimination . . . It is impossible to ignore the fact that the Anthropocene's strata are also social strata. It is not by accident that some propose to name it Capitalocene, stressing the fact that its map is shaped by the same dynamics of violence and unequal protection that mold the maps of environmental justice (Haraway 2015; Moore 2014). As Marco Armiero suggests in his essay "Of the Titanic, the Bounty, and Other Shipwrecks," we might well say that we are all on the same boat, but the truth is that, on this boat, not all of us are first-class travelers: "Class matters in the Anthropocene" (2015, 52).

The Anthropocene can thus be read also in the way it stratifies in human bodies, in how these bodies respond to these challenges. Its landscape is made of continuous cities swallowed by their own metabolism; it is a land swathed by an asphalt-and-concrete crust, a territory covered in rubble or knitted by wires. It is the atmospheric universe of atomic radiations; it is a landscape in which everybody is jointly liable to some extent—but in which some pay a higher price than others for this eco-geological shift. It is a world in which nature is so fuzzy and out of sight that it is hard for children to recognize real trees or real cows. This landscape closely resembles the one depicted by Calvino in *Invisible Cities* or in his works from the second half of the 1940s to the early 1960s. Here we find all the extraordinary strata of the Italian Anthropocene: atmosphere, soil, biosphere, society. Because Calvino's global imagination and even his most audacious constructions are deep-seated; his stories sediment into Italian ground.

Layers of the (Italian) Anthropocene

Italy joins the Anthropocene landscape after the war. In those early republican years, cities change, economy changes, industry is "reloaded," and here, too, the Great Acceleration begins. Increasingly, the destruction wrought on the peninsula by bombs—whether dropped by former friends or former foes—is followed by the destruction wrought by reconstruction. With dramatic speed, after being for centuries a living repository of collective memory, the landscape ceases to be a common good and, more and more often, it is turned into a "passive resource" for building developers (Settis 2013, 11). Industrial growth, although necessary, has its socio-environmental costs. In the northern industrial outskirts, where immigration, exploited labor, and poor housing go hand in hand, pollution infiltrates elements and places. Class matters in the (Italian) Anthropocene. Elsewhere, in apparently still bucolic settings, alien species invade autochthonous ecosystems, and the atomic radiations of war- and peacetime bombs, traveling across planetary skies since 1945, occupy the global landscapes of bodies and discourses, reverberating in Italy, too.

Calvino perceives all these mutations around him and, although obviously unaware of their geological implications, he seems to be quite cognizant of the environmental ones. His testimony begins in the period delineated by Zalasiewicz's golden spike. In the short piece "Le capre ci guardano" ("Goats are looking at us," 1946), commenting on the Operation Crossroads—in which the Bikini Atoll was used by the United States for atomic testing—the twenty-three-year-old intellectual draws attention to the animals sacrificed in the experiment, and in wars in general. He writes: "Have you ever asked yourselves what the goats on Bikini must have thought? And the cats in bombed houses? And the dogs in war zones? And the fish struck by torpedoes?" (2001, I, 2131–32). The stance, ethically and ontologically, is post-anthropocentric. One immediately understands that his viewpoint is that of all those nonhumans, "casualties" of our inhuman (peacetime) wars. But what one also understands is that the scope of his perspective is wide. And this is what makes the report on Bikini's goats historically apocalyptic. Providing a large-scale setting for his Italian stories, Calvino's article indeed entails *in nuce* the revelation of what will happen very soon to living species and to the global atmosphere in a landscape drowned by the interlaced dynamics of technology and power.

We see this with clarity in *Smog* (1958). In this short novel Calvino tells the story of a journalist living in a northern industrial city swallowed by pollution. This anonymous young man writes for *Purification*, a pseudo-environmental magazine aimed at "reassuring" the population about the effects of industrial smog. Paradox is the novel's pivot: smog is indeed a ubiquitous molecular presence saturating literally every corner, especially in and around the protagonist's body. Even more paradoxical, however, is that *Purification* is published by the same multinational corporation that produces pollution and whose goal is to manipulate information about the state of the air. The corporation is therefore responsible for a double, material and discursive pollution, an affront not limited to this unspecified city, unquestionably modeled on Turin. In an incredibly prophetic passage, the journalist, whose article on atomic radiation in the atmosphere has just been censored by the chief editor, says: "The cloud of smog now seemed to have grown smaller, a tiny little puff, a cirrus, compared to the looming atomic mushroom. . . . I avoided any mention of atomic explosions or radioactivity in the headlines, but . . . every day my eye fell upon statistics of terrible diseases, stories about fishermen overtaken in the middle of the ocean by lethal clouds, guinea pigs born with two heads after some experiments with uranium" (Calvino 1983a, 155–56). And, anticipating climate change, he adds: "The normal order of the seasons seemed changed, intense cyclones coursed over Europe, the beginning of summer was marked by days heavily charged with electricity, then by weeks of rain, by sudden heat waves and sudden resurgences of . . . cold. The papers denied that these atmospheric disorders could be in any way connected with the effects of the bomb; only a few solitary scientists seemed to sustain this notion" (156).

Although the hypothesis that there might be links between global warming and atomic radiation is not supported today by climatologists, the debate on possible climatic alterations, especially in the form of a "nuclear winter," has been for a while a lively one (Turco et al. 1983).[1] Sensible to the intertwined mutations in the landscape of elements and powers, however, Calvino saw the many changes occurring above and around him, and his stories reflect the connecting dots of this material narrative. And elsewhere he was further connecting the dots of trans-corporeal relations between technosphere and biosphere. In a novel titled *The Watcher* (1963), set in a Turin hospital for physically and mentally disabled people, he openly asked what happens in the long run to human genes when they are exposed to the effects of invisible anthropogenic forces: What unpredictable metamorphoses does "the material of human race" risk "each time it reproduces itself"? How exposed is it to "the risk . . . which is multiplied by the number of the new snares: the viruses, poisons, uranium radiation" (Calvino 1971, 17–18)? Here Calvino was explicit: this risk is not only a threat for individuals but also a "path evolution might yet take . . . if atomic radiations do act on the cells that control the traits of the species" (1971, 22). If the Anthropocene changes the stories embedded in the DNA of living beings, this cellular and evolutionary landscape is yet another of its horizons.

While the atmosphere was becoming saturated with pollutants old and new, under the sky a crust of concrete was forming, thickening the Anthropocene's lithic stratum. This is the subject of *A Plunge into Real Estate* (1957). With remarkable accuracy, this novella mirrors a historical watershed in the phenomenology of the Italian landscape, completely redesigned by the forces operating in the postwar economic boom. The interesting point of the story is that the rise and expansion of the new layer of concrete on the peninsula's body represents the rise of new financial powers as well: the landscape's mutation is also linked to an anthropological mutation, itself related to new, unexpected complicities. We see here ex-partisans become contractors and intellectuals become speculators who, in spite of ideology, values, or family traditions, now enter into business together. The protagonist Quinto, for example, converts his discomfort about the cementification of "*his* district, that amputated part of himself" into an insight that marks per se the golden spike of the beginning of a new epoch: "If everybody's building, why don't we build, too?"—Quinto says to his brother Ampelio. "Oh, no, my poor garden!"—cries their mother (Calvino 1983a, 166). But, as the reader sadly realizes, she belongs decidedly to another geological time. From the very beginning of the novel, indeed, one can observe that the transformation affecting places (here the Riviera Ligure, and notably Calvino's hometown Sanremo) is something more than simply a reconfiguration of the built environment. It is a complete natural-cultural metamorphosis that starts like a local infection—"the Riviera was gripped by a fever of cement" (163)—and then spreads, finally besieging the land, which ends up "being overwhelmed by cement" (165).

The novel opens with a provincial vision, whose limited scope does not make it less uncanny: "in the little towns on the terraced hillsides the new buildings played piggyback with one another . . . , the bulldozers were churning up the soil . . . , picks were demolishing the two-story residences, the ax was at the broad-leaved palm trees, which fell with a papery scrunch from the sky so soon to be filled by the desirable, three-room, all-convenience, sunny homes of tomorrow" (164). After a while, however, we understand that this perverse makeover is not affecting a mere portion of the landscape but is literally mutating its life. The territory, indeed, "had taken on a new life, abnormal and graceless perhaps, but *for that very reason* . . . it was more alive than ever before" (166, emphasis in the original). This hybrid "new life" of the territory is a mix of human and material agency, an unprecedented combination of disordered urban development and specific territorial features that will lead to today's hydro-geological imbalances affecting Italy in general and the Liguria region in particular. According to the Istituto Superiore per la Protezione e la Ricerca Ambientale's 2015 report on hydro-geological risk, 57.9 percent of the region's territory is at risk for landslides and other disasters, with a level of danger from moderate to extreme (ISPRA 2015). The risk depends on a mix of factors: deforestation, abandonment of former areas of agricultural land, and above all excessive building development. Sometimes structures are even erected on previous riverbeds. Combined with the effects of climate change and the high levels of seismicity, this leads to periodic floods, landslips, and structural collapses. In the post–World War II period the number of new buildings in Italy skyrocketed: from 1956 to 2001 the urbanized surface in Italy increased by 500 percent, and the yearly consumption of soil amounted to 244,000 hectares (World Wide Fund for Nature Italia 2009). Referring to Liguria—one of Italy's most cementified regions—these figures confirm the historical accuracy of Calvino's novella. As Monica Seger points out, during the 1950s "Liguria boasted one of the highest rates of Italian housing development, along with Lombardy and Emilia-Romagna. In

1959, for example, more than 50 dwellings were built in the region for every 1,000 residents. As a measure of comparison, Tuscany gained 30 to 40 new dwellings from every 1,000 residents" (2015, 30). In contrast with today's uninterrupted megalopolis of concrete, as Calvino clearly saw it, all this was the beginning of a post-*humane* landscape.

But the landscape of the Anthropocene is not only aboveground and not only urban—especially because one of the features of this epoch is that it "unnaturally" reconfigures the balance and life of ecosystems, putting us in very close proximity with species that, due to human traffic, step out their evolutionary biomes and come to invade other niches, including ours. This is the subject of *The Argentine Ant* (1952). There is historical terrain in this case, too. As Calvino writes to Goffredo Fofi in 1984, *The Argentine Ant* "describes with absolute precision the situation of cultivated lands in Sanremo and in most parts of the Riviera di Ponente, invaded by Argentine ants when I was a child" (Calvino 2000, 1511). And the arrival of this small and destructive ant, *Linepithema humile*, native of the Paraná region and ranking "among the world's 100 worst animal invaders" (Lowe, Browne, and Boudjelas 2000) was indeed a plague tied to the very fortune of the Riviera, where the import-export of plants was (and still is) one of the main sources of income. The invasion started around 1920. The detail that Calvino "mercifully omits," Domenico Scarpa reports, is that his father (a professor of agriculture and a small plantation manager) might have been personally responsible for the importation of these intrusive aliens: "the ants arrived in the Riviera along with the exotic plants that Mario Calvino had brought with him as he moved back to Italy" from Cuba, where he was working and where Italo was born (Scarpa 1999, 128). This hypothesis, conveyed by Calvino's wife, Esther, in private conversations and possibly believed to be true by Calvino himself, makes the story even more intriguing.[2] However, Mario might be innocent: already in 1923, two years prior to the return of the Calvino family to Sanremo, the city council had issued a public alarm about the ant invasion, and there are sources that date the infiltration back to 1919 (Paoli 1923; Castello n.d.). This gives the sense of how *Linepithema humile* was a very tangible presence in the landscape of Calvino's youth—and of how this landscape was already showing precursory signs of the Anthropocene.

The novella develops in a crescendo of anxiety from the discovery of these tiny black spots to the sense of powerlessness that their uncontainable presence inspires. Suddenly, what seemed firm and predictable—home—is exposed in its fragility and threatened by unforeseen foes. The protagonist and his family find themselves "face to face with an enemy like fog or sand, against which force was useless" (Calvino 1971, 151). And actually, bolstered by the abuse of chemicals in agriculture and land management (of which it was both cause and effect), the invasion is a typical example of the "magic-bullet approach to getting rid of 'pests'" resulting in a "feedback loop" (Morton 2016, 49), causing familiar environments to reveal their dark side:

> I was following the line of ants down the trunk, and saw that the silent and almost invisible swarm continued along the ground in every direction between the weeds. How . . . shall we ever be able to get the ants out of the house when over this piece of ground, which had seemed so small yesterday but now appeared enormous . . . , the insects formed an uninterrupted veil, issuing from what must be thousands of underground nests and feeding on the thick sticky soil and the low vegetation? . . . In certain places . . . there was a guarding crust of ants stuck together like the black scab of a wound. (Calvino 1971, 150)

The invasion is clearly another epitome of nonhuman agency, here emphasized by the singular, "the Argentine ant" (146). And this is also an epitome of how the agency of *bios* intra-acts with geology in the Anthropocene. With a supercolony spreading from Liguria to Portugal, *Linepithema humile* indeed transforms the underground of a huge portion of Mediterranean lands, as it also does in other parts of the world (Giraud, Pedersen, and Keller 2002; Wild 2004). These colonies constitute an actor of what geologists call "bioturbation": a process through which "living organisms affect the substratum in (or on) which they live" (Kristensen et al. 2012, 285). In principle, there is nothing wrong with this: underground landscapes coevolve with their biological residents. In *Linepithema*'s case, however, the point is that its bioturbulent presence has not coevolved with the local ecosystem, being rather a side effect of human intervention. Among the "telluric actors," Serpil Oppermann observes, "the so-called anthropos . . . is literally altering the foundational script itself" (Oppermann, forthcoming). And this, of course, happens on all scales and in all realms, from gigantic insect colonies to the subterranean maps of planetary extractivism.

In *Marcovaldo, or The Seasons in the City* (1963), all of these issues come together: industrial pollution, exacerbated urbanization, transformed natures and resources, pervasive alien agencies. In a world whose emblem is the factory, nature is an unrecognizable and yet resilient ontological horizon that can only emerge in the forms of natural-cultural hybrids: city mushrooms, chemical fish, poisonous rabbits, mutant plants, and "stubborn" cats. But these twenty stories also pose an important question: Who is the *anthropos* of the Anthropocene? When used to aggregate "all humans" to assign an identical share of liability, this disembodied concept "fails to account for unequal human agency or unequal human vulnerabilities" (Adamson 2016, 160). A book apparently destined for children and dressed in irony and lightness, *Marcovaldo* makes clear that the "epoch of the human," instead, is above all a class issue, thus qualifying as Calvino's most unequivocal environmental justice work. The protagonist and his family display all the features of environmental justice discourse: social marginality, poor individual health due to poor environmental conditions, labor exploitation, malnourishment, poverty. In a scene where the city is an "agglomerate of synthetic matter that confine[s] Marcovaldo's days" (Calvino 1983b, 98), not only is there no room for pastoral idylls, however accidental and deceptive (such as a "holiday" on a bench or a trip with cows), but even a children's game like creating soap bubbles is swallowed up in the horizon of the factory (96).

That Calvino treats these topics using the "comic mode" does not change the fact that he is describing a tragic reality. His is an industrial reality, experienced by an "immigrant" lost in a sooty landscape of mineralized human lives (Calvino 2003, I, 1233). Marcovaldo thus confirms that the "carbon embedded in geological strata is our newest mode of autobiography" (Cohen 2016, 25). Moreover, the more he struggles against the city's alienation from the natural world, the more Marcovaldo himself becomes an alien in the city, increasing his marginalization. Every time he wants to live "naturally" and use natural "resources" (animals or food, "good air" for his children's health, or sand for his rheumatism) not only is he forced back into his social niche by his superiors, but the natural itself congeals in its thickness of "strange stranger" (Morton 2010), revealing its erratic agency. And so, the mushrooms he finds at the bus stop turn out to be toxic, the fish taken by his children "where the river is more blue" are contaminated by a factory's chemical dumping, and even the rabbit he kidnaps from the hospital (where the animal is used for testing) is "poisonous" (Calvino 1983b, 67–70, 51–59). The nature Marcovaldo searches for is thus both craved and feared, hunted and haunted, threatened and threatening. Breaking all pastoralist clichés, what Marcovaldo encounters is "a mischievous . . . , counterfeit Nature, compromised with artificial life" (Calvino 2003, I, 1233). This compromise is the essence of the Anthropocene, here embodied by the city as a setting at once typically Italian and globally unspecified: "for some aspects, it could be Milan, for other . . . it could be Turin . . . This indeterminacy . . . signif[ies] that this is not *a* city, but *the* city, any industrial metropolis" (1235). But if the Anthropocene is both a landscape and a discourse, *Marcovaldo* is not only a historical and sociological reflection on Italian and global landscapes of the economic boom; it is also a reflection on the human, on human environmental porosity and ecology of mind, on the human-nonhuman relationship, and on the hybrid forms that the human takes on in epochs of change.

The narrative stratigraphy of the Anthropocene I have attempted to sketch temporarily stops around 1963. But imagine Italy half a century later. Imagine that northern city today, because it is from there that I am writing this essay. The streets are no longer so uneven: asphalt covers these once bumpy pavements, and it is here to stay—a bitumen memo for the next millennium. It's a warm winter, so far the warmest of the century. The air is still polluted in this now postindustrial city, and you don't see so many horses around. Today's Marcovaldos are migrants from Syria or Libya, and the planet is "full of refugees, human or not, without refuge" (Haraway 2015, 160). Still, you see bicycles. You see fewer plastic bags. Fresh locally grown vegetables in the resurfacing local markets. Little by little, you see awareness rising, even as more layers and rubble accumulate. The Anthropocene revealed, whether by literature or by this bodily text we call the world, means that at least some people are starting finally to decipher this landscape and its stories. And this is the challenge, if we want to make this as thin a stratum as possible in the history of the earth.

NOTES

1. I thank Luca Mercalli for this information.
2. My gratitude to Domenico Scarpa for this otherwise inaccessible, fascinating detail.

WORKS CITED

Adamson, Joni. 2016. "We Have Never Been 'Anthropos': From Environmental Justice to Cosmopolitics." In *Environmental Humanities: Voices from the Anthropocene,* edited by Serpil Oppermann and Serenella Iovino, 155–73. Lanham, MD: Rowman & Littlefield.
Armiero, Marco. 2015. "Of the Titanic, the Bounty, and Other Shipwrecks." *intervalla* 3: 50–54.
Calvino, Italo. 1971. *The Watcher and Other Stories.* Translated by William Weaver. San Diego: Harcourt, Brace & Company.
———. 1997. *Invisible Cities.* Translated by William Weaver. New York: Vintage.
———. 1983a. *Difficult Loves. Smog. A Plunge into Real Estate.* Translated by William Weaver. London: Picador.
———. 1983b. *Marcovaldo, or The Seasons in the City.* Translated by William Weaver. San Diego: Harcourt Brace Jovanovich.
———. 2000. *Lettere 1940–1985.* Edited by Luca Baranelli. Milan: Mondadori.
———. 2001. *Saggi 1945–1985.* Edited by Mario Barenghi. 2 vols. Milan: Mondadori.
———. 2003. *Romanzi e racconti.* Edited by Claudio Milanini. 2 Vols. Milan: Mondadori.
Castello, Giancarlo. n.d. "Storia di un'invasione: la formica dell'Argentina." *Bollettino Insetti.* http://www.uomoinerba.it/formiche.htm.
Cohen, Jeffrey Jerome. 2016. "Posthuman Environs." In *Environmental Humanities: Voices from the Anthropocene,* edited by Serpil Oppermann and Serenella Iovino, 25–44. Lanham, MD: Rowman & Littlefield.
Crutzen, Paul, and Eugene Stoermer. 2000. "The 'Anthropocene.'" *Global Change Newsletter* 41: 17–18.
Giraud, T., J. S. Pedersen, and L. Keller. 2002. "Evolution of Supercolonies: The Argentine Ants of Southern Europe." *Proceedings of the National Academy of Sciences USA* 99: 6075–79.

Haraway, Donna. 2015. "Anthropocene, Capitalocene, Plantationocene, Chthulucene: Making Kin." *Environmental Humanities* 6: 159–65.

Istituto Superiore per la Protezione e la Ricerca Ambientale (ISPRA), ed. 2015. *Il consumo di suolo in Italia*. Rome: ISPRA.

Kristensen, Erik, Gil Penha-Lopes, Matthieu Delefosse, Thomas Valdemarsen, Cintia O. Quintana, and Gary T. Banta. 2012. "What Is Bioturbation? The Need for a Precise Definition for Fauna in Aquatic Sciences." *Marine Ecology Progress Series* 446: 285–302.

Latour, Bruno. 1991. *We Have Never Been Modern*. Translated by Catherine Porter. Cambridge, MA: Harvard University Press.

Lowe, S. J., M. Browne, and S. Boudjelas. 2000. "100 of the World's Worst Invasive Alien Species." IUCN/SSC Invasive Species Specialist Group. Auckland, New Zealand: ISSG.

Moore, Jason. 2014. "The Capitalocene. Part I: On the Nature and Origins of Our Ecological Crisis." http://www.jasonwmoore.com/uploads/The_Capitalocene__Part_I__June_2014.pdf.

Morton, Timothy. 2010. *The Ecological Thought*. Cambridge, MA: Harvard University Press.

———. 2016. *Dark Ecology: For a Logic of Future Coexistence*. New York: Columbia University Press.

Oppermann, Serpil. Forthcoming. "The Scale of the Anthropocene: Material Ecocritical Reflections." *Mosaic*.

Paoli, Guido. 1923. *La formica dell'Argentina: Descrizione, costumi, mezzi di lotta. Istruzioni e decreti*. Sanremo, Italy: Conti & Gandolfi.

Ruddiman, William F. 2003. "The Anthropogenic Greenhouse Era Began Thousands of Years Ago." *Climatic Change* 61: 261–93.

Scarpa, Domenico. 1999. *Italo Calvino*. Milan: Bruno Mondadori.

Seger, Monica. 2015. *Landscapes in Between: Environmental Change in Modern Italian Literature and Film*. Toronto: Toronto University Press.

Settis, Salvatore. 2013. *Il paesaggio come bene comune*. Naples: La Scuola di Pitagora.

Turco, R. P., O. B. Toon, T. P. Ackerman, J. B. Pollack, and C. Sagan. 1983. "Nuclear Winter: Global Consequences of Multiple Nuclear Explosions." *Science* 222 (4630): 1283–92.

Wild, A. L. 2004. "Taxonomy and Distribution of the Argentine Ant, Linepithema humile (Hymenoptera: Formicidae)." *Annals of the Entomological Society of America*. 97: 1204–15.

World Wide Fund for Nature Italia, ed. 2009. *L'anno del cemento: Dossier sul consumo di suolo in Italia*. Rome: WWF Italia.

Zalasiewicz, Jan. 2016. "The Extraordinary Strata of the Anthropocene." In *Environmental Humanities: Voices from the Anthropocene*, edited by Serpil Oppermann and Serenella Iovino, 115–31. Lanham, MD: Rowman & Littlefield.

Zalasiewicz, Jan, Mark Williams, and Colin N. Waters. 2016. "Anthropocene." In *Keywords for Environmental Studies*. Edited by Joni Adamson, William A. Gleason, and David Pellow, 14–16. New York: New York University Press.

VIKTOR BERBERI

Resisting Erasure: Landscape, Folklife, and Ethics in the Calabrian and Arbëreshë Novels of Carmine Abate

One of Italy's southernmost regions, Calabria is far removed from the nation's dominant political, cultural, and economic centers, as geographical isolation has often contributed the region's marginalization in the selective course of Italian national history. As the nation's deep south, the region continues to be associated with poverty and neglect. The Calabrian landscape is a site where images of an unspoiled nature collide with the reality of illegal toxic dumping, unregulated development, and the region's inability to address the challenges of wastewater treatment. Calabria's striking natural beauty has been marred by unregulated development, *ecomostri*, unfinished buildings, and the proliferation of foreign- and Italian-owned wind farms.[1] While elements of this onslaught against the environment are relatively recent phenomena, the rhetoric of stark contrasts into which they are inserted is quite old. These Calabrian tropes involve an awareness of space, marking the contiguity of the richness of the landscape's natural beauty and the harsh poverty of its human inhabitants, but they may also take on a temporal sense. This occurs, for example, when the remnants of a glorious past, the Magna Graecia, are juxtaposed with present decay and abandonment, or when a fading contemporary Arbëreshë culture figures its past as a time of greatness.[2] Moreover, notions of Calabrian identity, whether constructed in the accounts of outside observers or embraced by members of the local communities, are not only tied to an understanding of place (regional identity is precisely that: regional) but indeed emerge from a reading of the surrounding landscape. Which is to say that the moment we read any landscape for its cultural significance, the natural and cultural become irretrievably entangled. As Tullio Pagano writes: "The 'constructed' nature of landscape is nowhere more palpable than in Italy, a country where virtually every inch of land has been transformed to suit the needs of the inhabitants. Landscapes may be seen as a palimpsest, where one only has to scratch the surface in order to detect the signs left by previous generations, often concealed under the deceiving naturalness of the scenery" (2011, 402).

Such a recognition reminds us, however, that while our sense of the land may be largely imaginary, our destiny as human beings is nevertheless tied to that of the environment we inhabit in very concrete ways. This is quite clearly the case in Calabria, given the historical difficulty of subsistence farming (and the resulting struggles over land ownership), the unsuccessful attempts at industrialization, and the recent investment in tourism as source of regional revenue—all of these being phenomena that carry with them a range of assumptions regarding the ethical and sustainable use of land.[3] If the landscapes of Italy can be seen as palimpsests, then a key element of an ethics of landscape will involve our ability to read these textual layers. This ability is akin to the sense in which Serenella Iovino uses the notion of "cognitive justice" in discussing ecocriticism as a practice of resistance and liberation. Distinguishing her understanding of cognitive justice from the term's use in postcolonial studies, Iovino calls for "a more radical form of justice based on the right to know, and to choose accordingly." She continues: "Like in many other countries, layers of missed cognitive justice in Italy involve the health of the land, as well as that of working places" (2016, 8). In the case of southern Italy, landscape has often been constructed in a way that thwarts this cognitive justice or undermines what Gloria Pungetti and Thomas Oles have described concisely as the "right to landscape," the right of people not only to live in safe environments but to "determine the shape and meanings of the places they inhabit" (2011, 291).[4]

This essay examines the literary works of contemporary Italophone Arbëreshë writer Carmine Abate (b. 1954), from the early novels set in Arbëreshë communities to the recent *Il bacio del pane* (The bread kiss, 2013), tracing the interpenetration of landscape and folklife as a way of instilling in the protagonists an evolving sense of social engagement and resistance.[5] Abate carries on a tradition inaugurated by Ernesto De Martino, and continued by Rocco Scotellaro and others, one that reconnects with the cultures of the agricultural south and strives to identify the specific, historically determined ways its people have given meaning to the world around them.[6] In chronicling the lives of Calabria's small towns, Abate acknowledges a history of caricatured portraits of Calabrian environments, where the land and its human inhabitants stand as irreconcilable presences, yet he moves beyond these categories to propose other modes of engagement with the natural world that bring forth the cultural, symbolic, and social, as well as ecological, value of the land. While each novel develops these human/nonhuman interactions in a unique direction, they all uncover resources for rethinking the challenges of environmental degradation and cultural erosion. Most importantly, attention to the layered texts offered to us by the landscape helps counter the lack of cognitive justice that Iovino decries. In the family saga *La collina del vento* (The hill of wind, 2012), the Arcuri family's relationship with the Rossarco hill yields parallel narratives, as each one over time generates a story of the recovery of a buried past. In *Il bacio del pane,* where a forest retreat calls up shared experiences of youthful rebellion and renewed political engagement, contact with natural spaces that harbor the memory of a previous generation's impulse to resist enables individuals to push back against organized crime. In both settings, individuals overcome the impasse presented by static depictions of southern Italy's past and current woes by opening themselves up to the agency of the landscape and the eloquent force of the material world.[7]

The most successful contemporary writer to emerge from southern Italy's Arbëreshë communities, Abate endeavors to create in his novels a sense of Calabrian, and specifically Arbëreshë, culture as an embattled ideal, one rooted in traditional cultural elements related to language, cuisine, family structure, folk wisdom, and oral tradition. In the backdrop of Abate's narrative, we see the arrival of Albanian exiles to southern Italy in the fifteenth century, the historical land occupations and the struggle against the *latifondisti* of the mid-twentieth century, and the contemporary threat of coastal development.[8] The world he depicts emerges through a dialogue with the surrounding landscape, as titles such as *Tra due mari* (Between two seas, 2002) and *La collina del vento* suggest. Abate's landscapes are saturated with cultural narratives, from the quasi-mythical Greek settlement of Krimisa to the hill around which the family saga of *La collina del vento* revolves. These settings—hills, ravines, forests—are always named, further indicating that they are never anonymous, untouched natural spaces but constitute strong cultural presences bound up in an imaginary process involving a community's sense of self.

As a diasporic community, the Arbëreshë are especially conscious of their lived experience of place. The story of the survival of minority ethnic and linguistic communities is often one of geohistory. When the first waves of Albanian refugees arrived in Italy in the second half of the fifteenth century, following the invasion of the Balkans by the Ottoman Empire, the southernmost Apennines presented a familiar landscape. Experience with malarial plains in Albania and strategic reasons of defense meant that the great majority of these Arbëreshë settlements were located at higher elevations. Over time, geography facilitated the preservation of the language and other aspects of Arbëreshë culture in these villages, whereas in low-lying settlements the Italian language supplanted Albanian entirely.[9] Given the awareness of this history, together with the threat of contemporary emigration, it is understandable that the Arbëreshë might perceive space analogically, weighing the qualities of the places of distant origin, of current habitation, of inevitable departure, one against the other. The perception of current emigration is intensified by the sense of repetition, as the landscape tells stories not only of the dislocation of early Albanians, but of the disappearance of Greek settlements, whose presence had been met with greater mistrust by existing communities.

Along with the significance of mountain peaks as a crucial part of these environments, the sea also punctuates several of the novels. As characters regularly descend from Calabrian hill towns to nearby beaches, we sense that the reality of migration is never far from their minds: a father's painful decision to emigrate for work in the north and abroad, the younger generation's waves of departure in search of opportunity, and the distant memory of the flight from their homeland of those first Albanian refugees after Skanderbeg's defeat all bear traces of a preoccupation with fluidity and movement.[10] The wind, too—the wind of death and fatalism, but of fertility and regeneration as well—that admonishes and guides the Arcuris in *La collina del vento* over the course of generations, resonates with the experience of forced migration, calling to mind the wind that according to oral tradition would keep the Turkish army at bay and protect those fifteenth-century refugees on their way to the Italian coast.

Taking up the tradition of the Arbëreshë rhapsodists which has faded in recent decades, Abate's novels read like narrative palimpsests through which we see reenacted deeds familiar from Albanian oral tales. *Il ballo tondo* (The round dance, 2005), for instance, is structured around four rhapsodies depicting the stories of Kostantini i Vogël (the young Constantine), Doruntine, and two episodes from the life and death of Skanderbeg. In the more recent novels, where the rhapsodist is absent, stories narrated by an older family member perform a similar function. The acts of Arbëreshë self-representation that he incorporates into the novels are strongly rooted in a connection to the land and stand at odds with the attempts of outsiders to engage the unique culture of these small Calabrian towns.[11]

La collina del vento takes the form of a family saga, spanning roughly one hundred years of the Arcuri family's history, as they hold their own against a series of threats posed to the family and its hill, the Rossarco. These range from the mystery of two skeletons found buried on the hill (the remains of men who had attempted to rape the narrator's grandmother), to the crash of an English plane during the Second World War, to the coercion of developers scheming to buy the land for the installation of wind turbines and a resort hotel. Much of the narrative is driven by an archaeological excavation led by Paolo Orsi, who was in fact responsible for the discovery of a number of major sites in Sicily and southern Italy, including some near Cirò Marina in the late 1920s, where the ancient city of Krimisa was believed to have been located. In the novel, the sympathetic Orsi becomes a protector of sorts for the Arcuri family, attempting to intervene to secure the father's early release from internal exile under the Fascist regime and offering to pay the family for artifacts found on their land.[12]

In *La collina del vento*, landscape is enlisted in the struggle to find a connection to a community's past, as anxiety over the erosion of culture runs parallel to an awareness of a threat posed to the land. This focus on the relation between the discursive and the material points to new modes of resistance to cultural loss. The Arcuri family wants desperately to find in their hill archaeological evidence of the ancient Krimisa. Such a (material) discovery would function much in the same way that stories of Skanderbeg do in novels like *Il mosaico del tempo grande* (The mosaic of the time of greatness, 2006) and *La moto di Scanderbeg* (Skanderbeg's motorcycle, 1999), stories that find Arbëreshë history so firmly rooted to the surrounding landscape. Here, the novel's two historical characters, Orsi and another archaeologist, Umberto Zanotti Bianco, are employed as elements in an interpretive process recalling what Axel Goodbody has referred to as "depragmatization": "Historical facts can be readily invested with new meanings. This linking of the real with the imagined facilitates the generation of new structures of cultural perception. Literary works typically seek to respond to a crisis or problem in the existing memory culture by focusing on forgotten aspects of the past, articulating as yet unformed memories, and making stories out of them" (2011, 58). The archaeologists' ability to read the landscape promises a richer sense of the region's past, restoring the memory of the Greek settlements mourned in the lines of Luigi Siciliani's poem "Capo Cremisseo": "Noi, che chiamati fummo greci, ma greci più grandi,/noi, ora siamo negletti in solitario abbandono" ("We, who were called Greeks, but greater Greeks,/now we are neglected in solitary abandonment"; 1905, 68).[13]

The archaeological project corresponds to oral tales that guide Abate's characters in their search for a grounding amid the inevitable fragmentation of their small communities. Indeed, the family members are often depicted as listeners, attentive to the tales told by parents and grandparents, and to those generated by the land. As the novel concludes, the father's ability to listen to the land allows him to predict the landslide that will bury the abandoned structures originally meant for a tourist resort, but now occupied by migrant squatters. The hill's response to development that fails to take into consideration anything but commodification tells of the fragility of migrant lives, mirrored in the fragility of the land itself. At the same time, the landslide unearths the long sought remains of Krimisa and provides the final piece in the narration of the family saga.[14]

As a result of the landslide which calls him back to the Rossarco, the narrator comes to a new understanding of the shared narratives of people and place: "The truth is that places, like jealous lovers, require absolute faithfulness: if you abandon them, sooner or later they show up to blackmail you with the secret history that binds you to them; if you betray them, they release it to the wind, certain that it will reach you wherever, even at the ends of the earth" (Abate 2012, 241; my translation). Abate goes beyond pathetic fallacy to draw the land into a relationship whose character is determined by a number of clichés associated with the south, but while his language resonates with a world of extortion, coercion, and *omertà* (the code of silence), the underlying message is a recognition of the interdependence of human beings and their environment.

Il bacio del pane also addresses the problem, already taken up in the earlier works, of extortion and organized crime, narrating the encounter between the young protagonists, Francesco and Marta, and Lorenzo, a victim of mafia violence. Lorenzo is hiding out in a nearby forest known as the Giglietto while waiting to testify against 'ndrangheta members who have threatened him and killed his brother. The Giglietto is a place of retreat and shelter from the present threat of death but also of a return to another time spent with *i capelloni* (hippies) in the early 1970s. Above all, it is here that Lorenzo finds the courage to resist: "What they call 'exemplary courage' matured slowly, day after day, night after night, in the solitude of the Giglietto" (Abate 2013, 172; my translation). For Francesco and Marta, the Giglietto also sparks the discovery of another time, when their parents' generation rejected, at least temporarily, the call of convention and consumerism in favor of a simple life lived closer to the land.

Rosanna Morace notes that the vivid description of smells and of the places associated with them suggests a clear connection between *Il bacio del pane* and *La collina del vento*, which, as they chronicle Arbëreshë and Calabrian life, contain recurring images from the local cuisine and products.[15] Here, the scent and taste of bread take on a clear, ethical weight, first creating a bond between the young couple and the older, diffident Lorenzo and eventually inspiring an attitude of commitment and sacrifice with regard to others and the land. *Il bacio del pane*, while recalling the significance of bread in a broader Mediterranean culture, refers more specifically to the practice of kissing bread that has been dropped to the ground. Abate compares the nine months it takes to grow wheat and produce bread to human gestation: "This book is born of a slap I received from my mother after I had kicked a slice of bread. I remember that my mother had me pick it up, and I kissed it.

With that gesture, I learned to appreciate effort and work, because bread, in addition to being one of the best foods that exist, is one of the most difficult to produce. It takes nine months to make bread, from planting the grain to the final phase. It is a gestation, we might say, that indicates the work and sacrifice involved" (quoted in Cusanno 2013, para. 3–4).

This gesture—much like the practice among older generations of prostrating themselves at the shore and kissing the beach—commemorates the insoluble bond between the community's heritage and the land.[16] Indeed, both this ritual kiss and the title kiss of *Il bacio del pane* serve as a way of closing the gap between the human and other than human and acknowledging our debt to a sustaining environment. Moreover, Abate's emphasis on taste and smell functions as a bulwark against a tradition in which landscape is put into the service of power, becoming, in the words of W. J. T. Mitchell, "a place of amnesia and erasure, a strategic place for burying the past and veiling history with natural beauty." In the dominant Western tradition, Mitchell continues, "landscape is something to be seen not touched. It is an abstraction from place and a reification of space. . . . A landscape, then, turns site into sight, place and space into a visual image" (2002, 265). Mitchell implies a shift away from landscape as distance, the colonizing impulse of the individual over the land—and, in particular, of the northern painter venturing into the unsettling landscapes of the far south—toward landscape as "concrete, historical, symbolic, and communal manifestation of cultural identities expressed in the land" (Bonesio 2007, 7).

While the nostalgia for a world that seems to be disappearing is undeniably present throughout much of Abate's work, the novels nonetheless aspire to answer Luisa Bonesio's positive formulation, offering a vision of a present-day Calabria as a place where renewal (both cultural and environmental) is still possible. It is telling that in one novel, *Gli anni veloci* (The fast years, 2008), two young lovers enjoy a picnic surrounded by fireflies, which Abate notes are not yet a rarity in the region. Abate reverses Pasolini's image, in what is known as the "Articolo delle lucciole" (The fireflies' article), of the disappearance of fireflies as an index of both environmental and cultural impoverishment in Italy, where agricultural and "paleo-capitalistic" values no longer count (Pasolini 1975, 129). The fireflies, like the eels, whose mysterious life cycle leads them from the Sargasso Sea to the streams of the Calabrian forest, and the trout that reappear in the Giglietto's stream at the conclusion of *Il bacio del pane*, together suggest the possibility of continuing resistance, of both environment and culture. The dialogue that results from a willingness to hear the stories embedded in matter counters the use of landscape as a mechanism for the manipulation of history and the burial of knowledge and allows human beings to find meaning in the places they inhabit.

NOTES

1. The term *ecomostri* (eco-monsters) is used to describe buildings seen as especially incompatible with their environment.

2. Here I have in mind Carmine Abate's novel *Il mosaico del tempo grande* (The mosaic of the time of greatness).

3. One tragic episode will find its way into Carmine Abate's novels: that of the massacre at Melissa in 1949, where three people were killed and over fifteen wounded by police when Calabrian farmers occupied the *latifondi* to demand that the owners concede land that had been left uncultivated.

4. Like Iovino's cognitive justice, Gloria Pungetti's right to landscape suggests the need to identify the threat posed by, for example, the so-called ecomafia and government corruption and collusion. For more about this idea, see the collection *The Right to Landscape*, especially Pungetti and Oles's chapter, "The 'Right to Landscape' from Hell to Heaven."

5. Abate's novels, which often depict the life of Calabrian Arbëreshë communities, like his native Carfizzi, are widely translated and have received several significant literary awards.

6. De Martino, in *Il mondo magico* (The world of magic, 1948) in particular, introduced a historiography that opens itself up to other cultures and seeks an awareness of its own cultural biases. Scotellaro's work, like Abate's, moved between fiction and socio-anthropology, depicting the lives of southern towns from within. See *L'uva puttanella* (Puttanella grapes, 1955) and *Contadini del sud* (Farmers of the south, 1954).

7. For recent insights into the force and agency of the material world, see especially Iovino and Oppermann (2014).

8. While the majority of Abate's novels are set in Arbëreshë towns, three are set in small towns in Calabria not marked as Arbëreshë, though I would argue that even in these novels, the author's voice is clearly shaped by an Arbëreshë oral tradition. For a discussion of the settings of Abate's novels, see Bovo Romoeuf (2008, 19–21). The *latifondisti* were the owners, often absent, of the large agricultural estates that existed in southern Italy until the land reforms of the early 1950s.

9. For a concise discussion of this early history, see Nasse (1964).

10. The fifteenth-century hero George Castriota, known as Skanderbeg (1405–1468), enjoys an unparalleled status in Albanian ethnic mythology and serves as a common point of reference for Albanian nationals and Arbëreshë alike.

11. Arbëreshë rhapsodists performed epics recounting the exploits of Skanderbeg, the flight of Albanians to Italy following defeat by the Ottoman Turks, and laments for the lost homeland, among other themes. Many of these were collected by the nineteenth-century poet Girolamo De Rada in *Rapsodie d'un poema albanese,* now in volume V of his *Opera Omnia* (2005).

12. For his depiction of the excavation in the novel, Abate relied largely on Orsi's own *Templum Apollinis Alaie ad Crimisa promontorium* (1933).

13. For a classic history of the early Greek colonies in Italy, see Pallottino (1991).

14. For the Arbëreshë, not only have Albanian epic poems held a place in the rhapsodists' performances on special occasions, but these same epics have been kept alive, at

least until recently, in lullabies telling of Costantino, who is forced to leave his bride to go off to war, and other laments over the separation from the homeland.

15. "There are two strong narrative elements that connect *La collina* with *Il bacio*: the smells (not only the smell of bread, but of the air, the place, with various characters sniffing the scents of the Giglietto, as the Arcuri and Paolo Orsi did on the Rossarco hill) and the centrality of place, which is not quite personified but is however a living organism, as if it had a soul, so much so that we sense the life of the Giglietto through its sounds, hidden echoes, the "murmur of the brisk wind, the sound of invisible water," the smells, the transformation of the vegetation through the seasons, and of the place over the course of years" (Morace 2014, 220).

16. "The older residents of Carfizzi tell of how their grandparents, on the occasion of Cirò Marina's traditional agricultural fair, lingered on the beach where the Albanian ancestors had landed. A symbolic kiss given to the shore of the Ionian Sea and songs in praise of the far-off homeland were part of a ritual that clearly expressed (and kept alive) a strong emotional connection with the places their ancestors had been forced to abandon in order not to submit to Ottoman domination" (Abate and Behrmann 2006, 175).

WORKS CITED

Abate, Carmine. 1999. *La moto di Scanderbeg*. Rome: Fazi.
———. 2002. *Tra due mari*. Milan: Mondadori.
———. 2005. *Il ballo tondo*. Milan: Mondadori.
———. 2006. *Il mosaico del tempo grande*. Milan: Mondadori.
———. 2008. *Gli anni veloci*. Milan: Mondadori.
———. 2012. *La collina del vento*. Milan: Mondadori.
———. 2013. *Il bacio del pane*. Milan: Mondadori.
Abate, Carmine, and Meike Behrmann. 2006. *I germanesi: Storia e vita di una comunità della Calabria e dei suoi emigranti*. Soveria Mannelli, Italy: Rubbettino Editore.
Bonesio, Luisa. 2007. *Paesaggio: Identità e comunità tra locale e globale*. Reggio Emilia, Italy: Diabasis.
Bovo Romoeuf, Martine. 2008. *L'epopea di Hora: La scrittura migrante di Carmine Abate*. Florence: Franco Cesati Editore.
Cusanno, Luciana. 2013. "Carmine Abate, dal premio Campiello a *Il bacio del pane*." *CoratoLive.it*, October 23. http://www.coratolive.it/news/cultura/251499/news.
De Rada, Girolamo. 2005. *Opera Omnia*. Edited by Francesco Altimari. Soveria Mannelli, Italy: Rubbettino Editore.
De Martino, Ernesto. 1973. *Il mondo magico: Prolegomeni a una storia del magismo*. Turin: Boringhieri.
Egoz, Shelley, Jala Makhzoumi, and Gloria Pungetti, eds. 2011. *The Right to Landscape: Contesting Landscape and Human Rights*. Farnham, UK: Ashgate.
Goodbody, Axel. 2011. "Sense of Place and Lieu de Mémoire: A Cultural Memory Approach to Environmental Texts." In *Ecocritical Theory: New European Approaches*, edited by Axel Goodbody and Kate Rigby, 55–67. Charlottesville: University of Virginia Press.
Iovino, Serenella. 2016. *Ecocriticism and Italy: Ecology, Resistance, and Liberation*. London: Bloomsbury Academic.

Iovino, Serenella, and Serpil Oppermann, eds. 2014. *Material Ecocriticism*. Bloomington: Indiana University Press.
Mitchell, W. J. T. 2002. *Landscape and Power*. Chicago: University of Chicago Press.
Morace, Rosanna. 2014. *Le stagioni narrative di Carmine Abate: Rapsodie di un romanzomondo*. Soveria Mannelli, Italy: Rubbettino Editore.
Nasse, George Nicholas. 1964. *The Italo-Albanian Villages of Southern Italy*. Washington, DC: National Research Council.
Orsi, Paolo. 1933. *Templum Apollinis Alaie ad Crimisa promontorium*. Rome: Società Magna Grecia.
Pagano, Tullio. 2011. "Reclaiming Landscape." *Annali d'italianistica* 29: 401–16.
Pallottino, Massimo. 1991. *A History of Earliest Italy*. Ann Arbor: University of Michigan Press.
Pasolini, Pier Paolo. 1975. *Scritti corsari*. Milan: Garzanti.
Pungetti, Gloria, and Thomas Oles. 2011. "The 'Right to Landscape' from Hell to Heaven." In *The Right to Landscape: Contesting Landscape and Human Rights*, edited by Shelley Egoz, Jala Makhzoumi, and Gloria Pungetti, 291–300. Farnham, UK: Ashgate.
Scotellaro, Rocco. 1954. *Contadini del sud*. Bari, Italy: Laterza.
———. 1955. *L'uva puttanella*. Bari, Italy: Laterza.
Siciliani, Luigi. 1905. *Capo Cremisseo: Versi*. Rome: Nuova Antologia.

SERENA FERRANDO

Terra in Dino Buzzati's Fantastic Landscapes

In Italian *terra* means earth, land, ground, soil, and dirt. In the works and thought of Dino Buzzati (1906–1972), *terra* is a mysterious hybrid landscape made of mountains and cities over which death hovers constantly and almost lovingly.[1] A native of the Dolomites area but Milanese by adoption, Buzzati's frequent descents underground (*sottoterra*) are mirrored by his heroic ascensions to the Dolomitic peaks: the vertical movement of his writing is a metaphor for his compulsive quest to answer the "everlasting question": What is death? This essay explores the materiality of Buzzati's love of his land and his fascination with death as they unfurl within his fantastic landscapes made of rock, sand, mud, and Dolomitic peaks. It also traces Buzzati's efforts to reign in the frightening openness and remoteness of an unknown existential space by turning it into a familiar place through the physical exploration of *terra*.[2] The rugged terrain of the Dolomites, so treacherous and mesmerizing, is the stage of this "primordial wild experience" of the earth (Bunting 2015, 613, 607, 610): his explorations are similar to those of the early travelers who assigned layers of significance to the new land they discovered. Buzzati superimposes new layers of meaning upon the strata of rock he travels through on his quest for the "invisible frontier" (Buzzati [1971] 2014, 170) where human territory and God's ultra-territory meet.[3]

Terra: Lust and Fear

The words *terra* and *territorio* both derive from the Latin *terra*. *Terrore* (terror) derives from the Latin *terror* and the verb *terrēre* (to terrify). These words are two main pillars of Buzzati's universe. Born in Belluno at the foot of the Dolomites, Buzzati was always fascinated by the mountains and wrote and thought about them incessantly. Their early charm is chronicled in a great number of drawings that accompany the many letters to his best friend, Arturo Brambilla. Starting with these early writings and throughout his work,

Buzzati describes the Dolomites as majestic and mysterious, full of insidious holes and rising from dark abysses eager to swallow those who climb their sides.[4] The danger of falling to one's death is constant in Buzzati's mountain tales: the rocks are dark, quiet, impenetrable, the peaks invisible, and death lurks in every precarious hold. Once at the top, however, the climbers achieve a fleeting moment of pure freedom in unison with the "divine crags" and bask in the pleasure of the conquest.[5] A type of sexual desire is, in fact, associated with the mountain, which in Italian is *montagna*, a feminine noun that the young Buzzati further feminizes and sexualizes. In a letter to Brambilla dated August 5, 1924, Buzzati jokes about killing himself by jumping off a "magnificent cliff" if he should fail his exams, then mentions the great happiness the mountains give him; he goes on to write about his frustrated desire to meet a woman immediately before he praises the famous guides "who had deflowered (*sverginato*) the most terrifying (*spaventose*) Dolomites" (Buzzati 1985, 153).

Sverginato and *spaventose* are important words here. Buzzati's relationship with the land is one of attraction and fear, and he has an overall "Pan-ic view" of the Dolomites, where the margin between terror and pleasure is extremely thin and porous. Pan is the half-man half-goat Greek god of mountains and nature. As early as the fifth century BC, he was portrayed as intent on various activities: chasing a shepherd, playing with nymphs, dancing and jumping around when Persephone appears from the underworld.[6] The Italian word *panismo* (translated into English as "spirit of nature") indicates an intense participation in the life of nature. Pan has also been worshipped as a universal god due to an erroneous interpretation of his name as "everything"; the Greek adjective *pan* refers to life as embodied in a collective universal organism.[7] The word *panic* (*panico* in Italian), derived from the god's name, means "a sudden overpowering fright," often causing a state of confusion and irrationality. It is synonymous with terror, alarm, consternation, dread, and fear. *Timor panico* is the mysterious and indefinable fear that our forefathers associated with Pan's presence.[8]

The Dolomites

Buzzati's *alpinisti* (climbers, from the word *Alps*) ascend to increasingly higher peaks, deflowering the mountains and defying the powerful spirits guarding them: "People say that the mountains need to be left alone. And San Nicola's bells must toll to chase the evil spirits away" ([1933] 2014, 4). Many dangers surround the crags, and they come in the form of ghosts, anthropomorphized animals, hunters, strong winds, the dark, ice, and falling rocks.[9] The mountains can be the stage of human conflict, as environmental historian Marco Armiero demonstrates, but for Buzzati their most important quality is existential. Armiero, who has written extensively about the Italian mountains, and Buzzati agree on three points: the mountains signify a boundary; a vast array of wild animals and strange creatures (witches, ghosts, and dragons) populate them; and the mountaineers who dwell in the Alps are as untamed as the landscape they inhabit (Armiero 2011). However, although both Armiero and Buzzati perceive the domestication of the mountain and its people in very negative terms, their views differ in political scope. Buzzati's interest lies in the universal forces that rule people and nature, while Armiero's focus is on the motives that drive groups of individuals to fight one another in the name of civic or partisan interests. This indicates that Buzzati's Dolomites stand outside history even though they are affected by time and historical, socioeconomic, and political factors.[10] His mountaineers are not political entities but a human group living on the material boundary between land and sky, and as such they are the closest people will ever come to unveiling the mystery of human existence. What is political concern in Armiero is existential anxiety in Buzzati. The taller the mountains, the greater the peril. In fact, every inch of civilization in Buzzati is under threat as described in "Il macigno": "A boulder sways above the beautiful villa where people live a carefree life.... Every once in a while, in the middle of the night, ominous thuds are heard from different sides of the valley, the windowpanes tremble. It means that some section of the mountain has come off and crashed down, it is possible that it has crushed a few houses" ([1955] 2011, 212–13). However, as a living thing, earth itself is threatened. Mountains, peaks, and glaciers are constantly shifting, eroding, and collapsing: "And what about the mountains? Oh, don't go and tell me that they have stayed the same. In the meantime, they have contracted. I remember, at a spot that I can point to you on the map, two ice-tipped needles, unbelievable, six or seven thousand meters tall; and now they've vanished" ([1955] 2011, 111).[11]

The Pulsating Life of *Terra*

While Armiero and, along with him, historian Peter Hansen (2013) underline the importance of the mountains as borders, Monica Seger (2015), although not focusing specifically on mountains, draws attention to the interstitial landscapes where nature and culture converge. The liminal space of the mountain peak is crucial in Buzzati for precisely this reason: it is where exceptional human beings (mostly alpine climbers) come into contact with the earth and the mixture of terror and ecstasy that it radiates and can hear its voice. It is a mystical experience in Buzzati's iconography, one in which experienced, successful climbers are portrayed as demigods. Buzzati's earth mysticism interprets man's relationship with the land (*terra*) as a meaningful yet failed conversation between human and supernatural forces through matter.[12] In

Bàrnabo delle montagne and *Il segreto del bosco vecchio*, for example, the earth speaks through nonhuman entities such as rocks, trees, the woods, the wind, and through wild animals. All children and a handful of men are able to hear its voice as long as they maintain a pure heart.[13] Earth grows silent when it is threatened by a whole array of frightening interlocutors such as ferocious hunters, killers, lumberjacks, or anyone who disrespects the mountains.[14]

Buzzati's *terra* is thus a sentient being and pulsates like an organism emitting a vital buzz. The rocks are alive, the mountains breathe, and the woods are filled with mysterious life: "The mysterious rustle of the garden, the countryside, the trees, the branches, the leaves, the lawn, the tiny voices of small animals, the stealthy trot of the foxes, of the rabbits, of the elves, the groaning of the crickets, the gurgling of the snails, of the small snakes, the impalpable squealing of the mole-crickets and the spiders" ([1971] 2014, 213).[15] *Terra* reveals its aliveness in various ways: it can transform and move, it can intimidate, it can kill, and it can cry.[16]

Verticality

The stratified geological history of the Dolomites, which formed around 240 million years ago, chronicles the mountains' intermittent movement between the depths of the sea and their current highest elevation (10,968 feet or 3,343 meters at Punta Penia).[17] Cyclically emerging from the waters and then submerged again, the Dolomites originated from the metamorphism of limestone into a sedimentary rock known as dolostone (Sperber, Wilkinson, and Peacor 1984, 609; Bosellini, Stefano, and the Società Geologica Italiana 1998). Their complex orogeny replicates the same imaginative vertical movement traceable in Buzzati's literary and existential explorations. His complex relationship with *terra* expresses a desire to move vertically away from the flatland of mortal life toward the peaks of immortality. It also includes the perception of the mountain as a barrier to an ascension toward God: "A pitiless barrier between us: on the other side my beloved countryside ... the mountains ... and on this side, just me" (Buzzati [1955] 2011, 128). Buzzati's painted story "Gli apriranno?" depicts a knight on horseback before a fortress-like mountain with the caption: "After such a long journey, after so many tribulations, after so much blood and thorns, he finally arrived at the yearned-for castle. But here all was shut and quiet" (2013, 64–65). Here the mountain stands as the obstacle preventing Buzzati from walking the distance from the concrete, comprehensible place of the familiar to the incomprehensible, abstract space of the unknown. Buzzati's underworld is also filled with similar hurdles. *Poem Strip* and "Viaggio agli inferni del secolo" ("A trip to the century's hells") chronicle a visit to hell (*sottoterra*), where death pulsates almost in unison with the life above ground (*sulla terra*). Steep staircases, elevators, and tunnels are typical features in Buzzati's metropolitan underworld and form a vertiginous vertical space. In a drawing from *I miracoli della Val Morel*, the anthropomorphized "satanic goat" flies in such a space and resembles a deconstructed Pan, whose mythical association with fear complements Buzzati's spelunking in the underworld ([1971] 2002, 71). Similar to his ascensional disposition above ground, the verticality of Buzzati's infernal travels is reminiscent of the Dolomites, particularly such crags (*crode*) as the Schiara and the Torre del diavolo (Devil's Tower), which also appear in *Le storie dipinte, I miracoli della Val Morel*, and many of Buzzati's paintings. Verticality is a constant element in Buzzati's topography of death: dying happens "from high to low, in a vertical direction," with death depicted as "a sweet abyss" and a "precipice" ([1966] 2012, 186–87). The abyss of Buzzati's underworld is an inverted *croda*, an empty cone of horror, ruled by the most human qualities of cowardice, selfishness, weakness, lack of respect, violence, and anxiety. It is a metropolitan wasteland entirely lacking nature (there are no animals and no gardens) governed by anthropomorphized devils. God or any benevolent, illuminated presence is entirely absent, and all upward movement is forbidden. The mountains' palpable existential fullness is mirrored by the mysterious emptiness of the underworld tunnels, and the peaceful solitude of the mountain peaks is counterbalanced by the urban crowdedness of hell.

Death and Time

Death hovers over Buzzati's literary universe, comprised between the extreme peaks of the Dolomites and the underground cones of hell. As described in *Il deserto dei Tartari*, Buzzati's novel about a military officer who dies right before he has had the chance to fight the enemy he has waited for all his life, time is the emissary of death, and this is an obsessively recurrent theme in Buzzati's world. In *God, Death, and Time*, Emmanuel Levinas argues that time is a relationship with infinity and death the necessary question to ask in order to establish such a relationship; it is tempting to adopt this conception of death and time (as a departure without return) as a possible philosophical basis for Buzzati's universe (Levinas 2000, 19). In Buzzati's city of death, the dead spin in an eternally frozen time, unable to resume the life on earth for which they long. In this fifth dimension, time is suspended and space is chaotic (in Greek the word *chaos* signifies emptiness and at the same time implies the uncontainable possibility of presence which in hell is never realized). The emptiness of the cones of the underground caverns mirrors the massive, rocky bodies of mountain peaks that are filled with the possibility of creating "an experience of death" without dying (Levinas 2000, 10). In their association with death and fear, Buzzati's mountains stand as the threshold between life and death or the point where place turns into unexplorable space and lies out of Buzzati's human reach. For this reason, the mountains have a sublime quality: even though they are visible and can be experienced in a tactile way, in Buzzati's work they always remain withdrawn and impenetrable as they guard the mystery of what lies above and beyond.[18] On these mountains, Buzzati finds the "absence of everything," which, in Levinasian terms, is the "plenitude of the voice, or the murmur of silence" that emanates from the Dolomites (Levinas 2000, 46). Buzzati's "disquietude" with death and the unknown echoes above and below his *terra* in the form of a question that, again in Levinas's terms, is "not convertible into a response" (16, 17). Space cannot be transformed into place, and Buzzati's "everlasting question" is bound to remain unanswered.

Buzzati's relationship with the territory echoes that of many ecopoets who respond "to the human-nature split" by attempting "to connect with the literal, local, physical places" (Bryson 2005, 33). Paraphrasing Scott Bryson's words about Mary Oliver's poetry, Buzzati attempts to turn the space of the mountain into a comprehensible, knowable, and localized place—while always remaining painfully aware of the failure of such undertaking. He aspires to create an intimacy with the territory while simultaneously embracing the logical impossibility of such closeness (Bryson 2005). Space is place before a connection to it has been formed, and in Buzzati, space and place are two "mutually exclusive perspectives" that can never be harmonized since space (like God) is forever out of reach (Bryson 2005, 25, 97). At the conjunction of *terra*, *territorio*, and *terrore* lies the forbidden frontier where Buzzati's characters fail to encounter God. *Terra* and *terrore* are intrinsic to the Dolomites: the mountains lure men up the crags with the promise of secret knowledge, but ultimately they dispense terror as such knowledge can only be imparted to those who fall into the abyss and die. In fact, such "temptation of death" radiating from the crevices of the earth inspires the need to "find comfort in something superhuman" (Buzzati [2010] 2012, 117). At the same time, Buzzati dissolves his religious experience into the realm of nature and suggests that the spiritual encounter with the *ultraterreno* must occur in nature by returning to the materiality of the rock. In his painting *Piazza del Duomo di Milano*, Milan's cathedral is transformed into a pinnacled Dolomitic fortress. A large grassy field in the foreground pushes the church far from the viewer's eyes and draws attention to the living soil on which it rests. The movement of the painting is upward, as if the transfigured rocky cathedral pushes against the frame in an effort to escape from it and transcend earth itself. The following passage captures the essence of Buzzati's lifelong affair with his *terra*:

> The extreme peaks of the Dolomites . . . the spectacle of the whole walls in their *frightening* and *beloved* solitude opened up before me, then I felt a

stirring both *painful* and *exquisite* inside of me . . . the old mountains, immediately recognized me and summoned me . . . No one has ever gone there, no one has ever climbed up the monk's head. You could do it . . . Up here you'll be happy . . . And, even with throbs of fear, without which the mountains would be just rocks . . . I ran to my friend . . . who was going to pull me up the buildings and the towers of that great mysterious city . . . Now . . . they don't call me with that silent voice that crawled into my guts. They stand there, immobile, cold, quiet, locked in a supreme indifference. What happened? Why have I become a stranger? ([1971] 2014, 169; emphasis added)

Buzzati keeps charging at the rocky fortress of a mysterious and unknowable God whose warning, "No one may see me and live" (Exodus 33:20), resonates all over his *terra*. Exploring the relationship between human beings and *terra* (or geology) is Buzzati's most successful attempt at accessing God or what lies beyond the "earthly experience of the land," and the Dolomites become the objective correlative of this endless quest (Scranton 2015, 15). Ultimately, by studying man's relationship with the materiality of the mountain as he tries to "cross the famous border," Buzzati explores what it means to be human (Buzzati [1971] 2014, 83).[19]

NOTES

I am indebted to my friend and colleague Anna Soffientini for her insights into Buzzati's *panismo* and her Ancient Greek expertise.

1. Dino Buzzati was an Italian writer, journalist, painter, and an avid alpinist. A number of his works, including the novel *Il deserto dei tartari* (1940; *The Tartar Steppe*, 1952) and *Poema a fumetti* (1969; *Poem Strip*, 2009), this latter being Italy's first graphic novel, have been translated into English. Several of his books feature drawings alongside text.

2. As defined by Scott Bryson, place is localized and connected to the person, while space is vaster and unconnected. Place is known, knowable, comprehensible, and concrete; space is unknown, incomprehensible, and abstract (Bryson 2005, 21, 25). On this topic see also Ursula Heise's *Sense of Place and Sense of Planet*, where, urging people to develop a consciousness of their surroundings, she quotes Paul Shepard: "Knowing who you are is impossible without knowing where you are" (Heise 2008, 28). See also Gary Snyder's (1974, 1990) and Edward Abbey's (1968) idea of the human body fused with its surroundings.

3. All his life Buzzati grappled with his inability to embrace religion and the Catholic God as evidenced, for example, by the poem he wrote shortly before dying from cancer: "Inexistent God, I pray to you/that at least on this great ship/that is taking me away/the cabins are well-aired" . . . "But if he does not exist, why are you praying?"/"He does not exist as long as I don't believe in him/until I continue living the way we all live/wishing, wishing/but if I call out to him . . . " (Buzzati [1971] 2014, x). Regarding Buzzati's mapping of the territory, one could argue that it provides a space where the agencies of *terra* and human beings interact as intermingled sentient beings (see Iovino and Oppermann 2012).

4. "The Croda dei Toni, full of mystery . . . I don't know what I'd give to spend a little more time among those crags." "Tomorrow I'm going with Augusto to the Formel, which is a hole in the mountain." "In the end the guide says we're here and we are at the top—with the largest abyss underneath" (Buzzati 1985, 61, 62, 65).

5. Buzzati often uses the term *divine* to describe the mountains: "The divine crags," "the divine wall of the Schiara," "the divine Dolomites" (Buzzati 1985, 153, 172, 179).

6. Enciclopedia dell'Arte Antica, s.v. "Pan," http://www.treccani.it/enciclopedia/pan _(Enciclopedia-dell'-Arte-Antica)/.

7. *Enciclopedia Treccani*, s.v. "Pan," http://www.treccani.it/enciclopedia/pan/. See also the original Greek Πάν (Pan, derived from the Greek *paein*, or to pasture), τὸ πᾶν (everything), and πᾶν (the accusative of the Greek adjective *pan* that means "all" or "everything").

8. Vocabolario Treccani, s.v. "Panico," http://www.treccani.it/vocabolario/panico_res -7c707877-002c-11de-9d89-0016357eee51/.

9. Here are some examples: "There is someone on the crags, where no one had ever been brave enough to climb" (Buzzati [1933] 2014, 30); "The evil spells of the woods," "The confused voice of the wind hosted an evil wrath, a pleasure to do evil" (Buzzati [1935] 2014, 44, 47); "In that exact moment, at the south-east end of the yard, in the shadow cast by the hornbeams, a trap door hidden below the grass began to open jerkily, shifting to one side and clearing the opening of a tunnel that disappeared underground. Suddenly, a thick and blackish being came out and started zig-zagging at frantic speed" (Buzzati [1966] 2012, 125).

10. See Buzzati's remarks in *Cronache terrestri* ([1972] 2012, 131–32) on how the legend of any unclimbed mountain is reduced to mere fact once its peak is conquered.

11. "I lupi nuotatori" (The swimming wolves) depicts the mountains as they disintegrate, as if pulled by a strange, powerful force (Buzzati 2013, 58).

12. I use the word *man* in the sense of male individual. In Buzzati, only men have a privileged relationship with the mountain and the land at large. Rarely are women mentioned in his articles and his stories about the mountains, and if so, they are almost exclusively portrayed in negative terms as if they lacked the capacity to relate to or the desire to connect with the land. Throughout his life and work, Buzzati's relationship with the other sex was marked by an inability (or unwillingness) to acknowledge women's equality to men, especially in regards to bravery and physical strength.

13. "And from the woods small mysterious voices begin to come out" (Buzzati [1966] 2012, 51); "That enigmatic groaning"; "They were thin voices, belonging to some small animals" (Buzzati [1935] 2014, 96, 62).

14. See "Secrets they are, guarded for eternity by the mountains" (Buzzati [1945] 2014, 128); "The top of Polveriera. Perfectly clear, icy, and silent" (Buzzati [1933] 2014, 34); "The solemn silence of the ancient woods" (Buzzati [1935] 2014, 71).

15. As he also writes elsewhere: "Before the door that opens onto the live rock"; "The breath of the mountain had flown over the Bersaglio fields" (Buzzati [1933] 2014, 4, 73).

16. "Look at this crag . . . last year it wasn't here. It seems impossible how the mountains change from one year to the next"; "Small gusts of wind. All is absolutely quiet. A few tiny rocks bounce from drop to drop. In front one can see the large towers of Lastoni di Mezzo with their frightening holds . . . The fear creeps up from underneath"; "A large

slab of rock came crashing down that if I'm not quick to move to the side, I will end up under it" (Buzzati [1933] 2014, 69, 35, 19). "A boundless scream rose from the earth" (Buzzati [1966] 2012, 51).

17. The Dolomites were named after French geologist Déodat de Dolomieu (1750–1801), who first determined their unique rock composition: calcium magnesium carbonate.

18. The word *sublime* derives from the Latin *sub* (up to) and *limen* (threshold): reaching the highest threshold (*Vocabolario Treccani*, s.v. "sublime").

19. On the impossibility of logical or empirical answers to the question of individual mortality see Scranton (2015, 20).

WORKS CITED

Abbey, Edward. 1968. *Desert Solitaire: A Season in the Wilderness.* New York: Simon and Schuster.

Armiero, Marco. 2011. *A Rugged Nation: Mountains and the Making of Modern Italy.* Cambridge, UK: White Horse Press.

Bosellini, Alfonso, Marco Stefano, and the Società Geologica Italiana. 1998. *Geologia delle Dolomiti: Atti della 78ª Riunione Estiva della Società Geologica Italiana.* Rome: Società Geologica Italiana.

Bryson, Scott J. 2005. *The West Side of Any Mountain: Place, Space, and Ecopoetry.* Iowa City: University of Iowa Press.

Bunting, Ben S. 2015. "An Alternative Wilderness: How Urban Exploration Brings Wildness to the City." *ISLE* 22(3): 602–22.

Buzzati, Dino. (1933) 2014. *Bàrnabo delle montagne.* Milan: Mondadori.

———. (1935) 2014. *Il segreto del bosco vecchio.* Milan: Mondadori.

———. (1940) 1999. *Il deserto dei Tartari.* Milan: Mondadori.

———. (1945) 2014. *La famosa invasione degli orsi in Sicilia.* Milan: Mondadori.

———. (1955) 2011. *In quel preciso momento.* Milan: Mondadori.

———. (1966) 2012. *Il colombre.* Milan: Mondadori.

———. 1969. *Poema a fumetti.* Milan: Mondadori.

———. (1971) 2002. *I miracoli della Val Morel.* Milan: Mondadori.

———. (1971) 2014. *Le notti difficili.* Milan: Mondadori.

———. (1972) 2012. *Cronache terrestri.* Milan: Mondadori.

———. 1985. *Lettere a Brambilla.* Novara, Italy: De Agostini.

———. (2010) 2012. *I fuorilegge della montagna. Scalate, discese e gare olimpiche.* Milan: Mondadori.

———. 2013. *Le storie dipinte.* Milan: Mondadori.

Hansen, Peter. 2013. *The Summits of Modern Man: Mountaineering after the Enlightenment.* Cambridge, MA: Harvard University Press.

Heise, Ursula K. 2008. *Sense of Place and Sense of Planet: The Environmental Imagination of the Global.* New York: Oxford University Press.

Iovino, Serenella, and Serpil Oppermann. 2012. "Theorizing Material Ecocriticism: A Diptych." *ISLE* 19(3): 448–75.

Levinas, Emmanuel. 2000. *God, Death, and Time.* Translated by Bettina Bergo. Stanford, CA: Stanford University Press.

Scranton, Roy. 2015. *Learning to Die in the Anthropocene: Reflections on the End of a Civilization*. San Francisco: City Lights Books.
Seger, Monica. 2015. *Landscapes in Between: Environmental Change in Modern Italian Literature and Film*. Toronto: University of Toronto Press.
Snyder, Gary. 1974. *Turtle Island*. New York: New Directions Books.
———. 1990. *The Practice of the Wild*. Berkeley, CA: North Point Press.
Sperber, Christine M., Bruce H. Wilkinson, and Donald R. Peacor. 1984. "Rock Composition, Dolomite Stoichiometry, and Rock/Water Reactions in Dolomite Carbonate Rocks." *Journal of Geology* 92(6): 609–22.

SOPHIA MAXINE FARMER

Aeropittura: Modern Aviation and the Fascist Idealization of the Italian Landscape

> It is imperative that we create; we, people from this epoch and this generation, because we have the duty to remake the face of the Fatherland both spiritually and materially. In ten years, comrades, Italy will be unrecognizable! This is because we will have transformed it, we will have made a new one, from the mountains which we will have covered with a green coat [of trees], to the fields which will be completely reclaimed. —Benito Mussolini, *Discorso del 30 ottobre 1934*

Although Futurism is often regarded as a movement that concluded with World War I in 1918, many scholars have recognized that there was a "Second Futurism" that followed the Great War and subsequently became associated with Fascism. Despite the death and abandonment of many of its founding members, Futurism continued to be a prolific movement under its leader Filippo Tommaso Marinetti (1876–1944) well into the 1940s. Many of the latent iterations of the movement further problematized the earlier sentiments of the historical avant-garde. Futurism condemned the widespread admiration for Italian tradition and ancient history in prewar manifestos. Nevertheless, as can be seen in writings and artistic works of the Fascist period, the Futurists came to embrace the aspects of Benito Mussolini's regime that were grounded in the intersections between aesthetics and politics, including historicized symbolism and style. The new forms of Futurism were even more complex and contradictory than earlier artistic iterations. In order to create utopic visions of the future, they recycled the iconography of the past. Moreover, the Futurists managed to gain the favor of the Fascist party through an exaltation of the new man, the cult of *il Duce,* and their seemingly incongruous obsessions with the Roman Imperial past and the technology of the future.

One sub-movement of this second wave of Futurism was *Aeropittura* or aeropainting. The imagery featured in the group's paintings, which focused on the airplane and the Italian landscape from an aerial perspective, among other things, also reflects the Fascist rhetoric that exalted a cultivated landscape. Yet to understand the shared conception of nature between Fascism and Futurism, the following questions must be addressed: Are the artistic movement's perfected representations in line with Fascist imaginings and notions of an idealized and cultivated nature? Do these imaginings of the conquered landscape help us to better understand the Fascist aesthetic and the regime's conception of nature? If so, how?

This essay seeks to tackle these issues by examining *Aeropittura* paintings from the 1930s, when most of the nature projects of a now well-established Fascist regime were instituted.[1] These projects involved three complex forms of *bonifiche* or reclamation: agricultural, human, and cultural. These three branches sought to remake non-Fascist nature—here seen as an uncultivated environment—according to an ideal, a nationalistic vision of culture (Armiero 2014, 242). As a result, the national program of *bonifica integrale* aimed at reclaiming both the people and the land, through technological innovations in agricultural programs, education, and technology (Caprotti and Kaïka 2008, 617). Thus Italy was engineered to be a newly perfected Italy, inhabited by the new idealized Italian. Typically, agricultural reclamation sought to salvage land that was viewed as unhealthy (usually swamps, river deltas, and coastal areas) by transforming them into productive agricultural, industrial, and semi-urban areas. During this period, agricultural reclamation projects like the draining of the Pontine Marshes were heavily documented through literature, photography, film, and newsreels. At the same time, the Futurist painters active throughout the second decade of Fascism created vibrant works to capture an idealized version of the Italian landscape. While historians such as Federico Caprotti, Marco Armiero, and Wilko Graf von Hardenberg have considered the film and literature of this era in conjunction with the Fascist ideas of nature, the connection between this topic and painting remains largely unexamined.

Rather than graphically representing Italian countryside as viewed from an airplane, the *Aeropittori* painted idealized imaginings that portrayed the fantasy of a conquered Italian land, as put forth by Mussolini and the Fascist regime. As the signatories of the *Manifesto dell'aeropittura* assert, their works portray, "the shifting perspectives of flight [that] constitute an absolutely new reality which has nothing in common with reality as traditionally constituted by a terrestrial perspective" (Rainey, Poggi, and Wittman 2009, 283).[2] In their paintings, the *Aeropittori* create poetic and aesthetically engaging symbols of a national identity associated with the transformation of wilderness into a bountifully productive agricultural landscape.

The utilization of aesthetics was paramount to a cultivated vision of an idealized nature in Fascist Italy. Like all other aspects of the regime, the idea differed greatly from the reality of nature in the Italian nation (Falasca-Zamponi 2000, 155). However, the conceptualization of nature was not a new discourse in the peninsula. Though the Fascist regime capitalized on aestheticizing the perception of nature as a nationalist characteristic, the concept of *natura* or nature has a long history in the nation even prior to the Risorgimento and national unification in 1861. The idea of an Italy that incorporated both cultural and natural aspects into a place of beauty and great fertility is a concept that dates back to the Roman era (Lazzaro and Crum 2005, 157). Furthermore, the Italian view of nature is contradictory but often tied to the concept of a cultivated and idealized landscape that is above all productive (Graf von Hardenberg 2006, 198). The Fascist ideal of nature has an entirely different meaning from the contemporary North American understanding of the term, which epitomizes wilderness. Certain aspects of nature, particularly agriculture, were viewed as a positive influence by the regime, but other features were viewed as unproductive and uncivilized (Caprotti and Kaïka 2008, 617–18; Binde 1999, 767). Uncultivated land was seen as unhealthy and dangerous, worthy of neither glorification nor consideration, until man transformed it into something more productive (Graf von Hardenberg 2006, 198).[3]

Therefore, in an effort to create a nature that fit the Italian ideal of a bountiful landscape the regime implemented land reclamation projects and major water management works (Graf von Hardenberg 2006, 198). The transformation of the Pontine Ager was the most notable land reclamation project. The marsh region which spanned about 75,000 hectares south of Rome was considered to be a high-priority area to be transformed for agricultural production (Caprotti and Kaïka 2008, 616). This stretch of land had been the subject of other failed attempts to repurpose it into a productive landscape dating back to the days of the Roman Empire. The Fascist regime saw the project as a continuation of the reclamation projects of the classical empire, and they promoted their success in the endeavor as an affirmation of the coming Fascist empire—a reestablishment of Imperial Rome (Caprotti 2009, 384).

As Per Binde asserts, the reclamation of the Pontine Marshes is a significant example of the Fascist struggle against nature (1999, 768). Within the regime the representation of violence was an important part of Fascist identity. Moreover, the threat of war, and the violence that inevitably went hand in hand with it, had a significant impact on the discourse on nature (Falasca-Zamponi 2000, 38). Wilderness was portrayed as something that needed to be conquered. The transformed marshes were upheld as an example of the regime's ability to conquer and colonize. This form of internal colonization prefigured the establishment of an overseas empire. It was even used in the campaigns for the war on Ethiopia in 1935 (Binde 1999, 768; Caprotti 2009).

Additionally, the development of the Pontine Marshes was linked to the larger project of the *battaglia del grano* or "battle of grains." Officially launched in 1925, the battle of grains was intended to increase the national wheat production as a means of reaching food autarky (Falasca-Zamponi 2000, 150). The campaign contributed to a significant body of propaganda as reclamation projects and the planting and gathering of wheat transformed these regions. Furthermore, the agricultural projects that contributed to the increased production of wheat on the peninsula were saturated with metaphors for military attack. The peasants taking part in the endeavor were referred to as "soldiers" or "troops" that "fought on the front lines." Unlike the coming invasion of North Africa, the enemy was not another group of people but nature itself, which was to be conquered and forced into cultivation (Binde 1999, 768).

Nature, for the Fascist, was promoted as a resource to exploit through the reutilized concepts derived from the Italian cultural tradition and symbolized the Fascist struggle for a radical transformation of Italian society. The Futurist conception of nature, on the other hand, was varied and pluralistic (Graf von Hardenberg 2006, 198). Despite the available discourse found in Futurist texts, there is little scholarly consideration of the depictions of a nationalized nature found in their imagery. Often, when discussed, nature is seen as something wholly rejected by the Futurists, but this is not entirely accurate. While many members of the Futurist movement exalted urban over rural spaces and mechanical beings over wildlife, some sub-movements embraced the natural as a means of achieving a utopic future. The *Aeropittura* generated both images of bountiful landscapes and visions of high-tech metropolises. Moreover, there are other less prominent sub-movements within the second wave of Futurism that even more directly engaged with the Fascist nature rhetoric, such as *Naturismo*, which advocated patriotism, virility, and individual heroism and valorized the qualities and resources of the land (Ialongo 2013, 410). At times, Futurist condemnations of nature and the natural were focused on a similar rejection of wilderness as that of the Fascist regime. However, Futurism's negation of nature originated from the expressed desire—if not realization—of eradicating the symbolist love for the untamed landscape, while Fascism's arose out of political calculation and was motivated by the rhetoric of conquest. When the *Aeropittori* spoke of nature, they focused on the act of going beyond the earth and its imperfect landscapes. As Fillìa (Luigi Colombo, 1904–1936), one of the founding members of the *Aeropittura*, stated in 1931: "In all Futurism there is a feeling of overcoming the terrestrial, not only with the action of the machine, but also through different interpretations of nature" (quoted in Miracco 2005, 13). With this pluralistic interpretation of nature, many group members came to embrace the Fascist discourse and focused on depicting idealistic landscapes as a product of man and the machine.

Marinetti, along with several other Futurist artists, wrote the *Manifesto dell'aeropittura* in 1929, launching the sub-movement that he referred to in the 1938 catalogue of the Venice Biennale as "the child of Fascist aviation and Italian Futurism" (quoted in Lazzaro and Crum 2005, 69). This was the first Futurist initiative to emerge alongside Fascist policy and showed the growing concerns about the role of aviation in Italy's future wars (Ialongo 2013, 402). Both Futurism and Fascism believed that aviation would bring Italy into the modern era and enable the country to compete on the world stage with regard to technological developments (Paluch-Mishur 2004, 42). Many members of the movement were actually aviators, and those who were not used whatever means they could to view the earth from an aerial perspective. While some relied on fellow members or connections to Fascist aeronautic programs to experience the joys of flight, others used the increasingly more accurate military aerial photography produced by the regime (Greene 2014, 272). The *Aeropittori* went beyond the depiction of the technological aspects of flight. Their images often portrayed idealized and cosmic visions of the Italian landscape and incorporated Fascist iconography. Additionally, they used the established Futurist techniques of well-known predecessors and contemporaries—such as Umberto Boccioni (1882–1916) and Giacomo Balla (1871–1958)—to portray the speed and power achieved through aeronautical flight.

Gerardo Dottori's (1884–1977) and Alessandro Bruschetti's (1910–1980) paintings are exemplary of the *Aeropittori*'s engagement with the concept of nature. Though the movement was composed of a large number of artists with far-ranging stylistic tendencies, as well as varied levels of engagement with the Fascist regime, the work of Dottori and Bruschetti tends to be on the figurative side of the spectrum of abstraction and therefore more clearly illustrates the treatment of nature. While *Aeropittura* primarily concentrated on representations of the experience of flight and often depicted cityscapes rather than rurality, the body of landscape paintings is extensive. Although the image of a new, productive Italy as described by *il Duce* was never truly realized in the Fascist state, despite expensive and questionable reclamation projects, it was realized pictorially in the idealized representations of the *Aeropittori*. *La Virata* of 1931 (figure 1), a work by the prolific Umbrian Futurist Dottori, aptly expresses the (mostly fabricated) Fascist story of conquest. This oil painting presents an Italian agricultural landscape devoid of modernization. It remains largely un-urbanized with the exception of one

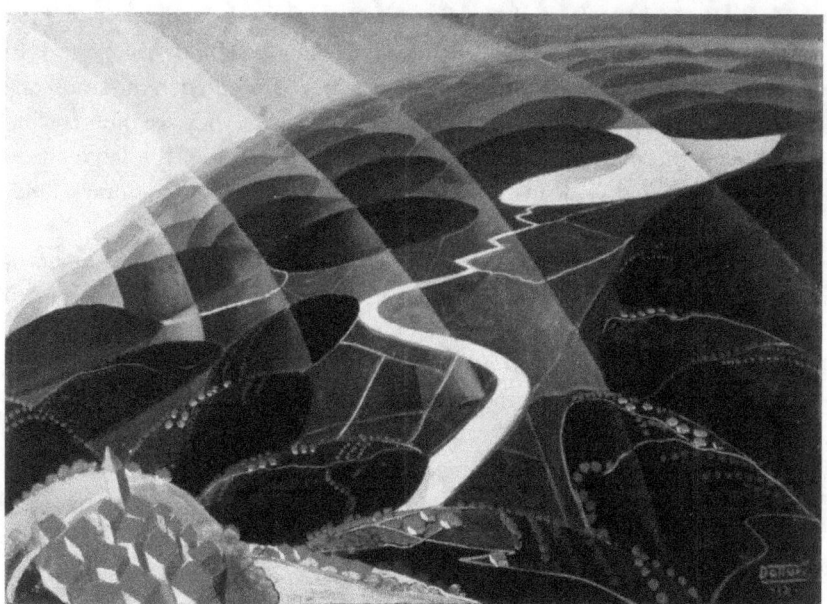

FIGURE 1. Gerardo Dottori, *La Virata* (1931), oil on panel. (Casa Museo Boschi Di Stefano, Milan. All rights reserved.)

prominent town in the foreground and a few red-roofed houses, which dot the circular hills. A river leads the eye across the landscape through bountifully green fields that indicate a fruitful harvest. Yet rather than meeting a straight horizon line, the landscape fades into the curvature of the earth with no indication of a sea or other lands. The sun edges out from the left-hand side of the work, casting the foregrounded town in light and the nearby hills with a rosy tone. Concentric lines radiate out from the light source mimicking the curvature of the earth in an opposing angle.

Unlike the early images of Futurism, *La Virata* appears calm, picturesque, and entirely removed from political discourse. However, there are aspects of this work that relate to Fascist nature and landscape rhetoric. First of all, the neat little town in the immediate foreground recounts the Fascist dialogue on urbanization. Although the notion of cities as sterile environments was prominent in Fascist rhetoric, it led to a policy of *ruralizzazione* that constituted a binary of negative and positive urbanism. Negative urbanism aimed to halt rural/urban migration and urban expansion, while positive urbanism included the state's active engagement in the creation and growth of new urban settlements, from neighborhood units to small villages and towns (Caprotti and Kaïka 2008, 618–19). These new settlements served to house agricultural populations in reclaimed areas such as the Pontine Marshes and were considered free from the corruption that affected the old cities, which were metaphorically swamped in cultural decadence (Binde 1999, 769). In Dottori's painting, although the Umbrian towns represented in the landscape are not the new towns of Fascist reclamation projects, they are uniform and perfected—therefore, free of the decadence and decay of the large cities. They are presented as idealistic and totally in service of the agricultural landscape that surrounds them.

Moreover, the presence of a perfected old town that has been modernized with clean lines and uniform roofs links the peninsula's ancient past to the future that the Fascist regime sought. Just as the aqueducts and other Roman agricultural projects shaped the face of Italy, so too did the regime seek to transform the landscape so that its reign would be evident in the land itself for years to come. In a speech to farmers and peasants in 1928 Mussolini stated: "The integral reclamation of our national territory is an enterprise the achievement of which would alone suffice to make the revolution of the Blackshirts glorious down the centuries" (quoted in Schmidt 1938, 73). Thus, the landscape presented in *La Virata* is not one that existed but one that signified the glorious, conquered, and perfected landscape the regime sought to achieve through land reclamation. Further, the landscape extends to the curved horizon line, giving Italy the appearance of encompassing a large portion of the globe. As Armiero has suggested, one of the key aspects of Fascist rhetoric was utilizing nature as a form of propaganda for future military conquests (2011, 109–54). This *Aeropittura* painting, created as early as 1931, presents an Italy that achieved an empire of cultivated lands.

Alessandro Bruschetti's 1933 painting, *Aeroveduta con laghi vulcanici* (figure 2), even more directly presents the use of agricultural metaphors for military attack. More specifically, the work displays a duality between an aerial battle above and the illustration of the success of the battle of grains below. The work displays a dogfight raging between two airplanes over a serene agricultural landscape. The planes fire at one another in the sky as a turbulent swirl of clouds surrounds them, yet below, the bushes, houses, lakes, hills, trees, and beaches are perfectly repetitious and uniform. Volcanic lakes, so perfect they seem man-made, are surrounded by the small settlements of this hilly region. Though there are trees present they are not wild, or even forest-like, but rather line the agricultural plots and towns as if planted to create perfected circumferences around their borders. The homogeneity of the land stands in direct contrast to the loud and abrasive quality of the battle above. What connects the seemingly divided picture planes of *Aeroveduta con laghi vulcanici* is threefold. First, the clouds reach beyond the sky merging with the far-off landscape, bringing the concentric force from the planes to the ground. Second, the planes are precarious as they attempt to destroy one

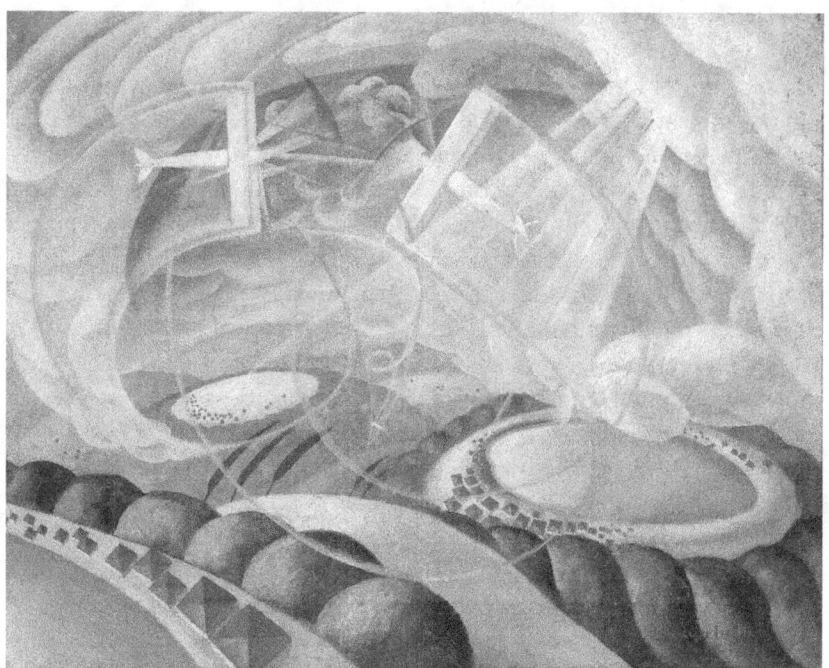

FIGURE 2. Alessandro Bruschetti, *Aeroveduta con laghi vulcanici* (1933), oil on canvas. (Private collection, Milan)

another, and a flaming part spirals toward the ground, indicating the imminent death of at least one pilot. Third—and most important—both the technology of the airplanes above and the cultivated land below are the product of man. The only part of the work that appears removed from man's touch is the few rays of light that manage to break through the clouds to illuminate the scene. Despite this element, the work gives the impression that the power of man, and more specifically the Fascist "new man," is nearly all-encompassing.

In Bruschetti's work, we see the parallel between agricultural battle and military conquest promoted by the regime. More precisely, this painting, which was created about six years after the battle of grains was announced, juxtaposes a concluded battle that has resulted in a perfected landscape with an ongoing one that, if successful, will result in similar bounty. The transformed land exemplifies the regime's victory over nature and moves beyond other propagandistic forms of representation to show an indisputable ideal that will never truly be achieved. *Aeroveduta con laghi vulcanici* corresponds to the reclamation of the Pontine Ager and the battle of grains, emphasizing the regime's ability to build life (portrayed below) from death (imminent to the pilots above) (Falasca-Zamponi 2000, 153).

Not only did Mussolini consider the Fascist regime to originate in the rural aspects of the peninsula—despite being founded, like Futurism, in the urban center of Milan—but he also promoted himself as one whose beginnings were that of agriculture and peasantry (Caprotti and Kaïka 2008, 618). Mussolini firmly linked himself and Fascism to the people of the country. He did so most importantly by promoting propaganda imagery that featured *il Duce* aiding in agricultural projects. The *Aeropittori* went further to depict the Fascist leader in direct dialogue with nature and the rural landscape. Marinetti wrote of Mussolini as a figure that was "radiant outside his body . . . a proud cosmic divinity of heroism and of invisible volcanoes" (quoted in Humphreys 1999, 76). Nowhere is this description of the Fascist leader more directly manifested than in Dottori's portrait of 1933, *Mussolini: Anno XI* (figure 3). In this oil painting, *il Duce* is not presented as a farmer or peasant but as an omnipotent being who either embodies the landscape itself or bends nature to his whims. Mussolini's superhuman bust rises out of the hilly landscape that was (and still is) characteristic of much of rural Italy. Futurist aircraft surround his famous bald head and chiseled jaw (McCloskey 2005, 91). Mussolini's shoulders merge with the hills that fade into the distance, the rest of his body appearing to exist just beneath the surface of the nation. His shirt has a dominant black tonality that is reminiscent of the Blackshirts of the *Fasci di combattimento*, which fades to green as he becomes more engrained in the landscape.[4] The fractured lines that radiate from his face merge *il Duce* with the surrounding scene, connecting him to the rural landscape below and the airplanes above and further emphasizing the duality and ambivalence of the Fascist state as it both looks back and seeks to modernize. Just as Fascist discourse dictates that nature must submit to the hand of man, so are the earth, the sky, and even the planes conquered by the masculine depiction of the Fascist leader in Dottori's painting. While he is one with the landscape, he is also central in respect to the Italy that is pictured around him. Moreover, he takes on the role of the sun, feeding the earth with his rays and lighting up the scene with his face.[5] *Mussolini: Anno XI* depicts the Fascist dictator as both the figurative and literal head of state. He is positioned centrally and is denoted, not by his whole body, but only by his head, the source of his "genius." The planes represent both the *Aeropittori*—who rotate around their leader and source of Fascist signification—and the state aeronautics programs at the forefront of the dictatorship's military strategies.

Historically, the Italian landscape has also been tied to the concept of national identity. Italy's pre-Fascist conception of nature highlighted John Ruskin's nineteenth-century idea that "the landscape is the beloved face of the fatherland" (quoted in Ercolini 2007, 315). This idiom was also relevant to the Fascist discourse on nature and the concept of beauty and is embodied in

FIGURE 3. Gerardo Dottori, *Mussolini: Anno XI (Ritratto del Duce)* (1933), oil on canvas. (Museo del Novecento, Milan. Copyright © Comune di Milano. All rights reserved.)

Mussolini: Anno XI. Mussolini is the beloved face of the new fatherland under Fascism and personifies the national Italian landscape. Moreover, this concept of national identity represented through Mussolini and the countryside can also be found in later landscaping projects of the regime. In 1938–39, about five years after Dottori's work was presented to the Italian public, the Fascist Forestry Corps planted pines to spell out a gigantic DUX on the slope of Mount Giano, Lazio (Armiero and Graf von Hardenberg 2013, 293).[6] While the regime did not have the ability to realize the ideal presented in *Aeropittura* painting, or the means to create an Italian version of Mount Rushmore, the impressive DUX is still readable today on the body of the land, just as Dottori's painting is still housed in the Museo del Novecento in Milan.

In 1926, Mussolini emphasized that "we must create a new art, an art of our time: a Fascist art" (quoted in McCloskey 2005, 90). The Futurists responded with the *Aeropittura* movement, which promoted not only the regime's interests in aeronautics but also illustrated the ideals of the Fascist discourse on nature. Although even before the founding of the Fascist party, Marinetti emphasized the need to perform a "reclamation of lands infested with malaria and drainage into newly created canals," it wasn't until the *Manifesto dell'aeropittura* that his and Mussolini's vision of a conquered landscape found a perfected visual source (Rainey, Poggi, and Wittman 2009, 250).

While the regime promoted many forms of representation from photographs and posters to films and newsreels to highlight their national program of *bonifica integrale*, these images presented a glossy and constructed version of reality that never truly matched the idyllic vision presented in Mussolini's rhetoric. *Aeropittura*, on the other hand, utilized painted media to represent this fictive and unachievable ideal in tangible form. The landscapes of the Fascist imagination were constructed through the material illustrations of perfected and bountiful country and extended this idealization of nature to the figure of man. Thus Dottori and Bruschetti's paintings not only highlighted aspects of agricultural reclamation but also reclaimed humans and culture to envision a utopic version of modern Italian society.

NOTES

1. *Nature* is a highly contested term, which encompasses a variety of meanings. For the purposes of this essay I will be using it to describe the Italian Fascist conception of nature, grounded in a dualistic vision of the negative wild and untamed environments and the positive cultivated and farmed landscape.

2. The manifesto's signatories were Filippo Tommaso Marinetti, Giacomo Balla, Benedetta Cappa Marinetti, Fortunato Depero, Gerardo Dottori, Fillìa (Luigi Colombo), Enrico Prampolini, Mino Somenzi, and Guglielmo Sansoni Tato.

3. The gendered term *man* is used in this text to denote human-made innovations, while also highlighting the misogynistic rhetoric of the Fascist regime.

4. The *Fasci di combattimento*, the "league of combatants," was an Italian organization created by Mussolini in 1914.

5. Many representations of Mussolini during this period depicted his role as aviator in a more literal manner. He posed for magazine covers, newspapers, and postcards seated in planes and standing next to them, donning the characteristic helmet and goggles of military pilots.

6. This image can be found at: http://www.bigodino.it/lifestyle/perche-sul-monte-giano-appare-la-scritta-dux.html.

WORKS CITED

Armiero, Marco. 2011. *A Rugged Nation: Mountains and the Making of Modern Italy*. Cambridge, UK: White Horse Press.

———. 2014. "Introduction: Fascism and Nature." *Modern Italy*. 19(3): 241–45.

Armiero, Marco, and Wilko Graf von Hardenberg. 2013. "Green Rhetoric in Blackshirts: Italian Fascism and the Environment." *Environment and History* 19(3): 283–311.

Binde, Per. 1999. "Nature versus City: Landscapes of Italian Fascism." *Environment and Planning D: Society and Space* 17(6): 761–75.
Caprotti, Federico. 2009. "Scipio Africanus: Film, Internal Colonization, and Empire." *Cultural Geographies* 16: 381–401.
Caprotti, Federico, and Maria Kaïka. 2008. "Producing the Ideal Fascist Landscape: Nature, Materiality and the Cinematic Representation of Land Reclamation in the Pontine Marshes." *Social and Cultural Geography* 9: 613–34.
Ercolini, Michele. 2007. "Il paesaggio (e la sua difesa) nella legislazione italiana dei primi del Novecento: origini, principi e protagonist." In *Paesaggio: Didattica, ricerche e progetti (1997–2007)*. Edited by Guido Ferrara, Giulio G. Rizzo, and Mariella Zoppi, 315–32. Florence: Firenze University Press.
Falasca-Zamponi, Simonetta. 2000. *Fascist Spectacle: The Aesthetics of Power in Mussolini's Italy*. Berkeley: University of California Press.
Graf von Hardenberg, Wilko. 2006. "Nature Rhetoric: Mediterranean Fascisms between Industrialization and First Preservation." In *Views from the South: Environmental Stories from the Mediterranean World, 19th–20th Centuries*. Edited by Marco Armiero, 187–208. Naples: CNR Istituto di studi sulle società del Mediterraneo.
Greene, Vivien. 2014. *Italian Futurism 1909–1944: Reconstructing the Universe*. New York: Guggenheim Museum Publications.
Humphreys, Richard. 1999. *Futurism*. Cambridge: Cambridge University Press.
Ialongo, Ernest. 2013. "Filippo Tommaso Marinetti: The Futurist as Fascist, 1929–37." *Journal of Modern Italian Studies* 18(4): 393–418.
Lazzaro, Claudia, and Roger J. Crum. 2005. *Donatello among the Blackshirts: History and Modernity in the Visual Culture of Fascist Italy*. Ithaca, NY: Cornell University Press.
McCloskey, Barbara. 2005. *Artists of World War II*. Westport, CT: Greenwood Press.
Miracco, Renato. 2005. *Futurist Skies: Italian Aeropainting*. Milan: Mazzotta.
Paluch-Mishur, Michelle. 2004. "'The Mutable Perspectives of Flight': Futurist Aeropittura and the 'Golden Age' of Aviation." PhD diss., University of Wisconsin, Madison.
Rainey, Lawrence, Christine Poggi, and Laura Wittman. 2009. *Futurism: An Anthology*. New Haven, CT: Yale University Press.
Schmidt, Carl Theodore. 1938. *The Plough and the Sword: Labor, Land, and Property in Fascist Italy*. New York: Columbia University Press.

FRANCO ARMINIO

On Places and Looking: Italy's Silent Epiphanies

I consider looking to be something we should do everyday, even at home. You don't need an elsewhere to trigger your thirst to see. Italy is the Mecca of the gaze. And disunity is its strength. So many different places coexist in a very small space. Take a city like Palermo: you change streets and the whole city transforms before your eyes. This is the time of places. Space matters more than time. Because whether or not history has come to an end, geography certainly hasn't. In his ancient Grand Tour, Strabo reminds us that "the usefulness of geography presupposes that the geographer be a philosopher, a man engaging in the pursuit of the art of living, or, in other words, of happiness." When we think of geography, we think of open spaces: mountains, rivers, valleys. Today, though, geography is a shelter, a site where you can protect yourself from the evanescence of the digital: geography as a substitute for psychology, and perception instead of opinion. Wander around where nobody goes, be the tourists of mercy, be the travelers who not only seek beauty, harmony, sunshine, but also the loneliest and most disconsolate places—places waiting for someone to look at them, to recognize them before they become bereft of their history as well as their geography.

With Leopardi's and Pasolini's Eyes

You might think that the impoverishment of nature reflects on the impoverishment of language. Today images, words, and rhythms are no longer suggested by Nature, but by the Web. And so we have a language and a politics that taste stale. Still, it's good to resist the temptation of looking apocalyptically at today's Italy. It's beautiful to look for the places that have never been filled, the places that didn't interest anybody, the poor, impervious, remote ones. In these places Italy still offers itself. And so you can be startled, watching the cows' snout in the Accettura forest, watching an old man in a vegetable garden in Salento, or a peasant plowing the fields on a Sardinian afternoon. The Italian journey has to be made without anxieties of complaisance or denigration. Going about, observing how cities and villages change. Turin today is very different from how it was in the seventies. L'Aquila is a double town: the town of monuments and that of ruins. And Taranto, too, is double—a sea town surrounded by the city of steel. When one looks at Italy one ought to hold together the gazes of Leopardi and of Pasolini—the Pasolini who held together Casarsa and Caravaggio and in 1959 wrote *La lunga strada di sabbia* [The long road of sand], a story of a coastline journey from Ventimiglia to Trieste, an act of love for the provincial Italy still untouched by the cultural genocide which produced the Italian landscape we now cross.

In Praise of the Countryside

Have a holiday
around a blade of grass,
give yourselves to silence and light,
to the mute lust of a rose

Despite the aberrant past decades, when Italy seemed to have turned its back on the train of the past, on the god of the migration paths and the gooseberry, the countryside still exists. Our grasses, honey, the air, silence, pottery, crochet: we must care for all the things belonging to these lands. The shape of a roof tile, the refrain of a song, a nickname, drinking in the fields, the inflection of a voice, a smile, wrinkles and tears, the harvested wheat, grapes on the vines: these are all things fast to decay. Especially when the great misunderstanding of progress rapidly dissolves the cement of intimacies and mutual assurances of looking and feeling which used to make the Italian countryside inhabitable.

All-out Masterpieces

Italy's beauty is the beauty of its historic piazzas. There are thousands of them, all different from one another, small and large, shaped like an arm, a cloud, a funnel, a ring of bread. Middle Ages and Renaissance, and then Baroque and the eighteenth century: Siena and Volterra, Milan and Fabriano, Rome, Naples, Pienza, and many others, all the way to the masterpiece of Padua's piazzas—one after another, an unbelievable sequence of proximal beauty in a city close to the miracle of Venice, close to Treviso, Vicenza, Mantua. In other parts of the world there are extraordinary cities, but they are one-act events. In Italy masterpieces are endless, and they condense themselves in small galaxies: consider the triangle Perugia-Arezzo-Urbino or the sequence of magnificent cities from Bologna to Parma. And there are places with the strength of things that have hardly spoken, of things neglected or disliked. Matera and almost all of Lucania are the emblem of this Italy where Italy has another face: think of the castles of Melfi and Lagopesole, of Venosa and Lucania's Dolomites—of the Pollino, of the ruins of Craco and Aliano's ravines.

The Country of Disenchantment

Rome is a big body on dialysis. Its blood has become dull. The city is no longer able to welcome, to blend. Tourists wander around, and so do the indigenous: to each and every one a pre-established path between monuments, restaurants, and offices. All this has no soul. Maybe the ruins of the great empire no longer emanate the allure they used to radiate at Goethe's time. It's decadence without lyricism, without the smallest streak of the sacred. Rome should be helped. It must reclaim its capacity to filter the spiritual misery that surrounds it today, like nature used to surround it in earlier times. Every big Western capital has its glories and miseries, and these immediately catch the eye. Maybe today Goethe would see Rome as corroded by the acid of people bereft of a heartbeat. Maybe all of Italy would appear to him as the country of discontent and disenchantment. Italians are more prone to look at the problems of the places where they live than at the solemn beauty still present almost everywhere. We must pass from a discouraged gaze to an enchanted one. It is for this reason that reading Goethe's *Italian Journey*—his serene disposition to marvel—might be tremendously helpful today.

The Pharmacy of Landscape

Today the beauty of place has become a drug to alleviate the discomfort that comes from the ambiguous and painful relationships between people. We must move around to get relief from the inflammation of residency, the mildew and the cold sweat of habits—one must move around because places still have an innocence that people no longer have. Maybe few today can afford the luxury of a Grand Tour; still, every day we can allow ourselves a Petit Tour, even in our neighborhood. Instead of going to the drugstore or seeing a therapist, we should just go out and look. There is a respectable voyeurism, the voyeurism of landscape. To spy on how, and where, things are: that gate, that geranium pot, the old man sitting on a bench, the parked car, the girl with her cell phone, the cathedral, the lonely tree. It's the wonder of the outside world, and we're animals that need air to live. There are just two things we should do whenever we can: walk and look.

There is a curious disease we all have: being slaves to ourselves. We have become slaves to business, and it doesn't matter if that business is improper or noble. We are subjugated by the idea of profit and make ourselves comply with a series of obligations that are part of our active life, obligations from which we expect compensation, rewards, a monetary or moral income. The way out of this slavery—slavery that forces us to continuously obtain something from ourselves—is to observe the things beneath the sky. To bring the outer world inside us was the move through which language was born. From body to metaphor. Here Giambattista Vico's formulation comes to mind: sensible living that transforms itself into linguistic living. Goethe wrote about this great Neapolitan historian: "It is wonderful for a people to have such a patriarch."

The Party of the Gaze

Among those—ever fewer, to be honest—who try to change Italy, and those who do everything to preserve it, there is a third way: the party of the gaze. This is an omnivorous gaze, collecting everything that was once beautiful and that looks beautiful now. Because, although the Italy of the Grand Tour is still here and worth visiting, yet another Italy has emerged. In Goethe's time nobody knew anything about Matera, Lecce, Cosenza. Today a landscape without warehouses and factories and gas pumps looks solemn and lyrical to our eyes. In Goethe's time all of Italy was so. The Po Valley was not what it is now, a big manufacturing site that encompasses towns and cities. Certainly Goethe would still like to visit Veneto, but he would be surprised to see houses and warehouses everywhere. And in Florence, he might spend even less time than the three hours he dedicated to the city. He might be fascinated by L'Aquila and Taranto, by the beauty combined with the destruction wrought by the earthquake and the factory. And it is difficult to guess what effect Naples would have on him today. Apart from the incredible concrete siege taking place on the foothills of Mt. Vesuvius, Naples is one of the few Western cities still immune to globalization. If today's Italy is characterized by the contiguity of décor and slander, if antiquity's glory and uncivilized modernity struggle to conquer every space, Naples is the apotheosis of all this. If Italy's urban development plan included silence, we would surely have more foreign visitors. And if Goethe wished to escape the noise of Italian cities, he should find refuge on the mountains, in the Alps and Apennines. We could then recommend to him a place like Trevico, where the density of silence is supreme—though it is a silence that only benefits those who experience it from time to time. But if you don't feel like queuing to see the Sistine Chapel, if your countryside bar is more central than the Spanish steps, then find a step for yourself, and rest with your face in the sun. Look with gentleness at those who stay, at those who walk. If there is one who speaks, listen to him, wait until it gets dark before you go back home, use the dusk as a ribbon to close your day; and let this be your gift to the ones who care for you.

(Translated by Serenella Iovino)

3

ECOLOGIES AND ENVIRONMENTS

MARCUS HALL

Thinking Like a Parasite: Malaria, Plasmodium, and Sardinia's Extraordinary Longevity

A journey across Sardinia makes one appreciate why this is a wild land brimming with extremes, being the Mediterranean's most inaccessible island, and its oldest geologically. High numbers of rare or unusual plants and animals thrive here, making it a biodiversity hotspot. Its people are one of Europe's most genetically distinct ethnic groups—harboring rarer sequences of DNA than almost any other group, for there has been little out-migration since early seafarers arrived on its shores some eight thousand years ago. Although many of these islanders enjoy such hardy advantages as dark, sun-resistant skin and remarkable endurance, they also suffer inordinately from rare genetic illnesses such as Celiac sprue, Wilson's disease, and favism, all of which demand special diets. As D. H. Lawrence described his own trip across Sardinia in 1920, "it is a strange, strange landscape, as if here the world left off" (1921, 102). No wonder anthropologists flock to the island. Human geneticists have made it a favorite study site. Demographers increasingly descend on its shores. Much more than other peoples, Sardinians and their habits are *indigenes*: of the place, born here, even evolved here.

Demographers come to study population trends, for another Sardinian superlative is human longevity. Sardinians are some of the longest-lived people on the planet. Due to genes or lifestyle—or despite genes and lifestyle—these islanders have apparently discovered the secret to longer living. A recent study concludes that in Sardinia, some 208 people out of 100,000 live past the age of one hundred, more than twice the rate of most Western countries. The mountainous interior of Sardinia is even more spectacular in promoting long life, nurturing twice the number of centenarians than the island as a whole. Only scattered villages in faraway Costa Rica or Japan's Okinawa archipelago vie with the interior of Sardinia for stacking up human years. In fact Sardinia is also a Guinness World Record holder for the world's oldest siblings, where at last count the combined age of nine brothers and sisters added up to 828 years. Such impressive demographics are highlighted in official reports and tourist brochures which note that certain of the island's Methuselah hotspots can count one centenarian for every two hundred people, which is twenty to thirty times the rate found elsewhere (Mattalia 2014; Merlini 2006). Perhaps Sardinia's secret has been the red wine or maybe *calcagno* and *gnemmerrìdde*— sheep cheese and sausage. Or maybe the secret has been malaria.

By the logic of chronology, many of the most elderly Sardinians are precisely those who as children confronted widespread infectious disease—with malaria topping the list. There is in fact another Sardinian superlative: disease experts have long considered the island to be Europe's most malarial place as tabulated by mortality and morbidity, as well as one of Europe's last malaria strongholds until the disease disappeared following massive DDT spraying. Surveys in the 1930s showed upward of 60 percent of Sardinians to be suffering from malaria. Another early traveler to Sardinia, William Henry Smyth, mused in 1828 that "it is surprising that with such inconvenient residences, and uncleanly habits, the natives should remain so generally healthy as they do" (168). These and other descriptions suggest that Sardinia's most stunning anomaly may not be its remarkable longevity or its horrific experience with malaria but rather the combination of both. In some fashion, Sardinians plagued by the age-old killer malaria have gone on to live spectacularly long lives. Is there something special about infectious disease, and malaria in particular, that confers robust health and long life on those who survive it? Can the micron-long malaria parasite transmitted by mosquitoes confer health as well as illness? In the following pages, we keep these questions in view as we shrink ourselves down, entering the matter and mind of the creatures who make us sick (Brown 1987, 162; Tognotti 1998; Packard 2007, 38; Hall 2011).

Thinking Hard about Our Bodily Creatures

In 1684, Tuscan naturalist Francesco Redi issued his *Osservazione intorno agli animali viventi che si trovano negli animali viventi* (Observations of living animals found within living animals) at a time when parasites were simply, as the title suggested, living creatures found living within other living creatures. Until then, parasites per se were not repulsive and slimy. Indeed they were not necessarily small or even inside of us or even biological. Anders Gullestad has traced the meanings of *parasite* to show that its connotations were initially anthropic, becoming organismal only in the eighteenth century, and that it was later still that a sponging human would take on the characteristics of an animal counterpart. Affluent Greeks two thousand years earlier hosted human parasites (*parà-sítos*, "eating beside") who enjoyed free meals and sometimes shelter in exchange for good conversation or entertainment.

As the *Dizionario Universale Storico e Critico dei Costumi, Leggi, Usi, Riti, e Costumanze* (1784) explained it, a parasite, "now considered mostly negative, was once an honorable title" (III, 313). In short, only in the last two centuries did our view of parasites begin morphing from the human to nonhuman, and only in recent times did we deem certain humans to be metaphorical parasites (Gullestad 2012).

Despite the growing tendency to see our internal creatures as freeloaders and, following Victorian naturalists such as Ray Lankester, as evolutionary degenerates—creatures that had "devolved" from higher forms—some scientists still sought to view parasites on their own terms. By 1875, when Belgian naturalist Pierre Joseph van Beneden published his classic *Les Commensaux et les parasites dans le règne animal* (*Animal Parasites and Messmates*), nonhuman parasites were becoming bona fide subjects of zoological study. Yet even Van Beneden could not resist anthropomorphizing this class of creatures when he taught that "the parasite installs himself either temporarily or definitively in the house of his neighbor; either with his consent or by force, he demands from him his living, and very often his lodging" (1876, 1). Here a parasite was characterized by its propensity to freeload, rather than by its preferred habitat, say, or its means of transmission or effects on hosts. Man had made parasites in his own image and then set out to study this creature for what it could tell him about the natural world. No wonder there was a difference of opinions about which characteristics of parasites made them parasitic.

Painstaking studies of these micro-creatures in the laboratory and in the field convinced Van Beneden to propose three categories of organisms living on hosts, categories that persist in biology textbooks to this day. It was Van Beneden who suggested that *mutualists* benefit themselves and their host, that *commensalists* benefit themselves while inflicting no harm on their host, and that *parasites* benefit themselves while harming their host. Yet he qualified that "the greater part of those animals which have established themselves on each other, and live together on a good understanding and without injury, are wrongly classed as parasites by the generality of naturalists" (1876, 2). Meticulous observations of parasites doing what they do led him to believe that not all parasites harmed their hosts, at least not all of the time. In fact a close reading of Van Beneden's text shows that he was distinctly sensitive to the benevolent side of creatures living in or on other creatures—even those he considered to be true parasites as defined by his third category: "The parasite is he whose profession it is to live at the expense of his neighbor, and whose only employment consists in taking advantage of him, but prudently, so as not to endanger his life" (1876, 85). Although prudence is not a trait one generally associates with parasites, Van Beneden was signaling with this word that a parasite aims to avoid harming a host else it may ultimately harm itself.

Regarding malaria, this illness captured the attention of Italy's medical providers and healers long before its naturalists turned their focus on our bodily co-travelers. In those early days, malaria was thought to stem mostly from evil convections and diseased currents. The etiologic agent of *mal'aria*—bad air—was ethereal, invisible, and supernatural but hardly organismal. Investigators also wondered what made Sardinians so susceptible to this disease, leading them to suspect such causative factors as poverty, pastoral life, diet, education, altitude, and even alcohol consumption. As one study conjectured, a village's per capita consumption of red wine correlated so closely with its rate of malaria that heavy wine drinking seemed to be the obvious cause of the disease. Such spurious correlations were not always easy to discount. The mystery of malaria fever, *la febbre*, was that it was so hard to link with mosquitoes since it might arise in winter far from mosquito-saturated swamps and conversely it might not arise even when and where the insects buzzed fiercely. In 1899, Lombardian malariologist Giovanni Battista Grassi boldly concluded that malaria only resulted when infected people and anopheles mosquitoes were simultaneously present, in a law christened with his name: infected people + Anopheles mosquitoes = malaria.

Remove either of the first two components, Grassi discovered, and malaria disappears. The precise nature of the infection was being elucidated in the same years, with British and Italian malariologists racing one another to identify the infectious agent. Sir Ronald Ross finally captured the Nobel Prize in 1902, but not without bitter mud-slinging between him and Grassi. While Ross had demonstrated the mosquito transmission of a malaria parasite to birds, Grassi had described life stages of several malaria parasite strains found in humans. The ensuing scientific rivalry ended by Ross calling Grassi "a cheap crook, a parasite who survived on the ideas of others" (Srinivas 2015, 1). The reputation of parasites was apparently sinking so low that they not only caused disease but could also steal academic prizes. The parasite's character of ill repute has never recovered to our day (Capanna 2006).

Sardinia for its part became a proving ground for parasite killing. With its high malarial rates, investigators from Italy and abroad came to test better ways to exterminate malaria parasites—the plasmodium—as well as the mosquitoes that transmitted these parasites, noting their successes for eventual application across the country and world. With their enemy definitively identified, malariologists distributed quinine, atabrine, and then chloroquine pills to stun the plasmodium in the bloodstream; they directed spray campaigns of crude oil, Paris Green, and then DDT to stun the mosquito in its habitat. They also drained wetlands, planted eucalyptus, and imported gambusia fish to cripple or kill still more mosquitoes during their various life stages. By 1950, the war on plasmodium was finally won, with the result that the face of Sardinia would never be the same (Hall 2004).

Plasmodium Landscapes

Indeed, in the quest to eradicate malaria, government-sponsored water reclamation projects drained or filled in Sardinia's mosquito-breeding marshes and planted eucalyptus while straightening its stream courses where physically possible: low-lying river valleys today are hardly recognizable from their counterparts of seventy-five years ago. The island's intensive mosquito-killing campaign also altered its economic landscape. When 32,000 DDT-sprayers and applied entomologists found precious seasonal employment in seeking to exterminate mosquitoes in those years, they injected wages into a cash-poor world. It seems that this expensive pesticide campaign served to jump-start a lethargic Sardinian economy, not only by ridding the island of its malaria scourge but also by distributing much-needed lire among those leading a subsistence way of life. Or as one elderly Sardinian later reflected in an interview about the DDT era, villagers in those days finally carried "coins in their pockets" (Hall 2009, 124). Even if this pocket change derived from United Nations relief funds that were directed by the Rockefeller Foundation, the primary mover was really the plasmodium. Like Michael Pollan's manipulative plants, such as tulips or marijuana, which by offering petal hues or intoxicants convince us to plant more of them, plasmodium transformed Sardinia's landscape by steering human efforts to accommodate this demanding parasite (Pollan 2001).

Certainly the malaria parasite had already sculpted Sardinia even before the final all-out insecticide campaign. The attentive traveler to the island detects plasmodium's imprint at nearly every turn. Town planning, building styles, social habits and rituals, even clothing fashions have been modified by this parasite as people struggled to avoid its periodic fevers and to deal with its cruel deaths. A century ago, so ubiquitous and recurrent was malaria that most Sardinians considered its symptoms to be inevitable sufferings: like sleeping with buzzing flies or eating moldy bread, malaria was a nuisance that came and went but was mostly unavoidable. These islanders could not so much prevent the disease as learn to live with it. In their effort to stay clear of *mal'aria*, they built their dwellings far from pestilential marshes, up on hillsides, often clustering them near other buildings in hill towns. Shepherds practiced reverse transhumance, which found them making permanent habitations in the highlands and leading their flocks to lowland pastures in winter when the malarious drafts abated (Hall 2010). Dress style was also influenced by the parasite, as when islanders fended off insalubrious airs by wearing thick garments even on hot summer days to minimize exposure of bare skin. In describing the heavy robes draped over Sardinian peasants, D. H. Lawrence remarked that "they say it keeps off the malaria. The men swathe shawls round their heads in the same way" (1921, 99).

The plasmodium also made its presence known when Sardinians were naming their most sacred shrines, such as Cagliari's Santuario di Nostra Signora Bonaria—the Sanctuary of Our Lady Good Air. Legend has it that in the fourteenth century, a Spanish ship was caught in a tempest offshore, whereupon the sailors began jettisoning cargo to save their lives. After one particularly heavy trunk was thrown overboard, the storm suddenly abated, averting catastrophe and allowing the sailors to keep their ship afloat. When local friars later found the heavy trunk washed upon the beach, they opened it to find a small statue of the Madonna, which they named after the adjacent Colle di Buenaire, or Hill of Good Air. Not only did the Aragon king later order a castle and basilica constructed there to commemorate the event, but Spanish conquistadores voyaging to South America named Argentina's capital city, Buenos Aires, after this Sardinian site. In these days before the germ theory of disease, it was the *buon'aria* that Sardinians sought and cherished, hoping that it would waft away the enervating wafts of *mal'aria*. Pope Pius X in 1907 proclaimed Madonna Bonaria the patron saint of Sardinia for her role in bringing good luck—and good air—to the island. In subsequent decades, Paul VI and John Paul II also made pilgrimages to Bonaria. From the architectural to the economic, from the physical to the spiritual, Sardinia's plasmodium has commanded even popes to come to the island.

The Parasite's Dilemma

One begins to realize that all parasitic creatures maintain an interest in keeping their hosts alive so that they can keep themselves alive. The parasite's dilemma is what Van Beneden felt was a parasite's propensity to act prudently: to take from the host but not to take so much that the host suffers. Researchers have found that through complex and sometimes convoluted ways, successful parasites often work hard to ensure that their hosts will also be successful. Even true parasites, which are defined as taking more than receiving, have been found to promote activities that benefit themselves through benefits they bring their hosts. The parasite's dilemma seems to be playing itself out in humans who host various species of intestinal worms that have been found to offer collateral benefits (Lederberg 1999). Such maladies as Crohn's disease or ulcerative colitis, and perhaps even asthma and multiple sclerosis, are found to be alleviated with helminthic therapy, or the ingestion of roundworms that were once common in our gut before today's hygienic lifestyle scoured us of these organisms. Physicians now perform fecal transplants for replenishing some of the intestinal diversity that was lost during childhood antibiotic treatments. Indeed from a parasite's perspective, it may seem that it is the host who is the primary beneficiary of the relationship. Or as Michel Serres points out, "it might be dangerous not to decide who is the host and who is the guest, who gives and who receives, who is the parasite and who is the *table d'hôte*, who has the gift and who has the loss, and where hostility begins within hospitality" (2007, 15).

A successful parasite therefore gives and takes, just as its host gives and takes, to such an extent that "symbiosis" seems the best descriptor of most host-parasite relationships. Consider the classic case of intestinal shark worms that live in and feed upon their host shark's nutriments: at first glance the worms (*Anthobothrium sp., Paraorigmatobothrium sp.*) appear to be freeloading off the shark (*Carcharhinus dussumieri*), while offering nothing in return. Yet recent evidence shows that such worms also absorb poisonous heavy metals from their host, thereby serving to detoxify the sharks (Kaplan 2007). A relationship that was once considered parasitic is now viewed as symbiotic—mutually useful to each. In fact, many host-parasite unions are increasingly being relabeled by ecologists as symbioses, with the precise advantages for each member still being worked out. As another example, the mistletoe that grows on juniper trees and consumes some of their nutrients may in a new light be providing services to the trees by attracting nesting birds that help disperse the tree's seeds (Van Ommeren and Whitham 2002). The mistletoe is offering its host something in return for the benefits it reaps.

In the case of malaria's parasites, one suspects that plasmodium is also doing more than simply inflicting illness and death. Fortunately for Sardinia, as for the world, most malaria victims eventually recover, now and in the past: rates of malaria's morbidity have always outpaced malaria's mortality. There are, moreover, even higher numbers of individuals who carry the plasmodium and show no ill effects. For reasons not entirely understood, some individuals are not susceptible to plasmodium, while others have developed or else inherited immunities against its ill effects. To offer numbers, it is estimated that each year about one out of 16,000 people currently succumb from malaria worldwide, while 470 others contract but survive this disease (World Health Organization 2015). Exact numbers of asymptomatic, parasitaemic malarial individuals are harder to come by, but the best estimates suggest that there are at least as many people who get sick from malaria as those who carry the plasmodium without experiencing any malarial symptoms. All told, such statistics mean that (1 + 470 + 470) or some 900 to 1,000 people out of 16,000 carry plasmodium in their blood, or one-sixteenth of humanity. If we consider Sardinia of a century ago when today's centenarians were being born, more than half of the people suffered from malaria, suggesting that nearly everyone on the island was carrying the parasite in their veins. One wonders what all those parasites were up to (Doolan, Dobaña, and Baird 2009).

The Benefits of Being Parasitized

Of course it is almost unspeakable to suggest that malaria can bring anything but suffering to the human species. This disease is consistently ranked as a leading killer that, along with AIDS and tuberculosis, is among humanity's most deadly infectious diseases, slaughtering at least 438,000 people last year, many of them children, many of those in Africa. Only a decade ago, malaria's yearly death toll reached one million or more. If one considers the long sweep of human history, some researchers suggest that malaria has killed more individual human beings than any other infectious disease. Multiplying malaria's annual proportion of victims by the number of years people have walked the earth will produce estimates of total malaria victims in the billions (Livingstone 1971).

Yet against this specter of death, there is the undeniable possibility that malaria parasites may also be providing direct or indirect benefits to the human species. Such benefits will be colored by whether we look through lenses that are medical, ecological, or cultural. A case in point is the medical benefit of contracting malaria stemming from its tendency to induce high fevers, thereby making life difficult for other, more pathogenic microbes. So-called malariatherapy, a widely practiced procedure during the World Wars for alleviating the effects of syphilis, depended on transmitting plasmodium and inducing malaria in a patient for the purpose of raising the body temperature in order to debilitate the syphilitic pathogen. Malariatherapy's discoverer, Julius Wagner-Juaregg, won a Nobel Prize for recognizing the beneficial effects of a parasite. One realizes it is often better to host combinations of microinhabitants than just the most pathogenic ones. Stated differently, plasmodium can both exacerbate and ameliorate disease.

An ecologist eyeing a parasite might consider disease to be a necessary condition of life. Sickness and death by parasitism are forces that allow life to evolve and develop new adaptations, including the production of new parasites. Amazingly, biodiversity enthusiasts estimate that upward of 70 to 80 percent of all creatures on earth are parasites. Just as astonishing is to find out that most healthy human bodies host between forty and four hundred different kinds of macroscopic parasites. We are in effect superorganisms—walking bundles of parasites and symbionts—which taken together shape what it means to be human (Dobson et al. 2008).

Beyond medical and ecological considerations, our cultural achievements, our lifestyles, indeed our very beliefs and aspirations would themselves be impoverished if not for our bodily co-travelers. Plasmodium brought misery and death to Sardinia, but it also modified sheep herding practices, clothing fashion, architectural styles, and spiritual traditions. This influential parasite brought more than just bad; it produced emotions high and low, new ideas, timeless literature, and high art. Grazia Deledda, Sardinia's Nobel laureate of literature, often made malaria the backdrop of her novels. As one critic described her best-known *Canne al Vento* (1913; *Reeds in the Wind*, 1999), "Deledda beautifully captures the rough, malaria-ridden Sardinian setting, where superstition vies with theology, folklore has a strong hold on the imagination and 'the sound of the accordion fills the courtyard with moans and shouts'" (*Publisher's Weekly* 2009). Constantly present in old and young alike, the parasite of malaria goes to the core of what it means to be Sardinian.

Living with Our Co-travelers

As today's ambitious Human Microbiome Project is demonstrating, each of us carries millions upon millions of distinct organisms, from simple bacterial cells (and viral DNA packets) to multicellular protozoa, flatworms, and even arthropods. When painting mascara across our eyelashes in the morning, we should realize that just one in fifty of us do *not* host eyelash mites (*Demodex sp.*) in those hair follicles. Such bodily fauna varies according to diet, age, ethnic group, place, century, and many other factors. Each person is a veritable fingerprint of microbial composition. Microbiologists also point out that there are ten times more nonhuman than human cells in each of our bodies, so that a human being can also be viewed primarily as a repository of reproducing, interacting, symbiotic creatures. Our digestive rhythms, our muscular movements, our very moods and emotions and ideas, are intimately connected to the microbial diversity that composes us. Laboratory mice sterilized of their intestinal microfauna are found to live shorter lives than those that maintain a rich parasitic diversity (Human Microbiome Project Consortium 2012).

All of this brings us to wonder, finally, what Sardinians may expect now that plasmodium is no longer circulating in their blood? How will their island change now that malaria has been erased from this land? And will Sardinia's stunning rates of human longevity become a thing of the past? One can only be sure that a large vacuum has been opened in Sardinia's landscape and lifestyle now that this key parasite is gone. Sickle-cell anemia, thalassemia, and favism have all become more problematic across the island since those who harbor these genetic anomalies no longer reap advantages in carrying them. More serious may be the fact that Sardinians, and Mediterranean people generally, now suffer from higher blood pressure than ever. It turns out that malaria's most deadly "pernicious" (or cerebral) form results from complexes of plasmodium-red cells being pushed through the host's brain capillaries to cause lesions and even death. Under such conditions, it seems that long-term fitness would be awarded to those plasmodium that protect their hosts—and so protect themselves—by lowering blood pressure in the host. A recent study highlights biochemical mechanisms by which plasmodium can lower blood pressure. In fact there is a chillingly close overlap between former malarial areas and current zones of hypertension. It seems that with plasmodium now gone, dangerous hypertension runs free across Sardinia, and indeed across many other formerly malarial areas (Gallego-Delgado and Rodriguez 2014, 121).

Long an agricultural people who avoided the coasts, Sardinians in recent decades are witnessing modernity arrive rudely and abruptly to their azure beaches, with summer tourists from the continent seeking pristine sunshine and luxury hotels. But modernity has also reached into the hearts and veins of the islanders, picking out the little protozoa that for millennia brought fevers, nausea, headaches, anemia—and also helped lower blood pressure. While there is much to celebrate in bidding adieu to malaria's terrible debilitations, one must also wonder what disease does to life, or what is lost when an ancient disease disappears.

Humanity's intimate relationship with plasmodium reveals why we need to recount not just histories, but co-histories: human stories entwined with those of our co-travelers. Alongside domesticated animals and cultivated plants that foster human civilizations are the creatures that live in and on us, some of them lethal but others innocuous or even beneficial. Far from being a simple disease agent, a malaria parasite does not merely infect the human body, to grow, multiply, and debilitate its host before traveling to the next unsuspecting host. Instead, our plasmodium seeks to live with us and adapt supremely to our habits and lifestyles so that it can go on living. Plasmodium takes from us, but it does not take everything. Plasmodium may have little concern for an individual human life, but it is deeply concerned about the fate of the human species.

WORKS CITED

Brown, Peter J. 1987. "Microparasites and Macroparasites." *Cultural Anthropology* 2(1): 155–71.

Capanna, Ernesto. 2006. "Grassi versus Ross: Who Solved the Riddle of Malaria?" *International Microbiology* 9(1): 69–74.

Dizionario Universale Storico e Critico dei Costumi, Leggi, Usi, Riti, e Costumanze Civili, Militari: e Politiche, e delle Cerimonie, e Pratiche Religiose, e Superstiziose, sì Antiche che

Moderne, di Tutti i Popoli delle Quattro Parti del Mondo, Contenente Ciò Che V'è d'importante . . . in Bassano. 1784. 5 vols. Venice: Remondini.

Dobson, Andy, Kevin D. Lafferty, Armand M. Kuris, Ryan F. Hechinger, and Walter Jetz. 2008. "Homage to Linnaeus: How Many Parasites? How Many Hosts?" *Proceedings of the National Academy of Sciences of the United States of America* 105: 11482–89.

Doolan, Denise, Carlota Dobaña, and Kevin Baird. 2009. "Acquired Immunity to Malaria." *Clinical Microbiology Reviews* 22(1): 13–36.

Gallego-Delgado, Julio, and Ana Rodriguez. 2014. "Malaria and Hypertension: Another Co-Evolutionary Adaptation?" *Frontiers in Cellular and Infection Microbiology* 4: 121.

Gullestad, Anders. 2012. "Parasite." *Political Concepts: A Critical Lexicon.* http://www.politicalconcepts.org/issue1/2012-parasite/.

Hall, Marcus. 2004. "Today Sardinia, Tomorrow the World: Killing Mosquitoes." *Bard-Politik: The Bard Journal of Global Affairs* 5: 21–28.

Hall, Marcus. 2009. "World War II and the Axis of Disease." In *War and the Environment: Military Destruction in the Modern Age.* Edited by Charles Closmann, 112–31. College Station: Texas A&M University Press.

Hall, Marcus. 2010. "Environmental Imperialism in Sardinia: Pesticides and Politics in the Struggle against Malaria." In *Nature and History in Modern Italy.* Edited by Marco Armiero and Marcus Hall, 70–86. Athens: Ohio University Press.

Hall, Marcus. 2011. "Le ultime battaglie contro la malaria in Italia: Una guerra in sangue e metafore." *Ricerche Storiche* 41(3): 50–70.

Human Microbiome Project Consortium. 2012. "Structure, Function, and Diversity of the Human Microbiome." *Nature* 486: 207–14.

Kaplan, Matt. 2007. "Parasites Suck Toxins from Sharks." *Nature,* June 25. http://www.nature.com/news/2007/070625/full/news070625-1.html.

Lawrence, David Herbert. 1921. *Sea and Sardinia.* New York: Thomas Seltzer.

Lederberg, Joshua. 1999. "Parasites Face a Perpetual Dilemma." *ASM News* 65(2): 77–80.

Livingstone, Frank. 1971. "Malaria and Human Polymorphisms." *Annual Review of Genetics* 5: 33–64.

Mattalia, Daniela. 2014. "La vita oltre i cento anni." *Panorama,* April 17.

Merlini, Paolo. 2006. "Comuni Blue zone, 6 paesi sardi conquistano il marchio doc della lunga vita." *La Nuova Sardegna,* March 6.

Packard, Randall. 2007. *The Making of a Tropical Disease: A Short History of Malaria.* Baltimore: Johns Hopkins University Press.

Pollan, Michael. 2001. *The Botany of Desire: A Plant's-Eye View of the World.* New York: Random House.

Publisher's Weekly. 2009. Review of Grazia Deledda, *Reeds in the Wind* (1999). http://www.publishersweekly.com/978-0-934977-63-0.

Serres, Michel. 2007. *The Parasite.* Minneapolis: University of Minnesota Press.

Smyth, William Henry. 1828. *Sketch of the Present State of the Island of Sardinia.* London: John Murray.

Srinivas, Bevinje. 2015. "Ronald Ross." *Malaria Site,* February 25. http://www.malariasite.com/ronald-ross/.

Tognotti, Eugenia. 1998. "Malaria in Sardinia." *International Journal of Anthropology* 13(3–4): 237–42.

van Beneden, Pierre Joseph. 1876. *Animal Parasites and Messmates*. New York: D. Appleton. Originally published as *Les Commensaux et les parasites dans le règne animal* (Paris: Librairie Germer Baillière, 1875).

van Ommeren, Ron J., and Thomas G. Whitham. 2002. "Changes in Interactions between Juniper and Mistletoe Mediated by Shared Avian Frugivores: Parasitism to Potential Mutualism." *Oecologia* 130: 281–88.

World Health Organization. 2015. "10 Facts on Malaria." http://www.who.int/features/factfiles/malaria/en/.

LUCA BUGNONE

Ascending Underground: An Ecocritical Way through the Susa Valley

Lithophilia/Bodies of Rock

Consider wax, land, and stone as a flux of unshaped matter, energy flourishing, flowing and fading. Consider bees, trees, and us. "Each living thing remakes the world through seasonal pulses of growth, lifetime reproductive patterns, and geographies of expansion," Anna Tsing states. "We are surrounded by many world-making projects, human and not human" (2015, 21). Hands, roots, and jaws produce forms and ideas. Air, water, and soil are altered so that workable living arrangements may come to matter. By establishing its ecological niche, "each organism changes everyone's world" (Tsing 2015, 22). Regarding human activities, the Italian humanist Leon Battista Alberti depicted the ability to mold matter—let's call it sculpture—in *De Statua,* a brief treatise written in 1445. "In the pursuit of perfection," Alberti maintained: "some added and took away, as do those who work in wax, plaster or clay. . . . Some others began by only taking away and, by removing that material which is deemed superfluous, they sculpt, revealing in the marble a form" (2013, 10).

Michelangelo fancied the block of stone as allegory for the human body, a vehicle or container for the soul. He attacked the stone and released what was imprisoned within. For him, the form was the captive's ideal yearning for release, as defined by Renaissance thought. The world of matter had to be modeled, liberated, or portrayed. In Japanese culture, the *karesansui* or "dry landscape" garden also perfectly sums up such dynamics. The main elements of Japanese rock gardens are rocks and sand, with the sea symbolized not by water but by sand raked in patterns that suggest rippling water. They are intended to imitate nature and to serve as an aid to meditate about the meaning of life. Artists see landscape painting as a genre depicting vistas of natural surroundings, as mediated land arranged by their vision, whereas modern ecologists see landscape as analogous to a text with a language of its own (Lindström, Kull, and Palang 2014, 110). Jeffrey Jerome Cohen claims that "we create art with stone because we recognize the art that stone discloses: fossils, a museum of strata, lustrous veins, faceted radiance" (2015, 21). Stone discloses queer vivacity; stone aggregates, attracting disparate matter, varied rhetorical devices and narratives (2015, 6). Rocks jump and glide, and lava fields and landslides compose plastic, fluid shapes: indeed matter can unveil its potential by itself. "Landscapes are not backdrops for historical action, they are themselves active," says Tsing. "Watching landscapes in formation shows humans joining other living beings in shaping worlds" (2015, 125); "history, then, is the record of many trajectories of world making, human and not human" (135). Matter is the protagonist of stories rather than the silent setting of human history.

I will venture an interpretation of world making as a sculpting technique—something reminiscent of Michelangelo's *non finito*—thus heeding the stories built into the lithic bodies. I will focus on the stone I know: minimally refined matter rather than the products of human shaping. "To wander in search of stone's stories is to wander in its enduring company," Cohen has noted (2015, 12). To me, stone has always been a companion: I grew up in the mountains. Hence, let's begin with them. Let's take a step back to the origins of the Alps.

Ninety million years ago, as tectonic plates collided, mineral waves arose from the scorching waters of the Tethys Ocean—the ancestor of the present-day Mediterranean Sea; they stretched themselves, broke apart and merged together. During the Quaternary, these rocks were filled, carved, and smoothed by ice sheets, whose melting revealed a kaleidoscope of valleys with steep sides and flat bottoms. One of those, among the western part of the alpine ridge, is the Susa Valley. The valley extends for over 80 kilometers from the French border toward the city of Turin, forming the watershed between the Graian and the Cottian Alps. A clear pathway through the immovable petric plenitude, over the centuries it has been trodden by the armies of Constantine, Charlemagne, and Napoleon. Here the Romans traced the Via Cottia, which was renamed Via Francigena during the Middle Ages. Although it has always been depicted as a passageway—"via"—the valley also was a shelter for people who, in turn, deeply changed that landscape. Among these people are the *picapera*, a Piedmontese word literally meaning "stone-beaters." The *picapera*'s work consisted of stacking wooden poles inside the vein of a rock—its spine—and spraying these poles with water so that they expanded; as the rock snapped, it was ready to be modeled. The peasants built up reinforcing walls and canals and paved trails by means of the sediment carried by the Dora River. The shepherds crowded the peaks with summer pastures and constellations of wayside shrines, the *piloni*, which incarnated ex-voto, saints, beloved dead. Each one of these bodies of rock was named and infused with a story. They whispered the truth of the common origin of all matter or that, as Carl Sagan once argued, we are made of stars: "We are the local embodiment of a Cosmos grown to self-awareness. We have begun to contemplate our origins: starstuff pondering the stars; organized assemblages of ten billion billion billion atoms considering the evolution of atoms; tracing the long journey by which, here at least, consciousness arose" (Sagan 1980).

Here, on these heights, we entrusted our flesh to the lithic flakes. They led our stories to a larger cosmology.

Lithophagia/Stone-Eaters

"In any art or discipline, one extracts from Nature certain principles, perfections, and rules, which if we examine them with care and diligence, and utilize them, we will undoubtedly do all we set out to do. . . . Nature also shows us certain guides and certain means by which we may, with a solid step and sure principles, proceed as we wish." So Alberti claimed (2013, 11). The populations of the high regions cleverly unearthed those principles and rules, which they utilized in order to fabricate havens that endured from the Renaissance until the Industrial Revolution. Afterward, massive technological advances in transportation and communication marked the beginning of a different relationship with the alpine environment. The star stuff progressively turned into a resource: it was domesticated, if not subdued, and the commandment to "proceed as we wish" resulted in pillaging. The body of Turin, Italy's first capital, is a patchwork of copper, iron, gneiss, and marble wrenched out of the Alps: each and every *piazza, portico,* and *palazzo* is made out of alpine rocks and clay dredged from the rivers winging through the plain. Environmental historian Marco Armiero argues that "nationalising mountains implied imposing meanings, appropriating resources, enforcing authority of the State, redefining boundaries between wild and tamed, wise and irrational, beautiful and ugly"—it meant, literally, "to make Italians out of soil and rocks" (2011, 6). Three centuries after the Renaissance the government of the newborn kingdom of Italy had ceased to see the Cottian Alps as a quarry. However, the Susa Valley remained exploitable, albeit in a different way. After the creation of the unified kingdom in 1861, construction of new railroads intensified. The political agenda pushed international trade to prevent the country from being cut off from the global flow of goods. And since the mountain passes were only open for six months a year, the Alps were seen as obstacles to economic growth: they needed to be *perfected.*

During the parliamentary debate about the approval of a railway tunnel that would connect Italy to France, Prime Minister Camillo Benso of

Cavour portrayed the challenge of piercing the Mount Cenis massif as a choice between "improving or perishing" (*Atti* 1873, 2775). The member of Parliament Ferdinando Isola, for his part, stressed the need to "rip the guts out of this mountain range" (*Atti* 1873, 2736). Despite his vehemence, however, nobody knew what was hidden underground. Scientists did not exclude the possibility of stumbling upon incandescent rocks, subterranean streams, even monsters and dragons. Today we know that asbestos is one of these monsters: the tectonic structure of the Western Alps in the Susa Valley zone is very complex, having been involved in various geological events. Heavy concentrations of asbestos can be found in many serpentinite rocks. Tremolite veins are common in small masses of serpentinite schists in the Piedmont area, especially in the upper part of the valley (Clerico et al. 2014, 6).

It took fourteen years of explosive charges and new pneumatic rock-drilling machines, plus the loss of thirty human lives, to drill the 13 km long tunnel beneath the massif. When it opened on September 17, 1871, the Fréjus tunnel was the first of the large tunnels to pierce its way through the Alps. The chronicler Edoardo Barraja labeled this enterprise a "fight against the rock," whose protagonist had been the foresighted statesman Cavour and whose "apostles" were the engineers Germain Sommeiller, Severino Grattoni, and Sebastiano Grandis (1921, 65, 73). Describing the machines patented by Sommeiller as flaming snakes, Barraja turned the story that the lithic world had inspired *against* the lithic world itself. In 1879 a monument was erected in Turin using the stones extracted from Mount Fréjus. The raw boulders are piled on top of each other. Seven marble giants lie on them in utter despair. A bronze winged genius tops the pyramid, conveying a sense of calm and triumph. According to Barraja, the monument celebrates the debacle of the mountain and the outright victory of humankind: "The sinister aptitudes of Titans, signs of a subjugated brutal force, contrast with the Genius's pure serenity, symbol of the undefeated perseverance that enlightens the dark bowels of the earth with the ray of divine insight. . . . Those boulders wrenched out by the deep womb of the giant mountain are the simulacra of a crushed field" (90–91).

It would probably be too much to call the monument to the Fréjus tunnel the embodiment of the pernicious idea of a dead or at least instrumentalized matter that has fed human hubris "and our earth-destroying fantasies of conquest and consumption" (Bennett 2010, 9). Luckily, the positivist meaning has been superseded by another: today the monument testifies to the suffering endured by the miners to carry out the work. Still, chasing the glow of the Genius's star we disfigured the starry ground. We became stone-eaters. Nowadays we dig mountains and dredge rivers, chewing gravel and sand to feed our posthuman Stone Age with concrete. We blend sand, water, oil, and gravel like bees blend tree resin, wax, and pollen. Bees produce propolis (from the Greek *pro-polis*, "before the city"), very suitable as sealant, whereas we produce walls, city blocks, highways, and idols. Without stone, humans could not endure. The valley is no longer trodden and carved: it is enslaved and consumed. The Susa Valley's stone has been transmuted into the floor of a massive, overpopulated infrastructure inextricably connected with global trade. It is traversed by a railway and three motorways; a new road tunnel under Mount Cenis opened in 1980. More than 90,000 residents populate the area. Nonetheless, a network of seven natural reserves—the Parks of the Cottian Alps—has been established at higher altitudes and, ironically, the construction of a viaduct in Chiomonte unearthed the Neolithic site of La Maddalena, which was nestled in a beautiful wooded terrace planted with vineyards. The whole area lies along the *Strada Reale dei Vini Torinesi* (the royal wine road of Turin's wines), a broad itinerary featuring winegrowers that runs throughout the province of Torino and is dotted with cellars and important cultural and historical sites. In Chiomonte vintners harvest and process Avanà grapes, the most important vine in the Susa Valley, grown for centuries in the vineyards surrounding the village. Until a few years ago I would visit the vines, the caves, and the archaeological museum. I lay in the grass and gazed at the stones, fantasizing about my ancestors, people reluctant to accept abrupt changes and whose habits we have forgotten altogether. It felt good to be there.

Unfortunately, La Maddalena happens also to be an area of "national strategic interest." In 2010 the Italian government, led by Silvio Berlusconi, chose this place as the site of the umpteenth tunnel for a high-speed railway line to link Turin and Lyon, part of the pharaonic Corridor 6, also called Mediterranean Corridor, a high-speed freight line about 1,800 miles long that will hypothetically run from southern Spain to the Ukrainian border. The European Commission website describes the Italian section in these terms: "Together with the Gotthard-Monte Ceneri axis in Switzerland and the Brenner Corridor, the Lyon-Turin rail connection will establish a complex of high-capacity rail links. They will help achieve the environmental objectives set by the European Union and ensure the modal shift from road to rail so necessary for the future of the ecologically sensitive Alpine region" (Tuszyńska 2016).

The planned TAV (Treno Alta Velocità, high-speed train) line has been the source of heavy criticism. Since the 1990s, an intense mobilization has spread from the Susa Valley all across Italy under the banner of the No TAV movement. The first No TAV national march happened in 1995. The TAV project has since enjoyed unwavering political support from the "ecologically sensitive" members of parliament, right-wing and left-wing alike.

Several preliminary drafts have been overturned in the attempt to quell a three-decades-long clash with the communities, a clash that most of the local people depict as "resistance," latching on to the partisans' epic stories of endurance against the Nazi scourge that took place in the valley.

Amid ballooning costs, repeated delays, and uncertainty over funding, the railway project has changed shape repeatedly. Only one thing has remained the same: its aim. The obstinacy of the governments has led to an escalation of the intimidation tactics employed by both factions. In 2011 La Maddalena was declared a "red zone": it was occupied by police after struggles and riots, its museum was converted into a site for military barracks, and the necropolis and ancient shelters were devastated by crawler excavators. Since then, agricultural workers have been obliged to submit a safe-conduct to move past checkpoints and get to their vineyards.

There is not adequate funding for this major infrastructure—a so-called *grande opera*—whose cost of about $8 billion will surely increase the public debt. Moreover, the freight traffic through the valley has inexorably decreased during the last twenty years. In March 2015, the European Commission and the Swiss Federal Office of Transport provided a detailed description of the transalpine freight flow in *Observation et analyse des flux de transports de marchandises transalpins: Rapport annuel 2013* (Observation and analysis of the transalpine freight transport: Annual report 2013). The actual trade flux recorded in the report diverges from the prodigious forecasts the Italian government made in 2011. It is also worth pointing out that only 20 percent of the existing railway line capacity is currently used.

Nobody except politicians, contractors, and poorly informed people endorse the high-speed train project, which an increasing proportion of the public sees as an example of corrupt politics deaf to its citizens' needs and another violation of the exhausted alpine environment. The practice of public supply contracts has raised questions regarding accountability and financial transparency, particularly in view of the fact that an investigation by the European Anti-Fraud Office (OLAF) is currently looking into the huge cost overruns and allegations of mafia links in Italy. An investigation in 2014 revealed connections between the 'ndrangheta, an Italian organized crime network, and one of the companies in charge of building the tunnel. The No TAV movement is likewise facing investigations by the public prosecutor's offices of Turin. Twenty activists are currently in custody or subjected to other supervisory measures, charged by the police with possession of weapons, resistance to a representative of public authority, and personal injury, plus disrupting public order and security. Furthermore, a year after writer Erri De Luca was tried and acquitted due to his public support to the protests, Roberta Chiroli, a graduate student within the Department of Anthropology at Ca' Foscari University of Venice was accused of being "morally complicit" with the movement as a result of her involvement in 2013 demonstrations. Although she maintained she took part in the protests to make use of the widely accepted methodology of participant observation during the drafting of her thesis, she was sentenced to a two-month prison term.

The conflict has obviously been exacerbated. But the No TAV movement is a resilient organism. It has channeled its energy into proactive and propositional activities. At the local level, it has opened new sites of struggle in the valley (protests against the Beltrame steel plant and the enlargement of the Fréjus tunnel). At the national level, it promotes alliances with other local movements within the *patto di mutuo soccorso*, a methodology of struggle based on principles including mutual aid, information sharing, and active solidarity. The No TAV movement has therefore managed to extend a struggle over territorial issues into a broader and more complex critique of this model of development, at the same time leading to experiments in new forms of democratic participation and new practices in degrowth theory. Nevertheless, in March 2016 the French president François Hollande sealed the TAV project as "irreversible." No dragon, or even the risk of asbestos contamination, will stop the diggers. An entire ecosystem is being trampled on, but the lithic stories, roaming around like glacial erratics, might breach this wall of obstinacy.

Lithophany/Waves of Liberation

Serenella Iovino and Serpil Oppermann (2014) have brilliantly enlightened the mutual permeability between matter and imagination. Material things are imbued with stories that demand to be read and thus liberated from their silence (Iovino 2016, 1). "Storied matter" also bears texts that can "add new layers to a society's ecology of mind, thus supplementing its ethical and ontological vocabulary with new words" (Iovino 2016, 4–5). Stories are tools. All organisms have the power to bestow form on inorganic matter, and words emerging along trajectories across a stage of space-time-matter have the power to shape new worlds. If we start seeing matter as lively—or "vibrant"— then "the status of the shared materiality of all things is elevated," writes Jane Bennett (2010, 12–13). I wonder whether stories about mutual aid between humans and stones can reverberate on a global scale; whether interacting forms of resistance—like, for example, civil disobedience against paradoxical politics of growth carried out in a narrow land embedded in the Alps—can be construed as the flapping of a butterfly's wings. Sometimes a battle is just one blip in the war; still, other times it shifts the course of history.

In 1944 the valley was under military occupation by the Nazi Fascist troops. The resistance here had flourished, and the partisans were numerous and well-organized. In spite of this, on July 8 the Walter Fontan brigade was ambushed on the high pastures near Balmafol. Running out of ammunition, the partisan fighters followed the advice of a local shepherd's son, who suggested that they push boulders off the cliff. And so they did, thus routing the enemy. Almost sixty-seven years later, on July 3, 2011, sixty thousand people undertook a march on Chiomonte after the expropriation and militarization of the site. I was there. I saw the demonstrators in the vanguard argue and then split, since a sizable group intended to reach and besiege the work site using the old trails. What I saw when we finally entered Chiomonte was excruciating. The protesters were being repelled by policemen, who were firing tear gas at head height a few steps from elderly people and children. The woods and the vineyards were covered by thick smoke. My eyes started to sting. I found myself incapable of anger: I just felt sad and petrified. Then I saw some people renewing and enlivening the old stories inhabiting these places. I saw them throwing stones over the barricades.

Wonders coexist with burdens. Wonders dwell in boulders. Italo Calvino used a metaphor to define the stylistic challenge of expressing the world's complexity in words: "to pour the sea into a funnel" (1961, 9). I think that the material counterpart of Calvino's conceptual funnel lies in the Alps, right here, in the lithic body of the Susa Valley. Like Dante, we need a guide to attempt the journey, someone familiar with silence and darkness: a *picapera*. Only a heart of stone can transform this fall into a descent through memory and lead us "to see the stars again" (*Inferno* 34, 139).

Chiomonte's coat of arms shows the quote "*Jamais sans toi*"—"Never without you"—between two bunches of grapes, one white and one black, and the sun, meaning that sunlight is necessary for the grapes to ripen. The cultivation of vines and the making of wine are closely connected to Chiomonte's abundance of water. Chiomonte is known as the "town of seven springs" since in the past there were seven fountains which used to meet the needs of all the districts in the municipality. Among the ones that are left, one is particularly interesting. It was made by combining three other fountains and features a stone dating to 1562 united with a stone column from an 1888 fountain displaying an anthropomorphic figure. The richness of Chimonte's waters is principally due to the contribution of Colombano Romean.

Colombano was born in Chiomonte in the second half of the fifteenth century. He learned excavation techniques working in France. When he returned to his native village, he found that for years the population had been considering building an aqueduct to convey the waters of the heights to the hamlets of Ramats and Cels in the Exilles municipality because they had no water and thus the land was barren. But drilling was too difficult, and so the project had been abandoned. The fifty-year-old Colombano volunteered for the excavation works, ensuring the inhabitants that he would "finish the tunnel . . . as soon as possible." In addition to the salary, the locals would come up with additional gifts: "good and common rye and good and common wine." Between 1526 and 1533, Colombano dug the 430-meter *pertus*—that is, a hole. As the legend goes, his dog carried him food and wine daily from the town. Colombano mined sixty meters per year using a simple awl. The tunnel is uniform and refined with particular care. In it, we find artfully carved recesses for oil lamps, plus incisions and bas-relief representing human heads and lilies. He sculpted the rock gently, slowly, until water started to flow, creating something that would quench the valley's thirst for a long time. In fact, the *pertus* remained an important aquatic network for Chiomonte through the first half of the twentieth century, and it still works.

The parable of the miner and the dog emerging from the starry abyss of the Alps is an astonishing example of an intimate relationship with the nonhuman and of the humility it takes to be truly human. "Dogs and people figure a universe," Donna Haraway has written (2003, 21). Fed by his dog, Colombano Romean devoted his life to bettering his harsh petrous universe. He brings to mind Libertino Faussone, the protagonist of Primo Levi's *The Monkey's Wrench* (*La chiave a stella*, 1978), a Turinese man who travels the world building and fixing cranes, bridges, and towers. Faussone is a life-lover whose passion for work shines through his stories, while reminding us of the paramount importance of feeling and being useful. A man whose best friend, incidentally, was a little chimp. Voicing Faussone's enthusiasm for his job, Levi writes: "Day by day . . . it was like seeing a baby grow. I mean a baby that isn't yet born, when it's still inside its mama . . . This is a real satisfaction, like when they made the Frejus tunnel, and it took thirteen years, but then the Italian hole and the French hole met, without any error, not even twenty centimeters, so afterward they raised that monument, the one that's all black, in Piazza Statuto, with the flying lady on top" (1987, 15–16).

As Levi says, "if we except those miraculous moments fate can bestow on a man, loving your work (unfortunately, the privilege of a few) represents the best, most concrete approximation of happiness on earth" (79–80). I think Colombano Romean was one of these few people. His authentic *grande opera*, accomplished beneath the earth near today's high-speed train tunnel, reconciles the conflicting vocations of the Susa Valley: a passage, a political body, a masterpiece born from the sea and sculpted by ice, hands, roots, and words. Only by shifting environmental exploitation into a responsible material and discursive intra-action between human and nonhuman will our bodies continue to cross this passage. It will happen only if we slow down, remain silent and humble, and let our matter, too, be carved softly by the waves of liberation breaking on the mountain cliffs.[1]

NOTE

1. A video presentation including images of the issues investigated in this article is available at https://www.youtube.com/watch?v=GSZribXVAh8.

WORKS CITED

Alberti, Leon Battista. 2013. *On Sculpture*. Translated and commentary by Jason Arkles. Jason Arkles, publisher.

Armiero, Marco. 2011. *A Rugged Nation: Mountains and the Making of Modern Italy*. Cambridge, UK: White Horse Press.

Atti del Parlamento Subalpino, Discussioni della Camera dei Deputati, V Legislatura, Sessione 1857 (07/01/1857–16/07/1857), Volume (V) 3A delle discussioni della camera dei deputati dal 20/05/1857 al 16/07/1857. Rome: Eredi Botta, 1873.

Barraja, Edoardo. 1921. *Il traforo del Frejus: Storia di uomini e glorie*. Turin: Fedetto.

Bennett, Jane. 2010. *Vibrant Matter: A Political Ecology of Things*. Durham, NC: Duke University Press.

Calvino, Italo. 1961. "Natalia Ginzburg o le possibilità del romanzo borghese." *L'Europa letteraria* 2: 9–10.

Clerico, Marina, Luca Giunti, Luca Mercalli, Marco Ponti, Angelo Tartaglia, Sergio Ulgiati, and Massimo Zucchetti. 2014. "Railway Related Impacts: The Turin-Lyon High-Speed Rail Case." *Fresenius Environmental Bulletin* 24(5a): 1–9.

Cohen, Jeffrey J. 2015. *Stone: An Ecology of the Inhuman*. Minneapolis: University of Minnesota Press.

Haraway, Donna. 2003. *The Companion Species Manifesto: Dogs, People, and Significant Otherness*. Chicago: Prickly Paradigm Press.

Iovino, Serenella. 2016. *Ecocriticism and Italy: Ecology, Resistance, and Liberation*. London: Bloomsbury Academic.

Iovino, Serenella, and Serpil Oppermann, eds. 2014. *Material Ecocriticism*. Bloomington: Indiana University Press.

Levi, Primo. 1987. *The Monkey's Wrench*. Translated by William Weaver. New York: Penguin. Originally published as *La chiave a stella* (Turin: Einaudi, 1978).

Lindström, Kati, Kalevi Kull, and Hannes Palang. 2014. "Landscape Semiotics: Contribution to Culture Theory." In *Estonian Approaches to Culture Theory*, vol. 4, *Approaches to Culture Theory*, edited by Kalevi Kull and Valter Lang, 110–132. Tartu, Estonia: University of Tartu Press.

Sagan, Carl. 1980. "Who Speaks for Earth?" *Cosmos: A Personal Voyage*. Episode 13, aired December 21. Television.

Tsing, Anna Löwenhaupt. 2015. *The Mushroom at the End of the World: On the Possibility of Life in Capitalist Ruins*. Princeton, NJ: Princeton University Press.

Tuszyńska, Beata. 2016. *Research for Tran Committee: Alpine Transport and Tourism in Austria, Germany and Italy*. Brussels: European Parliament. http://www.europarl.europa.eu/RegData/etudes/BRIE/2016/573459/IPOL_BRI(2016)573459_EN.pdf.

ELENA PAST

Thinking on Foot in the Hydrocarbon Sublime: Paolo Sorrentino's Petrocultures

I used to think of Italy as a place where one travels on foot. That was likely because cobblestones, tourists, sidewalk cafés, and narrow medieval streets make driving and parking far more complicated in Siena, where I studied abroad, than in sprawling Beeville, Texas, where I grew up (Beeville has no sidewalk cafés and no tourists). That was before I had read Italo Calvino's "L'inseguimento," an energetic, paranoid, high-speed chase kind of a story where the entire "chase" takes place in a traffic jam at an intersection, and neither pursuer nor pursued move. It was before I had seen Federico Fellini's *Roma* (1972), or the documentary film *Sacro GRA* (The sacred Great Ring Road, directed by Gianfranco Rosi, 2013), both of which spend long hours in heavy traffic on the multilane ring road, the Grande Raccordo Anulare, that circles Rome. And it was before Fiat came to bail out Chrysler while Detroit, the Motor City and my university home, weathered bankruptcies and crises of postindustrialization. I now know that Italians own more cars per capita than any other population in Europe except Luxembourg (Ficocelli 2015), that the economic boom spurred impressive urban traffic jams, and that parking in most large Italian cities requires saintly patience or the intervention of the saints.

In her history of walking, Rebecca Solnit contextualizes the idea of a walkable Italy (and the American tendency to idealize it), noting that the absence of highways and parking lots in the city centers make the street "the pivotal social space, for meeting, debating, courting, buying, and selling" (2000, 179). Italian cinema, in Solnit's account, has captured some epochal walkers, like Cabiria in *Nights of Cabiria* or Antonio and Bruno in *Bicycle Thief* (2000, 180). In these films, socially engaged stories unfurl on the lively, lived streets, justifying the notion theorized by Cesare Zavattini that neorealist cinema should be "pedinamento," or stalking the cinematic subject on foot.[1] Yet Italian cinema has also traced the alienating effects of automobilization on these spaces, the "empowering and excruciating experience" of twentieth-century modernity that has shifted and often undermined patterns of meeting, debating, buying, and selling (Duffy 2009, 1). Director Dino Risi's film *The Easy Life* (1962) offers one clear example of the existential and material risks of automobiles and speed, and there are many others. So perhaps we might hypothesize that, since the economic boom, Italy has been the site of particularly intense encounters between those who walk and those who drive, making it a stage on which is performed the drama of urban landscapes built for humans and their nonhuman companions, and now full of automobiles. Further, Italian cinema has often foregrounded the collaboration between human walkers and film itself as pedestrian, inviting us to widen our notion of agency to envision both cinematic stories *and* the energy that powers kinesis as active partners in our petroleum culture.

Today, the way we frame stories of petroleum culture matters, because the way human bodies (and privileged human bodies in particular) move through and occupy space is one of the central questions determining the future of a warming planet. Contemporary transportation networks, war machines, construction industries, and energy-intensive leisure activities depend on vast reserves of hydrocarbons to fuel development, movement, and consumption. As Ian Angus writes, "capitalism and fossil fuels have spectacularly expanded human health and wealth for two centuries. Now they are overwhelming the planetary processes that have made Earth hospitable to civilization and our species for 10,000 years. They are thrusting us into a new and dangerous epoch" (2016, 108). Whether we call this perilous time the Anthropocene or the Great Acceleration, scientists warn that the faster we go, the more our fate is entangled with that of the planet:

> Hitherto human activities were insignificant compared with the biophysical Earth System, and the two could operate independently. However, it is now impossible to view one as separate from the other. The Great Acceleration trends provide a dynamic view of the emergent, planetary-scale coupling, via globalisation, between the socio-economic system and the biophysical Earth System. We have reached a point where many biophysical indicators have clearly moved beyond the bounds of Holocene variability. We are now living in a no-analogue world. (Steffen et al. 2015, 94)[2]

In *Facing the Anthropocene: Fossil Capitalism and the Crisis of the Earth System*, Angus discusses this crisis as a biophysical and socio-ecological phenomenon; Steffen and colleagues also identify clashes of socioeconomics and biophysics. Yet as environmental humanists know, this is an eco-cultural problem, too, enmeshed in conflicting stories being told by vibrant subjects of all kinds. Anthropic narratives, and the media we use to tell them, cannot be left out of analysis of the crisis, nor must they be forgotten as we sketch possible futures. Italian films have helped document the shape and speed of petroleum culture, but Italian films are also stories being told by petroleum culture. Cinema can help us to unfurl the story of why petroleum culture seduces us and provide critical and affective tools for understanding its effects.

This essay considers a series of films directed by Paolo Sorrentino that track different paces and modes of transit, including walking, driving, flying, and sailing: *The Consequences of Love* (2004), *This Must Be the Place* (2011), *The Great Beauty* (2013), and *Youth* (2015). Each production offers evidence of cinema's restless, petroleum-intense global reach, whether because it was filmed abroad or funded by international monies. One of the films, *This Must Be the Place*, features a road trip across the American Midwest and West. By engaging with the iconic landscapes of the West, this film discloses the importance of comparing notions of cinemobility transnationally: it participates in American hydrocarbon mythologies and considers the ways Italian film admires, resents, and perhaps revises these. Although Sorrentino's exquisite frames at times celebrate the landscapes they capture, beneath the surface of his films rumbles a deep awareness of the environmental and existential costs of individualism, of contemporary globalized nomadism, of cinema itself. Responding to Nadia Bozak's call to "locate the energy in cinema" (2012, 1), I suggest that Sorrentino's "hydrocarbon sublime" shows how ontological anxieties can trace deep roots in hydrocarbon culture, and how a cinema that "thinks on foot" can start to face them.[3]

Sorrentino's Petrocultures: The Hydrocarbon Sublime

Sorrentino has said that his films seek to "recount the mechanisms of power, which are solitude, arrogance, the tendency to build a life based exclusively on relationships of force" (Zaccagnini 2008, my translation). While this affirmation refers to the sometimes powerful and often lonely men at the center of his films, the mechanisms of power and relationships of force can also be read as interactions driven by petroleum. In fact Sorrentino's cinema shows us how petroculture is one of the primary drivers that moves and fractures our societies. A few examples: In *The Consequences of Love,* Titta Di Girolamo lives in exile in a hotel and never sees his family; he gives an expensive automobile to his love interest, who has been taking driving lessons, and she wrecks it, leaving him to contemplate a solitary future. In *This Must Be the Place,* Cheyenne has lived across the Atlantic from his father for more than thirty years and only returns for his funeral. In his journey across the American West, he encounters various members of a scattered family who complain that they rarely see their siblings, children, or grandchildren because they work across the globe and never come home. In *The Great Beauty,* a young man commits suicide by driving his expensive car with his eyes closed, leaving behind a disconsolate grieving mother. In *Youth,* we learn that a woman and her husband split at the airport, and later she awakens, screaming, as nightmares evoke her husband and his lover in speeding, exploding cars. Repeatedly, pervasively, the screenplays suggest that one significant part of the problem of existential isolation might be petroleum and the cultures of independence it fosters. Matthew Huber argues that oil fuelled the "mobile privatization" of society and wonders: "What if the most problematic relation to oil is the way it powers forms of social life that allow individuals to imagine themselves as severed from society and public life?" (2013, x, xi).

The alienating, mobile privatization of life is nowhere so evident as in *This Must Be the Place*'s journey through the United States. Cheyenne drives an oversized Dodge pickup, and the film crew captures his truck on lonely highways, traversing landscapes made iconic by Hollywood westerns in the style of John Ford. Empty roadways, dilapidated motor hotels, pickup trucks, semis, and road noise dominate, demonstrating the acoustic and bodily isolation of what Stephanie LeMenager calls "petromodernity" (2014, 67).[4] Petromodernity is more than just a setting for this film; in a multitude of ways obvious and not, petroleum culture produced it. Significantly, the cast and crew filmed not just in the West (New Mexico in particular) but also the Midwest, in Michigan, where the Internet Movie Database (imdb.com) credits filming in parking lots, small and large suburbs, and the historic Masonic Temple in the city of Detroit. Abandoned motels and crumbling infrastructure are part of Michigan's postindustrial landscape, which has become iconic in its own right, including in the genre sometimes called "ruin porn," an aestheticization of decay with roots in petroleum culture and the state's too-heavy investment in the globalizing auto industry. This landscape has been captured in a number of films seeking postindustrial and postapocalyptic settings, like *Gran Torino* (2008), *Red Dawn* (2012), *Batman v Superman: Dawn of Justice* (2016), and various of the *Transformers* franchise. *This Must Be the Place*, like many of these films, took advantage of a generous tax credit offered in Michigan from 2008 through 2015, which was intended to help replace lost jobs in the auto industry with jobs in cinema.[5] Ironically, more than a few of the films made with the tax credits, including Sorrentino's, capitalized aesthetically on the very collapse they were meant to help reverse. In ecological terms, the state attempted to fill in gaps left by one dirty, energy-intensive industry by calling in another: as Charles J. Corbett and Richard P. Turco show in their report *Sustainability in the Motion Picture Industry* (2006), the film industry consumes huge amounts of energy and emits significant quantities of greenhouse gasses.

Sorrentino's film productions in the American West did not continue, though; after the jaunt to the United States to film *This Must Be the Place,* he and his core crew returned to work in Europe. These films thus stage the push-pull of a transnational cinema that works to succeed on the terms established by a vast, Hollywood, American western scale, and a cinema that suspects that its greatest strength—and its greatest beauty—must be realized by doing something different. Within the stories of alienation, Sorrentino's films express the temptation to love petroleum time and time again in frames that capture something I call the "hydrocarbon sublime": moments of stark beauty that, like other sublime experiences, inspire awe underpinned by a sense of disquiet.[6] Here are a few significant moments, all captured in long and extreme long shots: a man sits atop a power transformer in the Alps near the end of *The Consequences of Love*; a flock of birds erupts across a sky traversed by a distinctive contrail in *The Great Beauty*; Jep Gambardella stands on the rocky shore of the Mediterranean Sea, contemplating the capsized *Costa Concordia* cruise ship; a motorboat speeds across the sea leaving a white wake behind it; in *This Must Be the Place*, Cheyenne's Dodge pickup truck catches fire suddenly, a spontaneous combustion perhaps caused by overfilling the oil reservoir; a mobile home sits in the middle of a stark landscape, and Cheyenne's new pickup sits nearby; in *Youth*, the cables of a gondola bisect a dramatic Alpine valley.

Although cinematographer Luca Bigazzi shows a fondness for the geometric grid structures of hydrocarbon culture, from power lines to construction cranes to long, straight highways, in many of these shots, the camera frames petroleum *residues:* contrails, wakes, flames, tire tracks. These residues, created in various ways by the relentless movement of fuel-powered engines, leave behind ephemeral visual traces that help recall the less ephemeral remnants left by burning fossil fuels. Here, the films help visualize cinema's own planetary residues, connecting the aesthetic experience to a material one. As Nadia Bozak recalls, from "vehicle to lights to the gas-powered generators used on location, to shipping film reels . . . , [t]he cinematic image, digitized or celluloid-based, is a manufactured or 'unnatural' resource" (2012, 58–59). She urges that "now, at this moment, the theory, history, and practice of making films can assume an explicit awareness of environment, that images, however intangible or immaterial they might heretofore appear to be, come bearing a physical and biophysical makeup, and leave behind a residue—a cinematic 'footprint,' as it were" (2012, 8).

Airborne and mobile, the contrails, wakes, and flames are in fact also visual signals of the substances that dissipate, envelop, and traverse our bodies, urging along a posthuman process of "unbounding" our human frames. We, after all, are partially made of petroleum; as Frederick Buell has pointed out, especially post–World War II, via chemical metamorphosis, fossil fuels "changed into what people dressed in, evacuated into, viewed, and even ate, not just what they put into their power machinery. Oil thus now reappeared as an agent of chemical *and* social metamorphosis. Bodies became literally oily" (2012, 290). Cheyenne, who applies and removes heavy makeup throughout *This Must Be the Place*, becomes the face of a willing partner in the human/petroleum hybrid when we recall the cosmetics industry's reliance on fossil fuels and mineral oil in particular. Via the hydrocarbon sublime and its juxtapositions of birds and contrails, power transformers and Alpine peaks, Sorrentino's films impel viewers to enter what Stacy Alaimo evokes as the "swirling landscape of uncertainty where practices and actions that were once not even remotely ethical or political matters suddenly become the very stuff of the crises at hand" (2010, 20).

But is talking about the sublime too anachronistic? In ecocriticism, the sublime has often been invoked to demonstrate the Romantic tendency to create binaries, to show human distance from nature. William Cronon argues that, for the Romantics, including Burke, Kant, and William Gilpin, "sublime landscapes were those rare places on earth where one had more chance than elsewhere to glimpse the face of God," where humans felt insignificant but also where they were working to tame that wilderness (1995, 73, 75). Greg Garrard suggests that the Burkian sublime was "always vulnerable to technological and cultural change" and that "European civilization largely mastered its mountains with trains, roads, and ski-lifts, whilst the exploration of the American West brought news of the Grand Canyon and the Rocky Mountains, making the wilderness of the Old World look decidedly tame" (2004, 66). Sublime nature is evoked in the ecocritical imagination to deconstruct it, to argue that such binaries blinded humanity to the fact that *we* created wilderness and that it "could hardly be contaminated by the very stuff of which it is made" (Cronon 1995, 69). And yet there are various reasons I think a perverse, posthuman, hydrocarbon sublime is relevant here. For one, Sorrentino's films focus on framing the material spaces where the sublime has famously been theorized: Rome, the craggy Alps, and the American West, a historical-cultural fact that underlies the entanglement of memory, matter, and meaning. More significantly, perhaps, speaking of the sublime offers us a means to talk about beauty when we are also aware of the consequences of its creation, and the consequences of positioning ourselves to witness it—or better, to consume it. Aesthetic beauty in Sorrentino's films (together with a good measure of irony, like a beautiful frame that shows Cheyenne gazing in wonder at an absurd roadside attraction, a sculpture featuring the world's largest pistachio nut) underscores that we humans have *not*, in fact, mastered or tamed our environment but rather that we are clumsily and often hubristically bumbling—or burning—our way through it.

Thinking on Foot and a Posthuman Cinema of *Pedinamento*

In elaborating his theory of the sublime, Burke notes that, "when danger or pain press too nearly, they are incapable of giving any delight, and are simply terrible; but at certain distances, and with certain modifications, they may be, and they are, delightful, as we every day experience" (1876, 67). In Sorrentino's hydrocarbon sublime and the wide, long frames that capture these images, distance is a key part of delight. The distance here can be measured from the objects creating wakes, contrails, and flames but also from the possible planetary disaster that may result from burning them: his are certainly not films about environmental crisis or apocalypse but instead view these and other crises with a degree of detachment. In fact I think that the "certain distance" and "certain modifications" which Burke traces—realized in Sorrentino's films through aestheticized beauty and irony—might also be construed as certain dangers of cinema (and cinematic scholarship), and also perhaps their potential. In the age of the Great Acceleration and the unfolding climate emergency, fear of inadequate response can lead even the most engaged thinkers to "disavowal" or to "impotent activities" (Alaimo 2012, 561). Alaimo suggests that, to counter these, we need actors who can "recognize that their own material selves are the very stuff of the agential world that they seek to understand" (2012, 561). The hydrocarbon sublime and Sorrentino's nomadic transnational cinema more widely call out various ways in which we are deeply implicated in the networks of petroleum-fired transit but also enmeshed in petroleum culture. And in fact, on closer inspection, his particular transnational cinematic archive incorporates visual evidence of some of the most pressing nature-cultural concerns in Italy, from resource-intensive cement manufacturing in *The Consequences of Love*, to the eco-disaster of the capsized *Costa Concordia* in fragile Mediterranean waters in *The Great Beauty*, to the oneiric sinking of Venice in *Youth*. Although peripheral, these more-than-human stories reinforce the suspicion that the Mediterranean is the site of a vibrant (and consequential) struggle between danger and delight. Burke claims that the Romantic sublime causes a "state of the soul, in which all its motions are suspended, with some degree of Horror" (1876, 78). In the perverse hydrocarbon sublime, though, motion is central to the experience, not suspended: kinesis, movement powered by fuel, underpins both the beauty and the fear these images inspire. The exquisite frames capturing the existential and environmental damage caused by petroleum modernity can lead to an experience of sublime aesthetic delight, a response that would be radically inadequate in seeking to change our cultures of excess. Yet these images also propose absorbing ways for us to envision ourselves as always already incorporated in those landscapes, implying in the process that we are both more fragile and more responsible. Most importantly, they allow us the time we need to take them in.

The sociologist and philosopher Franco Cassano argues that in order to challenge forms of modernity we must slow down and observe, critically, the "complex and manifold structures, permeable and subject to different interpretations, which depend, first of all, on the relationship that every tradition has with the environment that surrounds it" (2012, xlviii). From his Mediterranean perspective, he explains, in other words, that we need to "think on foot." Such thinking on foot, made possible in the fluid rapport between sociocultural and ecospatial forms, is still possible today in Italy, and in Italian cinema. Solnit points out that the evening *passeggiata*, an extra-slow kind of walking traditional in certain Italian town centers, "is not a way of getting anywhere, but a way of being somewhere" (2000, 66). This moving-in-place (proper also to the placeology theorized by Franco Arminio) describes a posthuman cinema of *pedinamento* that I am interested in, a cinema that envisions *specific* places on foot, even if place is part of a transnational cinematic landscape. In social and material counterpoint to lives fractured by petroleum culture, Sorrentino's protagonists are great walkers: Titta ambles around shopping malls and Swiss piazzas; Cheyenne walks everywhere in Ireland and returns home after his American road trip to travel on foot again (his face now, significantly, cleaned of the heavy layer of makeup he wore throughout); Jep strolls elegantly around Rome by night; Fred and Mick, the two central figures in *Youth*, spend their days walking slowly up and down a gravel road in the Alps. But Sorrentino's cinema also thinks on foot even when his protagonists aren't walking. Thinking on foot can be a formal technique, too, a Mediterranean form of resistance to the speed, obsolescence, and consumption driving the Anthropocene and a means for sharpening our ability to see and hear the world or for allowing it to permeate us in meaningful ways. At the end of *The Great Beauty*, the film thinks on foot by water, as the camera meanders down the Tiber River from the perspective of a slow-moving boat. In *Youth*, the film thinks on foot in acoustic terms when, in an Alpine pasture, an orchestra conductor decides to direct a symphony of bovine bells, mooing, and flapping bird wings. Slow pans, frequent use of slow motion, infrequent cuts, rich soundscapes, saturated color palettes make these and many other gentle, riveting scenes compel viewer attention for their beauty, push human protagonists to the periphery, and potentially draw human viewers into a wider understanding of what our world depends on—and what it runs on.

In *A Philosophy of Walking*, Frédéric Gros argues that when we walk, we are more apt to allow the landscape to become a part of us than when petroleum rockets us toward a destination: "it isn't so much that we are drawing nearer, more that the things out there become more and more insistent in our body. The landscape is a set of tastes, colours, scents which the body absorbs" (2014, 38). Although we usually watch films while seated, cinema, too, can help make experiences of contemporary reality insistent in our body, while its colors, sounds, and cinematic residues traverse us. Without denying Italy's own love affair with petroleum, or Sorrentino's love affair with Hollywood, I propose that his films dazzle us with the beauty of posthuman sublime landscapes fueled by our machines and our imaginations, landscapes that *are* us (if we are privileged Western global citizens), that our bodies have the cognitive time to absorb, and that our senses have aesthetic time to appreciate.

Writing about perception, the senses, and petrol fumes, among other things, eco-phenomenologist David Abram worries that climate change is a "consequence of failing to respect or even to notice the elemental medium in which we are immersed" (2014, 301). He evokes the hydrocarbon residues—factory smokestacks, exhaust from cruise ships, tankers, airplanes, and automobiles—when he notes that "even the most opaque, acrid smoke billowing out of the pipes will dissipate and disperse, always and ultimately dissolving into the invisible. It is gone. Out of sight, out of mind" (302). In Sorrentino's films, the hydrocarbon sublime intervenes to make sure that we remark our immersion in the elemental medium; the cinematic archive keeps a striking visual record of those residues. I hope that thinking through—and teaching students to notice—the beauty, fragility, and cost of such cinematic images might help in some small way to decelerate the conclusion that Italo Calvino sees for our human story, a conclusion that tells us that the process of bodily absorption goes both ways. In the short story "The Petrol Pump," Calvino reminds us that one day our bodies will form the organic deposits that will create the fossils to fuel some other, posthuman culture.

NOTES

1. The concept of "pedinamento," which became one of the underlying theories of neorealism, was described by Zavattini in one of his "diary" entries in the journal *Cinema Nuovo* where he writes of a woman he would like to film: "You need patience, you have to follow her [*pedinarla*], and when possible surprise her: it seems so clear to me that to make this kind of film you need a new technique, I think. It is a question of patience" (1952, 8).

2. In "The Trajectory of the Anthropocene: The Great Acceleration," Steffen and colleagues update the original, influential graphs that charted the Great Acceleration. Paul Crutzen is credited with defining the Anthropocene as the age (allegedly starting near the end of the eighteenth century) when human impacts on the Earth led to a new geological era. The Great Acceleration, on the other hand, refers to the period starting in the 1950s when the magnitude and rate of the "human imprint" increased dramatically. The graphs chart changes in major features of the earth's structure and functioning,

including: "atmospheric composition, stratospheric ozone, the climate system, the water and nitrogen cycles, marine ecosystems, land systems, tropical forests and terrestrial biosphere degradation" (Steffen et al. 2015, 83).

3. Hydrocarbons are a class of organic chemical compounds that are the main constituents of petroleum and natural gas; they are used for fuels and lubricants and are components in the manufacturing of plastics, rubbers, explosives, industrial chemicals, and more (Carey, 2011).

4. As LeMenager specifies, petromodernity is "modern life based in the cheap energy systems made possible by oil" (2014, 67).

5. The tax credit in Michigan was discontinued after various studies concluded that it cost far more than the revenues it generated (Thom and An 2017).

6. Giuseppina Mecchia has theorized the sublime aesthetics of *The Great Beauty*, arguing that "the *Aion*—the inhuman time of the cosmos—just won't be ignored: no party, no new loving attachment can avoid the immeasurable reach of a cosmic order that the city of Rome both hides and makes visible in the apparent eternity of a sublime survival" (2016, 184).

WORKS CITED

Abram, David. 2014. "Afterword: The Commonwealth of Breath." In *Material Ecocriticism*, edited by Serenella Iovino and Serpil Oppermann, 301–14. Bloomington: Indiana University Press.

Alaimo, Stacy. 2010. *Bodily Natures: Science, Environment, and the Material Self*. Bloomington: Indiana University Press.

———. 2012. "Sustainable This, Sustainable That: New Materialisms, Posthumanism, and Unknown Futures." *PMLA* 127(3): 558–64.

Angus, Ian. 2016. *Facing the Anthropocene: Fossil Capitalism and the Crisis of the Earth System*. New York: Monthly Review Press.

Bozak, Nadia. 2012. *Cinematic Footprint: Lights, Camera, Natural Resources*. New Brunswick, NJ: Rutgers University Press.

Buell, Frederick. 2012. "A Short History of Oil Cultures: Or, the Marriage of Catastrophe and Exuberance." *Journal of American Studies* 46(2): 273–93.

Burke, Edmund. 1876. *Essays*. London: Ward, Lock, and Tyler.

Carey, Francis A. 2011. "Hydrocarbon." *Encyclopaedia Britannica*. https://www.britannica.com/science/hydrocarbon.

Cassano, Franco. 2012. *Southern Thought and Other Essays on the Mediterranean*. Edited and translated by Norma Bouchard and Valerio Ferme. New York: Fordham University Press.

Corbett, Charles J., and Richard P. Turco. 2006. *Sustainability in the Motion Picture Industry*. Los Angeles: University of California, Institute of the Environment.

Cronon, William. 1995. "The Trouble with Wilderness; or, Getting Back to the Wrong Nature." In *Uncommon Ground: Rethinking the Human Place in Nature*, edited by William Cronon, 69–90. New York: W. W. Norton.

Duffy, Enda. 2009. *The Speed Handbook: Velocity, Pleasure, Modernism*. Durham, NC: Duke University Press.

Ficocelli, Sara. 2015. "In Italia 608 auto ogni 1000 abitanti, che record." *Repubblica*, January 6. http://www.repubblica.it/motori/sezioni/attualita/2015/01/06/news/quante_vetture_circolano_in_italia_-103859738.

Garrard, Greg. 2004. *Ecocriticism*. New York: Routledge.

Gros, Frédéric. 2014. *A Philosophy of Walking*. Translated by John Howe. New York: Verso.

Huber, Matthew T. 2013. *Lifeblood: Oil, Freedom, and the Forces of Capital*. Minneapolis: University of Minnesota Press.

LeMenager, Stephanie. 2014. *Living Oil: Petroleum Culture in the American Century*. New York: Oxford University Press.

Mecchia, Giuseppina. 2016. "Birds in the Roman Sky: Shooting for the Sublime in *La Grande Bellezza*." *Forum Italicum* 50(1): 183–93.

Solnit, Rebecca. 2000. *Wanderlust: A History of Walking*. New York: Penguin.

Steffen, Will, Wendy Broadgate, Lisa Deutsch, Owen Gaffney, and Cornelia Ludwig. 2015. "The Trajectory of the Anthropocene: The Great Acceleration." *The Anthropocene Review* 2(1): 81–98.

Thom, Michael, and Brian An. 2017. "Fade to Black? Exploring Policy Enactment and Termination through the Rise and Fall of State Tax Incentives for the Motion Picture Industry." *American Politics Research* 45(1): 85–108.

Zaccagnini, Edoardo. 2008. "Intervista a Paolo Sorrentino." *Close-up: Storie della visione*, October 11. http://www.close-up.it/intervista-a-paolo-sorrentino.

Zavattini, Cesare. 1952. "Diario." *Cinema nuovo* 1(1): 8.

ILARIA TABUSSO MARCYAN

Slow Food and Terra Madre: A Conversation with Carlo Petrini on Ecology, Rural Traditions, and New Food Cultures

How do local and global realities coexist and intersect today? In a world that is becoming more intensely globalized each day, where distances virtually do not exist and we learn, almost in real time, what is happening on the other side of the planet, we can observe that natural landscapes, food, and cultures related to food offer us a way to reconnect with our surrounding environments and local realities. In the last few decades, the rediscovery and appreciation of local food in the metropolis of the so-called First World has taken the shape of farmers' markets, urban gardening, and urban farming. These relatively new urban local realities—together with movements and organizations around the world that are engaged in reviving food cultures and traditional agricultural systems—are related, directly and indirectly, and support the ideas and values proposed by Slow Food, Terra Madre, and Carlo Petrini, the founder of both grassroots and nonprofit organizations.

This essay, with the help of my conversation with Petrini presented in the second section, traces the roots and stories of these two international organizations and their iconic founder. Moving from the northern Italian region of Piedmont, Petrini's homeland and where these organizations began, I will investigate how food, food producers, food cultures, and landscape influence each other. I will also consider how movements related to food and agriculture can raise consciousness regarding food, agrarian issues, climate change, and sustainability.

Slow Food is a nonprofit, international, grassroots association founded in 1986 in Italy. Petrini is a lifelong gourmand and wine expert. His comments in an article published in the 1980s in the historic Italian food and wine magazine *Gambero Rosso* and reprinted in *Slow Food Revolution*, contain the early seeds of the Slow Food movement and of all the different organizations born from it in the following years:

> I have the great luck of having been born and living in an extraordinary part of southern Piedmont, the Langhe, which borders on the end of the Ligurian Apennine foothills and is surrounded by the slow and sinuous course of the Tanaro River. In this sub-alpine part of our beautiful country, we grow up having conversations and discussions about good wine, the typical dishes of our tradition, and about food as a redemption from our ancient misery. Fenoglio, Pavese, Lajolo, and Nuto Revelli are our literary legends; in their works we can read our story, our way of being, and also the extraordinary development of the local wine industry, once poor and dispossessed. (Petrini 2006, 55)

In this passage, food is presented in a new, dignified form as the element that can redeem the land and its people. A sense of pride in belonging to the Langhe blooms into a sense of belonging to the local, a very important aspect that Slow Food further develops in its philosophy. Petrini, in fact, recognizes his cultural origins in the intellectual fervor of the postwar era, and the literary legends he is referring to are the ex-partisans and authors of the so-called literature of the Resistance. The Italian Resistance movement developed in northern Italy during World War II against Fascism and the German occupation. During the war many writers and intellectuals engaged in the partisan movement and the Resistance, and after the war many of them wrote novels and testimonials about the period. The authors that Petrini mentions are all from Piedmont. To Petrini, this body of literature is a means with which to root the organization's spirit of activism in the local history of resistance, a history that often includes hardship, as well as violence. As Serenella Iovino stresses, the Resistance in Piedmont, and the literature that emerged from it, discloses a violence that also includes ecological concepts: "This violence is not only the violence of the soldiers, but also that of vinedressers and peasants" (Iovino 2016, 130). Through Slow Food Carlo Petrini transforms the history of peasant poverty in northwest Italy into one of strength, thereby reclaiming its traditions through the culture of food.

Petrini considers peasants to be keepers of a cultural tradition who have the power to recuperate, rediscover, and revive the Italian agrarian past and Italy's culture of food. From the partisans' tradition of civil resistance during World War II, to the literature of resistance, Slow Food was initially known as a movement opposing the spread of McDonald's and other fast-food chains. While commercial food chains worked toward a standardized way of presenting, producing, conceiving, and consuming food, Slow Food understood that it was necessary to work on a local scale to counteract the virus of the sterile processed-food industry. Moreover, Carlo Petrini and Slow Food understood that the spread of industrial and fast food was not limited to Italian local food traditions but concerned a more global reality.

Today, Slow Food is present in 160 countries, has more than 100,000 members, and features thousands of international projects supporting local gastronomic traditions, food communities, and efforts toward ecological sustainability. In the last thirty years, with "local" as a key concept, Slow Food created over 450 presidia around the world, of which 262 are in Italy. These units sustain means of quality food production that risk extinction, revitalizing traditional food cultures, native breeds, and native plants. Today, the small red snail symbol on a food product is a guarantee of quality, both for those who produce and those who consume the food.

Vandana Shiva, past international vice president of Slow Food, has been engaged for the last thirty-five years as an environmental activist and intellectual in India and around the globe. In her preface to the Italian edition of *Slow Food Revolution*, Shiva compares her work as an activist to that of Carlo Petrini and acutely summarizes how, even if their premises are different, their efforts converge in ethics and values:

> Carlo Petrini started from the culture of food, I started from the ecology of food production; but it was inevitable that the celebration of taste would lead Carlo to biodiversity and to the small producers, and that the protection of biodiversity and sustainable agriculture would bring me to celebrate quality and taste. The convergence of the two movements connected to food—one originated from the land, the principles of ecology and sustainability, the other from the pleasure of the table, from the quality of food, from the variety and uniqueness of food cultures—has liberated new forces, new possibilities, a new creativity. (Petrini 2005, 9)[1]

Terra Madre is among the new forces to emanate from Slow Food. Founded in 2004, Terra Madre is an international network of food cultures and farmers that gathers every two years in Turin. It speaks directly to the need to recognize, make visible, and give space and a voice to food communities from all over the planet while supporting the idea of reviving local realities. As Petrini claims, "Terra Madre is a concrete way of putting into practice what has been defined as 'glocalism': a set of actions carried out on a local scale to generate major repercussions on a global scale" (2010, 1). Terra Madre has been thought of as a network linking rural communities, from farmers, to shepherds, to fishermen, to all those who, through their work, respect and support biodiversity. The first gathering of Terra Madre was held in 2004 and featured some five thousand people from 130 countries (see Petrini 2009, 22). During Terra Madre's biennial meeting, the international food communities meet to exchange and share their practices and knowledge. The term *global*, according to Petrini, can be understood using a more holistic approach, and, as Shiva claims, instead of a global system ruled by corporations and industry, *global* can refer to "our universal values as humans. . . . It can refer to humans as one species among many, which both differentiates us from, and connects us to, other species. We can experience the global belonging to the earth family" (Shiva 2005, 82).

In 2015, Slow Food and Terra Madre participated in several international events. The presence of Slow Food at the Milan World Expo, a six-month-long event whose theme was "Feeding the Planet, Energy for Life," helped counterbalance the general idea of food as a mere product to consume. Petrini also participated as spokesman for Terra Madre at the Second Global Indigenous Forum, organized by the International Fund for Agricultural Development (IFAD) in February 2015, confirming the fundamental role indigenous people play within the Terra Madre network.[2] If, on one level, Petrini's discourse at IFAD can be interpreted as a speech in praise of local and indigenous communities, in reality his words offer key points to reflect on his frequent assertion of a need for a paradigm shift. According to Petrini, the wisdom of indigenous people can be summarized in three main ideas: the sacred nature of food, respected and revered as a source and supporter of life; a life centered on the concept of community, be it the family, the village, or beyond; and finally, indigenous peoples' caring for the planet, which includes all forms of life. Considering a free market of food and food production as one of the weakest points of the current global economic system, and insisting on how our lives are based on greed and an indiscriminate consumerism, Petrini claims that the so-called First World and industrialized countries have lost touch with the complexity and potentials of food and that indigenous peoples can and must show us how to restore this connection. The paradigm shift here is therefore represented by a call from the First World to the Third World, meant to recapture lost principles such as the value of food and food producers, the sense of community, and of the planet we live on, in order to emerge from the current global economic, environmental, and social crises.

Simultaneously, in these moments of serious global ecological crisis, the First World appears to be starting to recognize these very principles. Due to the economic global crisis, but also thanks to a renewed environmental sensibility, many young people in Italy are choosing to return to the land. In 2014, agricultural studies saw a 72 percent increase in enrollment, and for the first time the University of Bologna had to introduce entrance exams to limit enrollments (see Segrè 2015, 11). According to a study led by Coldiretti, the leading organization of Italian farmers, in 2015 there was an increase in farming careers of 76 percent in women, 27 percent in men, under the age of thirty-four (Coldiretti 2016). According to the study, many of them are first-generation farmers. Half of them hold a university degree and are proud of their professional choices. Answering my question regarding the reality of new peasants and farmers in Italy, Petrini confirmed that the new generations are aware of what a rural life requires: "It is not the goal of these young generations returning to the land to invest in agriculture, and lead a wretched life like their predecessors. . . . They decide to undertake a profession that corresponds to a life style capable of offering a dignified life and, at the same time, in harmony with nature. . . . They often choose a multidisciplinary approach that allows them to integrate their revenue in diversified forms." This is the case, for example, of Genuino Clandestino ("Genuine Clandestine"). Founded in 2010 in Italy, Genuino Clandestino is a movement that fights for the right of "self-determination of food" (Potito and Borghesi 2015, 267). It is a self-organized, nonhierarchical movement based on practices of information, knowledge, production, and markets where producers and coproducers—the consumers—can meet and collaboratively create new forms of local resistance against industrial agriculture. It does not have a leader or spokesperson but is a matrix of several associations, small producers, farmers, shepherds, and other members of the rural economy throughout Italy who consider the land not only as a source of production but also and foremost a life choice. Genuino Clandestino rejects the notion that legislation regulating the food industry cannot and should not be applied to small-scale food production and packaging. As some of their members explain, the artisan characteristics of a product are expressed through the making of the product and its subsequent flavor. Such qualities are closely related to the place and cannot be standardized through a law. "How can you make a law governing the care, attention, aroma, in the porous asperity of an old wine cellar of a mountain village, or of a wood?" (Potito and Borghesi 2015, 34). Genuino Clandestino's questions evoke Petrini's holistic vision of the relationship between food, food cultures, and biodiversity, developed in projects like 10,000 Gardens in Africa or the Ark of Taste. Genuino Clandestino is also in line with the Gruppi di acquisto solidale or GAS (ethical purchasing groups), an economy developed in Italy in the late 1990s based on valuing the relationship between consumer and producer while practicing an ethical and environmentally conscious use of resources.

In 2015 Genuino Clandestino published a collection of stories of different Italian geographical areas, from Piedmont to Sicily. These pages narrate, through images and words, stories of sustainable practices of agriculture, respectful of and, as Petrini points out in his discourses on Terra Madre and Slow Food, in harmony with nature. This and other alternative economies, in Italy and around the world, support local and traditional knowledge and encourage a sense of community and connection with the consumers, those who support and coproduce the food, and the lands where the food is produced.

The University of Gastronomic Sciences, an international institution located in Pollenzo, near Bra, in Piedmont, exemplifies how Slow Food's ideas may enter the academy while maintaining a grassroots character. Established in 2004, the same year as Terra Madre, the University of Gastronomic Sciences is the first university to focus entirely on the intersection between food and food cultures. Its programs offer undergraduate and graduate degrees in disciplines related to gastronomy, food cultures and heritage, food ecologies, and many other areas of study related to food. As Petrini hosted and introduced the 2016 honorary degree ceremony dedicated to Michael Pollan—never forgetting that food quality is strictly related to those who produce it—he could not fail to remind his university students of the peasant origins of food and how academic theory has to be integrated with practice and experience: "We need the thoughts of the many who are around the World and we need the thoughts, not only of the intellectuals but also of those who are humble, the peasants, the shepherds and the nomads. . . . You know very well that these people represent the true intellectuality of the relationship with the land and food" (University of Gastronomic Sciences, 2016). Terra Madre's biennial gathering in Turin has the same focus.

In 2016 there were some crucial changes. The two biennial events, Salone del Gusto, which promotes quality and diversity of food, and Terra Madre, both supported by Slow Food and hosted during the same period in Turin, Piedmont, became one single event under the name "Terra Madre—Salone del Gusto." The purpose of unifying the two events was to make clear that "there cannot be gastronomic pleasure without responsibility and sustainability." In addition, the event was not enclosed in the space of a convention center but took place at some of the most prestigious historical sites in Turin. The thousands of farmers and food producers from around the world met and mingled with the city residents and made, as Petrini hoped for, "visitors and foreigners even more aware of the need to preserve our common heritage."[3] The common heritage is not only the local region of Piedmont, with its vineyard landscapes, hills and mountains, history and culture, but also our host planet, with its rivers, oceans, woods, valleys, plains, deserts, mountains, and nonhumans inhabitants. Starting from food, a very practical and material human need and source of pleasure, Slow Food, Terra Madre, and Carlo Petrini propose a new intellectual perspective and material culture: a political, social, economic, and, more importantly, ecological paradigm shift coming from below, from the margins, from the South of the world, wherever that might be, as a form of liberation from poverty, hunger, inequality, and ecological and human exploitation (see Petrini 2013, 7).

A Conversation with Carlo Petrini

Ilaria Tabusso Marcyan: In 2014, the vineyard landscapes in Piedmont in the area of Langhe-Roero and Monferrato were named world heritage sites by UNESCO, becoming the fiftieth Italian site with this recognition. This acknowledgment not only considerably impacts tourism in the area but also confirms how this landscape provides an outstanding example of human interaction with the natural environment. What was the cultural, historical, and environmental landscape when Slow Food was formed and started its journey? What is the relationship between the landscape as it was then and as it is now? How have the environmental and cultural ecologies of those places changed since Slow Food began, and how did Slow Food contribute to Italy's (and beyond) ecological vision of the places to which it relates?

Carlo Petrini: The Slow Food adventure started at the end of the eighties, in a cultural landscape very different than today's. Economic growth, an increase in consumption, and the availability of goods were the forces energizing society at the time. After World War II, the increase of intensive industrial agriculture changed the shape of our countryside, especially in the more modern areas of the Po Valley, while the marginalized areas were inevitably depopulating. Everything was changing, but we Italians seemed to be anesthetized, not fully aware of the eventual price to pay. The prevailing social ambition was to abandon the countryside to look for a better life in the city. In the collective imagination, the rural areas had always represented poverty, ignorance, and a life of toil.

Nevertheless, the first signs that something was going wrong were already becoming visible. We began to lose vegetable varieties and animals that, according to the new standards, were not producing enough. When peripheral areas were abandoned, we lost the distinctiveness of those areas. The vanishing of these less productive varieties led to the gradual disappearance of the typical products and dishes of these areas, a phenomenon that initially didn't seem too serious. It took a while to connect the dots, to understand that to lose peasant culture also meant to weaken local economies, to change farming and landscapes, to forget and destroy traditional forms of knowledge in the space of a few generations, and to consequently weaken the rural social fabric. There is still a long road ahead, but today there is more awareness of these topics. If Slow Food contributed to the changing perspectives on issues like production chains and landscape, I also hope that it helped us to value rural areas as a source of culture, as spaces of environmental safeguard, of a "real" economy.

ITM: Who are the new peasants and farmers in Italy today? What is the role of new migrants and how are they integrated into the Italian agricultural landscape?

CP: Italian rural reality today is very diverse. Most importantly, we are seeing young people return to the land, both in Italy and in other parts of the economically developed world. These young generations don't invest their lives in agriculture in order to lead a wretched life like their predecessors. They may have experienced the failure of the contemporary economic system and know that they don't identify with that model. Instead, they decide to take an uncharted path, one they are not unprepared for.

Today many educated young people return to the land because they understand that it is important to consider the quality of life when calculating for the future. They choose a profession that permits them to live a dignified life and, at the same time, one in harmony with natural rhythms. That is why those who decide to invest their lives in agriculture opt for more respectful farming techniques. They often choose a multidisciplinary approach that allows them to integrate their revenue in diversified forms (for example, by not just growing but also processing food, or by expanding their business to include hospitality and catering). And yes, there is the question of immigrants, without whom the renowned edibles "Product of Italy" could no longer be produced. There are more than 36,000 legal immigrants in Italy today, plus all those who are undocumented. These range from the Sikhs who take care of cattle in the Po valley, to the Macedonians who work in the vineyards, to people from the Maghreb who tend the mountain pastures, to the Africans in the fields of southern Italy. It is therefore a diversified landscape, complex and changing dramatically. As a civil society, it is our duty to make it possible for young people, and for immigrants, to envision a future of this kind. We could, for example, facilitate access to the land for those who have not inherited from their families, and monitor contracts in order for farmers to avoid living a life of abject poverty, if not that of a slave.

ITM: From the beginning, Slow Food has worked to protect and valorize farming and the production of local food. To have a Slow Food trademark on a food product marking a region or a specific area today is a guarantee of quality and goodness, both for those who sell and those who buy the product. Although your work and position have a democratic purpose, how would you answer the critiques of those who accuse you of promoting a message of elitism? What voice, visibility, and space do your producers have? By which culture is Slow Food inspired? What is the position of Slow Food with regard to the South (both Italian and global)?

CP: Quality food is not more expensive, it is simply more expensive than industrial food obtained from poor-quality raw materials. The real issue today is that food has lost its value. We can only recognize its price, and it has become a commodity. Yet this is not accurate. Being a source of life, food has, and needs to continue to have, a value of its own. If we don't eat, we die. We are what we eat. That is why, when we choose a food product to eat, it is important to think about what we are buying, what are we paying for. Are we paying for good, quality food, produced while respecting the environment? Do our food purchases respect the people working in the production chain? Do they support the local economy, safeguard the land, and keep the artisan knowledge that otherwise risks disappearing? Or are we choosing industrial food produced using more productive animal and vegetable species, food that undermines organoleptic and environmental quality? Food that creates profits for only a privileged few, while exploiting people and the environment? I rarely hear people complaining about the price of a cell phone. I believe we need to rethink our priorities. Today the industrial production of food is one of the primary causes of global pollution. This is a price that we are probably leaving for future generations to pay, but I can tell you right now, we are not saving money.

ITM: We live in a world in which local and global realities intersect, sometimes integrate, creating new cultural and culinary synergies. Today it is often possible to find exotic and international food items with competitive prices in local supermarkets. What is the position of Slow Food and Terra Madre regarding the relationship between traditional food and innovation, local and global food, in a world where distances become shorter and shorter, and where you can find pineapples and avocados in the fresh market of Porta Palazzo in Turin?

CP: The principles of sustainability that Slow Food supports do not aspire to the total autocracy of regions and nations. Throughout the history of humanity, goods have always traveled the world, creating infinite opportunities for contact and exchange between people.

In the same way, we cannot forget that a tradition is a successful innovation. Think, for example, of tomatoes, corn, or potatoes. They came from the Americas and today are the cornerstones of our gastronomy. Traditions change, evolve, and grow together with our history and stories. The pace of this change is not sustainable today; goods that are traveling today are not just the ones with a high surplus value. All kinds of simple fresh products, like fruits and vegetables, reach our tables after traveling across half the globe. The fact that these food products are cheaper than those cultivated locally cannot but make us reflect on the perversions of this system, a system that exploits, pollutes, and obviously does not provide a reasonable living wage to the workers in the production chain.

Slow Food wants to support sustainable production, to help the producers value their products, to support those who, in their daily work, perform a public service by safeguarding local gastronomic biodiversity. This is what Slow Food works for: to provide alternatives that allow people to make sustainable, edible choices.

NOTES

1. All translations in this essay are mine.
2. IFAD is a specialized agency of the United Nations established in 1977 to finance agricultural projects for food production in developing countries. More information can be found at www.ifad.org. Carlo Petrini's speech is available at https://www.youtube.com/watch?v=n-4PC6s35ZE.
3. Both quotes can be found in the announcement regarding the event, posted by Slow Food on December 1, 2015, with the title "Terra Madre Salone del Gusto 2016 Steps Outside!" See http://www.slowfood.com/terra-madre-salone-del-gusto-2016-steps-outside.

WORKS CITED

Coldiretti. 2016. "Lavoro: Coldiretti, con +76% è boom ragazze in campagna nel 2015." http://www.coldiretti.it/News/Pagine/77---4-Febbraio-2016.aspx.

Iovino, Serenella. 2016. *Ecocriticism and Italy: Ecology, Resistance, and Liberation*. London: Bloomsbury.

Petrini, Carlo. 2005. *Slow Food Revolution: Da Arcigola a Terra Madre. Una nuova cultura del cibo e della vita*. Milan: Rizzoli.

———. 2006. *Slow Food Revolution*. Translated by Francesca Santovetti. New York: Rizzoli International.

———. 2009. *Terra Madre: Come non farci mangiare dal cibo*. Bra, Italy: Slow Food Editore.

———. 2010. *Terra Madre: Forging a New Global Network of Sustainable Food Communities*. Translated by John Irving. White River Junction, VT: Chelsea Green Publishing.

———. 2013. *Food and Freedom. How the Slow Food Movement Is Changing the World through Gastronomy*. Translated by John Irving. New York: Rizzoli Ex Libris.

Potito, Michela, and Roberto Borghesi. 2015. *Genuino Clandestino: Viaggio tra le agri-culture resistenti ai tempi delle grandi opere*. Florence: Terra Nuova Edizioni.

Segrè, Andrea. 2015. *L'oro nel piatto*. Turin: Einaudi.

Shiva, Vandana. 2005. *Earth Democracy: Justice, Sustainability and Peace*. Cambridge, MA: South End Press.

University of Gastronomic Sciences. 2016. "Happy Birthday Carlo Petrini." Published on June 23. https://www.youtube.com/watch?v=jMw877PUeaA.

BODIES AND POLLUTIONS

4

MARCO ARMIERO

An Environmental Historian among Activists: The Political, the Personal, and a Project of Guerrilla Narrative

It was August 15, 2012. As always in the summer, Naples felt like a furnace; the streets on the outskirts were almost deserted. Egidio led us on his motorcycle; we followed in our car, crossing neighborhoods packed with cheap houses and dotted with shopping malls. Being a historian, I am not used to following my sources by car. I can follow a thread in the archive, I might even imagine the streets where the people I am writing about lived, but trying not to get lost while following them is not something I was trained for. Approaching a roundabout with a container covered with murals of the Chiaiano movement, we had to stop.

Traffic was blocked, and tables and chairs occupied the road. For once, this was not the neighborhood's usual picket line. Chiaiano is a working-class district in Naples's northern outskirts where in 2008 the special agency for Campania's waste emergency decided to open a gigantic landfill in the middle of a regional park. In response, a large part of the community began to mobilize, organizing legal actions, civil disobedience, and street blockades (Sgueglia 2015; Armiero and Sgueglia n.d.). Although the opposition to the landfill was fierce, including violent clashes with the police, ultimately, the landfill was opened. Most of the mobilization against the dump happened precisely in that roundabout, one of the innumerable traffic circles dotting a periphery with no *agora*, just high-speed roads leading to shopping malls. Just how the struggle against the landfill had transformed that roundabout into a lively place was appearing clearly before my eyes and, actually, nose. In fact, instead of the pungent smell of burning garbage there was the inviting aroma of Neapolitan cuisine. Many people were there, waiting to celebrate five years of resistance against the Chiaiano dump. It was a peculiar landscape, difficult to classify. The tables covered with traditional food suggested a folk festival rather than a political demonstration; however, the setting was neither a bucolic landscape nor some classic Italian historical neighborhood.

We ate among parked cars, under an urban sky of tall, cheap buildings and parabolic antennas. Here and there was the logo of the Chiaiano resistance: an angry tree holding a banner saying "Jatevenne"—"Go home" in Neapolitan dialect.

Indeed, in the lot behind those cheap buildings a wonderful forest had survived despite the rampant expansion of the metropolis, to become first a regional park—unfortunately understaffed and rather unknown—and later the location of a 700,000 ton landfill. Hence an angry tree inviting people to go home and leave the forest alone. Sitting at the tables were young activists from the local social center Insurgencia (Insurgency), middle-aged women who had been on the frontlines in the struggles against the dump, some older leftist militants, and two academics, my partner and me.[1]

The political ecologies of the struggles for environmental justice in Campania appeared before us, materializing in that hybrid urban landscape. The cheap and often illegal buildings told the story of the making of a subaltern neighborhood, compressed between the remains of a rural past—the forest—and the ruins of the urban present. The container with its graffiti and posters, the angry tree with its banner, testified to the struggles for environmental justice, while I directly experienced the making of a resistant community re-appropriating the urban space. Only a few years after that gathering, the same community—with Insurgencia as a leading political actor—would occupy a piece of land that used to belong to the camorra, the Neapolitan mafia, and transform it into a cooperative farm and a collective space for sociability. Not surprisingly, among activists the farm is known as the Selva Lacandona—the stronghold of the Zapatistas' insurgency; after all, isn't it an autonomous zone at one of the peripheries of global capitalism?

When I arrived at that gathering, I was an exotic guest from a professional and geographic elsewhere. I had lived abroad since 2005; I did not know that in following Egidio on his motorcycle I would enter a new territory that would change my way of thinking about my work and myself. Egidio introduced me to the participants as the one who told them who they were. Speaking in front of all these people he said something like: "What happened is that we were busy fighting and mobilizing, and then this guy from the US arrived and told us who we are and what we are doing." Egidio referred to a series of seminars I had offered on environmental justice (EJ) to the Neapolitan activists. I very much liked the way Egidio pictured me, how he explained who I was. It was in tune with my passion for storytelling. I was—and still am—more at ease being a storyteller than being a theory maker.

The festival of August 15, 2012, is a good place to start this essay. I was an environmental historian among activists, and it was a wonderful party.

Affected Researchers, or Keep the Windows Open

Apart from following Egidio on his roaring motorcycle, how did I end up at that party? And, more broadly, how did I find myself as an environmental historian among activists? Basically, I can tell two stories to explain this outcome. The most effective probably is what I call "the windows story," which, as any good foundational myth, has several variations. It goes something like this: I had started to envision a research project on waste in Naples, inspired by what occurred during a class with Donald Worster, one of the world's major environmental historians. In January 2009 we were together in Naples to teach a doctoral seminar, but Worster's class was heavily disturbed by the protests against the government's plan to deal with the waste emergency in Campania. His lecture was drowned out by the angry voices that erupted through the classroom windows, even louder than the usual Neapolitan traffic. He told me that instead of trying to insulate the room, it was better to let the confusion in, because after all environmental history was made to address those very issues. The day after Worster's class, I organized a tour of some waste facilities in the town of Giugliano for the PhD students. A group of activists drove us into the hell of mud and stink, explaining the links connecting toxic waste, the camorra, the emergency regime, and their private lives.

From a professional point of view the present is not my time. Throughout my career as a scholar I have always wondered about the past, as for example when I studied environmental conflicts related to the privatization of forests and the end of common property (Armiero 1999), or when I worked on the Vajont disaster, interpreting it as a major case of environmental injustice (Armiero 2011). Now, however, the voices from the street entered not only our classrooms, but also my head; the mud and the stench of Giugliano clung to my clothes, my ideas, my projects.

The windows story—however it actually happened—has all the ingredients of the classic activist's epiphany or conversion: a deeply sensorial experience penetrates into the everyday life of a "regular" person, changing it forever. But epiphanies and conversions do not happen in a vacuum. What the windows story does not say is why I was teaching environmental history with Donald Worster in the first place, and why I was ready to throw myself into the noise, mud, and stench of Campania's waste crisis.

The Historian, the Political Ecologist, and the Militant, or Looking for Something Finally Coming through the Window

I have never believed that things occur by chance; rather it seems to me that people fall into the stories they were looking for. I always had the impression of living in the wrong time, and who knows whether I would have ended up studying history were it not for this perennial chronological displacement. In the mid-1980s, having desperately looked for the slightest sign of political life during my high school years, I enrolled in the School of the Humanities in Naples, persuaded, with the arrogance of strong conviction, that I would become a historian, following the great tradition of Italian Marxist historiography. But my sense of temporal displacement continued; I discovered that labor and social historians were endangered species in the academic ecosystem, their near-extinction mainly due to their dramatic repentance rather than some harsh persecution. Maybe that is why I ended up looking to environmental history. I confess that I did not have a particular ecological sensitivity. The antinuclear movement was as far as I had gone into the realm of environmentalism. The option to take up environmental history was instead dictated by my hunger for a militant history that had not surrendered to the misery of the so-called end of ideologies, that continued to believe that an alternative story was possible. My personal history led me to be sensitive to the voices from Campania's environmental justice movements. It was the voice I was looking for.

I wrote up my research project, *Lares—Landscape of Resistance: Science, Power, and Environmental Justice in the Struggle over Garbage and Incinerators in Contemporary Naples, Italy* with great hesitancy; many advised me to soften the tone, to preserve an academic *super partes* aura, doubting that the European Union would finance a "militant" proposal. I chose another route, and for once the strange roulette of grant making favored me and my project. The most relevant part of my research was an oral history project with activists about their experiences in the struggles over waste. Rather than doing methodologically orthodox interviews, I was assembling a collection of oral histories, very open in form and substance. This choice marked a strong departure. I was studying people in flesh and blood: I learned not only that they were there with their voices, faces, diseases, and feelings but also that my words, my way of thinking, my face, my political history, even my car and the neighborhood where I grew up in Naples, became a piece of the research. The investigation became a practice of mutual disclosure.

A Guerrilla Narrative Project, or Stories Are Axes to Be Unearthed

When I arrived in Naples, I brought many readings on the movement for environmental justice with me from the United States. In 2009—10, the concept of environmental justice was almost unknown in Italy—with some exceptions (Iovino 2004). In fact, many of the people I contacted thought environmental justice was a branch of environmental legislation, rather than a social movement that has contributed to understanding environmental problems with attention to race, class, and gender. The assumption of environmental justice is that environmental costs and risks are not equally distributed among different social groups; some pay the bill for the welfare of others by being more exposed to contamination and pollution. In the United States ethnic minorities have become the ultimate dumping ground for all types of infrastructures and unwanted production, and that is why activists and scholars talk about environmental racism (Bullard 2000; Pulido 2000). The movement for environmental justice has voiced a radical critique of mainstream environmentalism and even the very idea of nature that it proposed (Melosi 2000). Instead of campaigning for the defense of patches of uncontaminated nature, endangered species, and the creation of parks, the movement for environmental justice focused attention on the environment closer to home, on the mixed ecologies of working and daily life and on the link between environment and health. The causal relationship between environmental exposure and illness is always difficult to prove and clearly demands awareness of the constructed statute of scientific knowledge and its epistemological legitimacy. Experts and scientists have the tools to reveal what is hidden from view, but they are not always willing to follow the complicated paths that connect objects, modes of production and consumption, toxic substances, and social inequalities. Often activists have become experts, producing and questioning knowledge, thereby forcing legitimate scientists to address uncomfortable issues. This was the case in Campania when grassroots organizations shifted attention from urban waste to toxic contamination (D'Alisa and Armiero 2013) or when they have been able to place the "Land of Fires" on the agenda of scientific and legislative institutions (Bonatti 2015). In his *Street Science* Jason Corburn tells a similar story about how citizens' organizations have been able to force the Environmental Protection Agency to change its opinion regarding the amount of fish in the diet of immigrants living in Brooklyn's Greenpoint/Williamsburg neighborhood (2005, 79–109). Examples like these demonstrate that environmental justice has been central to a significant paradigm shift that has questioned mainstream environmentalist cultures, the production and legitimization of knowledge, and broadly speaking the progressive narrative of economic growth and improvement of living conditions for all.[2]

With those readings in mind, I dove into the stories of waste in Campania. Obviously, I never thought of applying this unmediated model to the Campania case. However, that idea of environmental (in)justice helped me to see things that would otherwise have remained hidden, like the dioxin present in soils and bodies that only becomes visible when one looks for it. I started looking for injustice, going beyond the usual narrative about the waste crisis in Campania as a product of managerial inefficiency, corruption, and the camorra.

Despite many differences, I have also detected similarities between Campania and environmental justice cases in the United States. The most evident is the so-called path of least resistance, namely, the fact that in Campania, as for example in Chester, Pennsylvania, corporate and political powers have selected poor communities to become the ultimate dump, assuming that they would not have the resources to resist.[3] The role of activists in developing alternative knowledge—what Corburn (2005) has named "street science"—is another staple in environmental justice cases on both sides of the Atlantic. The same can be said about the role of women in those movements. In my fieldwork the centrality of women has emerged clearly; the great majority of the activists I interviewed were women, and I argue that this proves both their strong presence in the movement and their open and inclusive approach to mobilization. Nonetheless, gender identity does not obliterate any other difference. I have personally witnessed the conflict between those who have embraced motherhood as the main motivation of their mobilization—as for instance the grassroots groups called Mamme Vulcaniche (Volcanic mothers)—and others uncomfortable with conflating their identity as women activists with that of mothers.[4] In my research I have explained the centrality of women in the Neapolitan waste struggles on the basis of their social function within the community, often characterized by little outdoor work and an expectation of care within the family and in neighborhood relations, an explanation similar to the one offered by Adam Rome in relation to the participation of women in the 1960s US environmentalism (2003, 538).

In meeting with these women I realized that my academic attempt to build a different narrative of the waste crisis in Campania was not enough. Using interviews with activists for my publications seemed limited, even exploitative. Several considerations led me to conceive a different project. First was the idea of my experience as coresearch, in which the binary separation researcher/researched was blurred; coauthoring with activists was the logical consequence of that approach. In order to avoid any form of intellectual piracy, that is, the usual exploitation/extraction of communities' knowledge and concepts and their privatization as researchers' produced knowledge, I have coauthored several pieces with activists (Armiero 2014; Armiero and Fava 2016; Armiero and Sgueglia n.d.), and I plan to continue in that direction. Nonetheless, the very boundary between activists and scholars became porous and quite ambiguous. In my experience of coresearch, the transmutation of identity went in both directions, with activists who chose to pursue PhDs and scholars, as myself, who rediscovered a strong militant commitment.

However, these interviews were not merely sources in the hands of the knowledge producer, an instrumental tool for other aims. Rather the interviews were knowledge per se, and the very process of gathering them produced a counter-narrative of activists' collective history and identity. In this sense, by gathering my oral history collection I not only created my sources but also dialectically interfered with the making of a collective identity. One of the most important slogans of the American environmental justice movement says: "We speak for ourselves," meaning that activists do not want to be represented by anyone. For me that slogan also has another meaning: it refers to the narrative character of the movement. Activists speak in the first person and tell their stories, transmitting what they have learned and challenging the system that produced injustice by way of their stories. In her book *Ecocriticism and Italy* Serenella Iovino (2016) underlined the significance of collective storytelling in challenging the narrative monopoly and developing practices of liberation. Narrating means producing counter-narratives, because environmental injustice is not only imposed with tanks and truncheons but also with a narrative that eradicates any possible alternative, that requires an official truth, that criminalizes those who oppose.

Wu Ming, the Italian collective composed of radical novelists, has written that "stories are axes of war to be unearthed" (Ravagli and Wu Ming 2005). The idea of storytelling as an instrument of resistance is at the heart of my guerrilla narrative project *Teresa e le altre* (Teresa and the others, Armiero 2014). By the expression "guerrilla narrative" I mean the occupation of mainstream organized memory with counter-hegemonic storytelling and the sabotage of toxic narratives, that is, of narratives which reproduce or silence injustice (Barca 2014).[5] For a historian like myself, reclaiming the power of storytelling as means for resistance and social change has enormous appeal. Instead of trying to invent some kind of societal impact connected to policy making (as is ever more frequently requested in the carousel of grant applications), I took a chance and claimed that storytelling can be a powerful means for transformation. In the documentary (2009) inspired by her book *Shock Doctrine* (2007), Naomi Klein states that the shock doctrine is imposed not only through violence but also by erasing the stories of the targeted communities. Lois Gibbs (2014), the well-known leader of the Love Canal protests, anticipated Klein's argument when she said that the most precious weapon a community has to resist contamination is its own story. In *Teresa e le altre* nine women from the areas around Naples fraught with toxic and political pollution tell their autobiographies of struggle and contamination. These stories intertwine the personal and the political, the biological and the social. This is the case of Nunzia's illness and the painful contrast between the attachment to her community and the need to create some distance. She writes: "The experience of being sick has changed my life drastically. I had to strike a new balance between my civic engagement and my private life. . . . My departure from Marigliano [Nunzia's hometown] has been a difficult, painful choice, but it was needed for myself and my well-being" (Lombardi 2014, 39–40).

Illness is also present in Novella's writings when she explains how cancer has entered her daily familiar landscape through the growing number of female friends marked by the scars of chemotherapy. In Campania, Novella writes,

> we are all in the trenches, even those who do not realize it or pretend they do not know it. You can realize it from so many signs; from the dark smocks and the stink of the burning garbage. . . . You realize it by looking at the so many women who wear headscarves in order to cover the scars of chemotherapy. . . . Once, one of my neighbors told me that three out seven of her friends had a mastectomy. . . . Denying the truth is a war strategy. But then something will occur to your family, or to your friends or to you, something that will fling you into this waste war. (Vitale 2014, 128)

Both Doriana and Gigliola confess the naïveté of the dream they each had to buy a little corner of safety and well-being in some Neapolitan suburb, discovering soon that their single-family houses were built on the edges of massive dumps. For Gigliola the awareness of the environmental disaster hidden under the surface of the perfect American-style suburb materialized slowly: "We left the city and came to live here about twenty years ago. We were following our dream of a little house in the countryside, but close enough to the city, where we could raise our children. For many years we believed that our dream had come true. We had our single house with a nice backyard where we could play soccer and keep our dogs. Later we discovered another reality" (Izzo 2014, 65). Doriana, however, realized the power of the dump over her life almost immediately when she left the upper-class district of Posillipo to enter her new house in the Pianura neighborhood: "It was when we brought there our furniture that we started to feel it. The stink, the terrible, queasy, sweetish smell, which now is so familiar to me. This was how we discovered that our house was at less than one kilometer as the crow flies from the dump" (Sarli 2014, 103).

For all of these activist-narrators, the environmental injustice that they have suffered passed through diverse narratives that knit together their lives, communities, and environments.

In stories of conversion the protagonists must change dramatically their lives. Either you fall from a horse or follow Egidio's motorcycle; the transformation must be radical. In my case as well as in the biographies of several activists, what may be seen as a conversion is rather the reactivation of dormant passions and choices. The trope of conversion goes beyond personal biography and affects the very idea of what it means to be a politically engaged scholar.

Too often, it seems to imply a sort of transfiguration; one must stop being a scholar and become something else, maybe a journalist, a lobbyist, or a politician. I argue, instead, that the challenge is to be politically engaged specifically as a scholar. What is more political than telling the histories of oppression and resistance which are invisible in the mainstream narrative? As an environmental historian my aim is not only to analyze the relationships between humans and nature but to see how power or, more particularly, gender, class, and race have informed the socio-ecological formations of societies. Studying the mountain communities resisting the privatization of the commons, hydro-capitalism imposing dams and reservoirs, or entrepreneurs and mafia contaminating poor neighborhoods in southern Italy is political. Speaking truth to power is a political act. This is what environmental history looks like, whether listening to the voices of the Vajont massacre or following Egidio to an urban picnic.

NOTES

1. The Centri Sociali (Social Centers) are old, abandoned buildings squatted by young activists and transformed into centers for political, cultural, and recreational activities.
2. On these topics, see Agyeman, Bullard, and Evans (2003) and Sandler and Pezzullo (2007).
3. On this, see the documentary *Laid to Waste: A Chester Neighborhood Fights for Its Future* (Bahar and McCollough 1996).
4. On the debate over essentialism in feminist studies, see Gaard (2011).
5. For the concept of toxic narratives I am indebted, once more, to Wu Ming.

WORKS CITED

Agyeman, Julian, Robert D. Bullard, and Bob Evans. 2003. *Just Sustainabilities: Development in an Unequal World*. London: Earthscan.
Armiero, Marco, ed. 1999. *Il territorio come risorsa: Comunità, economie e istituzioni nei boschi abruzzesi (1806–1860)*. Naples: Liguori.
———. 2011. *A Rugged Nation: Mountains and the Making of Modern Italy*. Cambridge, UK: White Horse Press.
———. 2014. *Teresa e le altre. Storie di donne nella Terra dei Fuochi*. Milan: Jaca Book.
Armiero, Marco, and Anna Fava. 2016. "Of Humans, Sheep, and Dioxin: A History of Contamination and Transformation in Acerra, Italy." *Capitalism Nature Socialism* 27(2): 67–82.
Armiero, Marco, and Leandro Sgueglia. n.d. "Wasted Spaces, Resisting People: The Politics of Waste in Naples, Italy." Manuscript.
Bahar, Robert, and George McCollough, producers. 1996. *Laid to Waste: A Chester Neighborhood Fights for Its Future*. Berkeley, CA: Berkeley Media LLC (DVD).
Barca, Stefania. 2014. "Telling the Right Story: Environmental Violence and Liberation Narratives." *Environment and History* 20(4): 535–46.
Bonatti, Valeria. 2015. "Mobilizing around Motherhood: Successes and Challenges for Women Protesting against Toxic Waste in Campania, Italy." *Capitalism Nature Socialism* 26(4): 158–75.

Bullard, Robert D. 2000. *Dumping in Dixie: Race, Class, and Environmental Quality.* Boulder, CO: Westview Press.

Corburn, Jason. 2005. *Street Science: Community Knowledge and Environmental Health Justice.* Cambridge, MA: MIT Press.

D'Alisa, Giacomo, and Marco Armiero. 2013. "What Happened to the Trash? Political Miracles and Real Statistics in an Emergency Regime." *Capitalism Nature Socialism* 24(4): 29–45.

Gaard, Greta. 2011. "Ecofeminism Revisited: Rejecting Essentialism and Re-placing Species in a Material Feminist Environmentalism." *Feminist Formations* 23(2): 26–53.

Gibbs, Lois. 2014. "October 4, 2014—West Lake Landfill—Teach-In: Lois Gibbs, CHEJ [Center for Health and Environmental Justice], and Love Canal." https://www.youtube.com/watch?v=SfjoeWIRJ6s.

Iovino, Serenella. 2004. *Filosofie dell'ambiente: Natura, Etica, Società.* Rome: Carocci.

———. 2016. *Ecocriticism and Italy: Ecology, Resistance, and Liberation.* London: Bloomsbury.

Izzo, Gigliola. 2014. "Dal presidio di Taverna del Re sono tornata cambiata." In *Teresa e le altre: Storie di donne nella Terra dei Fuochi,* edited by Marco Armiero, 65–72. Milan: Jaca Book.

Klein, Naomi. 2007. *The Shock Doctrine: The Rise of Disaster Capitalism.* New York: Macmillan.

———. 2009. *The Shock Doctrine: The Rise of Disaster Capitalism.* DVD. Directed by Michael Winterbottom and Mat Whitecross. Pdxjustice Media Production.

Lombardi, Nunzia. 2014. "Il mio nome è Nunzia." In *Teresa e le altre: Storie di donne nella Terra dei Fuochi,* edited by Marco Armiero, 19–42. Milan: Jaca Book.

Melosi, Martin. 2000. "Equity, Eco-Racism, and the Environmental Justice Movement." In *The Face of the Earth: Environment and World History,* edited by J. Donald Hughes, 47–75. Armonk, N.Y.: M. E. Sharpe.

Pulido, Laura. 2000. "Rethinking Environmental Racism: White Privilege and Urban Development in Southern California." *Annals of the Association of American Geographers* 90(1): 12–40.

Ravagli, Vitagliano, and Wu Ming. 2005. *Asce di guerra.* Turin: Einaudi.

Rome, Adam. 2003. "'Give Earth a Chance': The Environmental Movement and the Sixties." *Journal of American History* 90(2): 525–54.

Sandler, Ronald D., and Phaedra C. Pezzullo, eds. 2007. *Environmental Justice and Environmentalism: The Social Justice Challenge to the Environmental Movement.* Cambridge, MA: MIT Press.

Sarli, Doriana. 2014. "Da Posillipo a Pianura, solo andata." In *Teresa e le altre: Storie di donne nella Terra dei Fuochi,* edited by Marco Armiero, 101–12. Milan: Jaca Book.

Sgueglia, Leandro. 2015. "Generi, Commoning e diritto alla città. Il caso dei movimenti urbani della periferia nord di Napoli." PhD diss., Università degli Studi di Napoli "Federico II."

Vitale, Novella. 2014. "Nessun veleno in nessuna terra." In *Teresa e le altre: Storie di donne nella Terra dei Fuochi,* edited by Marco Armiero, 124–40. Milan: Jaca Book.

ANDREA HAJEK

We Will Not Tremble: Healing the Body Politic in Post-Earthquake Emilia-Romagna

It was 4 a.m. when the cats woke me up—they wanted to go out, rather urgently. Nothing out of the ordinary; sadly their weak bladders are a common feature of our night lives. As I started back up the stairs, my sleepy eyes eager to return to the land of dreams, the muteness of the countryside suddenly turned to a hellish howling as the house started to shake and roar. My first, semi-rational explanation for this terrifying noise was that we were being bombed by some mysterious enemy, while the irrational part of my brain told me the house was haunted and had come alive. Subsequently I realized that what was really going on had nothing to do with political science fiction or the supernatural and that I had best get myself to safety. At the end of the night it was simply an earthquake.

Thus, in May 2012 the allegedly non-seismic region of Emilia-Romagna literally woke up to a nasty surprise: in the course of only ten days, two heavy earthquakes struck the predominantly agricultural hinterland of Bologna, the region's capital.[1] Although fatalities were limited and the material damage not nearly as dramatic as in the case of the L'Aquila earthquake of 2009, which saw the historical center of the ancient city almost entirely destroyed, the very significant productive force of Emilia-Romagna was severely damaged, with thousands of companies forced to reduce labor force, temporarily relocate, or close down all together.[2] Within six months of the earthquakes in Emilia-Romagna, 40,752 workers in 3,738 production units found themselves collecting unemployment insurance. Clearly the earthquake had affected a part of the country that draws on a very strong industry and agriculture, and as such it distinguished itself from previous earthquakes in Italy, which often occurred in less densely inhabited and less productive areas. It was also one of few earthquakes of this dimension to have struck the northern part of Italy, and because the region was not officially at risk of seismic activity, it was a particularly destabilizing event.[3] Finally, we must take into consideration the specific historical moment in which the 2012 quakes occurred, that is, when the financial crisis was already affecting the region's productive force.

In addition to the severe blow to the region's agriculture and industries, 42,000 people had to be evacuated and were moved to *tendopoli* camps run by the Protezione Civile, the Italian Civil Protection Agency. The agency had suffered a bad reputation since the L'Aquila earthquake in 2009; the rigid and hierarchical management of this earthquake by the Protezione Civile had nullified any possibility of democratic reconstruction. Most significantly, the affected citizens were relocated to hotels far away from their community or into the so-called New Towns, which both isolated people from the urban context and eliminated collective places of socialization. The Italian political class and the state had also failed the citizens of L'Aquila: they were unable to prevent acts of negligence and corruption and contributed to the overall mismanagement of the reconstruction process, with the near complete abandonment of Abruzzo's capital in subsequent years. L'Aquila thus served very much as a negative example or warning for Emilia-Romagna, yet at the same time it offered a positive and constructive model of how to deal with such a traumatic event and rebuild the local body politic.

In this essay I will discuss two such initiatives that were promoted in the wake of the 2012 earthquakes in Emilia-Romagna. The first was a grassroots project launched by two politically engaged youth centers (the so-called *centri sociali*) based near the area most affected by the earthquakes, which aimed at breaking the rigid schemes of the Protezione Civile and offering an alternative form of emergency management more in harmony with the emotional and social needs of the disrupted community. The second project was promoted by a cultural association from L'Aquila and was more focused on the idea of symbolically and visually healing the wounds of the affected community, both in its material and human manifestations. The two initiatives demonstrate how the earthquake changed the citizens' living and working environment, forcing them both to defend their political environment and to reconstruct their social environment in an unprecedented and highly unexpected situation. As Serenella Iovino observes in *Ecocriticism and Italy*, when an earthquake hits a community "a world is undone," and citizens are called "to reconstruct their emotional and material dimension" and "re-inhabit a world literally suspended on its own end" (2016, 85–86). Similarly, Giacomo Parrinello in *Fault Lines*, "disasters should be seen as 'processes' rather than 'events,' for they are rooted in the long-term interplay between the features of a human settlement and society and its biogeophysical environment" (2016, 4). They are therefore more than mere geographical events: they are "historical patterns of institutional response to and 'social memory' of hazardous events," and consequently they are always "the product of the historical interplay between geophysical forces and features..., but also the social and economic resources of the population" (Parrinello 2016, 4). These historical patterns have been strongly at play in the case of Emilia-Romagna, and in this essay I will discuss the impact of the social memory of the L'Aquila earthquake (and its mismanagement by the Protezione Civile) on communities and institutions in Emilia-Romagna, as they develop new understanding and practices in their response to the 2012 earthquakes.

Learning from L'Aquila

The L'Aquila earthquake occurred on April 6, 2009, with a magnitude between 5.8 and 5.9 and with the epicenter near the city. The quake killed 309 people, injured 1,600 people, and left 65,000 homeless. It caused 10 billion euros of damage. Other than the mismanagement of the emergency situation, the L'Aquila earthquake left what Iovino calls a "landscape of wounds: material wounds inflicted on the historic urban fabric as well as on important portions of the natural heritage; and moral and social wounds inflicted to the citizenship's political fabric and cultural identity" (2016, 84). As such it is a good example of "slow violence," when destruction "unfolds over time, pushing communities (especially agricultural ones) back in their 'evolutionary' path of economic progress" (Iovino 2016, 85). Consequently, the reconstruction process in L'Aquila has led to strong tensions between institutional aid, coming from above, and community interventions from below (see Petrei 2012). The former is reflected primarily through the intervention of the Protezione Civile, the *tendopoli* camps, and the New Town projects.

The Protezione Civile was created in 1992 with the aim of safeguarding citizens from damage (or the risk of damage) afflicted by natural disasters and catastrophes. It wasn't long until the Protezione Civile became assimilated with the politics of former prime minister Silvio Berlusconi, who increasingly employed the Protezione Civile for the management of major political and sporting events (Hajek 2013, 629). According to Fabrizia Petrei, it seems to have contributed to the creation of "a unanimous consensus block at national and international level which gives credibility to the idea that it is possible to emerge from the drama [of the earthquake] thanks to the intervention of a team (that of the Protezione Civile), which has a strong symbolic value and which proposes itself as an a-politic actor, as a neutral and operating mediator, in which citizens can confide with 'trust' and hope" (Petrei 2012, 42–43).

It allowed Berlusconi to become the leading figure and personal spokesperson for the government after the L'Aquila earthquake, turning it into a highly mediatized event. This is illustrated perhaps best by Sabina Guzzanti's satirical imitation of Berlusconi in her critical documentary, Draquila: Italy Trembles (2010), where Berlusconi/Guzzanti makes the following declaration:

"This earthquake has been a great success. No other earthquake has drawn so much audience as that of L'Aquila."

Part of this attempt to impose on citizens, from above, a system of reconstruction that would create consensus for Berlusconi's leadership was the way the *tendopoli* camps were organized. Drawing on Franco Basaglia's denunciation of the institutionalization of the mentally ill, Emanuele Sirolli introduces the concept of "syndrome of institutionalization" to describe the situation in the *tendopoli*, where control from above is felt constantly and also physically, in the first place through the presence of soldiers and the existence of rules and curfews limiting movement (Sirolli 2012, 63–64).[4] The very concept of the *tendopoli* implies that the inhabitants of the camps are isolated and in a sense "expelled" from society. Moreover, the formal and centralized organization of the *tendopoli*, with their rigid spatial and temporal rituals, contributes to the effect of institutionalization, "passivization," and what Alberto Puliafito calls "the infantilization of the displaced people" (Puliafito 2010, 22). This enhances the persistent sense of trauma, or the "slow violence" of earthquakes. Scholarly research has argued that an event's impact, and not the actual event in itself, constitutes trauma, if we understand trauma not in its original, clinical meaning of a psychological and neurological condition but as a socially mediated attribution that can affect a group of people. This depends on the importance the event is given in the public sphere and, more generally, the way it is managed within a community. Here the displacement and isolation of people from their original environment, along with the political and economic power games that have marked the post-earthquake process, disrupt the relation between private and public bodies. As Iovino explains, a "'galvanization of power' . . . takes place as central and local governments are called to rule the emergency, transforming political reality into a perennial state of exception corporeally played on the body politic" (2016, 85). In other words, when the process of material reconstruction fails to comply with a psychological and social reconstruction of the body politic, the trauma persists (see Sirolli 2012, 65).

In a similar way, the New Towns—a mass of nineteen buildings in a peripheral area for some 15,000 displaced people—again isolated people from the urban context. Nor did they offer much opportunity for social aggregation activities (see Sirolli 2012, 61). This resulted in a sense of "disorientation" (Carnelli 2012, 70–71) or displacement, both literally (that is, in a geographical or spatial sense) and psychologically, as people felt lost on the territory itself but also within their community. Consequently the New Towns reflect an imposition of a sudden change of life styles and, as such, represent the "slow violence" of the post-earthquake situation. The L'Aquila reconstruction process also produced a series of incidents of political corruption, economic speculation, and negligence. All this shows once again that earthquakes don't come alone and that geology reacts in combination with politics and society: "top-down decisions over people and territories, in landscapes and ecosystems gradually sacrificed to 'reconstruction,' and in the formation of new political and economic elites, which are often corrupted and not rarely criminal" (Iovino 2016, 85).

The fact that the political system has proven unable to guarantee territorial well-being resulted in a "democratic deficit" (Calandra 2012, 28), thus illustrating the shattering of what historian Giovanni De Luna has called—in a different yet not entirely unrelated context—a "pact of citizenship," that is, a pact between citizens and the state "on the basis of which the State guaranteed truth and justice in return for loyalty and trust" (2008, 16). In general, the relationship between citizens and the state has been problematic in Italy ever since its unification in the nineteenth century. John Foot speaks about this in terms of a legitimation crisis which has given space to "unwritten 'rules' that have institutionalized patronage, clientelism, and informal modes of behaviour and exchange" (Foot 2009, 29). It also forced Italians to solve their own problems, as David E. Alexander suggests in his work on natural disasters, where often "self-help was the only form of aid" (2002, 167–71). In the case of earthquakes a similar "pact of citizenship" regards the relation of citizens with politics and especially with their territory, which can only be reestablished by a new form of political action where those who inhabit the territory play an active role (Calandra 2012, 30, 33). The need for people to participate, actively, in the reconstruction of their homes and the return to a daily routine that was lost is indeed crucial for people to overcome the trauma of an earthquake, which represents not only an individual but also a collective wound, as sociologist Kai Erikson observes when he explains that collective trauma is "a blow to the basic tissues of social life that damages the bonds attaching people together and impairs the prevailing sense of communality" (quoted in Alexander 2004, 4). Moreover, in the case of earthquakes the wound is also a very material wound, visible in the landscape and in the fabric of the affected cities, as we will see in this essay.

This has occurred in many post-earthquake situations in Italy. As Iovino explains in her essay on the three earthquakes of Belice (1968), Irpinia (1980), and L'Aquila (2009), there is often a "repercussion on community life and narratives, and the creative ways of social self-representation they have enacted" (2016, 4). Indeed, a number of such community activities developed after the earthquake in L'Aquila, mostly through the use of new technologies and citizen journalism. One example of this is the Noi, L'Aquila website created only a few months after the earthquake, which collects memories, stories, and photographs by citizens. The very title ("We, L'Aquila") suggests a convergence of human subjects and the affected territory itself, and as such reflects the need for the private and the public bodies to become one again. In their study of the commemorative website, Manuela Farinosi and Alessandra Micalizzi demonstrate how, in the stories published on the website, public places or places "traditionally linked with the community memory of the city" prevail over other locations. They argue that "local memory websites, combining digital media, memory and locality, offer citizens a space to collect and share their narratives about particular places or experiences in their city, helping to maintain an indigenous story . . . and contributing to the social sustainability of a given community" (Farinosi and Micalizzi 2015, 93).

In doing so Noi, L'Aquila contrasts with the national, mainstream media that focus on the tragedy of the earthquake, giving very little space to individual voices and only in terms of passive victimhood. Farinosi and Micalizzi conclude from this that storytelling represents a "powerful and useful tool for the processing of trauma" (2015, 95).[5] Other forms of political activism that originated after the L'Aquila earthquake were open government, which implies openness and transparence in communal administrations, and co-working. This transformed citizens from passive recipients of decisions into active social actors in a bottom-up process (Petrei 2012, 47). In what follows we will focus on two different forms of engagement that took shape in Emilia-Romagna after the 2012 earthquakes, one more radical and with a political undertone, the other more creative and engaging a wider community, yet both aimed at rebuilding the community's body politic. Here the very idea of a body politic, that is, the sense that the community exists as a corporate entity much like the human body, is particularly relevant due to the blow to the very material and geographic unity—or body—of a community, as well as the material *identity* of the affected region, and through that the community's political, economic, and ecological identity.

Rebuilding the Body Politic: *Dal basso alla bassa*

The reconstruction process in Emilia-Romagna drew strongly on a social memory of previous earthquakes and, in particular, that of L'Aquila, and by fear of a "repeating pattern" in Italy's seismic history (Iovino 2016, 110). Moreover, the still very active presence of radical left-wing protest groups in Emilia, especially in cities like Bologna and Modena, as well as the communist legacy of what Togliatti once called "red Emilia," may also explain why several forms of grassroots activism rose up to defend the local body politic and avoid a fate similar to L'Aquila, where seven years later more than 11,000 people were still homeless (Arduini 2016).

The first project that developed in the wake of the two earthquakes was launched by the social center Guernica from Modena, which received support from a *centro sociale* based in Bologna. *Dal basso alla bassa* was a grassroots project offering citizens a bottom-up solution to the emergency situation, in stark contrast with the rigid schemes of the Protezione Civile.[6] Thus, the self-managed *tendopoli* Guernica set up in one of the most affected areas was meant as a sort of counter-space to the camps run by the Protezione Civile and as such centered not so much on the provision of food, clothes, and other basic necessities but on "the promotion of a sense of continuity and community that had lacked in post-earthquake L'Aquila" (Hajek 2013, 634). As one of the organizers of the alternative camps commented in a video for the independent online news portal *Infoaut*, the camps became "a moment of social cooperation free of the protezione civile and other more institutional organisms."[7] The organizers explain the activities as follows: "Other than the material distribution, we started to organize playful or socializing initiatives, like a BBQ on the day of the inauguration of the storage room, which saw over 150 participants. In fact we think it is important to also create occasions of relaxation in a severely damaged territory."[8]

The task of re-creating a sense of normality and daily routine, fundamental for a community affected by a natural disaster, was carried out not only through the "playful" initiatives and social moments in the actual camps but also on social media such as Facebook and in a photographic exhibition, which offered a very different perspective on the earthquake (as opposed to mainstream media): it showed people as more than mere victims and evacuees who have lost their homes. In other words, both the offline and online activities promoted by the *centri sociali* focused on the social reconstruction process, mostly by creating different, more fluid spaces with stronger ties to the actual territory, as opposed to the isolating spaces in post-earthquake L'Aquila. They therefore tried to prevent the imposition of that sense of "disorientation" that the Protezione Civile had afflicted on people in L'Aquila and, accordingly, the traumatic effect that the management of the L'Aquila earthquake had provoked. Instead, the grassroots project emphasized "the importance of creating spaces and occasions of social aggregation by capturing daily life moments" (Hajek 2013, 635).

That this specific approach to the post-earthquake situation is due to the strong presence of a social memory of the L'Aquila earthquake becomes evident in the following statement: "Once again the State vanishes in the fog when it comes to the emergency, and abandons the citizens to the solitude of the devastation. . . . The memory of L'Aquila is still alive: the government and the protezione civile (with their cameras) only showed up after the Aquilans, left to themselves, started pulling out of the ruins the first lifeless bodies."[9]

We should not, however, lose sight of the political agenda that is always at the basis of the *centri sociali*, and which resurfaces in the Dal basso alla bassa project as well. Indeed, I would argue that the latter had an explicit political connotation which went beyond the mere aim of bringing humanitarian aid. Thus the *centri sociali* extend their criticism of the Protezione Civile to building speculation, corruption, and the wider economic consequences of the earthquake on local workforce (Hajek 2013, 636–37). More interestingly, Guernica used a space that was illegally occupied by the *centro sociale* for the storage of the collected material that was to be distributed among the evacuees of their alternative *tendopoli*. In other words, the project seemed to serve the purpose of something of a protection shield against the continuous risk of eviction by local authorities. Hence, although Dal basso alla bassa represents a good attempt at rebuilding the community's body politic, to some extent I believe there was a political and slightly self-referential strategy behind the project.

Mettiamoci una pezza

A second project that developed in the wake of the 2012 earthquakes was again strongly linked to L'Aquila. It was in fact promoted by a local association from L'Aquila itself, Animammersa, created in November 2009, which describes itself as the "affirmation of the social and cultural identity of L'Aquila."[10] Founded by five local artists, it has promoted a number of cultural initiatives (mostly theatrical or musical performances) that narrate the experiences of the city and its inhabitants as they struggle with a natural and economic disaster and in doing so give value to the local heritage.[11]

Perhaps the best example of the community rebuilding by healing their wounds was the initiative called "Mettiamoci una pezza" ("Let's patch this up"). The initiative consisted of bringing to Emilia-Romagna colored patches of wool or cotton to literally cover the damaged or destroyed buildings of the most affected towns. In a symbolic yet literal sense, the wounds of the landscape were patched up by small pieces of artwork knitted by people from across the country and attached to the fences encircling damaged buildings. Moreover, the use of woollen yarn and the patchwork technique gave the initiative an additional meaning of solidarity and collectiveness. Much like the famous AIDS Memorial Quilt created in memory of AIDS victims, the initiative was inspired by the practice of urban knitting and reflects an attempt to confront the trauma of the earthquake as it is felt on a daily basis by the local community. This is also a very tangible trauma, where buildings and other parts of the city (trees, statues, benches) become hurt bodies that need to be safeguarded. Interestingly, some of the patchwork contains illustrations or photographs of damaged buildings in their original state, for example, in a child's drawing of the tower of Finale Emilia. The patchwork thus helped reenvision the buildings in their original and "healthy" pre-earthquake condition.

The initiative had been promoted a year earlier in L'Aquila and was then exported to Emilia in 2013. The patches—being sown by people from all over the country—reflected the solidarity of the entire country with the locals and through that the idea of a body politic that extended beyond the single region. To use the words someone knitted on a piece of patchwork, "We are each of us *angels with* only *one wing*, and we can only fly by embracing one another." Undoubtedly the sense of disorientation suffered extensively by the L'Aquila citizens after the 2009 earthquake urged them to seek wider networks across the country and to stand by their brothers and sisters in Emilia-Romagna. The patches also served, though, as an explicit denunciation of the slow violence that continued to affect L'Aquila: "The city of L'Aquila and its slow reconstruction returned in the eye of the media, thanks to the fitting of over 6,000 patches on the monuments of the historical city centre that needed protection or on the ugly and grey parts that needed to be cancelled out."[12]

Finally, the idea of visually covering or "patching up" the material wounds of the damaged buildings through mosaics of colored patches served the purpose of reweaving the ties of the fractured community and thus again to rebuild the body politic in a symbolic way. In sum, the project reflects those "new expressive energies of resistance" that Iovino describes as: "re-weaving the warps of their existences and knitting them with the woof of their lands in even stronger fabrics" (Iovino 2016, 86–87).

Haunted/ing Houses

Although our home had not suffered serious material damage, the emotional impact of the earthquake lingered. The house remained haunted for several days after the earthquake, in particular on one rainy night—worthy of the best of crime novels—when we slept in our car, and I literally sneaked through the abandoned house when it was my turn to empty my bladder. Two years later I still got goose bumps whenever the Glasgow subway passed under my flat in the West End. Today I am reminded of the tragedy whenever I walk by the crumbled, medieval tower of my town hall.

I guess this is part of the slow violence that accompanies earthquakes and which the two projects discussed here tried to deal with in their own ways. Their challenge was primarily to prevent the displaced people in Emilia-Romagna from falling victim to the democratic deficit that marked the reconstruction process in the case of L'Aquila and which so strongly damaged the pact of citizenship that holds together different private and public bodies, as illustrated by the bitter words of L'Aquila's former mayor in 2013: "One does not abandon a piece of the community like this." Both projects aimed at rehabilitating the body politic by rejoining the material territory, the social environment, and the community at large. In other words, they set out to reweave the ties of the fractured community by addressing the challenges not only of material reconstruction but, more importantly, the reconstruction of the natural and social environment fundamental for the survival of a community's identity.

NOTES

1. The two quakes on May 20 and 29, 2012, registered magnitudes of 5.9 and 5.8 (on the Richter scale) respectively and caused the deaths of twenty-seven people. The first quake was at a depth of 6.3 km, and its epicenter was Finale Emilia, in the province of Modena (although the adjacent provinces of Ferrara and Bologna were also severely affected); the second quake was at a depth of 9.6 km, with the epicenter in Medolla, again in the province of Modena.

2. Emilia-Romagna is one of the most productive agricultural and industrial regions in Italy, with over 420,000 mostly small and medium-sized companies, and its GDP is among the highest in the country. The area affected by the earthquake counts 550 thousand inhabitants and almost 50,000 companies from all economic sectors, for a total of 190,000 employees. See http://www.jobbe.it/it/lemilia-romagna-in-cifre/; and http://www.regione.emilia-romagna.it/terremoto/sei-mesi-dal-sisma/approfondimenti/il-documento-completo-della-regione-emilia-romagna.

3. One exception is the Friuli earthquake of 1976, with a magnitude of 6.5. It killed almost one thousand people and left 45,000 homeless.

4. Franco Basaglia was a radical Italian psychiatrist and mental health reformer, known best for having closed psychiatric hospitals in Italy.

5. On the idea of storytelling, see Iovino (2016).

6. The title of the project literally translates as "From below to the lowland area," in the sense of reaching out to someone; *basso* refers to the grassroots character of the project (from below), and *bassa* is the colloquial term for the agricultural lowland area that was struck by the earthquake.

7. See https://youtu.be/F44erTkqnFc.

8. Accessed originally at http://www.infoaut.org/index.php/nodi/modena/item/5132-dal-basso-alla-bassa-cosa-stiamo-facendo; page since removed.

9. Accessed originally at http://www.infoaut.org/index.php/blog/varie/item/4848-dal-basso-alla-bassa-anche-a-; page since removed.

10. See https://mettiamociunapezza.wordpress.com/chi-siamo/.

11. For "Lettere da L'Aquila," for example, stories by locals were gathered and transformed into performances, drawing on songs from local traditions. https://mettiamociunapezza.files.wordpress.com/2012/02/animammersa-presentazione-spettacolo-lettere.pdf.

12. See http://mettiamociunapezza.wordpress.com/il-progetto/.

WORKS CITED

Alexander, David E. 2002. "The Evolution of Civil Protection in Modern Italy." In *Disastro! Disasters in Italy since 1860: Culture, Politics, Society*, edited by John Dickie, John Foot, and Frank M. Snowden, 165–85. New York: Palgrave Macmillan.

Alexander, Jeffrey C. 2004. "Toward a Theory of Cultural Trauma." In *Cultural Trauma and Collective Identity*, edited by Jeffrey C. Alexander, Ron Eyerman, Bernhard Giesen, Neil J. Smelser and Piotr Sztompka, 1–30. Berkeley: University of California Press.

Arduini, Clelia. 2016. "L'Aquila, la ricostruzione e i segni di rinascita." Touring Club Italiano. http://www.touringclub.it/notizie-di-viaggio/laquila-la-ricostruzione-e-i-segni-di-rinascita.

Calandra, Lina M. 2012. "Territorio e democrazia: considerazioni dal post-sisma aquilano." In *Sismografie. Ritornare a L'Aquila mille giorni dopo il sisma*, edited by Fabio Carnelli, Orlando Paris, and Francesco Tommasi, 27–35. Rome: Edizioni Effigi.

Carnelli, Fabio. 2012. "Esserci a Paganica (L'Aquila), II anno d.T." In *Sismografie. Ritornare a L'Aquila mille giorni dopo il sisma*, edited by Fabio Carnelli, Orlando Paris, and Francesco Tommasi, 67–78. Rome: Edizioni Effigi.

De Luna, Giovanni. 2008. "Introduzione: Violenza, verità, giustizia." In *La piuma e la Montagna: Storie degli anni '70*, edited by Francesco Barilli and Sergio Sinigagli, 11–31. Rome: Manifestolibri.

Farinosi, Manuela, and Alessandra Micalizzi. 2015. "Geolocating the Past: Online Memories after the L'Aquila Earthquake." In *Memory in a Mediated World: Remembrance and Reconstruction*, edited by Andrea Hajek, Christine Lohmeier, and Christian Pentzold, 90–110. Basingstoke, UK: Palgrave Macmillan.

Foot, John. *Italy's Divided Memory*. 2009. New York: Palgrave Macmillan.

Hajek, Andrea. 2013. "Learning from L'Aquila: Grassroots Mobilization in Post-Earthquake Emilia Romagna." *Journal of Modern Italian Studies* 18(5): 627–43.

Iovino, Serenella. 2016. *Ecocriticism and Italy: Ecology, Resistance, and Liberation*. London: Bloomsbury.

Parrinello, Giacomo. 2016. *Fault Lines: Earthquakes and Urbanism in Modern Italy*. New York: Berghahn.

Petrei, Fabrizia. 2012. "Democrazia e comunicazione pubblica nel post-sisma: verso quale partecipazione all'Aquila?" In *Sismografie: Ritornare a L'Aquila mille giorni dopo il sisma*, edited by Fabio Carnelli, Orlando Paris, and Francesco Tommasi, 41–48. Rome: Edizioni Effigi.

Puliafito, Alberto. 2010. *Protezione Civile SPA: Quando la gestione dell'emergenza si fa business*. Rome: Aliberti.

Sirolli, Emanuele. 2012. "L'Aquila istituzionalizzata." In *Sismografie: Ritornare a L'Aquila mille giorni dopo il sisma*, edited by Fabio Carnelli, Orlando Paris, and Francesco Tommasi, 59–66. Rome: Edizioni Effigi.

MONICA SEGER

Thinking through Taranto: Toxic Embodiment, Eco-catastrophe, and the Power of Narrative

According to Greek mythology, Taras was born from the union between the sea god Poseidon and the nymph Satyrion. As a young man he was rescued from a sinking ship by a dolphin, which he rode across the Mediterranean Sea to a stretch of curving coastline in what is today southern Italy. There, in 706 BC, the Spartans founded a thriving colony and named it in his honor. The land has been known as Taranto ever since. Images of a bare-chested Taras astride his aquatic savior, often with his father's trident in hand, can still be seen throughout the modern-day city, from embroidered banners draped outside of cultural centers to the crudely painted paneling of roadside food trucks. The spirit of Taras, adventurous hero and chosen friend of the dolphin—long viewed as a harbinger of peace from the more-than-human world—can initially seem harder to find. Despite rich histories of agricultural production, maritime trade, and artistic expression, today's Taranto is largely in a state of despair, struggling to survive amid deadly, decades-long industrial pollution.

Due to its strategic coastal setting, Taranto has developed over the past sixty years into one of contemporary Italy's largest industrial centers. It has also become Italy's most significant site of toxic emissions, including various minerals, steel particles, and cancerous chemical compounds. Taranto houses a sizable cement plant, an oil refinery, and a naval base, but it is dominated, physically and beyond, by the Ilva steelworks. First opened in 1965, Ilva's operations extend for fifteen square kilometers immediately behind the densely populated Tamburi neighborhood, just past Taranto's central train station. Its towers can be seen from just about anywhere in this city of two hundred thousand residents, and its tiny, airborne, red steel particles notoriously paint the sky a deep pink at sunset.[1] As Cristina Zagaria writes in her novel *Veleno* (Poison), "the air is saturated with slivers of minerals that reflect the last rays of sunlight: it's like looking at a computer screen with the contrast on maximum. Metal sky. Artificial sunset" (2013, 103).² This "metal sky" regularly leaves a fine trace of visible dust across the stationary surfaces of everyday life—parked cars, patios, and playgrounds—just as it coats the leaves of plants and enters the lungs of animals, nonhuman and human alike. As a result, Taranto's residents have long faced startlingly excessive mortality rates compared to the general Italian population, and talk of tumors is a daily occurrence at the city's neighborhood bars.³

In recent years, while tumors have grown, residents have also borne witness to a thriving narrative renaissance, as authors, filmmakers, dramaturges, and visual artists from within the city and beyond seek to tell Taranto's many tales—largely of illness and ecological devastation but also of heroic histories and new beginnings. They do so in realist coming-of-age novels such as Flavia Piccinni's *Adesso tienimi* (Now hold me, 2007), speculative short fiction films like Davide Ippolito's *Taranto dopo l'Ilva* (Taranto after Ilva, 2015), and hybrid performance pieces like those crafted by the artist collective Nonperdono, Movimento trasversale d'avanguardia artistica (*non perdono* means "I do not forgive" (or alternately, "nonforgiveness"), Transverse avant-garde artistic movement). Through a vast range of storytelling practices and methods of circulation—including both mainstream publishers and free video-streaming websites—these contemporary descendants of Taras give voice to the living subjects of today's Taranto. Telling stories of singular protagonists and expansive communities, they explore what it means to have inherited stark legacies of risk and toxic embodiment as well as rich cultural traditions and unscripted futures. In this they breathe new creative energy and a renewed sense of agency into a city that desperately needs it. What's more, they usher in a potentially vast audience to affective response and fuller cognition of an urgent ecological reality. Inviting readers and viewers into rich storyworlds, they alert us to the eco-catastrophe actually unfolding in Taranto, which is not unlike so many other potential and real catastrophes throughout the world.

Narratologist David Herman defines storyworlds as "mentally and emotionally projected environments in which interpreters are called upon to live out complex blends of cognitive and imaginative response, encompassing sympathy, the drawing of causal inferences, identification, evaluation, suspense and so on" (2002, 16–17). These are tales, he explains, that ask for our active involvement. As contemporary work in eco-narratology suggests, such involvement can help foster deeper ecological awareness through both rational and feeling response, cognitive sense making, and affective recognition.⁴ When we enter fully into a place-based storyworld through imaginative experience, we gain greater understanding of particular circumstances, just as we access greater empathy for diverse environmental realities and greater concern for the damage they enact on human and nonhuman animal health.

At times, as Erin James (2015) has examined in postcolonial texts, these realities may be otherwise inaccessible to readers or viewers due to geography or other barriers, be they spatial or cultural. Such is largely the case when it comes to Taranto, nestled into Italy's heel along the Ionian Sea. The southern city is difficult to reach by public transport, with few scheduled routes leaving from hubs like Rome, and buses and trains are often long delayed or simply canceled without notice. It is only rarely featured on tourist itineraries and regularly overlooked by Italians further north as though it were worlds away, its toxic emissions containable within city limits.

Thanks, however, to the circulation of new texts and the worlds they contain, the Tarantine experience can now be intimately accessed by nonlocal actors and audiences, too.[5] One method of such access or entry is physical, as in Cosimo Argentina's *Vicolo dell'acciaio* (Steel alley, 2010). Like Piccinni's aforementioned *Adesso tienimi*, this novel features an angsty teenage narrator who repeatedly identifies neighborhoods and streets, while physically traversing them and while contemplating his working-class community's possible futures and real health crises. When he describes an evening out with friends mid-text, the whole adventure is guided by identification of place—street names, neighborhoods, nightclubs. Casually listing locations as though we too should be familiar with them, he invites readers in to the jumble of names, reinforcing both our imagined intimacy with Taranto and our actual disorientation as outsiders: we can follow along on his adventure but we must remain active readers to do so successfully.

Earlier, in a fraught conversation about the thought of Ilva's closure, this same narrator cries: "And in streets like via Toscana, via Emilia, corso Italia . . . via Temenide, via Pisanelli and all the other streets that come to mind . . . what would the people do?" (Argentina 2010, 32). Again he provides the necessary coordinates for readers to create a mental map of the city. Even more significantly, though, he reminds us of the tenuous balance between health and employment in a factory town, and the connection between material environment and the fates and futures of those that inhabit it: "I look at via Calabria and I see all those zombies and wannabe-future-vice-zombies. Thousands of 'six months to live's scurrying left and right" (41). With this offhand reference to the mundane nature of terminal health diagnoses in his community, Argentina's narrator evokes one of the most dominant threads of contemporary Tarantine texts: crises of creaturely health and the flows of toxic substances from steelworks to soil to animal.

Emblematic of this flow, Giuliano Foschini's hybrid reportage *Quindici passi* (Fifteen steps, 2009), the experimental documentary film *Non Perdono* (2015) by Roberto Marsella and Grace Zanotto, and Carlo Vulpio's book-length study *La città delle nuvole: Viaggio nel territorio più inquinato d'Europa* (The city of clouds: Journey to the most polluted land in Europe, 2009), all include the story of the real-life Fornaro family. In 2008, Angelo Fornaro's 605 sheep, long pastured near Ilva grounds, were ordered slaughtered due to the discovery of extreme levels of dioxin in their flesh and milk. His son Vincenzo now cultivates hemp, celebrated by many as a detoxifying agent, on that same land. *Non Perdono* makes striking use of the Fornaros' story by interspersing interviews with Angelo, as he speaks of his mother's death from cancer and his own recent tumor removal, with silent shots of his family territory, Ilva's chimneys always in the background. These are then further intercut with sensuous images of an anonymous figure, masked and hooded in reference to a local tradition of religious pageantry, who caresses both small explosive devices and lush olive branches while a jazz score plays. Here the connections between industry, agriculture, and illness are all neatly tied together in a practice of primarily visual storytelling—alongside a suggestion of potential dramatic change.

By briefly demonstrating the ways in which narratives can teach us about an actual reality, I do not wish to reduce the creative verbal and visual work of world building via story to an exclusively edifying practice—explaining how Taranto is shaped, who there is ill and who is to blame. Rather, I wish to underline the ways in which narrative practice and storyworld experience provide crucial space for the imagination necessary to make sense of challenging contemporary realities. Storyworlds are particularly crucial when it comes to reminding external audiences that industrially shaped eco-catastrophes affect real living creatures, individual human (and nonhuman) beings with feelings, families, and futures to consider. In the words of Martha Nussbaum, "narrative imagination is an essential preparation for moral interaction. Habits of empathy and conjecture conduce to a certain type of citizenship and a certain form of community: one that cultivates a sympathetic responsiveness to another's needs, and understands the way circumstances shape those needs" (1997, 90). A retained awareness of community is fundamental to approaching contemporary eco-catastrophe, when the involvement of large-scale industry and circulation of abstract figures can easily depersonalize and distance outside observers.[6]

The sharing of storyworlds can thus also work to actively counter dominant narratives created by state and industry. Such action is often so necessary in cases such as Taranto's, when national economic interest may dictate a mainstream narrative. As Marco Armiero writes in this volume, "Narrating means producing counter-narratives, because environmental injustice is not only imposed with tanks and truncheons but also with a narrative that eradicates any possible alternative" (169). While the Italian government has recently begun to acknowledge the environmental injustice in Taranto, both it and

Ilva have long downplayed reports of toxicity and obfuscated data on health and mortality as they promote the steelworks' national and regional economic importance.[7] By privileging and personalizing experiences of ongoing environmental illness, many of the authors and artists crafting contemporary Tarantine storyworlds instead propose that employment at Ilva is no longer worth the grave damage the steelworks has caused to environment and community, thus upsetting the long upheld official narratives that Taranto needs Ilva to survive and that employment alone is enough to constitute well-being.[8] Gaetano Colella's play *Capatosta* (Dogged, 2015), for example, addresses these contrasting narratives through lengthy dialogue between a veteran Ilva worker and his new colleague as they go about their workday. Ruefully echoing the message of their employer, the older man explains early on, "The steel that we make is much more important than all of our lives put together: mine, yours, your father's. Everyone's" (21). Yet in sharing the lives of these two Tarantine characters through theatrical representation Colella disproves that message, privileging the telling of stories over their steelworks setting, which serves as mere backdrop for intimate exchange.

While all of Ilva's abusive emissions are troubling, it is the release of dioxin and dioxin-like compounds that has caused greatest concern among area activists, as well as the authors and artists considered in this essay. Rather than intense isolated exposure—as in the historic Seveso disaster of 1976, in which a chemical explosion at a factory site produced the highest-known immediate dioxin exposure of a residential population to date—Taranto has borne the brunt of steady long-term emissions.[9] It has witnessed the sort of "slow violence" that Rob Nixon theorized in his book of the same name—an ecological and corporeal violence that "occurs gradually and out of sight, a violence of delayed destruction that is dispersed across time and space, an attritional violence that is typically not viewed as violence at all" (2011, 2). As a result of this "attritional violence" Taranto's dioxin output may be significantly more detrimental than Seveso's to the environment and long-term health of area residents. In both scenarios, however, whether released in mass quantities all at once or slowly over time, dioxin possesses an intriguing temporal, and ultimately narratological, identity. It persists in nonhuman matter such as soil for decades, bio-accumulates for an unpredictable number of years once it enters human and animal bodies, and may or may not manifest in eventual illness, all while remaining imperceptible without the aid of costly chemical analysis.

In its free flow between matters and bodies, dioxin forces a reckoning with what Stacy Alaimo has called trans-corporeality, the "material interconnections of human corporeality with the more-than-human world" (2010, 2). Dioxin brings subjects into awareness of the ways in which our bodies are permeable, not entirely within our control but rather deeply entangled with all sorts of "vibrant matter" and the social, economic, and industrial processes that envelop it (Bennett 2010). As Serenella Iovino has explored in relation to Seveso, dioxin has a certain "epiphanic" power as "an alien materiality that interferes and co-acts with the bodies of living organisms and living land, exposing . . . the social and ethical blind spots of social constructs and political practices" (2013, 42). In this, Iovino explains, dioxin demonstrates its own particularly narrative agency, including traits of linearity, chronology, cause and effect. Entering the bodies of Taranto residents, and especially those living in the working-class neighborhoods closest to the steelworks, Ilva's dioxin traces out an all too common story of perceived national economic interest privileged over one community's well-being. It is indeed a very physical tracing. We read in *Veleno*, "every dioxin leaves an imprint that links back to whoever produced it. . . . It's as though little murderous hands were placing themselves on us, touching us, each choosing a part of our bodies . . . lungs, head, ovaries, skin, throat . . . in order to then devour it, leaving only their little imprints" (Zagaria 2013, 161–62). Writing here in the voice of the real-life Daniela Spera, Zagaria traces dioxin's path from industrial producer to human body. She underlines its dependent origin (it was "produced" by some other agent or process) just as she confirms both its destructive agency and our human mutability.

Dioxin is not the only cause for ecological concern in Taranto, of course. Polychlorinated biphenyl, benzene, hydrochloric acid, polycyclic aromatic hydrocarbons, and benzo(a)pyrene, among other substances, also exit Ilva's chimneys at alarming rates. And yet, dioxin is the substance of highest concentration and greatest duration in the region's air, soil, and so much more. As Foschini writes, "dioxin was not only in the air. Or perhaps in the flesh of sheep or in cheese. Dioxin had made it all the way into the breasts of Tarantine women" (2009, 40). Not only entering bodies but also passing intergenerationally between them, dioxin is such a fluid reminder of our constant becoming, in ways both physical and more. In this it serves as a strikingly apt symbol for the city and residents of present-day Taranto, cut through with deep histories and grappling with unknown next steps. Like the toxic emissions moving through its land and people, today's Taranto is bound up in the sort of insecure temporality that Elizabeth Grosz has elaborated as being "directed to a future that is unattainable and unknowable in the present" (1999, 1–2). It is precisely now in this insecure present, when residents do not know what will come of the Ilva steelworks, or of their community, land, or personal health—that the authors and artists (re)shaping Taranto's tales can have the greatest effect, by reaching out to readers and audiences far and wide through the creation of storyworlds. Recalling the spirit of Taras, they recognize Taranto's inherent richness, as well as the great work that must be done to recover and preserve it.

Long intrigued by the relationship between dioxin and narrative, especially in contemporary Italy where both are so dynamic, I spent much of 2015 reading and viewing what Taranto-based texts I could find. Through that immersive experience, I came to feel firsthand the power of entry into environmentally situated storyworlds. I began to think through Taranto—to traverse its streets, mourn for its sick children, relish its salty sea air, and wonder about its future with or without Ilva. In the summer of 2016 I had the opportunity to physically visit Taranto as well, confronting the real city with its image in my head. What I found through long walks and longer conversations was in many ways the same Taranto I had already come to know, only spilling over with yet more stories and narrators than I had even imagined. It was as overwhelming as it was inspiring.

I arrived in Taranto from Rome late at night. As my second train of the long journey down slowly rolled into the city, industrial lights visible through the dark, I realized that I carried a sort of fan-girl excitement mixed with palpable apprehension. I was physically entering into a space and community with whom I already felt somehow bonded, having inhabited that space and those relationships through so many texts. The next morning, I embarked on an exploratory walk through Taranto's "old town," a slip of an island flanked on both ends by bridges that divide the city's small bay into two halves. It was quieter than I had anticipated from my narrative wanderings, hardly another person in sight, and yet Taranto's physical shape, the curve of its coastline, was just as I knew it to be. As I looked out at the section of bay leading to the Ionian Sea, I almost felt Piccinni's teenage narrator pass by on her scooter, as she so often does in *Adesso tienimi*. Later, I couldn't stop myself from gasping with odd glee when I came across a simple drinker's tableau: a dilapidated office chair and spindly wooden side table set against an alley wall, an empty Raffo beer bottle perfectly perched. This was, I knew well, the locals' beer of choice.

What I found in the coming days continued to confirm my storyworld knowledge in ways both eerie and exciting while also, of course, surpassing it. I was profoundly struck by the oppressive weight of the air—a combination of midsummer heat, the city's slow pace, and the raw impact of seeing firsthand Taranto's environmental and health crises. During our shared wanderings, the local folklorist Angelo Cannata repeatedly made offhand jokes about dioxin "getting to the heads" of local acquaintances. I caught myself wondering if it had gotten to me as well: by the end of my second day of walking and talking with the cultural advocates and environmental activists I had come to meet, I felt a guilty desire to board the next train out. The situation seemed so desperate, the contrast so acute between the reality in

Taranto—where talk of Ilva's potential sale, gross environmental violations, and children's tumors passes daily across the lips of neighbors—and the rest of the country, taken up with other concerns.

I stayed on, of course, and as I continued to meet willing interlocutors and to let Taranto seep into my real-world consciousness, I discovered a still expanding world of creative communication even more dynamic than I had first understood. I also heard heartening reports of affirmative response. I had gone to Taranto in particular to meet Daniela Spera, whom I felt I already knew through Cristina Zagaria's *Veleno*. Over the course of a late morning coffee that somehow turned into night, Daniela described to me how her work as a pharmacist, in which she hears daily of local illness, led her to become one of Taranto's most outspoken environmental health advocates. She told me about the chemical makeup of dioxin and why long-term studies are more revealing than monthly peaks in reported emissions, about her mother's recent sudden death, and about her own attempts to communicate Taranto's realities on levels both local and international. When I asked her what it was like to have circulated the world in story, she was less forthcoming, almost embarrassed. But when I asked her about reaction to *Veleno* she beamed, telling me, "As a novel . . . this created a sensibility in many young people. In fact, there were a few girls who wrote to me, saying: I study at the university in Pisa now—I chose environmental science. I'll tell you even more: I'm going to graduate from Pisa and then I'll go back to Taranto, because I can go back to Taranto possessing *knowledge*."

NOTES

1. As in any factory town, the relationship between the Ilva steelworks and Taranto is close and complicated. So too is the relationship between Ilva and the national government, which has offered the steel producer tireless legislative and financial aid despite significant rebuke from the European Commission. In July 2016 the Italian senate approved one more in a series of "Save ILVA" decrees, the tenth in response to a period of major financial crisis that reached its peak in 2012, when Ilva's Taranto plant was partially closed due to extreme violations of EU environmental regulations. Since 2015 the steelworks have been under temporary administration of the Italian government. Once secured, incoming owners will take on a debt totaling nearly 3 billion euros and have until 2019 to complete a court ordered environmental cleanup.

2. All translations from the Italian are my own.

3. According to the SENTIERI study on mortality and pollution, based on data collected from 1995 to 2002, Taranto residents face significantly excessive mortality rates from a host of particular illnesses as compared to average Italians. This includes an excess 30 percent mortality rate due to lung cancer, an excess 50 percent mortality rate for men and 40 percent for women due to serious respiratory disease, and an excess 15 percent mortality rate for men, 40 percent for women due to digestive disease (Lucifora, Bianco, and Vagliasindi 2015, 16–17).

4. Along with James's recent study, see work by Lehtimäki (2013) and Heise (2002, 2008).

5. As an example of such access, author Cristina Zagaria states in our personal correspondence that *Veleno* had sold more than three thousand copies by 2016.

6. The discourse of risk is thus very relevant in the case of Taranto but omitted from the current brief study due to space concerns. For more, see recent work by Ursula Heise (2008), Kate Rigby (2015), and Molly Wallace (2016).

7. As of 2015 approximately 12,000 people were directly employed at Ilva's Taranto plant, with additional thousands employed as subcontractors. A report prepared for the European Parliament's Committee on Environment, Public Health and Food Safety from that same year raises concerns, however, about the economic impact of "the environmental problems caused by emissions from the plant," with cows and sheep repeatedly ordered slaughtered, the cultivation of various crops prohibited, and tourism impeded (Vagliasindi and Gerstetter 2015, 7).

8. At the time of this writing, Prime Minister Matteo Renzi has just completed a much publicized visit to Taranto, during which he again emphasized the steelworks' primacy of place to economic survival in the region (July 28, 2016).

9. Seveso's extreme case of concentrated exposure ultimately helped to shape EU environmental policy through the Council Directive 82/501/EEC of June 24, 1982, also know as the Seveso Directive, and subsequently amended in 1996 and 2012, the later in response to environmental abuses at Ilva's Taranto plant. The disaster produced both immediate and long-term consequences for the local environment and health of area residents. As Laura Centemeri notes, "In Europe, the dioxin crisis at Seveso marked the appearance of a new kind of environmental damage—one that might produce delayed rather than immediate effects. Damaging chemical effects might extend to future generations" (2010, 200–201).

WORKS CITED

Alaimo, Stacy. 2010. *Bodily Natures: Science, Environment and the Material Self.* Bloomington: Indiana University Press.

Argentina, Cosimo. 2010. *Vicolo dell'acciaio.* Rome: Fandango.

Bennett, Jane. 2010. *Vibrant Matter: A Political Ecology of Things.* Durham, NC: Duke University Press.

Centemeri, Laura. 2010. "The Seveso Disaster Legacy." In *Nature and History in Modern Italy,* edited by Marco Armiero and Marcus Hall, 195–211. Athens: Ohio University Press.

Colella, Gaetano. 2015. *Capatosta.* Unpublished manuscript.

Foschini, Giuliano. 2009. *Quindici Passi.* Rome: Fandango.

Grosz, Elizabeth. 1999. *Becomings: Explorations in Time, Memory, and Futures.* Ithaca, NY: Cornell University Press.

Heise, Ursula K. 2002. "Toxins, Drugs, and Global Systems: Risk and Narrative in the Contemporary Novel." *American Literature* 4(4): 747–78.

———. 2008. *Sense of Place and Sense of Planet: The Environmental Imagination of the Global.* Oxford, UK: Oxford University Press.

Herman, David. 2002. *Story Logic: Problems and Possibilities of Narrative*. Lincoln: University of Nebraska Press.

Iovino, Serenella. 2013. "Toxic Epiphanies: Dioxin, Power, and Gendered Bodies in Laura Conti's Narratives on Seveso." In *International Perspectives in Feminist Ecocriticism*, edited by Greta Gaard, Simon C. Estok, and Serpil Oppermann, 37–55. New York: Routledge.

Ippolito, Davide. 2015. *Taranto dopo L'Ilva*. Independent release (DVD).

James, Erin. 2015. *The Storyworld Accord: Econarratology and Postcolonial Narratives*. Lincoln: University of Nebraska Press.

Lehtimäki, Markku. 2013. "Natural Environments in Narrative Contexts: Cross-Pollinating Ecocriticism and Narrative Theory." *StoryWorlds: A Journal of Narrative Studies* 5: 119–41.

Lucifora, Annalisa, Floriana Bianco, and Grazia Maria Vagliasindi. 2015. *Environmental and Corporate Mis-compliance: A Case Study on the ILVA Steel Plant in Italy*. Catania, Italy: University of Catania.

Marsella, Roberto, and Grace Zanotto. 2015. *Non Perdono*. Video. https://www.youtube.com/watch?v=vT9m2jP2KYE.

Nixon, Rob. 2011. *Slow Violence and the Environmentalism of the Poor*. Cambridge, MA: Harvard University Press.

Nussbaum, Martha. 1997 *Cultivating Humanity: A Classical Defense of Reform in Liberal Education*. Cambridge, MA: Harvard University Press.

Piccinni, Flavia. 2007. *Adesso Tienimi*. Rome: Fazi Editore.

Rigby, Kate. 2015. *Dancing with Disaster: Environmental Histories, Narratives, and Ethics for Perilous Times*. Charlottesville: University of Virginia Press.

Vagliasindi, Grazia Maria, and Christiane Gerstetter. 2015. *The ILVA Industrial Site in Taranto: In-Depth Analysis for the ENVI Committee*. Brussels: European Parliament. http://www.europarl.europa.eu/RegData/etudes/IDAN/2015/563471/IPOL_IDA%282015%29563471_EN.pdf.

Vulpio, Carlo. 2009. *La città delle nuvole: Viaggio nel territorio più inquinato d'Europa*. Milan: Edizioni Ambiente.

Wallace, Molly. 2016. *Risk Criticism: Precautionary Reading in an Age of Environmental Uncertainty*. Ann Arbor: University of Michigan Press.

Zagaria, Cristina. 2013. *Veleno*. Milan: Sperling and Kupfer.

MARCO MORO

Room with a View (of a Landfill): The Making of Verdenero

"Tommi looked out of the living-room window. From the eighth floor there was a good view of the landfill, in particular the sections with the incinerators and the one next to the *putrida* (the rotting swamp). He saw the fire and ran to open the windows, letting the cold air and the smell of burning in" (Bucciarelli 2010, 58). In *Corpi di scarto* (Discarded bodies) by Elisabetta Bucciarelli, the image of a disfigured country draws closer, representing the place where I live, Milan. And although the novel depicts a landfill that does not really exist near the Navigli, my neighborhood, the smell that often stagnates in the air makes the fictional scenario convincing. I don't see landfills or incinerators from my living room window. However, I can hear the noisy garbage trucks that clean my street after the market on Mondays. They are less threatening than the vehicles that go back and forth to the dump site where Bucciarelli sets her story of human and nonhuman waste, less threatening than the bulldozers that reshape the landfill's topography, every day shifting the map of the precarious idea of "livability" which orients the lives in the place where the city hides every kind of junk. It is plausible. It is true.

Here, where I live, a group of citizens regained access to an abandoned green area, transforming it into a shared, community garden. This garden is alive. It hosts parties, concerts, courses, picnics . . . or it is simply a place of relaxation. However, here one cannot grow a vegetable garden unless one plants seedlings in well-raised garden beds, which are then tended by the children attending a nearby school. The reason for this solution is that metal, glass, and plastic scraps keep surfacing from the dirt in the garden. I don't know how deep one must dig to get rid of the contaminated soil. It was a no-man's land and had become a landfill. Beyond the garden fence there is more abandoned green space, an urban wasteland inhabited by the community's "refuse." The gap between fiction and reality is minimal.

Corpi di scarto is one of the approximately twenty volumes that constituted an editorial project called "Verdenero" which, as it developed, offered an original, accurate picture of the physical and human landscape in contemporary Italy. The Verdenero project was conceived as a campaign to raise awareness through literature. It is also the product of an encounter between two phenomena with strong national connotations. The first is the widespread penetration of organized crime into the economy and the administration of Italy. The second is the popular success of noir fiction in a publishing industry that otherwise finds itself in deep crisis. This idea formed thanks to the long collaboration between Edizioni Ambiente (an Italian publishing house entirely dedicated to documenting environmental themes and sustainable development) and the foremost national environmental organization, Legambiente. Their initial, common goal was to substantially improve the community's awareness about the processes of environmental and social degradation which, despite being close by and pervasive, were also barely understood in their real extension and impact. *Ecomafia*, a term invented by journalist Enrico Fontana in 1994, describes these phenomena and has become a fundamental object of investigation on the part of Legambiente.

From Reporting to Noir

First of all, let's define *ecomafia*. This term describes activities in which the presence of organized crime is pervasive and from which criminal organizations derive substantial sources of income. The phrase "organized crime" refers to the main Italian criminal organizations: mafia, camorra, 'ndrangheta, and so on. Each of these has its own peculiarities and specializations, which include: trash management (all the activities linked to the illegal disposal of waste, in particular toxic or dangerous waste); cement management (illegal building and polluting the process of public procurements), and "minor" entries such as "archeomafia" (traffic of archaeological finds and artworks), "agromafia" (control of agricultural activities, food adulterations, etc.), and "zoomafia" (this includes everything to do with animals, from smuggling protected species to clandestine horse races).

The merit of Legambiente was to clearly identify a combination of activities that share a common denominator: aggression toward the land, nature, and various cultural assets (including Italian food). Not by chance, these all play a substantial role in creating the image and "imaginary" of Italy, including at the international level. Legambiente's work basically converged into a single object: the *Ecomafia Report*. This annual volume, which is hundreds of pages long, documents the results of the investigations carried out by different branches of law enforcement and by Legambiente itself, region by region and field by field, with data and lists of involved criminal clans. However, the report's readership was primarily limited to those already working in law enforcement agencies, government ministries, and the local administrations where Legambiente directly distributed it. This situation highlighted a (paradoxical) default both in the communication and the perception of mafia phenomena and of their penetration and distribution throughout the Italian territory. Such phenomena were so widespread that they became almost invisible. They suggested the presence of a sort of "mafia next door" which was concealed in a social and political context that paid little attention to environmental issues. Here, environmentalism was not part of the culture, or at least not as much as a tendency to petty unlawfulness and corruption.

The media hardly deals with anything that is not crime, with events that don't include somebody getting killed. However, people also die outside standard criminal scenarios. Does land contamination cause deaths? Yes, it does, but in order to prove the links, you need data about the onset of tumors to know and evaluate processes that develop slowly over time. This sort of event happens more slowly than extortion, homicide, gang warfare. And the related stories, with a few exceptions, do not have such a mediatic impact. And then there is the problem of representing environmentally related phenomena in their totality, which is the only way to convey their real scope (also in terms of the revenues of ecomafia). We are, nonetheless, always dealing with stories, with facts that—if you know how—can be recounted by finding an effective narrative register and genre. And there is little doubt that, in this case, the crime story and the noir are such genres.

In 2006, while trying to figure out how to balance costs and cope with the limited sales of the *Ecomafia Report*, we had a eureka moment: each report is potentially rich with inspiration for an author of detective stories. In Italy noir is a genre that enjoys wide success and has a large audience, one which, however, would never read a six-hundred-page report. Our next step was to contact the best Italian noir writers and convince them to participate in a project devised by an environmental association and an environmental publishing house, the latter certainly far from being a major player in the book market. Many authors enthusiastically adhered to this project: Sandrone Dazieri (the first to join), Carlo Lucarelli, Simona Vinci, Pietro Colaprico, Giancarlo De Cataldo, Massimo Carlotto, Eraldo Baldini, the three Sicilians Giacomo Cacciatore, Valentina Gebbia, and Gery Palazzotto, and Wu Ming. They all agreed to write following an unusual work pattern, one where both Legambiente and the editors in charge of the series would suggest themes to be developed into potential novels. Authors then had the possibility of choosing among the proposed ideas or suggesting a topic of their own. These writers constitute a particular segment within the national literary landscape. They write fiction but are also often crime/judicial news journalists or (ex-)magistrates whose investigations are also occasionally broadcast on TV. Additionally, they often are strongly attached to the place where they live, and they narrate its story and present situation through literary invention.

By the time the series was launched, two relevant examples of this kind of writing already existed. The most famous, Roberto Saviano's *Gomorrah*, came out in 2006 when the Verdenero project was close to its debut and is generally considered to be the foundation of ecomafia narrative. However, even though it is less well-known, the novel *Nordest* (Northeast) by Massimo Carlotto and Marco Videtta was actually published one year before *Gomorrah* and is even more legitimately associated with the noir genre. In *Nordest* the authors recount (and denounce) the degradation of the social fabric and of human relations, the business-fueled, moral drift of the then hyper-affluent communities living in the Italian northeast and, in particular, the Veneto region, Carlotto's homeland. The novel offers a portrait of unscrupulous homemade entrepreneurs willing to contract with organized crime in order to take care of services such as toxic waste disposal, which they found much more convenient to provide outside the rules of law. Carlotto's novel already mentioned the "Land of Fires" and the connivance between northern factories and "disposers" from the southern region of Campania.

The Verdenero project was therefore fed by a sensibility toward place that constitutes a common cultural background for many of these authors. When they were asked to tell stories of degradation, they had the opportunity to present a different face of their own places.

Ugly Neighborhoods: A New Materiality of Landscape

The image that emerges from the more than twenty narratives that form the main corpus of the series (which eventually moved toward the novel and the investigative report) is one of a country that lives basically unaware of what lies beneath, under the agricultural soil, under the sand on beaches or below the sea, under the ground below industrial areas or along rivers. The narratives depict an underground landscape in a parallel Italy, one that in some of the most audacious interpretations—as in the eco-fantasy *I dannati di Malva* (The damned of Malva), by Licia Troisi—is rendered as an explicit relationship between two worlds, one above ground and one below.

This underground laced with poisons conceals the true essence of an apparently fine landscape, which is still a fundamental component of a popular image of Italy (especially among politicians). And this is an image that falls under the rhetoric of the "beautiful country" (*bel paese*), whose roots were materially explored by Piero Camporesi in his 1992 book *Le belle contrade* (The beautiful neighborhoods), for example. As I mentioned, these narratives also give us an idea of what is concealed under the sea, the air, forests, rivers, cities, streets. They pay a renewed attention to material data that points to a miasmatic Italy (in a temporal loop that goes back to the times from which Camporesi drew his literary sources), that is to say, to a nation also made up of putrid waters, mud (i.e., *Solo fango* by Giancarlo Narciso, 2010), ashes, and waste and by the destruction and literal subtraction of pieces of landscape, of material chunks of the country. These are all matters for a noir: cement, trash, asbestos, fire, poisons. But even tomatoes and cultivated land can become part of a noir when one talks about the exploitation of clandestine workers on the job (i.e., *Bloody Mary* by Marco Vichi and Leonardo Gori, 2008). Ooze, dust, acid, and oily substances, hydrocarbons (defined as "Ur-shit" in *Previsioni del tempo* [Weather forecast] by the writers' collective Wu Ming); patinas that cover objects and people, corroding identities and breaking wills, as in *Sequenze di memoria* (Memory sequences) by Loriano Macchiavelli (written in 1976 and republished in the Verdenero series).

If there is a main sensory protagonist in these stories, I would say it is the sense of smell, like the scent of bitter almonds (linked to vinyl chloride or VCM) in *Con la faccia di cera* (With a wax face) by Girolamo Di Michele. And one should also breathe as little as possible when unidentified substances are mixed with both concrete and the lives of common people in *Rovina* (Ruin) by Simona Vinci, or when the air is pervaded with the pungent stink of electronic waste burned in some African forest in *L'albero dei microchip* (The microchip tree) by Francesco Abate and Massimo Carlotto.

Covering places with adjectives and covering, in turn, the materials that make and contaminate them did not only aim to create an atmosphere in which to set the plot. In these texts matter is a protagonist, an object, and the goal, the true substance of writing.

A Long Coda?

Verdenero's history coincides with a cultural and political initiative that contributed, at least for a while, to the discussion of the emergence of a new "social novel." In a sense, literature played a subsidiary role to politics. It was able to introduce into public discourse topics that were usually concealed by the gaps between national and local politics, between the official economy and the parallel one of organized crime. It was able to introduce these topics in a society alternatively sympathetic, inattentive, misinformed, or more or less consciously conniving. This history was born from the relation between noir, a highly commercial literary genre, and an equally dark reality that was just waiting to be narrated with the adequate instruments. The debate about the social novel quickly abated without a trace and never expanded beyond the small niche group of authors and critics who initially promoted it. What is worth remembering, though, doesn't actually have much to do with literature, criticism, or the publishing market. In 2015, after twenty years of proposals, discussions, and complaints, Italy approved a law against eco-crimes. Today crimes against the environmental patrimony are punishable according to the penal code and not just by enforcing an ineffective (and often inapplicable) financial penalty. We like to think that Verdenero has, in some small way, contributed to this outcome. Every text in the series ended with a short section entitled "I fatti" (Facts), curated by Antonio Pergolizzi, coordinator of Legambiente's National Observatory on the Environment and the Law, as if to say: what you just read is fiction, but here we describe the reality that inspired it.

And then reality often exceeded fiction, captivating our readers even more.

(Translation by Enrico Cesaretti)

WORK CITED

Bucciarelli, Elisabetta. 2010. *Corpi di scarto*. Milan: Edizioni Ambiente.

5

IMAGINATIONS AND (RE)VISIONS

PASQUALE VERDICCHIO

This Nostrum That Is Neither Sea nor Remedy: Mediterranean Re-visions

And we have created from water
every living thing.
—Qur'an 21:30

Sea, I will write upon your soul,
shattered among the plastic bags
of those who poison and decimate
your populations, your nature...
—Giuseppe Conte, "Non finirò di scrivere sul mare," *Poesie 1983–2015*

Asmat, "Names." This is the straightforward and emphatic title of Dagmawi Yimer's film dedicated to the "memory of all sea victims" and bearing a date: "Lampedusa, 3 October 2013"—a day that marks what at the time was the single most numerous drowning incident of migrants in their attempt to reach Europe from the shores of North Africa (Yimer 2014). Yimer's commemoration emphasizes and attempts to shed light on the invisibility of individuals whose deaths become only momentary distractions and statistics within the swirl of world events. The drowned become part of a submerged and unknown mass that slides out of the collective consciousness, sometimes even displaced by other refugee crises deemed more important according to national interests and international relationships. In fact, hardly spoken of outside of Europe, the North African migrations that have seen tens of thousands disembark in southern Europe (the Italian island of Lampedusa being a primary point of arrival) have receded even further in relation to the Middle Eastern influx into northern Europe.[1] In such a context, Yimer's film becomes more than a commemoration. The hauntingly beautiful visuals are backed up by a recitation of names that may have been those of the drowned and are doubly effective for their written versions in Amharic rising up from the sea bottom to fill the screen. It is a challenge to anonymity that by its process of naming consolidates the victims within our frames of conceptual knowledge even as it declares difference. By assigning names to unknowns that remain unseen, Yimer requires us to shift toward a different sort of epistemology, based on the acknowledgment and initiation of an unconventional relationship with the invisible. The dreadful fact of the tens of thousands of known deaths over the years as a result of migration further emphasizes the absurdity of the situation. Although fleeing from all different sorts of strife, the cause of their death translates systematic inadequacies and, in its shifts, rejections, abandonment of territories, and dangers of death, suggests a movement toward *rarefaction* and *extinction*, terms usually reserved for nonhuman species. While we might understand the first term as the diminishment of the migrants' status as humans physically, materially, and in relation to our ethical response to their plight and fate, *extinction* refers to the literal disappearance of individuals in large numbers.[2] The film suggests this in its representation of the drowned migrant bodies as disembodied voices, partially visible or portions of bodies, and veiled countenances from which the names rise to the surface. During the limited course of this essay, I extrapolate these two terms to suggest a correspondence in how we view and relate to human and nonhuman elements in the waters of the Mediterranean.

Irish satirist Jonathan Swift's notion that "vision is the art of seeing things invisible" (1745, 252) most aptly describes the shortsightedness of contemporary inhabitants of the northern Mediterranean shores through most of our historical relationship with the sea. We have in fact considered it to be nothing more than a security barrier, a defensive obstacle, not much more than a moat. Besides the more obvious political manipulations by a variety of actors on the Italian and European stage, this idea has even worked itself into the lyrics of the rocker Luciano Ligabue's "Buonanotte all'Italia" ("Goodnight to an Italy in need of respite/no worries, the sea keeps guard and the country in sight," 2007). Although we may have lost sight of the sea as a shared common space and today lean toward Ligabue's representation of it, we still have Swift's forward-looking proposal within our grasp. The geopolitical divisions that have defined our lack of vision have been determined by the exploitative need and search for natural resources and the human labor necessary for their extraction and processing. Such appropriations have been enacted in consecutive steps, from colonialism and its associated practices which extend subjugation, through the granting of "independence" as protectorates, to control via selected puppet regimes and so-called foreign aid programs. All such entanglements betray our inability or unwillingness to see and suggest that we may have lost or even become fearful of "the art of seeing things invisible."

The surface geography of this rather small, well-traveled, and much charted sea could stand as a synecdoche for the larger uncharted wilderness of its own unseen teeming biota and of the greater watery and terrestrial worlds it joins. Further, as Bertrand Westphal suggests, "for a sea like the Mediterranean, water is a synecdoche of land. Water precedes land; what is on land is a product of water" (Westphal 2013, 27; my translation). In her introduction to a special issue of *Ecozon@* dedicated to "Mediterranean Ecocriticism," Serenella Iovino draws attention to how the Mediterranean itself has served to establish a new Orientalism, namely, a hierarchy of power, influences, and alliances that repeat familiar divisive binaries, such as north/south, First/Third World, east/west. Iovino (2013) writes:

> The implications of Mediterraneanism as a "global hierarchy of value" are . . . not to be underestimated. Its effects are evidently marked not only on the body of Mediterranean natures and landscapes, transformed into new markets for global capitalism; but also—bio-politically—on the migrants' bodies, masses of humans who die in the desperate attempt to escape the poverty and despotism of their (Mediterranean) countries, in order to reach more prosperous and democratic (Mediterranean) lands. It is these "Southern" people and their environments that are chiefly affected by the self-representations of the Mediterranean as a "Mare nostrum": a proprietary expression where "nostrum" clearly refers to a Euro-Atlantic collective of forces. (5)

In fact, the terms of these relationships have been manipulated to benefit the interested parties who participate in strategic international exchanges around the edges of the sea, with little regard for its populations and cultures. Policy examples of such an appropriation in recent history are French ex-president Sarkozy's plan for the Union of the Mediterranean, meant to replace the 1995 Barcelona Process (Euro-Mediterranean Partnership), Italian former prime minister Matteo Renzi's vision of a Mediterranean as the new center of Europe, and even the activities of human traffickers who profit from the exportation of men, women, and children under the most deplorable conditions toward almost certain death. All of these realities appropriate the Mediterranean to specific functions and interests that contribute little to an understanding or reenvisioning of the sea as differentiated territories of struggle, survival, life, and death. In *Southern Thought* Franco Cassano (2012) outlines the need for an expansive opening of the terms by which we view the sea:

> the sea weakens every tie by escaping ownership, it is also true that when it overflows its borders the sea transforms this weakening of ties in a planetary uprooting: against the earth's fundamentalism stands the fundamentalism of the sea, which pushes toward nihilism and the uncontrollable unleashing

of technology. When the sea is transformed into an ocean . . . it becomes a place without shores, an absence of land that spills into an integral dependency on technology. Indeed, only technology can offer (artificial) forms of stability and protection in a world that, founding itself on the perennial mobility of the sea, is fully deterritorialized and has renounced every home and root. (17)

Working within a similar optic, as an attempt to bring balance to past definitions and representations of the Mediterranean, David Abulafia, in *The Great Sea: A Human History of the Mediterranean,* undertakes to set his sights on "the surface of the sea itself."[3] His approach distinguishes itself from Fernand Braudel's and others who have extended their consideration of the Mediterranean beyond the shores of the watery basin to include surrounding lands. Abulafia's proposal would also seem to contradict Braudel's suggested envisioning of the Mediterranean not as a unifying or unified common set of cultures but as a diverse and heterogeneous grouping defined by geology, geography, and, in our day, the artificiality of geopolitical projects. More often than not, the sea itself has been defined by the lands that surround it, relegating the body of water to an afterthought of sorts, to secondary or nonexistent status. While not ignoring the land and all that has occurred upon it, Abulafia makes it his task to "concentrate on those who dipped their toes into the sea, and, best of all, took journeys across it, participating directly, in some cases, in cross-cultural trade, in the movement of religious and other ideas" (Abulafia 2011, xviii).

Today, among the millennial transformations that Abulafia narrates within the pages of *The Great Sea,* we would have to insert the migrations of common folks that history past and present has tended to occult. These "other" migrant voyages did not, and do not, seek "to control the sea" or to utilize it as a vantage point through which to gain control over other territories but consider it a link for the acknowledgment of their physical and cultural existence and survival (Abulafia 2011, xviii). As such, aside from being the meeting point of habitats and elements, human and nonhuman presences, geopolitical realities, alliances and contrasts, the *mare* also provides points of encounter for a potentially intimate dialogue of cultures. The sea's polyvalent interstitial skin, its so-called surface, stands as a site of transition, a transformative border between air and water that introduces a defining space in line with Predrag Matvejević's description of the Mediterranean as "a vast archive, an immense grave" (1993, 23).

As an expanse "between lands," it is easy to imagine the loss of direction one might experience while floating away from any visible shore. It is therefore interesting to note how such an effect falls back onto the sea, itself invisible in its totality. And yet, it is in that apparent separation from everything, and the possibility it offers our imaginative powers, that by "taking distance from this little globe [we might] discover in the enormous distance our common condition" (Cassano 2003, 84). By that same token, the distance between land and sea, air and water is actually more a matter of perception than spatial. From fishing practices above and below the surface to ancient and contemporary popular culture, from Jacopo Sannazaro's (1966) *Piscatorial Eclogues* (initiators of a correspondence that bestowed equal value to the undersea "pastoral") to cinematographic representations, the proximity of these realms and the facility with which the crossing from one to the other is attained, a narrative has emerged that ranges from a conscious awareness and potential for dialogue among the various realms, to an exploitative and exploited series of interactions that depend upon, and often suffer from, the invisible dimensions of the sea. Forever marked by a mysterious aura that challenged him, the *viator* Odysseus's travels and trials reinforce the ways in which we tend to relate to the sea's realities and myths. Its thin surface layer separates the more comfortable space for humans above from what lies beneath and has historically generated fear, leading us to visualize the unknown as frightening rather than, as per Swift's encouragement, a potentially enlightening and empowering source of vision.

The following poem by Neapolitan actor and playwright Eduardo De Filippo is part of a culture intimately connected to the sea that counts among its lineage the previously mentioned Sannazaro, a number of anonymous compositions such as "Lo Guarracino" and "Michelemmà," the fisher folk of Santa Lucia, the emblematic image of the Gulf of Naples and, most importantly, the mermaid Parthenope that gave the city its name and identity. The poem's closing verse, "'o mare è mmare,/e nun 'o sape ca te fa paura," encourages readers to consider the sea as an agent whose *being* and actions are not reflective of human projections:

"'O mare fa paura"	"The sea is frightening"
. . .	. . .
"Che brutta morte ha fatto	"What an awful death
stu pover'ommo,	this man has suffered,
e che mumento triste c'ha passato."	and what a sad moment."
Ma nun è muorto acciso.	But he was not killed.
È muorto a mmare.	He died at sea.
'O mare nun accide.	The sea does not kill
. . .	. . .
Io quanno 'o sento,	When I hear it
specialmente 'e notte,	especially at night,

cumme stevo dicenno,	as I was saying,
nun è ca dico:	I don't mean:
"'O mare fa paura,"	"The sea is frightening,"
ma dico:	but rather:
"'O mare sta facenno 'o mare."	"The sea is being sea."
'O mare è mmare,	The sea is sea,
e nun 'o sape ca te fa paura.	and knows not that it is frightening.

The suggestion that the sea is merely the sea, an agent that acts of its own accord rather as a mirror for human sentiments and projections, is also a guiding principle in the narratives of the popular songs "Lo Guarracino" (ca. 1700) and "Michelemmà" (ca. 1600). The first one narrates the imagined love encounters between sea creatures of every species in a tarantella story that ends in a general free-for-all among factions of the aquatic population. The song's folkloric value, its elaborate list of sea life that is a source of nutrition and livelihood for the region, the descriptions of species and their niche interactions in the aquatic ecosystem have been found to be extremely accurate by contemporary scientists (see Boccardi 2003). We might also say that as an allegory, the dwindling ocean and sea stocks correspond to societal and international hierarchies in the same manner that migrants' points of origin, trajectories, and deaths do in a parallel relationship to Dagmawi Yimer's listing of names in *Asmat*. The second song, "Michelemmà," blends a love story with historical narrative in a mythical tale of the interaction of human and nonhuman actors and their qualities. The figure of Michela "nata 'n miezz'o mare" (born in the sea) is a hybrid being reminiscent of Parthenope, the mermaid who possesses both a mythical and a real cultural value for Neapolitans.

While it may seem insensitive to talk about migrant deaths alongside sea life and folk songs, the approximation of all these elements within one confluent discourse is enabled by Stacy Alaimo's suggestive notion of trans-corporeality as what "traces the material interchanges across human bodies, animal bodies, and the wider material world" (Alaimo 2014, 187). In terms of nonhuman life, the fossil evidence, folksongs, popular testimony, and activities provide a record that traces possible environmental changes over time. In terms of human life, our habit of separating ourselves from other realms in order to reify them generates a distance from the greater ecological cycles and as such tends to hint at a human ahistoricity that is stable and uncritical.

Jason deCaires Taylor's undersea sculptures might clarify what I am attempting to suggest. The groupings of sculptures placed in the Mediterranean waters of Spain and Greece, but also of Mexico, the United Kingdom, and Granada, engage human shapes constructed of nonhuman materials in the protection and regeneration of nonhuman elements and ecosystems such as coral reefs, vertebrate and invertebrate habitats. The fantastical figures made from an amalgam of materials, are "stable and environmentally responsive.... For example, in coral regeneration, the sculptures integrate a coral-promoting neutral pH cement and propagate damaged coral fragments found in the ocean into preset keys in his figures" (Scales 2014, 25–26). While the sculptures represent a commentary on environmental degradation and an effort at regeneration, they also suggest an unavoidable parallel commemoration of human tragedies associated with migrations and slavery. Although it is actually situated in the waters off Lanzarote, Spain, Taylor's sculpture *The Raft of Lampedusa* clearly pays homage to the same migrants referred to in Yimer's film. This speculative interpretation is supported by the fact that in making *The Raft* and other pieces, the sculptor used casts made from models who are themselves immigrants. The manner in which these sculptures come to inhabit the sea provides an indirect link to the migrants' crossings and deaths. The drowned migrants who do not wash ashore become part of the organic matter that generates new life in the sea, transitioning from human to more-than-human or nonhuman inhabitants of ecosystems. Taylor's shape-shifting sculptures illustrate the reconfiguration enacted by the sea life that adheres to them.

The interplay between human and nonhuman in Taylor's works, as well as in Yimer's film, denies the usual medium distinctions that separate them, as it undoes the suggested distance between atmospheric and aquatic spheres and the hierarchies that humans have imposed. Again, Alaimo's notion of trans-corporeality, especially if applied to marine contexts, is a useful point of reference, as it proposes an open and intra-active relationship of beings and elements:

> Trans-corporeality situates the (post)human as always already part of the world's intra-active agencies. For an oceanic sense of trans-corporeality to be an ethical mode of being, the material self must not be a finished, self-contained product of evolutionary genealogies but a site where the knowledges and practices of embodiment are undertaken as part of the world's becoming.... Trans-corporeality as an ethical practice requires not only that citizens seek out information, which may or may not exist in any trustworthy or usable form, about risks to their own health, but that they also seek out information about how their own bodily existence—their consumption of food, fuel, and specific consumer products—affects other people, other animals, habitats, and ecosystems. (Alaimo 2014, 193)

While this description holds true in general terms, when we consider that migrants and other marginalized populations and categories endure "a suspension of the human" (Allewaert 2013, 85), we are held to contemplate the inevitable emergence of an invisible gradient that moves through and links the disappeared migrants and the dwindling, dying bodies of subaqueous flora and fauna. Mediterranean waters are poor in sea life when compared to the nearby Atlantic, and particularly so in animal, plant, and plankton life because of the sea's high temperatures and a topography devoid of coastal shelves. The sea's wonderfully attractive, characteristic transparent blue color is a direct result of this dearth of life. Today, as the stocks of available sea life have become even scarcer from overfishing and pollution, a consciousness of interdependence seems to have finally become apparent for those who have sustained themselves through the sea. The destructive realities of toxic dumping and other industrial catastrophes, the failed attempts of migrating human bodies that seed its waters with death, might seem to inscribe the Mediterranean as a dying sea. However, if we take on the task suggested by Alaimo, to consider that "the material self must not be a finished, self-contained product of evolutionary genealogies but a site where the knowledges and practices of embodiment are undertaken as part of the world's becoming" (192–93), the need to delve into other possible variations—variations that could help us translate the finality implied by death into a contemplation on life—becomes apparent. Within this scenario, Rosi Braidotti's elaboration of "zoe" as "the dynamic, self-organizing structure of life itself (that) stands for generative vitality" may be recalled as a proposal through which to counter "the opportunistic political economy of biogenetic capitalism turns Life/zoe—that is to say human and non-human intelligent matter—into a commodity for trade and profit" (2013, 60–61).

The terms by which death is transformed into life require an "interrogation of how corporeal and non-corporeal, organic and inorganic materials and parts that compose being and places emerge" (Allewaert 2013, 18). In her study of the colonial/slave systems of the American tropics, Monique Allewaert argues that the term *parahuman* "might describe American slaves' categorization as neither human nor animal" (2013, 22). This term can be easily adapted to Mediterranean migrants since they too, although indirectly and in forms different from those described by Allewaert, are imposed upon by colonial narratives and are similarly designated as less than human. As I hope to have pointed out via my limited Neapolitan examples, parahuman forms are not foreign to Mediterranean cultures and, as such, illustrate an extant relationship to hegemonic/dominant cultures that provides different parameters for agency. A shift in our perspective from conventionally understood bodily forms tends toward decentering notions of personhood rooted in colonial hierarchies and moves away from the prioritization of human beings (understood as European). Pointing out that in the "Anglo-European cosmology . . . agency depends on the integrity of the animal body," Allewaert develops her discussion by referring to the mutilation, decapitation, and fragmentation of slave bodies as a colonial attempt at dehumanization (2013, 98). But it is in this very fragmentation, and in its reconstitution through Alaimo's version of porosity as osmotic trans-corporeality, or the recognition that bodies inter-are with economic, social, cultural, and ecological networks, that the parahuman does not lead to or aim for humanity but that it is "an identificatory category that recalls yet is also beside and after the human" (Allewaert 2013, 110). Not torn or mutilated in the manner that slave bodies were, the Mediterranean bodies are torn from their native situations to be cast asunder across lands and, here, the sea. What Allewaert describes as an "alternative materialism of the body" (2013, 3) begins to take shape at the moment of departure and is further emphasized by the sea crossing. Those who successfully make the crossing continue a transformative series of experiences that, although connected to some of the bodily conventions encountered, continue to live in conditions that previously and presently dehumanize them in conventional terms. Nevertheless they, along with the decomposed bodies of the drowned, bridge the assumed separation from the natural world and deny the traditional terms of distinction between human and nonhuman. In this sense, a different sort of agency is born, a new collective subjectivity that, although painful, is productive in ways that are nonnegotiable and not easily manipulated.[4] As Taylor's metaphorical representations, and Alaimo's and Allewaert's work suggest, these bodies (survived and drowned) are transformed by the act of migration from objects of capitalist processes of exploitation into subjects, protagonists, initiators of their own collective liberation and history.

To conclude my observations, I would like to restate a section from one of Antonio Gramsci's *Ordine Nuovo* articles, wherein we might cast the "choice" of migration in place of the Communist Party and the role it was to have played. This argument forms part of Gramsci's elaboration of the role and formation of intellectuals as an active modality:

> The Communist Party is the instrument and historic form of the process of intimate liberation, by which the worker from *executor* becomes *initiator*, from *mass* becomes *head* and *guide*, from arm becomes mind and will . . . becoming part of the Communist Party, the worker collaborates in "discovering" and "inventing" original ways of living, where the worker collaborates "voluntarily" in the world's activities, thinking, envisioning, is responsible, where the worker is an organizer and not organized, where the worker builds an avant-garde that brings with it the whole of the popular masses. (Gramsci 2015, 76–77)

The decision to undertake the elaborate and dangerous migrations to reach the shores of North Africa and then a Mediterranean crossing is thus indicative of taking action in order to "invent" a new way of being, a way to initiate and determine one's own faith. This differently established agency gives voice to the protest and activism of migrants and, like Yimer's commemorative work, gives names to formless manifestations of ecological solidarity, or that move toward "becoming world" (Braidotti 2013, 80).

NOTES

1. While the influx of Mediterranean migrants makes landfall on Lampedusa, the island itself does not necessarily represent the Italian south in the general imaginary. The city of Naples has tended to function in social, anthropological, political, and cultural representations (positive and negative), as a synecdochical example of southern Italy's relationship with the sea. Therefore, while Naples is only tangentially approached within the body of this essay, the city and Lampedusa are meant to function as bracketing terms rather than precise points of contrast. Lampedusa, a place of arrival and transit, represents the enormity of migrant arrivals but is not necessarily descriptive of their eventual relationship to Italy or Europe. Similarly, the recent documentary by Gianfranco Rosi, *Fuocoammare* (2016a), filmed on Lampedusa, represents the relationship of migrants to the residents of the island also tangentially, in other words, temporarily intimate. While the film is unquestionably "a work of art, above all an important work of art" that shifts "documentary as a form toward realism as creation," reviewers such as Nazzaro (2016), whose words I have just quoted, tend to relegate the migrants themselves as subjects at the service of the "work of art." Nazzaro describes the migrants as "those bodies, even for only momentarily, are not the bodies of other: they are the bodies of a vital rhythm that we see and hear pulsate, intuited in the alternating cycles of the sun and moon of Lampedusa, and that now lie lifeless," a description that deprives them of any sense of agency and casts them, once again, as a momentary appearance, contradicting the ongoing and enormously present migrations. Rosi himself has addressed and acknowledged this point in interviews; Lampedusa is for migrants a point of arrival and departure, where they are "processed" and transported elsewhere. The director further intimated that the true subject of his film is Lampedusa and its inhabitants, the constantly present population that receives and often rescues the migrants (Rosi 2016b).

2. Extinction also refers to the disappearance of species as a result of adaptation to changing environments, which signifies not a wholesale erasure but changes in traits that manifest as a new species, differing from its previous taxonomy. See Colwell (2009).

3. "My 'Mediterranean' is resolutely the surface of the sea itself, its shores and its islands, particularly the port cities that provided the main departure and arrival points for those crossing it" (Abulafia 2001, xvii).

4. Walter Benjamin and Asja Lacis's notion of "porosity" in relation to Naples is useful in this larger context, apparently appreciative of the city as a place of contradictions (see Verdicchio 2007). They define *porous* and *porosity* as qualities that arise "not only from the indolence of the Southern artisan but also above all from the passion for improvisation, which demands that space and opportunity be at any price preserved" (Benjamin and Lacis 2000, 35). While their use of *porous* tends to suggest a view of the city as less than civilized, we might nevertheless extract from it a sense that can be positively

developed. The population's aptitude for improvisation, and Benjamin's own observation that "everywhere is preserved a space that could potentially become a theatre of new and unforeseen constellations. Certainty and codification are everywhere avoided" (34), aid in our rescue of the term, where the avoidance of certainty and codification can be understood as an active signifier within the pages of my present essay.

WORKS CITED

Abulafia, David. 2011. *The Great Sea: A Human History of the Mediterranean*. New York: Oxford University Press.

Alaimo, Stacy. 2014. "Oceanic Origins, Plastic Activism, and New Materialism at Sea." In *Material Ecocriticism*, edited by Serenella Iovino and Serpil Oppermann, 186–203. Bloomington: Indiana University Press.

Allewaert, Monique. 2013. *Ariel's Ecology: Plantations, Personhood, and Colonialism in the American Tropics*. Minneapolis: University of Minnesota Press.

Benjamin, Walter, and Asja Lacis. 2000. "Napoli." In *Napoli*, edited by Enrico Donaggio, 31–41. Naples: L'Ancora del Mediterraneo.

Boccardi, Vincenzo. 2003. "Una finestra sulla biodiversità di un ecosistema marino del recente passato: L'originale testimonianza del canto popolare napoletano *Lo Guarracino*." *Didattica delle Scienze* 224: 5–12.

Braidotti, Rosi. 2013. *The Posthuman*. Cambridge, UK: Polity Press.

Cassano, Franco. 2003. *Oltre il nulla: Studio su Giacomo Leopardi*. Rome: Laterza.

———. 2012. *Southern Thought and Other Essays on the Mediterranean*. Edited and translated by Norma Bouchard and Valerio Ferme. New York: Fordham University Press.

Colwell, Robert K. 2009. "Biodiversity: Concepts, Patterns, and Measurement." In *The Princeton Guide to Ecology*, edited by Simon A. Levin, 257–263. Princeton, NJ: Princeton University Press.

Conte, Giuseppe. 2015. *Poesie 1983–2015*. Milan: Mondadori.

Gramsci, Antonio. 2015. *La Classe Operaia: Antologia di unità e di lotta*. Rome: Edizioni Centro Gramsci.

Iovino, Serenella. 2013. "Introduction: Mediterranean Ecocriticism, or, A Blueprint for Cultural Amphibians." *Ecozon@* 4(2): 1–14.

Ligabue, Luciano. 2007. "Buonanotte all'Italia." *Primo tempo*. WEA-Warner Bros. Records 514 4 24865 2. Compact disc.

Matvejević, Predrag. 1993. *Mediterraneo: Un nuovo breviario*. Milan: Garzanti.

Nazzaro, Giona. 2016. "*Fuocoammare*, il realismo come creazione" in *Micromega*, February 22. http://temi.repubblica.it/micromega-online/cinema-fuocoammare-di-gianfranco-rosi/.

Rosi, Gianfranco. 2016a. *Fuocoammare*. Video. Rome: 01 Distribution.

———. 2016b. "Intervista a Gianfranco Rosi, Orso d'Oro alla Berlinale 2016." Video. https://www.youtube.com/watch?v=Iya4JU1mmCs.

Sannazaro, Jacopo. 1966. *Arcadia and Piscatorial Eclogues*. Translated by Ralph Nash. Detroit: Wayne State University Press.

Scales, Helen. 2014. "From Polyp to Rampart: The Science of Reef Building and How Art Can Inspire a Sustainable Future." In *The Underwater Museum: The Submerged Sculptures of Jason deCaires Taylor*, 19–29. San Francisco: Chronicle Books.

Swift, Jonathan. 1745. *Thoughts on Various Subjects: Further Thoughts on Various Subjects.* London: Robert Dodsley.

Verdicchio, Pasquale. 2007. "'O Cuorp' 'e Napule: Naples and the Cinematographic Body of Culture." In *Italian Neorealism and Global Cinema,* edited by Laura Ruberto and Kristi M. Wilson, 259–89. Detroit: Wayne State University Press.

Westphal, Bertrand. 2013. "La Méditerranée ou la forme de l'eau." *Ecozon@* 4(2): 15–29.

Yimer, Dagmawi. 2014. *Asmat, nomi.* Produced by Comitato 3 ottobre and Archivio delle Memorie Migranti. Video. https://youtu.be/_EM-nUU_MyQ.

ENRICO CESARETTI

Eco-Futurism?
Nature, Matter, and Body in
Filippo Tommaso Marinetti

> We want to sing the man at the wheel, the ideal axis of which crosses the Earth, itself hurled along its orbit.—F. T. Marinetti, *The Futurist Manifesto* (1909)

> First of all, let's put an end to the boasted superiority of the human.—F. T. Marinetti, *The Nonhuman Poem of Technicalities* (1940)

Both epigraphs above accurately represent the often contradictory thought of Filippo Tommaso Marinetti, the champion of European Futurism: exaltation of speed and technological control over a submissive Earth mastered by "man" versus a rejection of the "boasted superiority of the human." It seems that we could hardly be further away from an ecological horizon. But is this really the case?

Certainly Marinetti's works do not display an environmental consciousness in the modern, common sense of the expression, and the term unsustainability could well describe his relationship with the natural world. He viewed nature as a resource to be conquered and civilized, a corpus to be mastered to enhance and affirm the bellicose virility of the masculine subject, or "the locus of the feminine and the maternal (which) must be opposed and displaced by both the machine, and its symbolic ally, matter (sheer dynamic physicality)" (see Härmänmaa 2009; Poggi 1997, 24). Nevertheless, a first step to reconsider the complex, interrelated notions of nature, matter, and body in Marinetti's work from a perspective that wishes to be open and receptive to current ecocritical concerns and theories might be to recall Anne Raine's remark that "the appreciation of and concern for the natural world may be more central to literary modernism than critics have recognized" (quoted in Garrard 2014, 99). At the same time, it helps to keep in mind the "Janus-headed configuration of literary and artistic Modernism" and the "paradoxical dynamics" characterizing European culture of the turn of the twentieth century, that is, one able to generate often contradictory and antipodal responses "with respect to social and cultural norms" (Moroni 2011, 117–22). Following this line, those rare occasions in Marinetti's texts when

Futurism's dismissal of nature is not straightforward and, rather, nature "becomes the hero (or heroine) that cruel, materialistic technology victimizes" become especially relevant (Sartini Blum 1996, 141). This is the path taken by Sartini Blum in *The Other Modernism*. In her book she convincingly discusses passages in several of Marinetti's works where the natural realm is positively and nostalgically associated with notions such as peace, seduction, the maternal, "the transforming power (as well as the danger) of progress," heroism, compassion, and regeneration (1996, 139).

Indeed, Marinetti occasionally praises and ultimately valorizes nature, or landscapes, using the technology and machines at his disposal (including the *techne* of his writing), rather than merely conquering or taming it. For example, a passage in the chapter "Green Throbbing Edges of Milan" in the autobiographical *Great Traditional and Futurist Milan* (1943) conveys this idea, as the poet finds himself outside the city in the green belt around Milan formed by the "countryside around Bergamo and Como" (Marinetti 1969, 155). He tells Jesus that he is there unexpectedly to make a humble offering: "We wandering artists are here offering the little we have that is art verses paintings dreams prayers of streams azure sculptures of incense . . . Before opaque beings come to trample on us we must well extol the fluent contacts of the best Italian landscapes" (Marinetti 1969, 155–56).[1]

Futurism's perception of landscape as a dimension that mediates between outside and inside, self and world, and subjectivity and objectivity finds its highest, and yet ambiguous, achievement with aeropoetry, Marinetti's creative solution to celebrate through poetry (and painting, with aeropainting, as Sophia Farmer illustrates in her essay, pp. 98–109), "the sensory drama of flight." As Daniel Mangano observes, at the base of aeropoetry there is a definitive ambiguity because if aeropoetry is a way to penetrate matter through the fusion with the machine, it is also an upward shift and, thus, a new distancing of the world (1996, 60–61). Particularly relevant to my discussion are his remarks that both Marinetti and, even more consistently, other Futurist aeropoets such as Gaetano Pattarozzi, Bruno Sanzin, and Paolo Buzzi, with his *Aeropoetry for Aeropainting*, were able to convey in their writings an identification between landscape, machine, and poetic self to reduce the distance between the world and the "I," bringing the latter closer to the "cosmic dimension of matter" (Mangano 1996, 61). As a matter of fact, Futurism's intuition that subjectivity and objectivity merge through the mediation of landscape indicates at least an aesthetic interest in the environment, whereby human beings and the world in which they live would aim to coexist symbiotically in a new, in-between artistic reality which is neither the traditional work of art nor the environment. But there is more. The implicit idea that subjects and objects, bodies and things, organic and inorganic matter belong to—and have an impact on—the same natural, universal dimension, strongly resonates with some postmodern, ecocritical theories that investigate the extension of human agency, the boundaries of human and nonhuman, nature and culture, and, in short, the intertwinements "of bodies, natures, and meanings" (Iovino and Oppermann 2012, 450).

In what follows, I thus consider Futurism's notorious fascination and "lyrical obsession" (Marinetti 1990, 50) with the notion of matter in conjunction with the recent development within ecocritical theory known as the material turn. The latter, in fact, has expanded ecocriticism's practical applications "beyond nature writing," beyond nature and a vision associating nature with human-centered concepts such as the "other than culture," "wilderness," or "the environment" (Iovino and Oppermann 2012, 449). Since this materialist ecocritical approach does not exclusively focus on and put nature, landscape, or the human at the center of the discourse, it is a more appropriate lens through which to examine a "hostile" context such as Futurism from an ecocritical perspective. In particular, I am interested in assessing to what extent Marinetti's representation of the multifaceted concept of matter may be posthumously contributing to the discussion originated by one of the fundamental questions posed by postmodernist material ecocriticism, that is, "how material are we," or better yet, "how material-discursive are we?" (Iovino and Oppermann 2012, 454).[2] It goes without saying that the body, as a privileged, environmentally interactive playground for matter's many narratives, remains central to such a question. Yet my main objective is not to provocatively extract Marinetti from his historical context and suddenly transform him into a precursor of posthuman, ecocritical thought.[3] Rather, I seek to draw attention to certain affinities, parallelisms, and, to use Deleuze and Guattari's term, "adjacencies" between the way Futurism imagined matter and some of the current positions of material ecocriticism (1986, 7–8).

Of course, the fundamental reasons behind Futurism's and posthuman/postmodern ecocriticism's common interest in matter are substantially different. In simplified terms, in the former case, such an interest is an ideal means to defeat time and the perishability of the organic body through the combination of the abolition of the "I" and the advent of a strengthened "multiplied man." In the latter case, it is a way to question precisely the primacy of bio-/logo-/anthropocentrism and to become aware of our nonhierarchical interrelatedness with a nonhuman universe.[4] Still, despite their clear ideological divergences, Futurism's and ecocriticism's respective explorations around the interrelations of human corporeality with a universe constituted by other-than-human elements illuminate each other. Specifically, the two discourses share a concern with the force and vibrant life of things and a desire to register the agency and the stories of both human and nonhuman entities. Furthermore, both positions indicate a fundamental, common interest in the precarious and not always central position of human beings in a rapidly transforming world, as they strive expose a continuity of the organic and the inorganic, of bodies and things, of beings and objects.[5] I am intrigued when, for example, in *Vibrant Matter: A Political Ecology of Things* Jane Bennett (2010) states that her aim is to stress the active role of nonhuman materials and thing-power in public life, thus inviting readers to develop the naïveté and sensibility to the outside which distinguish and are associated with vital materialism. My attention is similarly stirred when, within the same discourse, she encourages readers to rediscover the theoretical wealth of premodern philosophies of nature such as animism, vitalism, and anthropomorphism. And, finally, some of Futurism's own tales and positions keep "dangerously" coming to mind when Bennett asks us to direct all our attention to tales which, both ambitiously and naively, ask questions "that have been too readily foreclosed by . . . the fetishization of the subject, the image, the word" (2010, 19). In particular, I cannot help but think of Marinetti's many naïve remarks regarding the need to put an end to the superiority of the human, to "penetrate the essence of matter and destroy the dull hostility that separates it from us" and to operate on the discursive level of the text so that "literature enters directly the universe and becomes one with it" (1990, 52–53). I think, too, of Balla, Depero, and Prampolini's playful intention in their "Futurist Reconstruction of the Universe" (1915) to provide "skeleton and flesh to the invisible, the insubstantial, the imponderable, the imperceptible," thus articulating their desire to infuse a corporeality and a vital materiality even into the quasi-body of a universal vibration (Bennett 2010, xiii).[6]

The language of these few Futurist excerpts shows once again how crucial the body is in this context, and how the expansion (or reduction) of its perception resembles some of the positions of material ecocriticism. In other words, the notion of corporeality loses its familiar, fixed association with the human specifically. Instead, we can see corporeality here becoming a dynamic process that transits, is diffused to, and in turn, defines other potentially sentient entities beyond the human. In this scenario, it becomes reasonable to imagine that the nonhuman, too, can now be embodied. Such nonhuman embodiments may include a literature/text that must now actively become one, that must be integrated with the outside world (i.e., to make a body), or even an invisible vibration in the energy/matter of the universe that acquires a skeleton and flesh.

Marinetti and Futurism's invitations to embrace the "same life of matter . . . in order to provide the maximum amount of vibrations and a more profound synthesis of life" (Marinetti 1990, 73–76), their calls to diminish the ontological distance that separates human beings and things, and the poet's creative efforts arguably to convey what Bennett calls the "vitality intrinsic to materiality" (2010, xiii) are too numerous to include in the limited scope of this essay. In these circumstances, however, Marinetti's "plays of objects" aim to represent on the stage a series of animated, sentient objects removed from their traditional setting and situate them instead in an unusual condition. Here, by contrast, their astonishing essence, construction, and nonhuman life emerges, and they stand out as some of the clearest texts in which, ecocritically speaking, one may state that action is generated by the mutual collaboration between the human and the nonhuman. In the dramatic piece and play of objects *They Are Coming*, for example, the lives of the human and nonhuman characters—the majordomo and the servants, respectively—and the pieces of furniture (an armchair, a table, and eight chairs) are ideally interconnected since they belong to the same existential horizon and have equal performative standing on the stage's dynamic topology. Their interactive engagement as they inseparably move and are moved around, waiting and listening together for some mysterious guests to arrive, is that which provides dramatic tension and shapes the piece itself. As Marinetti wrote: "In *They Are Coming* I wished to create a synthesis of animated objects . . . the spectator . . . must feel that the chairs really live and move by themselves to get out" (1960c, 285). A similar intention to "convey the nonhuman life of objects" may be found also in *The Little Theatre of Love* (1960a, 345). Here the pieces of furniture—a cupboard and a sideboard—possess even a voice, and they exchange onomatopoeia-rich lines ("Cupboard: Cric. It shall rain in three quarters of an hour . . . Sideboard: Crac-crac. On the third floor the servant is going to bed") (342). Together with a little girl, they witness from their apparently wiser existential condition of thingness a depressing bourgeois scene of human love and betrayal between the girl's mother and the "first guy to come along" (342).

Marinetti's explanation of what happens in this play is particularly interesting, since he specifically points out the nonhuman origin of the vitalistic impulse that characterizes the objects on the stage: "In the Little Theatre of Love, I wished to convey the nonhuman life of objects. The most important characters are the little wood theatre, the cupboards, the sideboard, and they are not humanized . . . but nonhumanly convey the temperature, their expansions, the weight they can bear, the vibrations of the walls, etc." (1960a, 345). In other words, the vitality and animation of the inorganic is not just the result of a process of humanization or simple anthropomorphism but is inherent to matter itself, to the materials (i.e., the wood, metal, and paint) that constitute the bodies of these active objects that are also becoming, in effect, speaking subjects and "actants" in the play. In these short, experimental pieces, we thus see, with material ecocriticism, that "the old conceptions of matter as stable, inert and passive physical substance, and of the human agent as a separate observer always in control, are being replaced here by . . . models that effectively theorize matter's inherent vitality" (Iovino and Oppermann 2012, 465). In these examples, matter is not just "a vector of speed, a volatile, masculine substitute for . . . nature" (Poggi 1997, 24) and another instance of Marinetti's familiar animistic tendencies. It is also not merely something that helps the Futurist's fight to defeat time and "against rot" (Schnapp 2004, 230). Marinetti's interest in matter reveals rather both a pseudoscientific, esoteric fascination with "the incomprehensible and inhuman alliance of its molecules or its electrons" (Marinetti, 1990, 50–51) and a bent for a poetic, even mystical attitude of re-enchantment with, and wonder about, the nonhuman world. These different perspectives depend, ultimately, on us: we might chose to emphasize and view Futurism either through, respectively, a "theosophic" premodern lens (Cigliana 2002, 237) or an "onto-poetic" postmodern, material-ecocritical one (Iovino 2012b, 142).

Although in the previous texts matter possesses what Bennett calls the "quivering effervescence" of life (2010, 55), there is no doubt that it is its fundamental inorganic and other-than-human quality that allegedly prevents the decline over time of the individual (and political) body that especially fascinates Futurism. The "fabrics of modern times" discussed by Schnapp in his analysis of Marinetti's *The Nonhuman Poem of Technicalities*, together with a number of new modern, industrially produced materials from steel to plastics, helped energize and awaken such an individual body from its decadent torpor and functioned as "the prosthetic extension of the new multiplied man and woman" (Schnapp 2004, 233). Leaving aside fabrics, and adding some iron and concrete, a text like Marinetti's *Reconstructing Italy with Sant'Elia's Futurist Architecture* (1960b) suggests that those same materials are considered essential to reinvigorate the nation's body politic and health, especially when some of its parts, like the city of Venice, are thought to be weakened and dying because of their association with "passéism" (and thus need to be destroyed and then rebuilt according to Futurist principles). Marinetti's architectural "divertissement representable in many synthesis" thus promises to generate some conclusive reflections on the Futurist interactions between nature, bodies, and matter, as it expresses concern for the future of the Italian territory in general, and the city of Venice in particular.[7] Inspired by the polemical debate between rationalists and Futurists at the end of the twenties on the objectives and qualities of modern architecture, *Reconstructing* dramatizes the different and yet ultimately overlapping positions of the "Speedists," who stand for the Futurists, and the "Spatialists," who stand for the rationalists. These two conflicting groups eventually search for common ground, reconciliation, and victorious collaboration against the threat represented by the "Softies," namely, the traditionalists, who are attached to the past and to old-fashioned conceptions of urban architecture and landscape planning. On the one hand, this work necessarily reconfirms the author's distance from any modern idea of environmental or ecological consciousness. Vasto, the leader of the Spatialists, makes this immediately clear in the first synthesis "The Living Space," when he establishes a direct correspondence between the human and the national body. He states: "We, magnified men, need a magnified homeland. The peninsula will be augmented, at every tip of its edge, with 200 kilometers of reinforced concrete and iron that will cover the sea filled with the pieces of the razed-to-the-ground mountains" (Marinetti 1960b, 520).

Ballamar, one of the "spatial architects," echoes this position. While certainly not a supporter of the natural world, since he complains about the domination of "the line of the very beautiful sea" (Marinetti 1960b, 520) and outlines his plans to reshape it "through new kinds of waves" (523), he is also the proponent of an ephemeral, theriomorphic architecture which, in a familiar dynamic, betrays a persistent fascination with nature, its shapes and functioning principles: "The frameworks are wings . . . The buildings will have immense and sharp ostrich breasts and pirouetting balconies . . . the dams of the new harbors will have the synthetic shapes of waves and fish . . . Expansive architectures (made of diverse) matter will unite with the clouds, the rain, the snow, the fog, the darkness . . . Projectors, by weaving their beams of light into the clouds laid on the brow of the building, will complete the building itself with a splendid germination of luminous crystals" (523–24). Both Ballamar and Vasto, as well as the leaders of the Speedists (Furr and Vif-Glin), are confident in the powers of new construction materials. Their brief architectural debates revolve around the supposed eternity or ephemerality such materials should possess, and they eventually seem to like and compromise on the mutually agreeable solution of an "ephemeral spatial concrete" (524).

What seems particularly interesting in this passage is not only the deliberate effort to merge the inorganic aspect of the constructions with the organic one of the animals—to unite artificial and natural matter, or the fact that architecture becomes here a metaphor for human existence—but also the inherent vitality (and corporeality) of buildings which possess wings, breasts, and a forehead. The limited time span of concrete, its eminently lifelike quality, and, especially, the implication that the construction materials possess a dormant vibrancy of their own should also be highlighted. This vibrancy, once energized with the combination of natural elements (clouds, rain, etc.) and artificial ones (electric light) will contribute to an almost autogenic completion of the buildings themselves.

Beyond the surreal plot and self-serving propagandistic turn of the events depicted, the idea that human beings, habitats, and materials (i.e., bodies, nature, matter) share an interrelated, inner vitality is thus animating *Reconstructing*. As a consequence, this text also foregrounds the interactions between different kinds of living bodies and their entanglement with the more-than-human world in Marinetti's work.

While Futurism's main interests and goals do not include environmentalist concerns, the adjacencies of some of the developments of material ecocriticism to a selection of his works turn our attention to a new perspective from which to (re)consider Futurism's representation of nature, its thinking of the body, and its still unresolved relationship with the eloquence of matter. The idea that some of the aspects of the "vital materialism" discussed by Bennett can be traced in this modernist context allows us to navigate between seemingly incompatible views on Marinetti. Specifically, seeing in Marinetti's work the possibility of a nonhierarchical mutuality, interaction, and coexistence between human subjects and nonhuman objects, between bodies and things opens a path between two positions: on the one hand, those interpretations that perceive Marinetti as someone who gives "always more importance to matter, marginalizing and diminishing human beings" (Curi 2009, 296), and on the other, those affirming the poetic and vital anthropocentric prevalence of the creating subject over matter and things (Ceccagnoli 2009, 329). To conclude, it is worth noting that when Marinetti wrote that it is necessary for literature to directly enter the universe and become one with it, he was referring specifically to the linguistic need to eliminate syntax. With a little imaginative effort, however, his aspiration might also be interpreted as aiming to establish a cultural and existential poetic ecosystem in which the discursive and the material world are embodied together. Here, if nothing else, the long-term survival (if you wish, "aesthetic sustainability") of this ecosystem depends on the possibility that "humans share their narrative horizon with ... other things" (Iovino 2012a, 66). In other words, the notion of a corporeality no longer exclusively human or organic, but also material, finds one of its earliest and most intriguing manifestations in Marinetti's modernist work.[8]

NOTES

1. All translations from the Italian are mine.

2. With "material-discursive" Iovino (2012a) points to material ecocriticism's consideration of matter as a text in itself: "reality is read as a material text, *as a site of narrativity, a storied matter*. If discourse and meaning are co-extensive in the constitution of matter, reality can be discovered as an array of stories" (57–58, emphasis in the original).

3. On the relationship between Futurism and posthumanism, see Terrosi (2009); see also Ryan and West (2015).

4. "The main tendency of futurism is not to negate man or the human but to magnify it . . . thus maintaining a thread of continuity with the positions of humanistic renaissance" (Terrosi 2009, 268).

5. In her discussion on how Anglo-American modernism and ecocriticism can be productively engaged, Anne Raine (2014) points out that as early as 1998 Carol Cantrell argued that modernist texts are relevant for ecocriticism because modernist writers are self-conscious "witnesses to the profound changes in the human relations with the planet that ha[d] become visible in [their] century," sharing a sense of having experienced a "revolutionary change" in "'the given' we call nature" (101).

6. The following excerpt from the "Technical Manifesto of Futurist Painting," one of the Futurist texts that is closer to a posthuman aesthetic, is worth mentioning: "Our new conscience does not make us consider man as the center of universal life any longer. For us, the pain of a man is as interesting as the one of an electric lamp, which suffers, and agonizes, and cries with the most excruciating expressions of pain" (quoted in Terrosi 2009, 271).

7. *Venezianella e Studentaccio* is where Marinetti concludes his complex, lifelong poetic elaboration on Venice. In his introduction, Valesio (2013a) notes that the novel also "expresses . . . the desire to stabilize Venice, protecting it from the danger of sinking" (lxvii, n. 25), thus suggesting that a sui generis environmental sensibility may actually be present in Marinetti.

8. The "evocation of poetry as a privileged and ideal space, a haven from the ugliness of the world, traverses all of Marinetti's work, from its pre-futurist (i.e., symbolist) phase . . . to its futurist one, despite the various desecrating moves" (Valesio 2013a, lxv, n. 17).

WORKS CITED

Bennett, Jane. 2010. *Vibrant Matter: A Political Ecology of Things*. Durham, NC: Duke University Press.

Ceccagnoli, Patrizio. 2009. "'Necrofilia' e prosopopea della materia: La personificazione in Marinetti." In "A Century of Futurism: 1909–2009," edited by Luca Somigli and Federico Luisetti, special issue, *Annali d'Italianistica* 27: 309–31.

Cigliana, Simona. 2002. *Futurismo esoterico*. Naples: Liguori.

Curi, Fausto. 2009. "Marinetti, il soggetto, la materia." In "A Century of Futurism: 1909–2009," edited by Luca Somigli and Federico Luisetti, special issue, *Annali d'Italianistica* 27: 294–307.

Deleuze, Gilles, and Felix Guattari. 1986. *Kafka toward a Minor Literature*. Minneapolis: University of Minnesota Press.

Garrard, Greg, ed. 2014. *The Oxford Handbook of Ecocriticism*. New York: Oxford University Press.

Härmänmaa, Marja. 2009. "Futurism and Nature: The Death of the Great Pan." In *Futurism and the Technological Imagination*, edited by Günter Berghaus, 337–60. Amsterdam: Rodopi.

Iovino, Serenella. 2012a. "Material Ecocriticism: Matter, Text, and Posthuman Ethics." In *Literature, Ecology, Ethics: Recent Trends in Ecocriticism*, edited by Timo Müller and Michael Sauter, 49–68. Heidelberg: Universitätsverlag Winter.

———. 2012b. "Steps to a Material Ecocriticism: The Recent Literature about the 'New Materialisms' and Its Implications for Ecocritical Theory." *Ecozon@* 3(1): 134–45.

Iovino, Serenella, and Serpil Oppermann. 2012. "Theorizing Material Ecocriticism: A Diptych." *ISLE* 19(3): 448–75.

Mangano, Daniel. 1996. "Paesaggio e Futurismo." In *Dino Buzzati: Immagini del mondo*, vol. 9, 55–66. Nanterre, France: Université de Paris X.

Marinetti, Filippo Tommaso 1960a. *Il teatrino dell'amore*. In *Teatro*, edited by Giovanni Calendoli, vol. 2, 341–45. Rome: Vito Bianco Editore.

———. 1960b. *Ricostruire l'Italia con architettura futurista Sant'Elia*. In *Teatro*, edited by Giovanni Calendoli, vol. 3, 509–602. Roma: Vito Bianco Editore.

———. 1960c. *Vengono*. In *Teatro*, edited by G. Calendoli, vol. 2, 283–85. Rome: Vito Bianco Editore.

———. 1969. *La grande Milano tradizionale e futurista, Una sensibilità italiana nata in Egitto*. Milan: Mondadori.

———. 1990. *Teoria e invenzione futurista*. Edited by Luciano De Maria. Milan: Mondadori.

———. 2013. *Venezianella e Studentaccio*. Milan: Mondadori.

Moroni, Mario. 2011. "Beyond Matter: Futurism and Occultist Practices." In *Futurismo: Impact and Legacy*, edited by Giuseppe Gazzola, 117–24. Stony Brook, NY: Forum Italicum Publishing.

Poggi, Christine. 1997. "Dreams of Metallized Flesh: Futurism and the Masculine Body." *Modernism/Modernity* 4(3): 19–43.

Raine, Anne. 2014. "Ecocriticism and Modernism." In *The Oxford Handbook of Ecocriticism*, edited by Greg Garrard, 98–117. New York: Oxford University Press.

Ryan, Derek, and Mark West, eds. 2015. "Modernist Ethics and Posthumanism," special issue, *Twentieth-Century Literature* 61(3).

Sartini Blum, Cinzia. 1996. *The Other Modernism: F. T. Marinetti's Futurist Fiction of Power*. Berkeley: University of California Press.

Schnapp, Jeffrey. 2004. "Rayon/Marinetti." In *Science and Literature in Italian Culture from Dante to Calvino: A Festschrift for Patrick Boyde*, edited by Pierpaolo Antonello and Simon A. Gilson, 226–53. Oxford, UK: European Humanities Research Centre.

Terrosi, Roberto. 2009. "Futurismo e postumano." In "A Century of Futurism: 1909–2009," edited by Luca Somigli and Federico Luisetti, special issue, *Annali d'Italianistica* 27: 263–73.

Valesio, Paolo. 2013a. "Introduzione." In F. T. Marinetti, *Venezianella e Studentaccio*, vii–liv. Milan: Mondadori.

ANDREA LERDA

Nature's Creative Balance: On Italian Eco-art

As I penned this essay, Christo's most recent project, *The Floating Piers*, opened on Lake Iseo. This coincidence is important, since it offers the perfect pretext to begin the story that I would like to tell about ecocriticism in Italy, in the artistic realm. As has often been the case for the American artist of Bulgarian origins, the Italian event generated a lively debate. On social media, newspapers, and television art critics, historians, curators, and museum directors interpreted the work, offering infinite different points of view. On the one hand, some called it a great achievement in marketing, an "alternative to village festivals" (Agazzi 2016) or even a dangerous work, an ecological disaster. On the other hand, it has been celebrated as a unique experience. This is not the first time Christo chose to work in Italy. He last worked here in the 1970s, when an international artistic movement was taking root: starting in the 1960s, the foundations were being laid for Arte Povera. Regardless of the point of view, his work on Lake Iseo helped reawaken a focus on environmental culture and criticism in Italy.

The floating walkways—made of 70,000 square meters of fabric in a changing yellow shade, and 200,000 cubes of high-density polyethylene—raised ethical questions that go beyond the artistic context. According to what the artist has always affirmed, his works are carefully conceived, as are the procedures for dismantling the work. Yet this does not suffice; large installations like this one raise equally significant moral questions. The words of Lucretius come to mind, when, in *De rerum natura*, he recognizes (perhaps for the first time) the existence of an anthropocentric position and lays the foundation for a critical relationship between humans and the earth: "Fear grips all mortal men precisely because/They see so many events on the earth, in the sky,/Whose rational causes they cannot discern—/So they suppose it's all the will of the gods. But once we've seen that nothing is made from nothing/We'll find our path and see straight through to what/We search for:

we shall know that things can come/To be—and in what manner—without gods" (Lucretius 1995, 29). Lucretius continues, clearly expressing how, in nature, cultivated places have a greater value than uncultivated ones and that human actions generate the best fruit. The earth contains a vital force, but with our hoes and our arms, with the earth and the nourishment we give it, we help the seeds to germinate. The core of his work turns on just a few words, which are relevant today: "nothing is made from nothing."[1] The role of human action and the sense of responsibility are the key points that Lucretius raises in the poem, and which we find in the works of philosophers, writers, thinkers, and artists for centuries to come.

This leitmotif finds an audience in Italian artistic and intellectual thought. In the 1970s, such thought dialogued closely with the social and political scene. The person who best performed a lucid, careful, provocative analysis of the political, social, and economic transformation of Italy was Pier Paolo Pasolini, a poet, writer, director, intellectual, and visionary artist. Italy in the years following World War II experienced an anthropological shift, which Pasolini synthesizes in the literary image of the "disappearance of the fireflies." In an article published in the *Corriere della Sera* on February 1, 1975, "Il vuoto di potere" (The power void), and then collected in his *Scritti corsari*, Pasolini writes: "In the early 1960s, thanks to air pollution and, in the country, pollution of water (the crystal-blue rivers and clear canals), the fireflies began to disappear. The phenomenon was lightning-quick and striking. After a few years, there were no more fireflies" (1990, 129). What does the author seek to denounce? What crucial events are unfolding in Italy? Pasolini uses the disappearance of the fireflies as a metaphor to speak, rather than yell, of the radical transformation of a wicked society, of uncontrolled technical and economic progress, of unscrupulous capitalism, of the economic boom that in a short time destabilized the balance of a country that for many centuries had been a traditional agricultural society. This radical transformation destroyed landscapes and cityscapes, caused pollution and ecological devastation, and was characterized by cultural and anthropological decadence, the upsurge of mass culture, the standardization of lifestyles, and the death of the fireflies, those delicate "blazes of innocence" (Didi-Huberman 2009, 16) that represented the fragility of natural balance, marred by irrationality and the blindness of human cynicism.

This literary image was a fundamental part of the birth of Arte Povera. During the 1960s and '70s, it was the ideological answer to the violent uprooting of Italian society. At the same time, minimalism, pop art, and land art were asserting themselves in the United States. In Europe, the current shifted more informally toward *nouveau réalisme*; in Italy, the spatial works of Lucio Fontana, Alberto Burri, and Piero Manzoni were taking shape, along with the experimental work of Gruppo Origine, Gruppo Forma I, Movimento Arte Concreta, Gruppo T, and Gruppo N.

At the threshold of the 1960s, a group of Italian artists began to recognize the importance of affirming an "ethical choice, out of the dynamic vortex of techno-scientific progress, and reflecting on its deep roots in artistic experience, overstepping the contingent limits of the opposition tradition/modernity to reach, instead, more ancestral, universal results" (Lista 2011, 160). The Arte Povera movement was shaped around an experience of safeguarding the environment, not directly interested in ecological questions. Nevertheless, it had a fundamental role in creating an artistic and societal sensibility with a "poor" aesthetic, a "return to the origins," in a historical period characterized by the economic boom and the "cultural genocide" that Pasolini recounted in his "Fireflies" article. For the Arte Povera artists, Giovanni Lista has observed, "in the face of the physical and sensorial emptying of aesthetic experience, inaugurated and promoted by the language of the American avant-garde, art becomes . . . the scene through which to relocate a direct contact with one's origins, with one's roots, and with a historical tradition, with nature and with reality as spaces of physical relationships, in which to test the universal value of existence" (Lista 2011, 160)

The main theorist of the movement is Germano Celant. In the *Manifesto dell'Arte Povera* (Manifesto of Arte Povera), published in *Flash Art* in 1967, he reveals the presence of a new attitude "directed at locating the real meaning of the emergent human sense of living. An identification of human-nature, which no longer has the theological, medieval sense of *narrator-narratum*, but a pragmatic intent of liberation, of non-addition of objects to our ideas of the world, as we see it today" (Celant 1967, 36). Key words here are *slow down, proceed toward the origins*, the *primordial*, the motto "less is more." The protagonists of this new artistic scene move between two poles, Turin and Rome, which, at the beginning of the 1960s, are the principal creative forces of the *Bel Paese*. Without describing the movement in detail, I will show where it moved most significantly toward a rediscovery of the human-nature relationship.[2]

In Turin, Mario Merz worked on the organic structures of the vegetal world, on the intersection of primary and natural forces with contemporary objects. His first works, full of biomorphic influences, gave life to the symbolic figures that made him famous. First there was the igloo, an archetypal and archaic structure of human presence on earth, an "ideal organic form" (Celant 1967, 97) that represents, in three-dimensional space, the dynamism of the spiral (another cardinal point). A sign of cosmic movement, the igloo is based on the idea of the dynamic continuity of the universe, of human beings and the processes of the transformation of nature (*La natura è l'equilibrio della spirale* [Nature is the balance of the spiral, 1976]). Merz calls on an entire platoon of animals, and on the Fibonacci sequence, which is used to describe the laws of nature through the truth of numbers. The tree, that "miracle of spontaneity," also appears in his work to speak of balance as a conceptual act: *Un albero occupa soprattutto tempo, due alberi occupano il medesimo tempo ma uno spazio maggiore* (A tree mainly occupies time, two trees occupy the same time but more space, 1976).[3] Other artists also in Piedmont cast the critical "seed in the wind"—to recall the title of another of Merz's artworks (*Seme nel vento*, 1953)—that turned out to be central in the debates leading to ecological criticism and contemporary ecocriticism. In the 1960s, Giovanni Anselmo employed materials like wood, formica, rock, water, sand, cotton, sugar, bread, and, famously, lettuce, among other things. These are all elements related through the theme of energy, in a dialogue between visible and invisible, organic and inorganic. The work *Senza Titolo* (Untitled, 1968) is emblematic, as granite and copper wire meet a head of lettuce, triggering a relationship of dependence whereby "the work exists as long as it resists, each day with a new, refreshed form, until humans, with their behavior and gestures, take notice" (Lista 2011, 102). Lucretius's words come to mind, and a path is traced between past, present, and future. Pier Paolo Calzolari rediscovered art as a sensual, fantastic material "event." His works—made of ice, lead, moss, tobacco leaves, tin, felt, wax, animals, honey, and salt—present organic elements with which contact must be reestablished. In 1967, Pino Pascali proposed a material authentication and "behavioral sensism" with *2 metri cubi di terra* (2 cubic meters of earth) and *1 metro cubo di terra* (1 cubic meter of earth), a synecdoche of the natural world. With his zinc basins that hold "the sea," he attempts to reconcile the natural with the artificial. Through works like *Pozzanghere* (Puddles), *32 mq circa di mare* (About 32 square meters of sea), *Canali di irrigazione* (Irrigation canals) and *Campi arati* (Plowed fields), 1967–68, the artist put the primary elements of water and earth front and center. In the latter of these, he found a profound, benign Mother, giver of life and eroticism.

Among these artists, Michelangelo Pistoletto has a central role, with his various, apparently contradictory, polyform works directed toward a dialectic between art and life, object and behavior, daily reality and social aesthetic. The most important example in the ecological thread happened many years after Arte Povera, in 2003, when Pistoletto wrote the manifesto of the Terzo Paradiso (Third paradise) and created its symbol, a reconfiguration of the mathematical sign for infinity. What is the Terzo Paradiso? As Pistoletto explains:

> It is the fusion between the first and second paradise. The first is the paradise in which humans were fully integrated into nature. The second is the artificial paradise, developed by human intelligence to globalizing proportions through science and technology. This paradise is made of artificial needs, artificial products, artificial comforts, artificial pleasures, and every other form of artifice. . . . The Third Paradise is the third phase of humanity, realized as a balanced connection between artifice and nature. The Third Paradise is the passage to a new level of planetary civilization, essential to ensure the survival of the human race. (2010, p. 1)

The experience of these representatives of Arte Povera is thus a warning, the alarm, anticipating what was to come in their future and our present. These artists feel change in the air, they see beyond the limits of time and know what will happen in a future tragically near, from environmental disasters to ecological devastations even more grave than those Pasolini recounted—and the mind here unavoidably goes to the 1986 nuclear explosion at Chernobyl.

In my opinion, the principal actors in this drama are to be found in Piedmont, a region that fed the profound instinct to commune with the natural elements. A native of the Cuneo area, Giuseppe Penone gives form to the intimate, authentic, and sublime experience linking humans and nature. He is aware of the work of American land artists, of the historical, artistic, geographic, and environmental context in which his colleagues across the ocean are working. He knows that making a huge "hole" in the desert is thinkable for land artists, but that "in Europe, nature is already anthropomorphic: it is so anthropomorphized that such a gesture would be insignificant" (Lista 2011, 114). Here, where the landscape has been amply shaped by the interaction between human civilization and natural heritage, "no work of Land Art can be created in relation to this reality that is already culture and history" (Lista 2011, 114). Profoundly influenced by his country origins and by the environmental context where he is born and raised, Penone departs from what he knows and feels: nature, his knowledge of trees, streams, rocks, natural material. He imagines them as living, moving presences. Many of his works represent a specular relationship between humans and nature. The reason he gives is simple:

> Nature is not separate from the human, because the human is nature. If we think that the human is nature, there are no hierarchies. Only from a religious perspective are we drawn to say that after God there is man, and then everything else. But the human has the same value as a piece of wood or paper . . . since the human is no more eternal than anything else. If we respect this equal relationship with things, the relationships change, and we have another vision of possibility. (Lista 2011, 121)

The series *Alpi Marittime* (Maritime Alps), created starting in 1968 in the corner of the world where he was born, is one of the first works that clearly represents the artist's emblematic vision. In *Alpi Marittime: Ho intrecciato tre alberi* (Maritime Alps: I have woven three trees), three slender, growing trunks were interwoven to modify their direction of growth. In *Alpi Marittime: L'albero ricorderà il contatto del mio corpo* (Maritime Alps: The tree will remember the contact of my body), Penone leaves his mark on the trunk, marking it with dozens of nails. In the same series, *Alpi Marittime: Continuerà a crescere tranne che in quel punto* (Maritime Alps: It will carry on growing except in that point), after creating a steel cast of his hand, he leans it against the trunk of a tree which will grow around it, surrounding it and deforming itself to welcome this human presence. Penone opposes natural time and human time, one silent and infinitely long, the other noisy and decidedly faster. The *Alberi* (Trees), created starting in 1969, are perhaps Penone's most famous works. He uses wood beams of various lengths, cutting them to bring the original tree back to life, thus showing what the beam once was. As Giorgio Verzotti comments, "Penone's intent is to indicate the ontological foundation in nature, the origin of all cultural practice, a foundation and an origin that we are not always aware of" (1991, 47). Penone highlights the cultural bases of the relationship between humans and nature in an investigation that allows him to bring to light primary gestures, the "imprint" that a body maintains as a "trace" of the presence of the Other.[4]

While in Lombardy Giuliano Mauri reflects on the concept of environment and participation, dialoguing with the landscape by realizing site-specific works in nature anticipating the famous *Cattedrale Vegetale* (Vegetal cathedral, 2001), in Piedmont Ugo La Pietra analyzes the meaning of living in the city, invoking the need for a greater awareness to balance humans and nature. He proposes green space as a solution for the problem of street furniture, calling on the relationships between architecture and the social dimension of life.[5] Gruppo 9999 and Gianfranco Baruchello are also significant, as is the Piero Gilardi's work in Italy. Gilardi, an artist and political activist, created his first "natural carpets" in 1965. "I had the idea for these carpets one afternoon when I was discussing the landscape of the future with a friend," he explains (Biasutti 2008, 65). From this came the need to re-create what is absent, by way of the perfect forms of plastics. The artist uses polyurethane to re-create, on a one-to-one scale, compromised nature. His "synthetic" nature becomes a symbol of the contemporary world, produced in a series with deliberate inattention to the natural context. The use of the sponge is an emblem of a period characterized by the explosion of plastic objects, synonym of "a nature being lost. It is the rite for our fear of loss, to invoke our courage in the face of death, reconstructing with our poor hands the adventure of the defeat" (quoted in Biasutti 2008, 68).

From producing objects, Gilardi soon understood the importance of living art as a relational process, discovering the importance of new media in artistic practice. In Turin, he became one of the primary proponents of the environmental movement, and from the beginning of the 1960s, he led activist battles for public green space. Gilardi (2016) found that biopolitics creates "maxi-fights," performs "political actions" ["*animazioni politiche*"], using every available tool to create an environmental consciousness. The result, in 2008, was the creation of the PAV—Parco Arte Vivente (Living Art Park)—in Turin, an experimental space and a laboratory for ecological art. The space showcases the relation between art and nature, biotechnologies, through an artistic methodology based in experimentation and the production of living artworks, which the artist defines "bioart." Through his conversations with artists abroad, today Gilardi is the leading Italian artist in the area of ecological activism.

There is another figure who stands out in this area: Joseph Beuys, who, from 1972 until his death, worked in Abruzzo to realize the battle in *Difesa della natura* (Defense of nature). He chose Italy because its political landscape offered fertile humus for his work, but also because here he dialogued with people who were aware of the necessity to reopen the dialogue with nature: "In Italy, everything converges so that nature can become substance and protagonist" (De Domizio Durini 2008, 23). Beuys worked with Buby Durini and Lucrezia De Domizio, organizing an entire farm for the work in *Piantagione* (Plantation) that he calls *Paradise*. He experimented with organic agriculture, giving life to *Operazione Difesa della Natura* (Operation in defense of nature), the most emblematic of the German artist's projects. On May 13, 1984, on the occasion of the famous action "Defense of Nature," he planted the *Prima Quercia* (First oak), which was the beginning of the monumental work *7000 Eichen* (7,000 oaks) in Kassel, Germany. Through his charisma and his shamanic appeal, Beuys indicated that "our creative and productive abilities begin in the earth, and only the earth can unite us with the sky" (De Domizio Durini 2008, 24).

All of these experiences, which dialogue constantly with artistic projects beyond Italy, are born and sediment in a country historically marked by a strong agricultural tradition, direct contact with the earth, and an incomparable richness of landscape and nature. It is the land of the Grand Tour, a place that fascinated generations of artists, thinkers, and writers and that, in spite of various abuses and environmental disasters, has inspired a direct dialogue with the primordial energy of natural elements.

In this sense, it is important to recall the presence in Italy of Luigi Ghirri, who, although far from Arte Povera or land art, immortalized forgotten landscapes in photography, seeking to create a new idea of the Italian landscape, often cooperating with Gianni Celati, as Patrick Barron's essay in this book illustrates (pp. 17–27). Ghirri's work features places at the margins, in dialogue with existence, full of feeling and intimacy. Yet this "photographing nearly nothing" is, for Ghirri, an existential act, "the reflection of a gesture connected to the experience of human's living with the earth" (Bertola 2016, 15). This type of work, in my opinion, is also a fundamental moment in consciousness raising about the role of the landscape, and of nature, in our everyday lives.

New generations of artists have continued to work in the paths traced by the masters of the past. There are two principal themes that they follow: nature, seen through an ethical, aesthetic, and environmental lens; and landscape, which continues to interest many Italian artists and helps create an environmental awareness in natural and rural contexts. Andrea Caretto and Raffaella Spagna are the foremost interpreters of the need for an artistic ecocritical perspective, and they are, not by chance, from Turin. Their work uses natural science and anthropology to analyze the relationship between humans, living organisms, and the environment. They develop projects, performances, relational practices, and installations enriched by their different backgrounds: landscape architecture for Spagna and natural sciences for Caretto.

Works by younger artists are also extremely valuable in this context. Andreco, for example, has long been engaged in work related to the environmental problems of our times. An environmental engineer by training, he conducted postdoctoral research on the benefits of urban green space in collaboration with the University of Bologna, Columbia University, and NASA in New York City. For him, anthropic interference is the primary cause of environmental harm: from the constant rise of CO_2 in the atmosphere, the pollution of land and sea, climate change, and cementification. Without becoming propaganda or intending to condemn these processes too openly, his distinctive works offer reflections on alarming subjects that the viewer can discover and analyze. Following in the same line, Giorgia Severi, whose work has been defined as performing an ethics of responsibility, makes art that allows her to complete cultural, social, and political actions that connect humans and the earth.[6] The role of memory, connected to the loss of natural, cultural, and anthropological resources, underpins all of her work. Emanuela Ascari takes a similar approach, using direct contact with the earth to invoke the urgent need to rethink human impact on it. Her most recent projects stem from her analysis of problems in agriculture and suggest possible solutions. Also worth mentioning is a series of artists who, although eco-critique is not their leitmotif, realized works or entire projects on themes connected to nature and environmental questions. Among these artists are Stefano Cagol, Andrea Nacciarriti, Enrica Borghi, the Brave New Alps collective, Gabriella Ciancimino, Ettore Favini, Roberto Pugliese, Francesco

Simeti, Cristian Chironi, Pennacchio Argentato, Dacia Manto, Luana Perilli, Filippo Leonardi, Maddalena Ambrosio, Michele Dantini, Nicola Toffolini, Silvano Tessarollo, Elena Mazzi, Federica Di Carlo, and the list could go on.

This story shows that Italy is certainly one of the most important, stimulating places for artists, past and present, who find in the earth the place to encounter the natural universe: a place to discover, to which to listen, to understand, and to defend.

NOTES

1. These words were the point of departure for a critical reflection that led to the 2016 exhibit Silvano Tessarollo: Nulla nasce dal nulla (Silvano Tessarollo: Nothing is made from nothing), with the participation of Herman de Vries, in the Michela Rizzo Gallery in Venice, curated by Andrea Lerda.

2. For more on Arte Povera, see also Celant (2011) and Christov-Bakargiev (2014).

3. This work was made entirely of earth and neon. The Merz Foundation of Turin recently showed it in the exhibit La Natura è l'equilibrio: Mario Merz (Nature is balance: Mario Merz), July 4 to September 18, 2016, in Turin. The project was dedicated to analyzing the relationship between Merz's work and nature.

4. The idea of trace, sign, and imprint are at the base of historic works like *Clay Breaths,* in which the artist attempted to produce the form of his breath against his body; in the series Rovesciare i propri occhi (Turning your own eyes inside out, 1970), *Palpebre* (Eyelids, 1978), *Svolgere la propria pelle* (Unraveling your own skin, from 1970), *Patate* (Potatoes, 1977), *Zucche* (Marrows, 1978–79), and finally *Unghia* (Fingernail, from 1987). For more on Penone, see Gianelli and Verzotti (1991) or Maraniello (2016).

5. One of La Pietra's works observes that "between nature and architecture, nature always wins."

6. John Passmore was one of the first to use the phrase "ethics of responsibility" in the ecological debate, with the publication of *Man's Responsibility for Nature* in 1974.

WORKS CITED

Agazzi, Davide. 2016. "Philippe Daverio: l'opera di Christo? È una baracconata, come la donna cannone." *Bergamo News,* June 17.

Bertola, Chiara. 2016. "Il Fondo Luigi Ghirri: Un lavoro sull'eredità culturale." In *Paesaggi d'aria. Luigi Ghirri e Yona Friedman,* edited by Jean-Baptiste Decavèle, 15. Mantua: Corraini. 9–15.

Biasutti, Giuseppe, ed. 2008. *Piero Gilardi: Opere storiche 1964–1969.* Text by Martina Corgnati. Turin: Biasutti and Biasutti.

Celant, Germano. 1967. "Arte Povera: Appunti per una guerriglia." *Flash Art* 5 (November–December): 36.

Celant, Germano. 2011. *Arte Povera: Storia e storie.* Milan: Electa.

Christov-Bakargiev, Carolyn. 2014. *Arte Povera.* New York: Phaidon Press.

De Domizio Durini, Lucrezia. 2008. "Territori terapeutici." In *Buby Durini for Joseph Beuys,* edited by Lucrezia De Domizio Durini, 23–24. Milan: Silvana Editoriale.

Didi-Huberman, Georges. 2009. *Come le lucciole: Una politica delle sopravvivenze*. Turin: Bollati Boringhieri.
Gianelli, Ida, and Giorgio Verzotti, eds. 1991. *Giuseppe Penone*. Milan: Fabbri Editore.
Gilardi, Piero. 2016. *La mia biopolitica: Arte e lotta del vivente. Scritti 1963–2014*. Milan: Prearo Editore.
Lista, Giovanni. 2011. *Arte Povera: Interviste curate e raccolte da Giovanni Lista*. Milan: Abscondita.
Lucretius. 1995. *On the Nature of Things: De rerum natura*. Translated by Anthony M. Esolen. Baltimore: Johns Hopkins University Press.
Maraniello, Gianfranco, ed. 2016. *Giuseppe Penone: Scultura*. Milan: Electa.
Pasolini, Pier Paolo. 1990. *Scritti corsari*. Milan: Garzanti.
Passmore, John. 1974. *Man's Responsibility for Nature: Ecological Problems and Western Traditions*. London: Duckworth.
Pistoletto, Michelangelo. 2003. *The Third Paradise*. http://www.pistoletto.it/eng/testi/the_third_paradise.pdf.

TIZIANO FRATUS

Walking Roots: Knitting Past and Future through Italy's Woods

I always like it when it rains. It feels like I'm drinking with the trees.
—Francesco Biamonti

Forgetting to close
The windows well so that the wind doesn't toss in
The leaves from the horse chestnut of my youth, thin vein by thin vein
I would have to recognize them
—Valeria Rossella

Roots and Roots: Reality between Neologisms, Definitions, and Experience

In Italy we've begun to walk again. In the mid-twentieth century, after centuries of labor and struggle, people from the country migrated to the suburbs. Men straightened their backs and put on blue coveralls; women left the stables and the stoves and dressed as office workers. Out of the ruins of 1946, in three decades Italy transformed itself into the Italy of the economic miracle: every housewife aspired to electrical appliances, and television soon supplanted newspapers, books, and the radio as the great linguistic educator and unifier. Walking was a stubborn relic of the past; in cities, you took public transportation or drove a car. Bicycles were for kids and priests. A deep rift developed between the lifestyles of those who stayed in the country, or returned years later, and those who adapted to the city. The economic and institutional crisis of the past ten years paralyzed the country. Even in the cities, work is a rare commodity, and more than a few people have returned to the rhythms of an existence that seemed to be lost forever. Several of my peers returned to live with their parents as forty-year-olds, after a failed marriage or having lost a job. Reshaped perspectives, together with a growing spirituality that isn't specifically confessional (in Italy even convinced atheists have Catholic roots) and a growing interest in the environment, nature, and the landscape, have contributed to forming a citizenry that has begun to walk again. Whether in the country or in the city, people love bicycling again; curious about the environment, they organize walks. Naturalist guides are finding more work than ever before in our country. I have been part of this movement, accompanying groups of walkers to discover important trees in parks, nature reserves, botanical gardens, and urban gardens.

In the 1980s, true, taciturn seekers of monumental trees began to appear in Italy: people who look, nod, measure, document, photograph, trace, think, catalogue. Impenitent dreamers, they find new instruments for loving our country, tracing botanical itineraries that illuminate the landscape; they draw together past and future. They transform our cities, populated by the *Homo economicus* species, into lived spaces inhabited by *Homo radix*. They are travelers interested in getting to know the creatures who have lived longest on the earth, and how they are, and where they are. Our Ents. Our green patriarchs. Our roots!

"Don't tell me which monuments are close to your house, but which trees," I often tell people who accompany me on one of my walks or come to hear a presentation. Whether we listen to him or not, there is a God of idioms and roots, a God who is born and reborn and reshapes himself with the passage of time, who accompanies the beings on this tiny planet at the margins of the galaxy, in a universe that continues to expand. Crossing the landscape in search of large trees makes a man a *chrononaut* (time traveler). I've had fun, as I sometimes do, creating a dictionary definition of this term that various writers and walkers have adopted:

> *Chrononaut*, singular, masculine (from the Greek Χρόνος, "time," and ναύτης, "navigator"). He or she who travels in time. 1. A traveler who, using a time machine, goes backward and forward in the centuries and eras of the Earth or another planet. 2. A seeker of centuries-old or monumental trees is a chrononaut since s/he approaches trees that have lived centuries or millennia. 3. Academics who work on extinct civilizations can be considered chrononauts, including anthropologists, historians, archaeologists, art historians, and the recently classified *paesologi* (placeologists) and *abbandonologi* (scholars of abandoned places).

When I encounter a man or a woman in a wood, we barely say hello. I wonder what we have in common. I've never understood it, but I can certainly say that, over time, I have discovered that I have more in common with people I don't know than with people I do. This is why my adopted family is composed of ancient trees and forests. When I'm in Milan, in the middle of a city of a million and a half people, the sap of the sycamores in the Parco Villa Litta calls to me. So does the high priest of the gardens of Porta Venezia, a huge specimen of *Taxodium distichum*. If I cross through the forests of the Apennines that innervate Tuscany and Emilia-Romagna, I return to visit the huge, hollow chestnuts, the beeches connected with the figures of some of our spiritual hermits, St. Francis and St. Romuald, who are both fathers of contemplative religious orders, the Franciscans and the Camaldolese. If I visit the large islands of the south, Sicily and Sardinia, I go to the ficuses of Palermo, which I've documented, measured—in centimeters—and described in a number of books. Under their aerial roots I've traveled in my imagination to their original environment, distant Australia. Or I return to the five hundred contorted olive trees of S'Ortu Mannu a Villamassargia, in Sardinia, a domain under the control of a frighteningly sculpted queen: Sa Reina, the locals call it, an olive tree whose trunk is eleven and a half meters in circumference and whose bark represents nine hundred years of cortical complexity.

My Italy is a landscape of ancient giants who listen but don't speak, don't recount anything, who exist so that we can admire them. In the silence of their hollow surfaces we come to hide our desires and our sins. They are filters for humanity and for the wickedness of the world.

I sketch more definitions, inspired by these associations. For example *dendrophony, pinosaurus,* and *dendrosophy*.

> *Dendrophony*—s.f. (from the Greek δένδρον, "tree," and φωνή, "sound").
> A composition achieved by recording the sounds and noises of a tree, sometimes in different atmospheric conditions, mixed and possibly accompanied by or inserted into music composed for the occasion.

> *Pinosàurus*—s.m. (pl. *pinosàuri*). 1. Specimen of the genus *Pinus*, part of a diverse group of species found at high elevations on mountain precipices and ridges; they have taken on spectacular, tortuous forms, recalling the striations and musculatures of certain large reptiles or the smooth forms of skeletons. 2. The Pinosàuruses of the Massif of Pollino belong to the Bosnian pine species (Pinus leucodermis or Pinus heldreichii), between Basilicata and Calabria. 3. The Pinosàuruses of the forest of Alevè, distributed between 1,700 and 2,900 meters from the forest of the Swiss pines (Pinus cembra) in Varaita Valley, Piedmont. 4. The serpentine-formed Pinosaurus of Roia, a monumental Swiss pine at 2,200 meters in Alto Adige, which fell and grew again in a curious form, taking the shape of a snake. 5. The Pinosauruses of the White Mountains in California, the oldest living trees on the planet, more than five thousand years old, which belong to the Great Basin bristlecone pine species (Pinus longaeva) and were studied for the first time in the 1950s by Professor Edmund Schulman.

Dendrosophy—s.f. (from the Greek δένδρον, "tree," and σοφία, "knowledge, awareness, love"). Dendrosophy is a field that unites different typologies of knowledge about history, biology, botany, forest studies, anthropology, literature, etc., as they relate to trees and woods. 2. A practice of meditation that calls for immersion in a natural environment, such as nature preserves, mountain landscapes, ancient forests, deserts, in order to nurture inner peace. 3. The person who practices dendrosophy is called a dendrosopher, from σοφός, "sage."

The maps of the world we inhabit and that we represent in our thinking are always an accumulation. Above all, a geographic accumulation: there is the Italy of our affections, the Italy of work, the Italy of passions, the Italy composed of the faces and places that we hear about in the news, the newspapers, culture. For me, the geographies are, above all, the passions and places I have inhabited: the Italy of great trees, Italy of woods and forests, Italy of natural parks, Italy of poetry, Italy of publishing, Italy of theater and dramaturgy. The worlds I have lived in over my twenty adult years. The further I advance in the seasons of life, the more I am convinced that objective reality exists, but it is not the one that we inhabit, concretely. We have in our blood the famous colored pill that the protagonist of the movie The Matrix took to awaken himself from his dream. Perhaps Nature put it there, or God, for those who want to believe in a certain version of the genesis of the world. Our brain isn't made to absorb acritically what the body registers and experiences. We need imagination and projections to resist, to conceal the crude reality of our existence on the planet. We are a web of breaths and glances in transit between the alpha of human history, birth, and the omega, death. We are transient, sentient creatures who do not seem destined to change the history of animate and inanimate things. We are nature, we are part of the world of beasts and wild creatures that we increasingly despise, that we cancel from our vital breath. We are nothing but nature; we are children of nature. And we hope not to witness one day the birth of a new species, more biologically evolved than ours: it could be the beginning of a new epoch of slavery.

Brief Guide to the Arboreal Crossroads of Little Italy

It is an interesting challenge to describe for the reader the forms and the characteristics, if not the sensations, when you arrive at the foot of certain green monuments. Italy hosts thousands of monumental trees, remarkable trees, and several dozens of probably millennial trees. It is a geography that has not yet been decrypted; mystery persists in our "reign of disorder." I will attempt, however, to trace a minute, essential geography of some of the trees and woods that must not be missed.

The Shepherd of Pietraporzio. Region: Piedmont.
Town: Pietraporzio. Province: Cuneo.

It sails high, over one thousand meters. At the top of a valley, having passed a rocky escarpment that zigzags along a waterfall, it appears along the path that leads to the Rifugio Zanotti, a solitary larch. It is the Shepherd of Pietraporzio, known locally as *Lou merze gros,* the big larch. The trunk is eight meters in circumference; an estimated age of more than six hundred years; a colossus with exposed roots that have become rigid feet, at the base. Arriving is an adventure, and waiting for the golden light of sunset is one of the most mournful and joyful things that humans can experience.

The Sculpted Forest of Lerosa. Region: Veneto.
Town: Cortina d'Ampezzo. Province: Belluno.

In the splendid province of Belluno, the land of two of our most popular writers—Dino Buzzati and Mauro Corona—there are many notable trees and some of our most fascinating forests, like the Cansiglio. There is a road departing from Belluno that flanks the area of the Vajont disaster and climbs through the larch woods and the villages of the Cadore region, emerging at Cortina d'Ampezzo, a fashionable holiday destination in the eighties and nineties. Near the city one of the most spectacular parks in Italy fans out, the park of the Ampezzan Dolomites. Walls of rose-colored rock full of ferrite, caves for spelunkers, waterfalls, summer pastures, and woodland parcels. One of these is at an altitude between 1,900 and 2,100 meters, near the Lerosa Plain. It is a residual forest of Swiss pines (*Pinus cembra*), and it survived the predation of soldiers who, in the crushing years of the Great War, dug trenches nearby.

The Miraglia Chestnut in the Wood of Camaldoli.
Region: Tuscany. Town: Poppi. Province: Arezzo.

The higher altitude regions of Emilia-Romagna and Tuscany are studded with large chestnuts, eight or nine meters in circumference. There is, for example, a large specimen probably planted by Matilda of Canossa in Zocca (near Modena), the town where the famous singer Vasco Rossi comes from. In the town of Camugnano (near Bologna), there is the Osteria del Bugeon (Tavern in a hole), a chestnut inside of which the owner created a tavern for his friends in the 1980s, complete with a little door and a table. The Miraglia chestnut is in the woods above the monastery of Camaldoli, which was founded one thousand years ago by Romuald. It takes its name from the wife of the general director of the Ministry of Agriculture, who built a house there. She would sit inside the tree, which is hollow. Here, we are in the region of the Parco Nazionale delle Foreste Casentinesi.

The Ornamental Plane Trees of the Villa Borghese Park.
Region: Lazio. Town and Province: Rome.

It is striking to walk through Rome and happen upon the entrance to the zoo, with the elephants' probosces sculpted over the arcs of the two columns at the entry. You realize that there is no marker to indicate that, a few steps away, in the first swath of forest, there are four-hundred-year-old trees. They are ancient creatures of the capital. A row of oriental plane trees, contorted and riddled with holes, thirteen poems written in wood that grow, year after year, decade after decade, from at least the beginning of the seventeenth century. Originally, there were forty. When you happen upon them, their Gothic aspect surprises you. Other trees of the same age can be found in the botanical gardens, near the staircase designed by Ferdinando Fuga: one is reduced in size because it was hit by lightning; the other is similar in size to the ones in the Villa Borghese.

The Garden of the Gods Where Lightning Carves Its Poetry in the Wood. Region: Basilicata and Calabria. Different Towns in the Provinces of Cosenza, Potenza, and Matera.

A piece of the Dolomites in the heart of the south: the Massif of Pollino, a park that marks the border between Basilicata—the region of ravines, the cliffs of Matera, and abandoned towns—and Calabria—a coastal region devastated by cement, a green heartland spread across three splendid areas, Serre, Sila, and Pollino. A scar, a forested spinal column that innervates the entire endpoint of the Italian boot. Five of the Massif's peaks are over 2,000 meters, and this is where you find the population of "ghosts" (dead trees) and resilient conifers, which are exclusively species of *Pinus leucodermis* or *Pinus heldreichii* or, commonly, Bosnian pines. Several years ago, a guide named the most spectacular point the "Garden of the Gods," and when you find yourself there that is just what you think. Immense pines with unimaginable deformations. The species was studied for the first time on top of the mountain of the gods par excellence, Olympus.

The Diffused and Australian Wood of Palermo.
Region: Sicily. City and Province: Palermo.

I fell in love with Palermo the first time I went there. A rough city with a theatrical aspect, dug by hand in the earth, cavernous sounds, popular neighborhoods flanked by ticky-tacky suburbs and dwellings from past eras, confusion of religions and sudden vegetal apertures, appearing silently from behind walls and beneath arches. Palermo is an ever-unfinished mosaic. And in these mosaics there appear enormous trees, the largest exotic trees by volume of the Old Continent: *Ficus macrophylla* or ficus of the Bay of Moreton, which were imported for the first time between 1840 and 1845 by the director of the botanical garden with the name *Ficus nervosa*, their name in France. Today, fifty or so trees of large dimensions are scattered across the city, and some are a world apart. One of these dominates the Garibaldi Gardens of Piazza Marina, near the old port, and the other is the heart of the botanical gardens. The foliage of this latter tree, if projected on the ground, occupies nearly 1,300 square meters. Forty-nine columns sustain its architecture. A giant that becomes a forest.

> *The Olive of Luras: If 3,000 Years Seem Like Nothing.*
> Region: Sardinia. Town: Luras. Province: Olbia-Tempio.

I will finish this mini-voyage through the Italian patriarchs in Sardinia, a region that is much more than just an island. It is a people, a language, a culture, another dimension. For us, it is Italy, but the truth is that Sardinia is Sardinia, period. In the northeast zone of the island, in the town of Tempio Pausania (a handful of kilometers from Luras, zone of cork oak), after 14 kilometers the road signs lead to the area called "Millennial olives." Today it is a protected reserve, and in summer you pay an offering to enter and a youth co-op puts it to good use. In winter you enter and hope for the best. Three large olive trees, one after the other; two giants. The third is estimated to be five hundred years old, and no one ever looks at it, squashed as it is by the mysterious, magmatic presence of the other two. The largest has soared across more than three thousand springs, and in the last few years has begun growing again, to germinate foliage. A sculpted trunk with two showy roots that stretch toward the visitor. They look like two dinosaur tails ready to sprout from the earth. The smaller has created a cupola around the center of the tree, under which we can walk, admiring it. Assuming the estimates are correct, three thousand years are an eternity.

Wishing you enlightening dendrosophies!

(Translation by Elena Past)

ROSI BRAIDOTTI

Afterword: The Proper Study of the Humanities Is No Longer "Man"

The international scientific community reached a consensus in August 2016 that the geological era we are living in is to be known as the Anthropocene, that is to say, a time when human action is having a lasting and negative effect upon the sustainability of the planet. In so far as the Anthropocene implies a reconsideration of the human and its place in the world, it intersects with the debate about posthumanism and the displacement of anthropocentrism. My argument is that we have entered a posthuman condition, and this is not only a crisis of belief in the future, but also and foremost a deep transformation: the productive aspects balance out the negative ones. My working definition of the posthuman condition is the convergence of posthumanism on the one hand and post-anthropocentrism on the other. The former focuses on the critique of the humanist ideal of "Man" as the universal measure of all things, while the latter criticizes species hierarchy and human exceptionalism. Their convergence is producing a trans-disciplinary field of posthuman scholarship that is more than the sum of its parts and points to the rise of the critical posthumanities, best exemplified by the environmental humanities (Braidotti 2013).

This positive approach is supported by the vitality of contemporary posthuman scholarship, which so far has displayed great transdisciplinary exuberance. For instance, the terminology has become more complex and nuanced: the nonhuman, the inhuman, the posthumanist; the post-anthropocentric, the multispecies; the trans-species; the "new" human as *Anthropos* today are circulating freely in academic publications. This discursive creativity reflects the explosion of the concept of life from *bios* to a myriad of nonhuman variations; *zoe* as a vital force emerges as the point of reference (Braidotti 2002).

As the essays gathered in this collection brilliantly illustrate, the environmental humanities offer different angles of approach. They do focus on the study of contemporary "medianaturecultures," a neologism that foregrounds the relational, self-organizing, technologically mediated, material systems of expression of forces that—before the Anthropocene—we used to call "nature." Complexity is the key to contemporary posthuman research, which feeds an exuberant discursive growth and tends to concentrate in a number of creative interdisciplinary hubs. Comparative literature and literary studies, in dialogue with cultural studies, science and technology studies, and disability studies, are building a new connection with urban studies and media studies to address computational and algorithmic cultures, issues of sustainability, and green citizenship. They are at the core of the new transdisciplinary assemblages that are rewriting the script of the posthuman condition. The generative transdisciplinary assemblage of the environmental humanities does not coincide completely with the traditional humanities disciplines in that it does not assume a concept of the "human" identical to the humanist "Man," nor is it compatible with anthropocentrism. This hybrid crossover formation rather builds a number of productive relations across a web of research areas.

This fast-growing scholarly landscape indicates that the consensus about "Man" as the basic unit of reference for the human has long been lost and that this figure is in trouble. It is time to speak of "former Man" and to give a posthuman core to the contemporary humanities. As this enlightening collection proves, the critical posthumanities are emerging today, as post-disciplinary discursive fronts not only around the edges of the classical disciplines but also as offshoots of the critical studies areas. They provide the answer to what the humanities can become, in the posthuman era, after the decline of the primacy of universalist "Man" and of supremacist *Anthropos*.

The critical posthumanities—as in the environmental humanities—are geo-centered and post-anthropocentric. They assemble the many others of "Man": the feminists and those who identify as LBGT+; the non-white, postcolonial, black, Jewish, indigenous, and native subjects; and the nonanthropomorphic—animals, insects, plants, trees, viruses, fungi, and bacteria. They connect them to the nonorganic force of technological automata and artifacts, and even to extraterrestrial bodies. This empathic bond to the nonhuman sets the tone for an anthropological exodus toward the posthuman.

This hybrid transversal assemblage is very striking when placed in the context of Italian literature and culture, in so far as Italy and humanism have often been taken as synonyms. The strength of this collection consists in honoring this aspect of Italian culture and literary history, while exploring its long and rich relationship to the nonhumans in all their shapes—from birds, to earthquakes, to hydrocarbon. Italian literature is full of monsters and chimeras, shiny metal things and pollution fumes. Moreover, Italian literature has dealt with the necro-political aspects of processes of government, both in terms of social disasters and, quite simply, in mobilizing deep familiarity with death and decline. These are posthuman *topoi* par excellence, which support a change of critical perspective in the direction of the environmental humanities.

The building block or plane of composition for the environmental humanities is the emphasis on matter as vital, dynamic, and self-organizing. Living matter as zoe indicates a geo-centered process of interaction with the techno-social, psychic, and natural environments. This posthuman approach composes transversal alliances. The subjects of the environmental humanities can therefore be redefined as nomadic, embedded, embodied, relational, and technologically mediated. Their relational capacity is not confined within the human species but includes nonanthropomorphic elements. They constitute complex assemblages of human and nonhuman, terrestrial and cosmic, given and manufactured forces.

Zoe-centered egalitarianism respects the nonhuman force of life as the transverse entity that connects across previously segregated species, categories, and domains. It can relate to contemporary informational and scientific practices but also resist the opportunistic trans-species commodification of life that is the logic of advanced capitalism. The posthuman zoe-centered framework of the environmental humanities sustains analyses of the new power relations carried by the posthuman condition and the social forms of exclusion and dominations perpetuated by the current world order.

The environmental humanities advocate an intensive shift outward, toward extra-disciplinary encounters in the real world. This expresses the relational nature of their epistemic core: a text gets redefined in terms of its transdisciplinary capacity for movement across different fields of knowledge production and toward the real-life world. Maybe because of this great vitality, the environmental humanities are reproducing rhizomatically across multiple discourses, missing links, and liminal spaces: they are the nomadic sciences of today. In this respect they design a horizon of posthuman becoming of the humanities—as an academic "minor science"—that the contemporary university and especially the academic world would do well to heed.

This opening out toward the world is multidirectional: it involves renewed attention to social and cultural movements, new kinds of economies and political systems, and multiple curiosity-driven knowledge practices. Consequently, posthuman critics today pursue the all too human task of speaking truth to power at a time when power is morphing into multimodal and multiscaled processes of domination and exclusion. Instead of new generalizations, we need sharper focus on the complex singularities that constitute our respective power locations. The aim is not to reunify humanity in new universals but rather to ground it in diversity by accepting the changing perceptions and formations of the human in the posthuman era. In this respect the environmental humanities give us a distinct foretaste of what we are in the process of becoming, as this enlightening volume so eloquently demonstrates.

WORKS CITED

Braidotti, Rosi. 2002. *Metamorphoses: Towards a Materialist Theory of Becoming.* Cambridge, UK: Polity Press.

———. 2013. *The Posthuman.* Cambridge, UK: Polity Press.

Contributors

MARCO ARMIERO is the director of the Environmental Humanities Laboratory at the Royal Institute of Technology, Stockholm, where he is also an associate professor of environmental history. His research interests encompass several themes, including nation and nature, migrations and the environment, and environmental justice and ecological conflicts. An associate editor of the journal *Environmental Humanities*, his articles have been published in *Left History, Radical History Review, Environment and History, Modern Italy, Journal of Political Ecology*, and *Capitalism Nature Socialism*, where he also serves as a senior editor. He is the author of *A Rugged Nation: Mountains and the Making of Modern Italy* (2011, translated into Italian in 2013), and coeditor of *Nature and History in Modern Italy* (2010) with Marcus Hall, *The History of Environmentalism* (2014) with Lise Sedrez, *The Environmental History of Modern Migrations* (2017) with Richard Tucker, and *Future Remains: A Cabinet of Curiosity for the Anthropocene* (2017) with Gregg Mitman and Robert Emmett.

FRANCO ARMINIO, a theorist of placeology, writer, and poet, was born and lives in Bisaccia, in Irpinia d'Oriente. He has published more than twenty books, including *Vento forte tra Lacedonia e Candela* (2008), *Terracarne* (2011), *Cartoline dai morti* (2010), *Geografia commossa dell'Italia interna* (2013), and *Cedi la strada agli alberi* (2017). He is also a photographer and makes documentary films. As a placeologist, he writes for various newspapers and online sources to defend small towns. Arminio is the technical spokesman for the *Progetto Pilota della Montagna Materana*, part of the *Strategia Nazionale delle Aree Interne*. He created and organizes *La casa della paesologia* (The house of placeology) in Trevico and the festival *La luna e i calanchi* in Aliano.

PATRICK BARRON is associate professor of English at the University of Massachusetts, Boston. He has received awards from the Academy of American Poets, the American Academy in Rome, the Fulbright Commission, and the National Endowment for the Arts. His edited and translated books include *Terrain Vague: Interstices at the Edge of the Pale* (2013), *Haiku for a Season; Haiku per una stagione,* by Andrea Zanzotto (2012), *The Selected Poetry and Prose of Andrea Zanzotto* (2007), and *Italian Environmental Literature: An Anthology* (2003). He has also published numerous scholarly articles, reviews, translations, and poems. His translation of *Verso la foce* (*Towards the River's Mouth*) is forthcoming in 2018.

DAMIANO BENVEGNÙ is a lecturer at Dartmouth College and an associate fellow of the Oxford Centre for Animal Ethics. His research focuses on representations of animals, animality, and the environment in modern literature, visual art, and philosophy. His new book, *Animals and Animality in Primo Levi's Work* (2018) deals with the ethical and aesthetic value of literary animals in the work of the Jewish-Italian writer and Holocaust survivor Primo Levi.

VIKTOR BERBERI is assistant professor of Italian at the University of Minnesota, Morris. His publications include essays on various aspects of twentieth-century Italian hermeticism and on the literature of migrant writers in Italy, along with translations of contemporary Italian and Albanian poetry. His recent research focuses on southern Italy and addresses the ethics of landscape in works of literature and film.

ROSI BRAIDOTTI is Distinguished University Professor and founding director of the Centre for the Humanities at Utrecht University. She was the founding professor of gender studies at the University of Utrecht (1988–2005) and the first scientific director for the Netherlands Research School of Women's Studies. She is one of the foremost exponents in the field of continental philosophy and epistemology, feminist and gender theories, poststructuralist and posthumanist thought. Her books include *Patterns of Dissonance* (1991), *Nomadic Subjects* (1994), *Metamorphoses* (2002), *Transpositions* (2006), *La philosophie, lá où on ne l'attend pas* (2009), *Nomadic Theory* (2011), and *The Posthuman* (2013). Together with Paul Gilroy, Braidotti has recently edited the volume *Conflicting Humanities* (2016). Her website is www.rosibraidotti.com.

LUCA BUGNONE graduated cum laude in comparative literature from the University of Turin. His thesis, titled *Heart of Stone: Metamorphism, Memory and Resilience in the Susa Valley,* which focused on the eco-narrative intersections of geology, politics, history, and literature in the Alpine site west of Turin, won the XXII Premio Piemonte Letteratura. His short stories and essays have appeared in anthologies and journals, including *Ecozon@, Culture della Sostenibilità,* and *Storyfilters.*

ENRICO CESARETTI is associate professor of Italian at the University of Virginia and a Mellon Humanities fellow (2016–17). His research deals with modern and contemporary Italian literature, with a focus on Italian modernism and the avant-garde. He is the author of several essays and two books: *Castelli di carta: Retorica della dimora tra Scapigliatura e Surrealismo* (2001), and *Fictions of Appetite: Alimentary Discourses in Italian Modernist Literature* (2013). His current book project, tentatively titled *Telling Matters: Narratives of Human and Nonhuman Entanglements in Modern Italy*, explores the narrative eloquence of some of the materials (concrete, steel, marble, petroleum) that—in their interaction with human beings' own corporality, agency, and imaginative stories—contributed to make (and simultaneously un-make) today's Italy.

ALMO FARINA is professor of ecology at the University of Urbino. His research aims to understand how environmental complexity influences the organization of communities, ecosystems, and landscapes. He has investigated landscape organization and how organisms perceive their subjective surrounding environment, especially through acoustic sensory mechanisms. He served as vice president of the International Association for Landscape Ecology (1995–98) and general secretary of INTECOL (1998–2000). He is among the founders of the discipline of ecoacoustics and is currently president of the International Society of Ecoacoustics. Farina published more than 270 articles on ecology, landscape ecology, theoretical ecology, and ecoacoustics, along with three books: *Ecologia del paesaggio* (2001), *Principles and Methods in Landscape Ecology* (2006), and *Soundscape Ecology* (2014).

SOPHIA MAXINE FARMER is a PhD candidate in the Department of Art History at the University of Wisconsin-Madison. She specializes in Italian modern art and the sociopolitical structures that affected the production of artwork during the late nineteenth and twentieth centuries. Her dissertation focuses on the intersections between early science fiction robots and the development of mechanical beings in Italian Futurist objects and imaginary.

SERENA FERRANDO is assistant professor of Italian studies at Colby College. She holds a PhD in Italian studies from Stanford University, a graduate certificate in digital humanities from the University of Victoria, Canada, and an MA in American studies from the University of Texas at Austin. Her book project is an ecocritical study of the element of water in the work of three contemporary Italian poets based in the city of Milan (Daria Menicanti, Alda Merini, and Milo De Angelis) and offers a literary-cultural narrative of the relationship between poetry and nature. She created and is currently curating the Navigli Project—a thick geo-temporal narrative composed of multiple layers of history, politics, literature, architecture, sound, visual arts, and geography that displays all the different factors that throughout the centuries have shaped the cityscape of Milan—a digital humanities project that complements her book.

TIZIANO FRATUS coined the concept of *Homo radix*, the practice of treeography, and the discipline of dendrosophy. Inspired by musician Arvo Pärt's concept of sacred minimalism, he practices daily meditation in nature, creates books and photographs, and writes the column *Il cercatore di alberi* for *La Stampa*. His published works include *I giganti silenziosi* (2017), *Manuale del perfetto cercatore d'alberi* (2013, 2014, 2017), *L'Italia è un giardino* (2016), *Il sole che nessuno vede: Meditare in natura e ricostruire il mondo* (2016), *Il libro delle foreste scolpite* (2015), *Ogni albero è un poeta* (2015), *L'Italia è un bosco* (2014), and the poetry collections *Vergine dei nidi* (2017), *Un quaderno di radici* (2015), and *Musica per le foreste* (2015). The book *Giona delle sequoie* and the poetry collection *Mitologia selvatica contemporanea* are forthcoming. He lives in Piemonte. His website is www.homoradix.com.

MATTEO GILEBBI holds a PhD in Italian from the University of Wisconsin–Madison. From 2009 to 2017 he taught Italian language and culture at Duke University, and he is currently a lecturer in the French and Italian Department at Dartmouth College. His primary area of research is the interaction between literature, philosophy, and media in modern and contemporary culture, with a particular interest in the representation of the human/animal divide. His recent publications take an ecocritical approach to Italian contemporary poetry, focusing on the representation of human-animal interaction and how an ecocritical analysis of such representations can help us understand the moral, political, and philosophical implications of confronting speciesism.

ANDREA HAJEK holds a PhD from the University of Warwick. From 2013 to 2016 she was a British Academy postdoctoral fellow in the School of Modern Languages and Cultures, at the University of Glasgow. She is the managing editor for the journal *Memory Studies* and an associate editor for *Modern Italy*. She is also a founding member of the Warwick Oral History Network and an affiliate member of the Centre for Gender History at the University of Glasgow. She is the author of *Negotiating Memories of Protest in Western Europe: The Case of Italy* (2013) and has coedited various special issues and published in a number of peer-reviewed journals.

MARCUS HALL is Privatdozent in the Department of Evolutionary Biology and Environmental Studies at the University of Zurich, where he is a group leader in environmental history and codirector of Environmental Humanities Switzerland. He and his students focus on the conceptual and historical foundations of ecological restoration, invasion biology, and disease ecology, examining geographical case studies from around the world. Among other projects, Hall is currently working on a cultural and evolutionary history of parasites in human affairs, with special emphasis on vector-borne diseases and the symbiotic benefits of parasitism. Hall has authored, edited, or coedited six volumes and some thirty articles and chapters.

SERENELLA IOVINO is professor of comparative literature at the University of Turin and past president and cofounder of the European Association for the Study of Literature, Culture and Environment. She has written on a wide range of topics, including environmental ethics and ecocritical theory, bioregionalism and landscape studies, ecofeminism and posthumanism, comparative literature and environmental humanities. Her recent publications include *Material Ecocriticism* (2014) and *Environmental Humanities: Voices from the Anthropocene* (2017), both coedited with Serpil Oppermann, *Ecologia letteraria* (2006, second edition 2015), and *Ecocriticism and Italy: Ecology, Resistance, and Liberation* (2016, winner of the AAIS Book Prize and of the MLA's Aldo and Jeanne Scaglione Prize for Italian Studies).

ANDREA LERDA is a gallery director, art historian, freelance curator, and the founder of the online portal Platform Green. He has collaborated with, among others, the Centro Sperimentale per le Arti Contemporanee di Caraglio, the Centro Studi sul Pensiero Contemporaneo di Cuneo, and the Associazione Culturale Marcovaldo. In 2015 and 2016 he organized *Per4m*, in the context of Artissima—Fiera Internazionale d'arte contemporanea di Torino. He has curated many exhibits, including *De Rerum Natura*, in collaboration with Angela Madesani; *Back to the Land*, at Studio La Città in Verona; and *Silvano Tessarollo: Nulla nasce dal nulla*, in collaboration with Herman de Vries, at the Galleria Michela Rizzo in Venice.

ROBERTO MARCHESINI, a philosopher and zoologist, is a leading scholar in the fields of cognitive science and epistemology. He is the director of the Study Centre of Posthuman Philosophy in Bologna, Italy, and has authored numerous books in the areas of posthumanism and nonhuman otherness, including *Fondamenti di zooantropologia* (2005), *Intelligenze plurime* (2008), *Il tramonto dell'uomo* (2009), *Modelli cognitivi e comportamento animale* (2011), *Epifania animale* (2014), *Etologia filosofica: Alla ricerca della soggettività animale* (2016), *Emancipazione dell'animalità* (2017), and *Over the Human: Posthumanism and the Concept of Animal Epiphany* (2017). His website is www.marchesinietologia.it.

MARCO MORO's interest in environmental subjects dates to the 1980s, when he worked as a civil servant with the Legambiente; he later trained and worked as an architect. He has served as the national director of an architectural association and has authored and edited works dedicated to sustainable architecture. Since 2006, he has been the editor-in-chief of Edizioni Ambiente, an Italian publisher that specializes in sustainable development and the environment. Since 2014, he has been the editor-in-chief of the bilingual magazine *Materia Rinnovabile/Renewable Matter*, the first international journal dedicated to bioeconomy and circular economy. He has also collaborated with the School of Design at the Politecnico di Milano, specifically in the field of communication design.

ELENA PAST is associate professor of Italian and associate chair of the Department of Classical and Modern Languages, Literatures, and Cultures at Wayne State University in Detroit, Michigan. She has published articles on the toxic waste crisis in Naples, Mediterranean cinema and ecocinema, and Italian crime fiction and film. She is the author of *Methods of Murder: Beccarian Introspection and Lombrosian Vivisection in Italian Crime Fiction* (2012) and, with Deborah Amberson, coeditor of *Thinking Italian Animals: Human and Posthuman in Modern Italian Literature and Film* (2014) and a special focus issue of the journal *Ecozon@, Animal Humanities*. Her book *Italian Ecocinema* will be published in 2019.

CARLO PETRINI is the founder and driving force of Slow Food and was recently acclaimed as a great innovator in *Time* magazine's list of European heroes. In May 2016, the United Nations named him FAO Special Ambassador Zero Hunger for Europe. A columnist for major Italian and international newspapers, his books in English include *Slow Food: The Case for Taste* (2003), *Slow Food Revolution: A New Culture for Dining and Living* (2006), and *Slow Food Nation: Why Our Food Should Be Good, Clean, and Fair* (2007).

MONICA SEGER is associate professor of Italian studies and the Sallie Gertrude Smoot Spears Term Distinguished Associate Professor of Modern Languages and Literatures (2017–2020) at the College of William and Mary. She teaches courses on Italian literature, film, and the environmental humanities and has recently published articles on television, toxicity, storytelling, and more. She is the author of *Landscapes in Between: Environmental Change in Italian Literature and Film* (2015).

ILARIA TABUSSO MARCYAN is visiting assistant professor of Italian at Miami University, Oxford, Ohio. She received her PhD in comparative literature from the University of California, San Diego, in 2016. Her essay "The Cervi Family: A Peasant Story" appears in the collection *Ecocritical Approaches to Italian Culture and Literature: The Denatured Wild* (2016). Her research interests include ecocriticism, deep ecology, bioregionalism, agroecology, twentieth- and twenty-first-century Italian literature and cinema, subaltern studies, and postcolonial studies. Tabusso Marcyan's research focuses on the ever-changing relationship between humans and the land.

PASQUALE VERDICCHIO is professor of Italian and comparative literature at the University of California, San Diego, where he teaches courses in film, literature, and cultural studies. As a translator, he has published works by Vivian Lamarque, Alda Merini, and Pier Paolo Pasolini, among others. His poetry, reviews, criticism, and photography have been published in journals and in book form, most recently *Looters, Photographers, and Thieves: Aspects of Italian Photographic Culture in the Nineteenth and Twentieth Centuries* (2011). He is also editor of the volume *Ecocritical Approaches to Italian Culture and Literature: The Denatured Wild* (2016) and, with Loredana Di Martino, *Encounters with the Real in Contemporary Italian Literature and Cinema* (2017).

Index

Abate, Carmine, 9, 78–86
Abate, Francesco, 198
abattoirs, 9, 47, 50–51. *See also* slaughterhouses
Abbey, Edward, 94n2
ableism, 2
Abram, David, 147
Abruzzo, 174, 231
Abulafia, David, 206, 212
Acoustic Complexity Index (ACI), 31
activism/activists, 7, 151, 178, 212; and art, 230; cultural, 11; ecological, 213; environmental, 152; in Naples 163–71; No TAV, 134; in Taranto, 188, 190
Adams, Carol, 48–49
Adamson, Joni, 9
Aeropittura (aeropainting), 9, 98–108, 216
Africa, 31, 101, 124, 154, 157, 203, 211
Agamben, Giorgio, 5, 44n9, 51–52, 63
Agazzi, Davide, 225
agency, 6, 11, 140, 159n2, 163, 185, 189, 210–12; human, 74, 217–18; of landscape, 80; material, 72, 85n7; more-than-human, natural; 4, 75; narrative, 189; nonhuman, 74, 218
Agosti, Stefano, 44n9
agromafia, 195. *See also* ecomafia
Agyeman, Julian, 171n2
Alaimo, Stacy, 144–45, 188, 208–11
Albania/Albanians, 9, 80–81, 85nn10–11, 85n14, 86n16
Alberti, Leon Battista, 129, 131

Alexander, David E., 177
Alexander, Jeffrey C., 177
Aliano, 112
Alighieri, Dante, 7, 136
Allewaert, Monique, 209–11
Alps, 89–90, 113, 130–33, 135–37, 143–44, 146, 230, 232
Amberson, Deborah, 7
Ambrosi, C. A., 30
Ambrosio, Maddalena, 233
American West, 141–42, 144
An, Brian, 148n5
Andersen, Karin, 62
Angelini, Aurelio, 7, 12n2
Angus, Ian, 140
animalization, 48, 52–55
animal studies, 61, 64
Animammersa (association), 180
Anselmo, Giovanni, 228
Anthropocene, 9, 10, 67–69, 71, 73–76, 97, 140, 146, 147n2, 242–43; Golden Spike, 70, 72. *See also* Great Acceleration
anthropocentrism/anthropocentric, 2, 4, 60, 62, 217, 222, 225, 242–43; nonanthropocentric, 4, 62; post-anthropocentric, 70, 242–43
anthropological machine, 52, 55, 63
anthropology, 8, 11, 59, 85n6, 134, 232, 238; zooanthropology, 59, 61, 64
Antonioni, Michelangelo, 21
ant(s), 73–74
Apennine mountains, 30, 80, 113, 237

Arbëreshë literature/language, 78, 80–83, 113, 237
archeomafia, 195. *See also* ecomafia
Arduini, Clelia, 178
Arezzo, 111, 239
Argentina, Cosimo, 186
Argentina, 122
Armiero, Marco, 6, 10, 69, 89–90, 99, 104, 107, 131, 163, 165, 167–68, 187
Arminio, Franco, 10, 146
art/artist/artistic, 9, 10, 11, 98–108, 125, 129–31, 185, 188, 204, 212n1, 216, 225–33, 236; Arte Povera, 11, 225–29, 233n2; bioart, 231; eco-art, 11, 225–33; minimalism, 226; *nouveau réalisme*, 226; pop art, 226
Arte Povera. *See under* art
Ascari, Emanuela, 232
Axel, A. C., 29

Bahar, Robert, 171n3
Baird, Kevin, 124
Baldan Zenoni-Politeo, Giuliana, 43
Baldini, Eraldo, 196
Balduino, Armando, 40
Balla, Giacomo, 102, 108n2, 118
Ballarini, Giovanni, 61
Barca, Stefania, 6, 169
Barcelona (Spain), 205
Barraja, Edoardo, 132
Barron, Patrick, 7, 9, 231
Baruchello, Gianfranco, 230
Basaglia, Franco, 176, 182n4
Basilicata, 237, 240
Bateson, Gregory, 8
battle of grains (*battaglia del grano*), 101, 104–5
Beeville (Texas, USA), 139
Behrmann, Meike, 86
Belice Valley, 6, 177
Belluno, 88, 239
Benjamin, Walter, 212–13n4
Bennett, Jane, 132, 135, 189, 218–20, 222
Benvegnù, Damiano, 9, 44n4
Berardinelli, Alfonso, 43
Berberi, Viktor, 9
Berg, Peter, 18
Bergamo, 216

Berger, John, 20–21
Berlusconi, Silvio, 133, 175–76
Bernardi, Ulderico, 44
Bertola, Chiara, 232
Beuys, Joseph, 231
Bevilacqua, Piero, 6
Biamonti, Francesco, 233
Bianco, Floriana, 191n3
Biasutti, Giuseppe, 230
Bibby, C. J., 33
Bigazzi, Luca, 143
Bignamini, Mauro, 44
Bikini Atoll, 70
Binde, Per, 100–101, 104
bioart. *See under* art
biodiversity, 29–30, 34, 37, 117, 124, 152, 154, 159
biome, 2, 29, 73
biophony/biophonic sounds, 19–20, 29, 31–32
biopolitics/biopolitical, 2, 7, 52, 205, 231
bioregion/bioregional, 17–18, 20
bioregionalism, 38
biosemiotics/biosemiotic, 28, 31–33
bioturbation, 74
BirdLife International, 37
bird(s), 8–9, 30–33, 37–45, 62, 120, 123, 143–44, 243
Bobryk, W. C., 30
Boccardi, Vincenzo, 208
Boccioni, Umberto, 102
body, 21, 25, 55, 62, 70, 94n2, 102, 106, 112–13, 124, 126, 129, 147, 189, 210–11, 212n1, 216–22, 230, 233n4, 238; of bird, 58; female, 48, 50–51, 54; of land, 71, 197; lithic, 136; Mediterranean, 295; politic, 10, 137, 173–81, 220; of sea/water, 11, 206; of Turin, 136. *See also* trans-corporeality
Boland, Philip, 18
Bologna, 59, 111, 153, 178–79, 182n1, 232, 239
Bonaparte, Napoléon. *See* Napoleon Bonaparte
Bonatti, Valeria, 167
Bonesio, Luisa, 84
Bordin, Michele, 42, 45n14
Borghese, Camillo. *See* Paul V, Pope (Camillo Borghese)

INDEX

Borghesi, Roberto, 154
Borghi, Enrica 232
Bosellini, Alfonso, 91
Bouchard, Norma, 148
Boudejelas, S. 73
Bovo Romoeuf, Martine, 85n8
Bozak, Nadia, 141, 143–44
Bra, 155
Braidotti, Rosi, 2–5, 11, 56n2, 63, 210, 212, 242
Brambilla, Arturo, 88–89
Brambilla, Mattia, 37
Braudel, Fernand, 206
Brave New Alps (artist collective), 242
Breda, Nadia, 6
Brenner Corridor, 135
Breu, Christopher, 4
Brooklyn (USA), 167
Brown, Peter, 118
Browne, M., 73
Bruschetti, Alessandro, 102, 104, 108;
    Aeroveduta con laghi vulcanici, 105
Bryson, Scott J., 93, 94n2
Bucciarelli, Elisabetta, 194
Buell, Frederick, 143
Buenos Aires (Argentina), 122
Bugnone, Luca, 10
Bullard, Robert D., 167, 171n2
Bunting, Ben, 88
Buonarroti, Michelangelo, 129–30
Burgess, N. D., 33
Burke, Edmund, 144
Burri, Alberto, 227
Buzzati, Dino, 9, 88–96, 239
Buzzi, Paolo, 216
Bystrak, D., 33

Cacciatore, Giacomo, 196
Cadore, 239
Caffo, Leonardo, 53
Cagliari, 122
Cagol, Stefano, 232
Calabria, 9, 78–86, 186, 237, 240
Calandra, Lina M., 177
Calvino, Esther, 73
Calvino, Italo, 9, 11, 67–76, 136, 139, 147
Calvino, Mario, 73
Calzolari, Pier Paolo, 228

camorra, 164–65, 167, 195. *See also* ecomafia; mafia; 'ndrangheta; organized crime
Campania, 10, 163, 165–68, 170, 197
Camporesi, Piero, 197–98
Camugnano, 239
Cannata, Angelo, 190
Cansiglio (forest), 239
Cantrell, Carol, 223n5
Capanna, Ernesto, 120
capitalism/capitalist/capitalistic, 42, 49, 55, 84, 140, 164, 171, 205, 210–11, 226, 244
Capitalocene, 69
Cappa Marinetti, Benedetta, 108n2
Caprotti, Federico, 99–101, 103, 106
Caravaggio, 111
Carbognin, Francesco, 39
carbon, 75
Caretto, Andrea, 232
Carey, Francis, 148n3
Carlotto, Massimo, 197
Carnelli, Fabio, 176
carnivorism, 48
Carson, Rachel, 37
Casarsa della Delizia, 111
Cassano, Franco, 5, 146, 205, 207
Castello, Giancarlo, 73
Castree, Noel, 3
Cavarero, Adriana, 5
Cavour, Camillo Benso, Count of, 132
Ceccagnoli, Patrizio, 222
Cecere, Jacopo, 37
Cederna, Antonio, 5
Celada, Claudio, 37
Celant, Germano, 227, 233n2
Celati, Gianni, 9, 17–26, 231
Celli, Giorgio, 58–59
Cels, 136
cementification, 71, 232
Cenis, Mount, 132
Centemeri, Laura, 192n9
Ceronetti, Guido, 1–2
Ceruti, Mauro, 60
Cesaretti, Enrico, 8, 11, 199
Charlemagne, 131
Chernobyl (Ukraine), 20, 229
Chester (Pennsylvania, USA), 168
Chiomonte, 133, 136–37
Chiroli, Roberta, 134

Chironi, Cristian, 233
Christo (Christo Yavachev), 225
Christov-Bakargiev, Carolyn, 233n2
Ciancimino, Gabriella, 232
Cigliana, Simona, 220
cinema, 7, 10, 24, 139–43, 145–46, 207.
    See also ecocinema
Cirò Marina, 82, 86n16
Clerico, Marina, 132
climate/climate change, 29–32, 34, 62,
    71–72, 147, 148n2, 150, 232
Cohen, Jeffrey Jerome, 75, 130
Cohen, Tom, 4
Colaprico, Pietro, 196
Coldiretti, 153
Colella, Gaetano, 188
Colombo, Luigi (Fillìa), 101, 108n2
Colwell, Robert K., 212n2
Como, 216
companion species, 53–54
concrete, 25, 69–70, 73, 113, 132, 198,
    220–21
Constantine, 131
Conte, Giuseppe, 203
Cooper, M. C., 29
Corbett, Charles J., 142
Corburn, Jason, 167–68
Corona, Mauro, 239
Cortina d'Ampezzo, 239
Cosenza, 113, 240
Costa Concordia (cruise ship), 143
Costa Rica, 117
Craco, 112
Croce, Benedetto, 5
Cronon, William, 144
Crum, Roger J., 100, 102
Crutzen, Paul J., 68, 147n2
Cuneo, 229, 239
Curi, Fausto, 222
Cusanno, Luciana, 84
Cyrulnik, Boris, 61

D'Alisa, Giacomo, 167
Dante. *See* Alighieri, Dante
Dantini, Michele, 233
Dazieri, Sandrone, 196
De Cataldo, Giancarlo, 196
De Domizio Durini, Lucrezia, 231

Deledda, Grazia, 125
Deleuze, Gilles, 11, 217
Della Porta, Donatella, 7
De Luca, Erri, 134
De Luna, Giovanni, 177
De Martino, Ernesto, 79, 85n6
De Mauro, Tullio, 44
dendrosophy, 11, 237–38, 241
Depero, Fortunato, 108n2, 218
De Rada, Girolamo, 85n11
De Sica, Vittorio, 67
Detroit (Michigan, USA), 139, 142
Diani, Mario, 7
Di Carlo, Federica, 233
Didi-Huberman, Georges, 226
Di Michele, Girolamo, 198
dioxin, 167, 187–92
Dobson, Andy, 124
Dolomites, 9, 88–96, 112, 239–40
Doolan, Denise, 124
Dottori, Gerardo, 102, 104, 106, 107–8,
    108n2; *Mussolini: Anno XI (Ritratto del
    Duce)*, 107; *La Virata*, 103
Duarte, M. H. L., 30
Duffy, Enda, 140
Dumyahn, Sarah, 27
Durini, Buby, 231

earthquake(s), 1, 6, 10, 42, 113, 173–82,
    244
ecoacoustics, 28–30, 32–34
ecocinema, 19. *See also* cinema
ecocriticism, 2, 79, 144, 217, 223n5, 225,
    228; material, 7–8, 11, 217–18, 220,
    222n2; Mediterranean, 205
ecofeminism, 172
ecology, 17, 28, 150, 152; literary, 7; po-
    litical, 7; of mind, 8, 75, 135; of voices,
    soundscapes, 28–34, 39
ecomafia, 1, 5, 85n4, 195–97. *See also*
    agromafia; archeomafia; camorra; mafia;
    zoomafia
Edizioni Ambiente, 11, 195
Emilia-Romagna, 10, 17, 72, 173–82
environmental crimes, 1, 199
environmental humanities, 2–11, 243–45
environmentalism. *See under* activism/
    activists

environmental justice, 10, 69, 75, 164–70, 187
environmental legislation, 1, 166
Environmental Protection Agency, 167
Ercolini, Michele, 106
Esposito, Roberto, 5
Eurocentrism, 2
Europe, 20, 31, 71, 117–18, 139, 143, 187, 203, 205, 212, 226, 229
European Commission, 133, 191n1
Evans, Bob, 171n2
Exilles, 136

Fabietti, Ugo, 61, 62
Fabriano, 111
Facebook, 179
Falasca-Zamponi, Simonetta, 100, 101, 105, 109
Farina, Almo, 9, 27, 28–32, 38, 39, 41, 43n1
Farinosi, Manuela, 178
Farmer, Sophia Maxine, 9, 11
Fascism, 98–99, 101–2, 106–7, 151
Fava, Anna, 168
Favini, Ettore, 232
Feld, Steven, 43, 43n1
Fellini, Federico, 42, 139
feminism, 5, 11, 171n4, 243
Ferrando, Francesca, 5
Ferrando, Serena, 9
Ferrara, 17, 21–24, 182n1
Ferrari, Ivano, 9, 47–56, 56n1
Ferrarini, E., 30
Ferrario, Davide, 18
Ferraris, Maurizio, 5
Ficocelli, Sara, 139
Fillìa. *See* Colombo, Luigi (Fillìa)
Finale Emilia, 180, 182n1
Fiorani, Eleonora, 61
Florence, 113
Fofi, Goffredo, 73
folklife, 9, 79
Fontana, Enrico, 195
Fontana, Lucio, 227
food, 1, 9, 10, 32, 49, 75, 84, 101, 137, 150–59, 159n2, 163, 179, 184, 192n7, 195, 209
Foot, John, 177
Foreman, Iain, 19

Foschini, Giuliano, 186, 189
France, 131, 136, 241
Francigena, Via (Via Cottia), 130
Fratus, Tiziano, 11
Fréjus, Mount, 132
Friuli Venezia-Giulia, 42, 182n3
Fuller, S., 29
Fumian, Carlo, 38
Futurism, 11, 98–99, 101–3, 106–7, 215–18, 220, 222, 223nn3–4. *See also* Aeropittura (aeropainting)

Gaard, Greta, 171n4
Gage, Stuart, 29
Gallego-Delgado, Julio, 126
Gane, Nicholas, 53
Gannon, Thomas, 43n1
Garrard, Greg, 144, 215
Gebbia, Valentina, 196
Gehlen, Arnold, 63
Gentile, Giovanni, 5
geophony, 19, 21, 28, 31, 32
Germany, 231
Gerstetter, Christiane, 192n7
Ghirri, Luigi, 17, 24, 25, 231–32
Gianelli, Ida, 233n4
Giano, Mount, 107
Gibbs, Lois, 169
Gilardi, Piero, 230, 231
Gilebbi, Matteo, 9
Gilpin, William, 144
Giraud, T., 74
Giugliano, 165
Glasgow (Scotland, UK), 181
Goethe, Johann Wolfgang von, 45n16, 112, 113
Golden Spike. *See under* Anthropocene
Goodbody, Axel, 82
Gori, Leonardo, 198
Gotthard-Monte Ceneri 133
Graf von Hardenberg, Wilko, 99, 100, 101, 107
Gramsci, Antonio, 211
Granada, 208
Grand Canyon (USA), 144
Grande Raccordo Anulare, 139
Grandis, Sebastiano, 132
Grand Tour, 8, 10, 110, 112, 113, 231

Grassi, Giovanni Battista, 120
Grattoni, Severino, 132
Great Acceleration, 67, 68, 69, 140, 145, 147. See also Anthropocene
Greece, 208
Greene, Vivien, 102
Gros, Frédéric, 146
Grosz, Elizabeth, 189
Gruppo Forma I, 227
Gruppo N, 227
Gruppo Origine, 227
Gruppo '63, 58
Gruppo 9999, 230
Gruppo T, 227
Guattari, Félix, 11, 217
Guernica (social center), 178–80
guerrilla narrative, 10, 163, 166, 169
Gullestad, Anders, 118, 119
Gustin, Marco, 37
Guzzanti, Sabina, 175

Hack, Margherita, 61
Hajek, Andrea, 10, 175, 179, 180
Hall, Marcus, 6, 10, 118, 121
Hansen, Peter, 90
Haraway, Donna, 53, 55, 56n2, 63, 69, 76, 137
Härmänmaa, Marja, 215
Hawkins, A. D., 30
Heidegger, Martin, 53
Heise, Ursula K., 38, 94n2, 192n4
Herman, David, 185
Hill, D. A., 33
Hollande, François, 135
Hollywood (USA), 142, 143, 147
Holocaust, 48
Holocene, 140
Homo radix, 236
Huber, Matthew, 142
Human Microbiome Project, 125
Humphreys, Richard, 106
hybridity, 2, 9, 12, 59–63, 72, 74, 75, 88, 144, 164, 185, 186, 208, 243
hydrocarbons, 10, 139–41, 143–45, 147, 148n3, 189, 198, 243. See also oil

Ialongo, Ernest, 101, 102
Ilva, 184–91, 191n1, 192n7, 192n9

infrastructure, 133, 134, 142, 167
International Institutes of Ecoacoustics, 30, 32, 34n2
Ionian Sea, 86n16, 186, 190
Iovino, Serenella, 3, 4, 7, 9, 18, 20, 38, 39, 43, 44n5, 79, 80, 85n4, 85n7, 94n3, 113, 135, 151, 166, 169, 174–78, 181, 182n5, 189, 205, 217, 220, 222, 222n2
Ippolito, Davide, 185
Ireland, 146
Irpinia, 177
Iseo, Lake, 225
Isola, Ferdinando 132
Istituto Superiore per la Protezione e la Ricerca Ambientale (ISPRA), 72
Italian Communist Party (PCI), 178, 211
Ivakhiv, Adrian, 19, 23, 24
Izzo, Gigliola, 170

James, Erin, 186, 192n4
James, P., 29
Japan, 117, 129
Jesus, 216
John Paul II, Pope (Karol Józef Wojtyła), 122

Kaïka, Maria, 99, 100, 103, 106
Kant, Immanuel, 144
Kaplan, B. M., 30
Kaplan, Matt, 123
Kassel (Germany), 231
Keller, L., 74
Klein, Naomi, 169
Krause, Bernie, 29
Krimisa, 80, 82–83
Kristensen, Erik, 74
Kull, Kalevi, 130

La Cecla, Franco, 5
Lacis, Asja, 212n4
Lagopesole, 112
La Maddalena (archipelago), 133, 134
Lampedusa, 203, 209, 212n1
Land of Fires (*Terra dei fuochi*), 167, 197
landscape, 1–2, 4–11, 17–23, 25, 28–30, 32–34, 37–39, 41–43, 43n1, 44nn4–5, 57, 67–76, 78–82, 84, 85n4, 88, 90, 98–108, 108n1, 111–13, 117, 121, 125, 129,

INDEX

130, 140–47, 150, 155–57, 163–64, 166, 170, 175, 177, 180, 195–98, 205, 216, 217, 221, 226, 229–32, 235–38, 243; architecture, 232; cultural, 5, 41, 156; economic, 121; historical, 156; intellectual, 11, 29, 243; painting, 129; photography, 6, 231; political, 231
landslides, 6, 44n13, 72, 82, 83, 130
Langhe-Roero, 151, 156
Lankester, Ray, 119
Lanzarote (Spain), 209
La Pietra, Ugo, 230, 233n5
L'Aquila, 111, 113, 173–82, 182n11
Latour, Bruno, 68
Lawrence, David Herbert, 117, 122
Lazio, 107, 240
Lazzaro, Claudia, 100, 102
Lecce, 113
Lederberg, Joshua, 122
Lefebvre, Henry, 18
Legambiente, 195, 196, 199
Lehtimäki, Markku, 192n4
LeMenager, Stephanie, 142, 148n4
Leonardi, Filippo, 233
Leopardi, Giacomo, 58, 110, 111
Lerda, Andrea, 11
Levi, Primo, 137
Levinas, Emmanuel, 92, 93
Libya, 1, 76
Ligabue, Luciano, 204
Liguria, 28–30, 72, 74, 151
Lindström, Kati, 130
Liri Valley, 6
Lista, Giovanni, 227–29
Livingstone, Frank, 124
Lombardi, Nunzia, 170
Lombardy, 72, 230
Lowe, S. J., 73
Lozano, A., 30
Lucania, 111–12
Lucarelli, Carlo, 196
Lucifora, Annalisa, 191n3
Lucretius Carus, Titus, 225–26, 228
Lunigiana, 9, 28–32, 34
Luras, 241
Lutwack, Leonard, 40
Luxembourg, 139
Lyon (France), 10, 133

MacDonald, Scott, 19
Machiavelli, Niccolò, 7
mafia, 83, 134, 164, 171, 195–96. *See also* agromafia; archeomafia; camorra; ecomafia; 'ndrangheta; organized crime; zoomafia
Magna Graecia, 78
malaria, 10, 80, 108, 117–18, 120–26
Mangano, Daniel, 216
Manto, Dacia, 233
Mantua, 47, 111
Manzoni, Alessandro, 7
Manzoni, Piero, 227
maquis, 30, 31. *See also* Mediterranean
Maraniello, Gianfranco, 233n4
Marchesini, Roberto, 5, 9, 53, 56n2
Marigliano, 169
Marinetti, Filippo Tommaso, 98, 102, 106, 108, 108n2, 215–22, 223nn7–8
Márquez, R., 30
Marsella, Roberto, 186
Massiccio del Pollino (Pollino Massif). *See* Pollino, Massif of
Matera, 111, 113, 240
Matilda of Canossa, 239
Mattalia, Daniela, 118
Matvejević, Predrag, 206
Mauri, Giuliano, 230
Mazzi, Elena, 233
McCloskey, Barbara, 106, 107
McCollough, George, 171n3
McWilliam, J. N., 30
Mecchia, Giuseppina, 148n6
Mediterranean, 1, 5, 6, 10, 11, 30, 33, 34, 74, 83, 117, 125, 130, 133, 143, 145, 146, 184, 204, 205–6, 208, 210–11, 212n1, 212n3; maquis, 30–31. *See also* ecocriticism; Mediterraneanism; migrants/migrations
Mediterraneanism, 205
Medolla, 182n1
Melfi, 112
Melosi, Martin, 167
Mengaldo, Vincenzo, 39
Mercalli, Luca, 76n1
Merlini, Paolo, 118
Messina, Strait of, 5
Mexico, 208

Micalizzi, Alessandra, 178
Michigan (USA), 142, 148n5
Middle East, 203
Midwest (USA), 141, 142
Miglietti, Francesca Alfano, 62
migrants/migrations, 1, 11, 31, 76, 81–82, 103, 111, 117, 157, 203–6, 208–12, 212n1. *See also* refugees
Milan, 17, 67, 75, 88, 93, 106, 107, 111, 153, 194, 216, 236
Miller, W. B., 29
minimalism. *See under* art
Miracco, Renato, 102
Mitchell, W. J. T., 84
Modena, 178, 182n1, 239
modernism, 215–16, 223n5
Monferrato, 156
Montagner, Hubert, 61
Montanari, Tomaso, 5
Moore, Jason, 69
Morace, Rosanna, 83, 86n15
Moreton, Bay of, 241
Morganti, N., 30
Moroni, Mario, 11, 215
Morri, D., 30, 31
Morton, Timothy, 74, 75
Mott, Glenn, 39
Mount Cenis, 132
Mount Fréjus, 132
Mount Giano, 107
Mount Rushmore (USA), 107
Mount Vesuvius, 113
Movimento Arte Concreta (MAC), 227
Mullet, T., 29
Munsterberg, Peggy, 37
Muraro, Luisa, 5
Mussolini, Benito, 98, 99, 104, 106–8, 108nn4–5

Nacciarriti, Andrea, 232
Napoleon Bonaparte, 130
Napoletano, Brian, 29
Narciso, Giancarlo, 198
NASA (National Aeronautics and Space Administration), 232
Nasse, George Nicholas, 85n9
Naturismo (naturism), 101
Nazzaro, Giona, 212n1

'ndrangheta, 83, 134, 195. *See also* camorra; mafia
Negri, Antonio, 5
neoliberalism, 3, 4
Neolithic, 68, 133
New Italian Theory, 5
New Mexico (USA), 142
New Towns, 174, 176
New York City (USA), 232
Nixon, Rob, 188
Nonperdono, Movimento trasversale d'avanguardia artistica (artist collective), 185
North Africa, 101, 203, 211
No TAV movement, 133–35
nouveau réalisme. See under art
Nussbaum, Martha, 187

Odysseus, 207
Ochoa, G. J., 29
O'Farrell, J. M., 29
oil, 1, 9, 120, 132, 137, 142–44, 148n4, 184, 198
Okinawa (Japan), 117
Olbia-Tempio, 241
Oles, Tomas, 79, 85n4
olive trees, 5, 30, 187, 237, 241
ontology, 3, 5, 7, 9, 59–63, 68, 70, 74, 135, 141, 219, 230
Oppermann, Serpil, 3, 4, 43, 68, 74, 85n7, 135, 217, 220, 251
organized crime, 11, 80, 83, 134, 195, 197, 198. *See also* camorra; mafia; 'ndrangheta
Orientalism, 205. *See also* Mediterraneanism
Orsi, Paolo, 82, 85n12, 86n15

Packard, Randall, 118
Padua, 111
paesologia. See placeology (*paesologia*)
Pagano, Tullio, 78
Page, B., 30
Palang, Hannes, 130
Palazzotto, Gery, 196
Palermo, 110, 237, 240
Pallottino, Massimo, 85
Paluch-Mishur, Michelle, 102
Paoli, Guido, 73

INDEX

parasites, 5, 8, 118–20, 122–24
Parco Arte Vivente (PAV, Living Art Park), 231
Parma, 111
Parrinello, Giacomo, 6, 174–75
Parthenope (ancient name of Naples), 207–8
Pascali, Pino, 228
Pasolini, Pier Paolo, 38, 84, 110–11, 226–27, 229, 234
Passmore, John, 233n6
Past, Elena M., 7, 10, 139–40, 142, 144, 146, 148, 241
Pattarozzi, Gaetano, 216
Paul V, Pope (Camillo Borghese), 122
PAV. *See* Parco Arte Vivente (PAV, Living Art Park)
Pavia, 1
Peacor, Donald R., 91
Pedersen, J. S., 74
Pennacchio Argentato, 233
Pennsylvania (USA), 168
Penone, Giuseppe, 229–30, 233n4
Pergolizzi, Antonio, 199
Perilli, Luana, 233
peripheries, 164
Perugia, 111
pesticides, 37
Petrei, Fabrizia, 175, 178
Petrini, Carlo, 10, 150–56, 159n2
petroleum. *See* oil
petroleum culture (Petroculture), 139, 141
petromodernity, 142, 148n4
phenomenology, 10, 71
Piccinni, Flavia, 185–86, 190
Piccioli, L., 30
Pico della Mirandola, Giovanni, 63
Piedmont, 10, 132, 150–51, 154–56, 228, 230
Pienza, 111
Pieretti, Nadia, 30–32
Pietraporzio, 239
Pieve di Soligo, 38–39, 44
Pijanowsky, Bryan, 19, 29
Pisa, 191
Pistoletto, Michelangelo, 228, 234
Pius X (Pope), 122
Pivato, Stefano, 29

placeology (*paesologia*), 10, 146
plasmodium. *See* malaria
Poggi, Christine, 99, 108, 215, 220
Pollan, Michael, 121, 155
Pollenzo, 155
Pollino, Massif of, 112, 237, 240
pollution, 7–8, 10, 20, 29, 67, 69–70, 74, 158, 167, 169, 184, 191, 210, 226, 232, 243
Pontine Ager, 100, 105; marshes, 99–101, 103
pornography, 48
Portugal, 74
Poseidon, 184
Posillipo, 170
posthuman/posthumanism, 7, 132, 143–48, 217, 223n3, 223n6, 242
posthumanities, 3, 8, 57, 242–43
postmodern/postmodernism, 11, 217, 220
Potenza, 240
Potito, Michela, 154
Po Valley, 6, 17–20, 113, 156–57
Prampolini, Enrico, 108n2, 218
Protezione Civile (Civil Protection Agency), 174–75, 179–80
Puglia, 11
Pugliese, Roberto, 232
Puliafito, Alberto, 176
Pungetti, Gloria, 79, 85n4

Raine, Anne, 215, 223n5
Rainey, Lawrence, 99, 108
Ralph, C. J., 33
Ramats, 136
Ravagli, Vitaliano, 169
Re, Anna, 7
reclamation (*bonifica*), 6, 99–101, 104–5, 108
Redi, Francesco, 118
refugees, 5, 80–81. *See also* migrants/migrations
Rega, C. C., 34
Remotti, Francesco, 61–62
Renaissance, 4–5, 111, 129, 131, 185
Renzi, Matteo, 192n8
resistance (movement), 1–2, 7–11, 38, 79, 82, 84, 134–35, 146, 151, 163–64, 166, 168–69, 171–72

Rete Rurale Nazionale, 37
Rigby, Kate, 192n6
Risi, Dino, 140
Risorgimento, 100
Rizzo, Michela, 233n1
Rocky Mountains (USA), 144
Rome, Adam, 168
Rome, 100, 111–12, 139, 144, 146, 148n6, 186, 190, 227, 240
Romean, Colombano, 136–37
Romuald, Saint, 237, 239
Rosi, Gianfranco, 139, 212n1
Ross, Ronald, 120
Ross, Silvia, 8
Rossella, Valeria, 235
Rossi, Vasco, 239
Roversi, Roberto, 60
Ruddiman, William, 68
Rushmore, Mount (USA), 107
Ryan, Derek, 223n3

Sagan, Carl, 131, 138
Saitta, Pietro, 7
Salento, 110
Salomone, Mario, 7
Sandler, Ronald D., 171n2
Sannazaro, Jacopo, 207
Sanremo, 72–73
Sansoni, Guglielmo (Tato), 108n2
Sanzin, Bruno, 216
Sardinia, 10, 110, 117–18, 120–28
Sarkozy, François, 205
Sarli, Doriana, 170
Sartini Blum, Cinzia, 216
Satyrion (nymph), 184
Saviano, Roberto, 197
Scales, Helen, 209
Scarpa, Domenico, 73, 76n2
Schmidt, Carl Theodore, 104
Schnapp, Jeffrey, 220
Scotellaro, Rocco, 79, 85n6
Scott, J. M., 33
Scranton, Roy, 94, 96n19
Sebald, W. G., 19
Seger, Monica, 7, 11, 21, 72, 90, 111
Segrè, Andrea, 153
Serre, 240
Serres, Michel, 123

Settis, Salvatore, 5, 8, 69
Severi, Giorgia, 232
Seveso, 188–89, 192n9
sexism, 2, 48–49, 51
Sgueglia, Leandro, 163, 168
Shepard, Paul, 94n2
Shiva, Vandana, 152–53
Siciliani, Luigi, 82
Sicily, 1, 5, 82, 154, 237, 240
Siena, 111, 139
Sila, Plateau of, 240
Simeti, Francesco, 233
Singer, Peter, 56
Sirolli, Emanuele, 176
slaughterhouses, 9, 47–55
Slow Food movement, 10, 150–59
slow violence, 175–76, 181, 188
Smyth, William Henry, 118
Snyder, Gary, 38, 94n2
Soffientini, Anna, 94n
Solnit, Rebecca, 139, 146
Somenzi, Mino, 108n2
Sommeiller, Germain, 132
sonic geographies, 18. *See also* ecoacoustics
sonotopes, 29. *See also* ecoacoustics
Soriani, Stefano, 37
Sorrentino, Paolo, 10, 139, 141–47
soundscapes, 18–19, 21, 28–29, 31–33, 38–43, 146
Spagna, Raffaella, 232
Spain, 133, 208–9
speciesism, 2, 48–49, 51, 53, 55
Spera, Daniela, 189, 191
Sperber, Christine M., 91
Srinivas, Bevinje, 120
Stefano, Marco, 91
Steffen, Will, 140, 147–49
Stoermer, Eugene F., 68
Strabo, 110
sublime, 58, 93, 139–49, 229
Sueur, Jérôme, 29
Susa Valley, 129–33, 136–37
Swift, Jonathan, 204, 207
Switzerland, 133
Syria, 1

Tabusso Marcyan, Ilaria, 10, 150, 152, 154, 156–59

INDEX

Taranto, 10, 111, 113, 184–93. *See also* Ilva; Taras (ancient name of Taranto)
Taras (ancient name of Taranto) 184–85, 189. *See also* Taranto
Tarpino, Antonella, 7
TAV (Treno Alta Velocità; high-speed train), 133–35
Taylor, Jason deCaires, 208–9, 211
technophonies, 28, 31. *See also* ecoacoustics
Tellini, Gino, 40
Tempio Pausania, 241
tendopoli, 174–76, 179–80
Terra Madre, 150–55, 157–59
Terrosi, Roberto, 223n3
Tessarollo, Silvano, 233
Thom, Michael, 148n5
Tiber River, 146
Tilman, D., 32
Toffolini, Nicola, 233
Togliatti, Palmiro, 178
Tognotti, Eugenia, 118
Tonutti, Sabrina, 61
Towsey, M., 29
trans-corporeality, 188, 208–9, 211. *See also* body
Trevico, 113
Treviso, 38, 111
Trieste, 111
Troisi, Licia, 197
Tsing, Anna Löwenhaupt, 129–30
Turco, R. P., 71
Turco, Richard P., 142
Turin, 10, 70–71, 75, 111, 130–34, 152, 155, 158, 227, 231–32, 233n3
Turri, Eugenio, 5–6, 20, 43n2
Tuscany, 28, 30, 73, 237, 239
Tuszyńska, Beata, 133
Tyrrhenian Sea, 30

Uexküll, Jakob von, 28
United Kingdom, 208
United States, 37, 70, 142, 166–68, 226
Urbino, 30, 111

Vagliasindi, Grazia Maria, 191n3, 192n7
Vajont Dam, 42, 44–45n13, 165, 171, 239
Valesio, Paolo, 223n7

Vallerani, Francesco, 6, 37, 43n2, 44n4
Van Beneden, Pierre Joseph, 119, 122
Van Ommeren, Ron J., 123
Varotto, Mauro, 43n2, 44n4
Veneto, 22, 25, 38, 113, 197, 239
Venice, 17, 102, 111, 135, 145, 220, 223n7, 233n1
Venosa, 112
Ventimiglia, 111
Ventura, Angelo, 38
Venturi, Francesco, 44n11
Verdenero (book series), 11, 194–95, 197–99
Verdicchio, Pasquale, 7, 11, 203–4, 206, 208, 210, 212
Verner, J., 33
Verzotti, Giorgio, 230, 233n4
Vesuvius, Mount, 113
Vicenza, 111
Vichi, Marco, 198
Vico, Giambattista, 113
Videtta, Marco, 197
Villalta, Gian Mario, 38
Villamassargia, 237
Vinci, Simona, 196, 198
Vitale, Novella, 170
Volterra, 111
Vulpio, Carlo, 186

Wagner-Jauregg, Julius, 124
Wallace, Molly, 192n6
waste, 1, 5, 10, 69, 163, 165–68, 170, 171n3, 194–95, 197–98. *See also* activism/activists; ecomafia
West, Mark, 223n3
West, Rebecca, 21
Westphal, Bertrand, 205
Whitham, Thomas G., 123
Wild, A. L., 74
wilderness, 99–101, 144, 204
Wilkinson, Bruce H., 91
Wimmer, J., 32
Wittman, Laura, 99, 108
Wojtyła, Karol Józef. *See* John Paul II, Pope (Karol Józef Wojtyła)
World Health Organization, 123
World War II, 39, 72, 143, 151, 156, 226
World Wide Fund for Nature Italia, 72

Worster, Donald, 165
Wu Ming, 169, 171n5, 196, 198

Yavachev, Christo. *See* Christo (Christo Yavachev)
Yimer, Dagmawi, 203–4, 208–9, 212

Zaccagnini, Edoardo, 141
Zagaria, Cristina, 184, 189, 191, 192n5
Zalasiewicz, Jan, 68–70
Zanetto, Gabriele, 37
Zanotto, Grace, 186
Zanzotto, Andrea, 9, 37–45
Zapf, Hubert, 3
Zavattini, Cesare, 139, 147n1
Zocca, 239
zoe/life, 210, 242, 244
zooanthropology. *See under* anthropology
zoomafia, 195. *See also* ecomafia
zoomorphism, 55
zoophilia, 59
Zunica, Marcello, 6

Recent Books in the Series
Under the Sign of Nature: Explorations in Ecocriticism

Kate Rigby
Topographies of the Sacred: The Poetics of Place in European Romanticism

Alan Williamson
Westernness: A Meditation

John Elder
Pilgrimage to Vallombrosa: From Vermont to Italy in the Footsteps of George Perkins Marsh

Mary Ellen Bellanca
Daybooks of Discovery: Nature Diaries in Britain, 1770–1870

Rinda West
Out of the Shadow: Ecopsychology, Story, and Encounters with the Land

Bonnie Roos and Alex Hunt, editors
Postcolonial Green: Environmental Politics and World Narratives

Paula Willoquet-Maricondi, editor
Framing the World: Explorations in Ecocriticism and Film

Deborah Bird Rose
Wild Dog Dreaming: Love and Extinction

Axel Goodbody and Kate Rigby, editors
Ecocritical Theory: New European Approaches

Scott Hess
William Wordsworth and the Ecology of Authorship: The Roots of Environmentalism in Nineteenth-Century Culture

Dan Brayton
Shakespeare's Ocean: An Ecocritical Exploration

Jennifer K. Ladino
Reclaiming Nostalgia: Longing for Nature in American Literature

Byron Caminero-Santangelo
Different Shades of Green: African Literature, Environmental Justice, and Political Ecology

Kate Rigby
Dancing with Disaster: Environmental Histories, Narratives, and Ethics for Perilous Times

Adam Trexler
Anthropocene Fictions: The Novel in a Time of Climate Change

Eric Gidal
Ossianic Unconformities: Bardic Poetry in the Industrial Age

Jesse Oak Taylor
The Sky of Our Manufacture: The London Fog in British Fiction from Dickens to Woolf

Michael P. Branch and Clinton Mohs, editors
"The Best Read Naturalist": Nature Writings of Ralph Waldo Emerson

Lynn Keller
Recomposing Ecopoetics: North American Poetry of the Self-Conscious Anthropocene

Serenella Iovino, Enrico Cesaretti, and Elena Past, editors
Italy and the Environmental Humanities: Landscapes, Natures, Ecologies

www.ingramcontent.com/pod-product-compliance
Lightning Source LLC
Chambersburg PA
CBHW071244230426
43668CB00011B/1575